THE COURAGE OF HOPE

John de La Mennais

1780-1860

Author

Br. Edmond Raymond Drouin, Phd

Editor

Br. Francis Blouin, Phd

Le Courage de l'Espérance

Jean de La Mennais

1780-1860

ISBN: 978-9970-445-03-5

Typeset and Printed by Marianum Press Ltd. P.O. Box 11, Kisubi, Uganda.
M VII 2012 650 JC 73/2012

Key to Footnote Abbreviations

PUBLICATIONS AND UNPUBLISHED MANUSCRIPTS

Chron   *Chronique des Frères de l'Instruction Chrétienne.* December 1874+.

ÉM   Études mennaisiennes. Avril 1988+. Irregular supplement to the *Chronique des Frères de l'Instruction Chrétienne.*

Cond F   La Condamnation de Lamennais. Dossier présenté par M. J. Le Quillou et Louis Le Quillou. (Paris: Éditions Beauchesne, c 1982. ISBN: 2-7010-1036-5754 pages.)

Cor gén F   Félicité de Lamennais. *Correspondance générale,* Textes annotés par Louis Le Guillou. Paris: Armand Colin, 1971-1981. 9 v.

Cor gén J   Jean-Marie Robert de La Mennais. *Correspondance générale,* Textes réunis et annotés par F. Philippe Friot. Rennes: Presses universitaires, 2001 +._v.

Lav   Laveille, Auguste-Pierre. *Jean-Marie de la Mennais* (1780-1860). Paris: Poussielgue, 1903. 2v.

Rop   Ropartz, Sigismond. *La Vie et les Oeuvres de M. Jean-Marie Robert de La Mennais.* Paris: Lecoffre, [1874].

REH   Rulon, Frère Henri-Charles, 1902-1981. "Études historiques sur les Frères de l'Instruction chrétienne en Bretagne: 1816-1830". [Studies completed between 1948 and 1964]. Typewritten manuscript. Monographs paginated individually. (Archives of the Brothers of Christian Instruction, No. 546.)

RPH "Petite Histoire des Frères de l'Instruction chrétienne, 1816-1860", [1964]. 528 pages. Typewritten manuscript. Paged continuously. (Archives of the Brothers of Christian Instruction, No. 547.)

SA (1960) Veneten. *Beatificationis et canonizationis ven. servi dei Ioannis Mariae Robert de la Mennais ... Summarium additionale ...* Typis Pologlottis Vaticanis, 1960. 700 pp. Sacrum Rituum Congregatio. Sectio Historica. (S. Hist. n. 107). Not published

Archives

ADCd'A Archives of the Department of Côtes d'Armor (formerly Côtes-du-Nord). (Saint-Brieuc, France).

AFEC Archives of the Brothers of the Christian Schools (Rome).

AFIC Archives of the Brothers of Christian Instruction (Rome).

AFP Archives of the Daughters of Providence (Cesson/Saint Brieuc)

ADM Archives of the Department of Morbihan (Vannes, France).

AMSB Municipal Archives of Saint-Brieuc (France).

AN Archives Nationales (Paris).

N.B.: The validity of these abbreviations is limited to this volume.

AUTHOR'S INTRODUCTION

Life opens for John de La Mennais hardly two years after the funeral of Jean Jacques Rousseau and François Marie Arouet, Voltaire. John lived through a century fascinated by the philosophers of his generation and tormented by the Revolution which followed. Renewal was imperative; he pledged his life to the cause while a new generation of ideologues dreamt of completing the dechristianization brutally undertaken by the Revolution. "On April 22, 1851 Auguste Comte prophesied: *"I am convinced ... that before the year 1860, I shall be preaching positivism at Notre Dame as the only real and complete religion"*. The courteous refusal of the French Jesuits offended the "founder" of sociology when he sent a friend to propose that they abandon obsolete Catholicism to promote his "invincible" positivism.

Rousseau theorized on education without knowing what to do with his illegitimate progeniture, but educators like John de La Mennais and their disciples opened schools. Voltaire championed progress and personal liberties, but frowned on the tuition-free schools of the Brothers of the Christian Schools for the education of youth. One century after Saint John Baptist de La Salle, it is John de La Mennais at work with a new generation of founders who provided Christian teachers for the neglected children of the working class.

When his disciples closed John De La Mennais' tomb at the end of 1860, the dechristianization anticipated by Comte had not occurred; Catholic priests were still preaching from the pulpit of Notre Dame, the diocese of Paris had not strayed from the successor of Peter and it was discontinuing its diocesan rituals to adopt the Roman liturgy. Though ingenious persecutions were revived against the Church, its message was gaining attention. Migne was beginning the publication of his monumental Greek and Latin patrology (1857), the Osservatore Romano was founded in Rome (1861). France enjoyed a resurgence of popular devotion, and religious practice was on the rise. It was also during this period that Lourdes was greeting its first pilgrimages and during all of this period, John had been faithfully at work with his leadership team.

Though he was hardly twelve when Louis XVI was guillotined, John cut a swath of hope through the confusion of his generation. Nine political régimes governed his country during the eighty years of his existence: the Old Régime, the phases of the Revolution and the First Republic (1792), the Directory (1795), the Consulate (1804), the Restoration (1815), the July Monarchy (1830), the Second Republic (1848) and the Second Empire (1852). John lived his adolescence during the revolutionary Terror; his priestly ministry began under the Bonaparte of the Consulate and ended during the Second Empire of Napoleon III. The violence of the century subverted the nation, battered the Church, frustrated his personal expectations without ever clouding his vision or bending his determination. Even the ecclesiastical conflicts which tormented his brother Félicité rumbled through his life without altering his course.

I started this biography with no other purpose than to summarize candidly an existence remembered for honesty, hope and daunting generosity. Biographers remain at a loss to explain everything in their story. I wrote in one volume what could reasonably be told in one volume, without claiming to leave unanswered questions. John de La Mennais filled his years with a wide variety of initiatives which newly discovered manuscripts help us better understand. I realized long before beginning this text that the light of a broadening documentation prohibited anyone from following available biographies too strictly. Researchers and historians have enriched our knowledge and their inquiries reveal the need for modifications to the traditional story; I would serve readers very poorly if I disregarded their work.

Brother Edmond G. Drouin

EDITOR'S NOTE

Brother Edmond Raymond Drouin had been working on the biography of Father John de La Mennais during more than ten years; however, illness prevented him from completing his work. Fortunately, except for a few chapters, most of the work had been completed before Brother's illness in 2005. I recently accepted to complete and edit the book, benefiting from the many resources collected by Br. Raymond Drouin. I enjoyed completing a work that represents a major commitment in the life of Br. Edmond Raymond Drouin.

Brother Francis R Blouin

LETTER OF SUPERIOR GENERAL

Dear Readers. Dear Friends,

A number of special events have underscored the 150th anniversary of the death of Father John Mary de La Mennais. The Anniversary provided the Brothers of Christian Instruction and the Mennaisian family an occasion to publicize their principal founder, helping to make him better known and loved.

Two biographies were written to commemorate this anniversary; one is in Spanish, translated into French and English, and one is in Italian. Though the biography that we present at this time is being published at about the same period, it represents professional research that took place during a twenty year period by Br. Edmond Raymond Drouin from the American Province. The work interrupted by illness, was recently completed though the cooperation of Br. Francis Blouin, also from the American Province.

Br. Edmond worked tirelessly in research, not satisfied until he had fully documented any statement of some significance; thus his work presents a text of great historical value. For the convenience of readers, the documentation is placed at the end of each chapter, fully authenticating the leadership role of our principal founder, and the historical situation in France following the traumatic years of the French Revolution.

We also wish to underscore the clarification presented in Br. Edmond's book of the significance played by Father Gabriel Deshayes as co-founder of the Brothers of Christian Instruction. Equally important in the text is the professional assessment of Felicite de La Mennais' role in the life of his elder brother, along with Feli's contributions and challenges to the Church. Br. Drouin has successfully navigated the shoals of a too simplistic rejection of Felicite's work, with an equally facile condemnation of the Church for its censure of a prophetic figure.

We are pleased to thank Br. Edmond Raymond for his steadfast determination in pursuing the story of John Mary de La Mennais, a text which speaks eloquently of his love for our founder. We equally appreciate Br. Francis Blouin's role in completing a work cut short by illness. Through their cooperation, we are blessed with a life of our founder with great historical validity.

We trust that many among us will use this text to deepen our commitment to our father whose love of youth motivated him to dedicate his life to their education. May Father de La Mennais' charisma continue to motivate his sons and daughters to continue his mission as educational leaders through the communities of the Brothers of Christian Instruction and the Daughters of Providence. Br. Yannick Houssay, s.g.

CONTENTS

CHAPTER 1

1. Saint – Malo (1780-1814)

A SEAPORT, A FAMILY

Bloodstains on the stone

The year was 1801; the city, Paris; the place, the dim solitude of a former Carmelite monastery church. Two men paced the room and stopped to gaze at a blood-stained wall. Though neither of them lived in Paris, personal reasons had unexpectedly brought them together from opposite ends of the country. The elder had recently come out of a long exile beyond the eastern border, the younger from the northwestern city of Saint-Malo.[1]

Gabriel Cortois de Pressigny (1745-1823) was Bishop of Saint-Malo at the outset of the French Revolution. The National Assembly had abruptly suppressed his diocese along with fifty-one others on August 24, 1790, and the prospect of invincible hostility had convinced him to flee. He had skipped through Paris, had quietly escaped into neighboring Savoie, had moved on from there and survived the fate of a fugitive until the return of peace.[2] John de La Mennais, (1780-1860) his companion of twenty-one, lived with his family in the Breton port of Saint-Malo. Determined to prepare for the priesthood, he allowed no other consideration to weaken his resolution as he found lodging at the Foreign Missions Seminary, *rue du Bac*. He had recognized the voice of his long missing Bishop at Mass, and he had stepped forward, identified himself and declared his intentions.

Uprooted, exiled, but not broken by a decade of wandering, the prelate listened. Revolutionaries without jurisdiction had ousted him. His ecclesiastical authority was still valid and he was prepared to deal with the reality of hard times. His tone was deliberate: *"Prepare for tomorrow, and I will make you a sub-deacon."* On the morning of December 21, 1801, de Pressigny led the young de La Mennais from the Foreign Missions Seminary to the Carmelite church, and reviewed the state of the nation with stark realism. The stains on the chapel floor and in the sacristy were the darkened trace of blood spilled during the September Massacres of 1792. The revolutionaries had assembled in this sanctuary, priests, religious and the faithful who had rejected the new religion of the Revolution. Between September 2 and 5, 1792, they had slaughtered 186 of them with calculated savagery, in the church, on the grounds, in the garden chapel and in related prisons.

The Bishop stared gravely at his young companion and observed: *"You want to be a priest. The men who did this are still living. Do you realize that they could start again at any time?"* John's answer was ready: *"I have seen priests step up to the guillotine in Brittany; their sacrifice inspired and strengthened my resolution."* The Bishop then accompanied the young Breton to a Ursuline convent within walking distance, ordained him to the sub-deaconate and celebrated mass in the quiet privacy of its chapel. Now, as in the early Church: *"Blood of martyrs, seed of Christians!"* John returned to Brittany with a new challenge. Before the events of 1789, he had lived a quiet childhood in the region of Saint-Malo; he was now called to an adult role in a very difficult time.

Fortress by the sea

Saint-Malo owes its name to a monk and colonizing bishop who led Welsh refugees from an England afflicted by the plague and oppressed by foreign rule. Angle, Jute and Saxon invaders from across the North Sea left their homeland in the fifth century to plant warring kingdoms upon English homelands. Ruled by intruders or caught between feuding rivals, the Celts gradually retreated west. From Wales and Cornwall, many sailed to exile in Brittany and made it their "little Britain" to the south.

Maclou, (also referred to as Mac Load, Maclow and eventually Malo) was but one of the colonizers who led migrants to resettle across southern waters, boat people of the sixth century dislodged by conquering hordes. Their new land had a prehistory of settlements, and memories of a Roman occupation. Saint Aaron came from England, established a hermitage on the rock which Malo's followers would soon occupy and temporarily left his name to it. Malo's own leadership and reputation of holiness later earned him and his new home the name of Saint-Malo.

Peaceful settlers at the entrance of the Rance River could neither erase the violence of a turbulent past, nor ward off that of the future. The majestic estuary of the Rance opened a wide welcome to sea rovers coasting southward along the western shores of Normandy and veering west toward Brittany. From time immemorial, its generous waters had lured raiders of the north shore with irresistible temptations. Thriving inland towns repeatedly overrun by conquerors from land and sea prospered along its banks. The raiders kept coming and the sentinel of the valley learned to anticipate the first strike on the river.

Saint-Malo proudly overlooks the sea from its granite base above the waves. To the north, the Channel, Britain beyond! South on the mainland across moors, marshes and shifting sand, roads leading from the Rance River through Brittany and eastward to the heart of France. Both island and port, Saint-Malo guards its identity in the combat zone where the sea challenges the supremacy of the land. Along the northwestern coast of France, Brittany defends its dominion against the restless Channel. Lines from a traditional ditty sing well of the island:

> To Saint-Malo we will go
> Merrymaking by the sea
> To the island we are off to play.[3]

Island? Yes, though the sea never fully made the city its own. The granite spike clung to the rock bed of the coast while a shifting sand bar linked the rock to the bank. Shore dwellers called it *le Sillon* (the furrow), for it seemed that a giant plow had raised the fragile ridge that never abandoned the city to the waves. The citizens determined not to let the stubborn tide shred the island's last moorings. In 1509, they built *le Sillon* into a firm passage; they widened it in 1733, then gradually built it into a stable causeway. Thus the island, sometimes compared to a ship at anchor by offshore observers, would never be cut off. The French kings honored the determination of the residents by crowning the rock with fortress walls.

Necessity, those walls! The peaceful refugees of the sixth century and their successors survived plundering marauders, and from the ninth century, they withstood the raids of Norman pirates. During the sixteenth and seventeenth centuries, the struggle for power cast the port between the warships of England and France; soon Saint Malo earned its reputation as a "nest of corsairs." The French kings called on its fleet and the stronghold became a prime target for the British Navy while the privateers of the ports, corsairs of legend, raced with blockade runners to loot British warships. Each captured cargo weakened the rival and invited retaliation.

Retaliations were mutual, reprisals no surprise. The citizens of the port enclosed their town within protective walls. From the twelfth to the sixteenth centuries, the ramparts grew in stages until they became the massive fortress which stood the offensives of the seventeenth, eighteenth and nineteenth centuries, a grave presence unmoved until the first half of the twentieth century. During World War II, the crossfire of German and American forces gutted the city, but left the walls. The city rose from the rubble as did the Saint-Malo residence of the La Mennais family, shelled during combat, later rebuilt on its original plan. Saint-Malo remains the, authentic historical seaside fortress of the north shore and the pride of the bay.[4]

Saint-Malo was rock, city and port to ambitious generations of achievers. Its citizens raised tall bastions and proud banners, but nothing could more commendably swell their pride than the native heroes whose names inspired the nation. The list was long, open, and glistening with names inviting new generations to enterprise and excellence. From here Jacques Cartier left to explore the Saint Lawrence River; René Duguay-Trouin plotted the corsair raids which captured some 360 enemy ships; the mathematician and geographer Pierre-Louis Moreau de Maupertuis honored his city by his science and his influence. An island burial off shore recalls the writings and services of François-René de Chateaubriand, a contemporary of the La Mennais children. Writers apparently found it impossible to evade Robert Surcouf, the ubiquitous corsair of that generation, but they would soon add the name of La Mennais into the history of their city.[5]

Enterprising ancestors

John's grandparents were from prominent families of Saint-Malo. Both **Robert** and **Lorin** were respected names among the leading bourgeoisie of the port. It was customary for the wealthy to keep secondary homes in the countryside and to mimic the nobility by adding the name of property holdings to their own. In the Lorin family, the title became *Sieur de La Brousse*. In the Robert family, the title changed from *Des Saudrais* to *La Mennais* when John's paternal great grandfather styled himself Sieur de *La Mennais*.[6]

Five generations before John de La Mennais, the head of the family was known as François Robert *(II)*, *Sieur de La Tourelle* (1624-1671) whose spouse, Josseline Michelot *Des Saudrais* brought new property, and a new title to the family. Descendants then chose to sign *Robert Des Saudrais* for two generations. François Robert (IV), *Sieur Des Saudrais* (1691-1742) married Marie Yver des Rivières (1691-1717). An estate named *La Mennais* in the hamlet of Trigavou (Côtes d'Armor)[7] came into the family by that alliance, and François, John's great grandfather, began to sign *Mennais Robert* or François *Robert de La Mennais*. The name of *La Mennais* did not outlast four generations as it disappeared with John and Félicité.

Sounds echoing from the La Mennais ancestry carry the chatter of families around the hearth, the transactions of merchants at the bargaining counter, the whisper of winds skipping through country estates, the patter of children's feet atop fortress walls, the flap of sails on the high seas, the accents of public officials debating civic affairs, and the thunder of war cannons from privateers. Mixed echoes indeed as the ancestors of John de La Mennais moved through such scenarios in times of peace and in times of war.[8]

Louis-François Robert, Sieur de La Mennais, (1717-1804) John's grandfather who lived in Saint-Servan, trusted his own fortune to the sea and handed a hefty enterprise to his heirs. On April 17, 1742, he married Marie Thérèse Padet du Dréneuf, (1718?-1744) his first wife. Two sons were born from that marriage: Pierre-Louis (1743-1828), John's father, and Denys-François (1744-1829), later remembered as the beloved uncle Des Saudrais. Marie Thérèse died only twenty-five months after marriage while giving birth to her second son, Denys-François.[9]

On September 5, 1775, the two brothers married two Lorin sisters in the Cathedral of Saint-Malo: Gratienne-Jeanne (1750-1787) and Félicité-Simone-Jeanne (1753-1794). Both wives were born in Saint-Malo, daughters of Pierre Lorin *Sieur de La Brousse,* (1719-1799) and Bertranne-Marie Roce. (1716-1803). The new households inherited a legacy of resourcefulness and civic pride which served them well during the Revolution. Denys-François took on the older title of *Des Saudrais,* from the name of an estate near Combourg. He and Félicité were childless and lived in close association with Pierre-Louis, Gratienne, and their children who would refer to them familiarly as uncle and aunt *Des Saudrais.* As the elder, Pierre-Louis, John's father, held the more recent title of Sieur de *La Mennais.*

The heads of the Lorin family had been lawyers and magistrates from father to son during several generations. Pierre Lorin, John's maternal grandfather, was a lawyer titled at the Parliament of Paris, and Seneschal of Saint-Malo. Both he and his spouse were Norman; Bertranne-Marie Roce was of Irish descent. According to family lore and available genealogy, her ancestry hopped islands through sea storms and briny mist before resting on Norman soil.

The family had Nordic roots reaching through Ireland, Scotland and Vikings conquerors. Descendants prided in their association with William the Conqueror, Irish opponents to Cromwell, privateers of the Robert lineage.[10] At her wedding, Bertranne brought into the family *La Chesnaie* in Plesder (Ille-et-Vilaine), a country estate south of Saint-Malo, off the road between Dinan and Combourg. The property was a blessing, a quiet haven, a nest sheltered by woodlands in the stillness of the Breton countryside; it was there where the Lorins would escape from the restlessness of the port to rekindle their family intimacy.

At the marriage of his daughters, Pierre Lorin held double office. He was counselor to the king and ruled as Seneschal, first judge and magistrate for the civil, criminal and police jurisdiction of Saint-Malo. He also accepted executive tasks as Sub-delegate to the king's Intendant, the overseer of the kingdom in Brittany. The role of Seneschal was full-time work, the sub-delegation a social service which disrupted his personal and professional life, a task he fulfilled until 1782.

Pierre Laurin's official correspondence reveals a man who abhors ambiguity, proceeds in truth and pursues his commitments to completion. In times of famine, his concern for the increasing number of poor moved him to recommend the establishment of stable, endowed public charities. Diplomatic, yet direct, he served beyond the limits of his obligations. He kept prudent measure in his commitments, declined tasks without clear duties and resigned the role of sub-delegate when he judged it incompatible with family life and primary obligations. The lawyer who succeeded him shouldered the burden only one year before returning to the less exacting, more lucrative pursuits of a full-time lawyer. Lorin then recommended his son-in-law, John's father for the office. [11]

Pierre-Louis Robert de La Mennais held a record of service. Three years before his marriage in 1772, royal executives had chosen him to supply grain to the Island of Belle-Isle off the southern coast of Brittany. During the war for American independence, he had been asked to send artillery and hospital supplies for the armies of Rochambeau. According to public testimony, when he was recommended for official titles of nobility, eight hundred wagons were requested, a task accomplished in eight days. He rewarded laborers for time, horses and wagons from his salary.

Famine struck Brittany again in 1782. Mr. de La Mennais had anticipated the emergency which was particularly severe in Dinan and Saint-Malo, and he was ready with 15,000 bushels of imported wheat. Scarcity had driven the price to twelve pounds a bushel; he sold the wheat at eight pounds rather than the ten offered to him, and he willingly repeated such services at a loss. Pierre-Louis Robert, Sieur de La Mennais accepted the responsibility of sub-delegation on August 28, 1782; John was not quite two at the time.

Oceanside home, riverside peace

Early in the 18th century, the La Mennais family was asserting its presence in Saint-Malo and along the banks of the Rance River. When life within the city walls seemed too confining, an open space awaited occupants in the vicinity. Saint-Servan was partly settled by an overflow of residents up river from the port city, to which it was subject until the French Revolution. Louis-François lived there despite heavy portside duties.

In 1778, he was listed as Captain of the First Company of the local militia; his son, Pierre-Louis, was listed as Captain of the Second Company. After his marriage to Marie-Thérèse Padet, he lengthened his signature *to Sieur de La Mennais en Trigavou, Des Corbières en Saint-Servan,* etc. The second title was the name of an estate brought to the family by his wife. He proceeded to increase its size by acquiring adjoining lots. When his sons married, he deeded Les Corbières to them and the domain grew under their management until it reached the river. At one point, the family of Pierre-Louis de La Mennais occupied it as a temporary residence. Saint-Servan by the Rance had its appeal; both Pierre Lorin and Denys Des Saudrais kept additional residences in the vicinity of the La Mennais land. [12] Malo or withdrew up river in rural freedom and family closeness at Les Corbieres.

The commercial firm of grandfather Louis-François was centered in Saint-Malo. He kept an active presence within the walls at 3, *rue Saint Vincent,* at least as early as 1759, by renting space from Guillaume Éon, a business partner. He first associated his two sons to his enterprise and later transferred all of it to them. The company was far from a shoddy survival affair. Pierre-Louis, John's father, sent fishing crews to the cod banks of Newfoundland. He even exported to Spain and the French colonies in the Caribbean Sea, cloth, sail, canvas, homegrown flax, hemp, and other merchandise from the vicinity of Dinan, Fougères and Saint-Malo while keeping trade links open with northern ports. His imports provided essential materials for the construction and armament of royal vessels. When harvests failed, his trade with England and Holland enabled him to haul in emergency cargoes of wheat against famine, flax and hemp to supply vital local industries, and survival fodder for the herds.

Meanwhile, a lively family flourished in the princely Éon mansion which his father rented at the corner of *rue Saint-Vincent* and *rue Sainte-Barbe,* within view of the *Saint-Vincent* Gate, a few streets away from the *Chateau.* His family could thus freely mix with the stirring gentry of Saint-Malo or withdraw up river to live in rural freedom and family closeness at *Les Corbiéres.*[13]

---

[1] **N.B.: To avoid lengthy repetitions, the more frequently cited works and archives are abridged in bold character footnote references. A quick access list of abbreviations and complete references is supplied in the pages preceding Chapter 1.**

[2] See Chapter 4.

[3] Author's version of the original: *Nous irons à Saint-Malo. Nous irons nous amuser. Nous irons jouer dans l'Île.*

[4] Edourd Prampain, Saint-Malo historique. Amiens: Piteux Frères, 1902. François Tuloup, *Saint-Malo, Histoire générale,* 2e éd., Paris: Klincksieck, 1970. Pierre-Jean Yvon, *Le Grand Saint-Malo,* Saint-Servan: ATIMCO [c1992].

[5] These lives range from the fifteenth to the nineteenth centuries: Jacques Cartier (1491-1557), René Duguay-Trouin (1673-1736), Pierre-Louis Moreau de Maupertuis (1698-1759), François-René de Chateaubriand (1768-1848), Robert Surcouf (1773-1827).

[6] From genealogical notes. **AFIC**, dossier no. 2.

[7] *Côtes-du-Nord,* at the time.

[8] A few examples are in order. François Robert, III, Sieur Des Saudrais (1664-1694/5) and his father-in-law, Jean Prairier, both died in the Caribbean in 1694. His father had died in Morocco, prisoner of the Barbaresques in 1633. Des Saudrais and La Mennais' ancestors, and most of their relatives include sea captains or successful merchants who fitted

■ ————————————————————————————— 9

out ships for the cod-fishing banks of Newfoundland and risked cargoes on the Atlantic. In times of war, their ships raced with blockade-runners and privateers.

[9] Christian Marechal, *La Famille de La Mennais sous l'Ancien régime & la Révolution,* Paris: Perrin, 1913. Pages 10-25.

[10] Genealogical notes from **AFIC**, 2. The complete genealogical trees for the La Mennais and Lorin families do not seem to have been thoroughly traced.

[11] *Marechal, La famille* ... op. cit., pp. 25-57.

[12] H.-C. Rulon, "Une propriété de la Famille La Mennais ignorée des. Historiens." **Chron**, no. 211 (July 1957): 224-231, and sequel in nos. 213 (January 1958):73-80 and 214 (April 1958): 146-152.

[13] Family vital statistics: *Maternal grandparents:* Pierre Lorin (1719-1799), Bertranne-Marie, (Roce) Lorin (1716-1803).

Paternal grandparents: Louis-François Robert, Sieur de La Mennais (1717-1804), Marie-Thérèse (Padet du Dréneuf) de La Mennais (1718(?)-1744). *Parents:* Pierre-Louis de La Mennais (1743-1828), Gratienne-Jeanne(Lorin) de La Mennais (1750-1784). *Uncle and Aunt de Saudrais:* Denys-François des Saudrais (1744-1829), Félicité-Simone-Jeanne (Lorin) Des Saudrais (1758-1794).

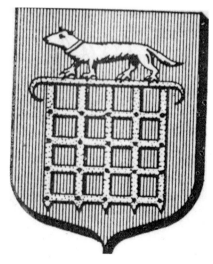

St. Malo

Chapter 2

JEAN-MARIE ROBERT DE LA MENNAIS (EARLY YEARS)

The family of Pierre-Louis and Gratienne

Jean-Marie Robert de La Mennais, familiarly known as *Jean-Marie* or *Jean* or **John,** was born in *Saint-Malo, Ille-et-Vilaine,* on Sept 8, 1780, and died in Ploërmel, *Morbihan* on December 26, 1860, the third child in a family of six, all born from 1776 to 1785.

Louis-Marie	1776 (Sept. 12)-1805 (Dec. 17)
Pierre-Jean	1778 (June 24) -1784 (?)

Jean-Marie 1780 (Sept. 8) -1860 (Dec. 26)

Hugues-Félicité 1782 (June 19) -1854 (Feb. 27). Known as *Féli* in the family.
Marie-Josephe 1784 (Feb. 24) -1851 (March 31)
Gratien-Claude 1785 (May 2) - 1818 (summer?)

Félicité and Marie shared many years of John's life, but by the summer of 1818, three brothers had passed away: the short-lived Pierre-Jeanin 1784, Louis-Marie, the eldest in 1805, and Gratien-Claude, the erratic youngest in 1818. John, the eldest of the three survivors lived 80 years, Marie passed away in her 67th year, and the ill-fated Félicité in his 71st.

The young family grew in vibrant togetherness. For Saint-Malo, the last years of the old regime were years of undisturbed peace which transformed the "nest of corsairs" into a whirring fellowship of thriving merchants. Never would the La Mennais enterprise fare better. The home at 3 rue *Saint-Vincent* called Mr. de La Mennais to paternal responsibility, but business preoccupations so often held him away that his wife managed the household. Her presence complemented the grave authority of her generous spouse with the love found only in a mother's heart. [1]

Gratienne had been educated beyond what was expected of a woman of her time. Her grandson Ange Blaize writes that his grandmother *"had read extensively, and gathered from her readings what could be useful to her children; she had personally written a plan for their education."* [2] Her premature death on September 22, 1787, deprived the family of her comforting presence. Félicité, her fourth son, was five at the time. He remembered only having seen her recite the rosary and play the violin. At seven, John was old enough to remember more and grieved her loss; he kept a few pages of her handwriting as relics all his life and occasionally showed them to close associates.[3]

We know little about Gratienne, but we catch a glimpse of her soul in her reflections on the De Profundis, Psalm 130. The inspiration of the psalm moves her to express her gratitude for our redemption: (Excerpts) *"I have lost sight of the divine perfection of a merciful God; Lord, do not reject my tears .We take little time to meditate on the rewards of the just, guided only by our senses, and at times degraded to the rank of an animal. It is from that state that you mercifully lead us to plead in trust: "Lord hear me!" How sad these thoughts, oh my God, for a heart that yearns to be entirely yours yet has not always been. As I experience your goodness, I yearn to remain entirely yours. -- You are the only good I seek, the only one I desire. -- The evils of the world have seduced me, yet with your strength, I no longer fear my weakness. A God dying for his creature is a mystery of love beyond my mind: I desire nothing than to speak of your greatness."*[4]

Providence provided caring guardians at Gratienne's death as her sister, Félicité, (from whom John's younger brother was named), remained an attentive neighbor known as "aunt Des Saudrais." Her intriguing and jovial husband, Denys, "uncle Des Saudrais," was always welcome as *Tonton* (child talk for uncle). Maid Villemain shared their life by loyally assuming her share of responsibility, earning the role of an affectionate and indispensable presence. After Gratienne's death, aunt Félicité Des Saudrais became a second mother to her sister's family. Marie remembered the lessons and examples of her mother and her aunt as she faithfully transmitted them to her own children.

Gratienne opened her children to life and helped them to open their first books. When the day came for more structured academic work, Mr. de La Mennais found a tutor in the person of Father Carré who prepared John and Félicité for the study of Latin authors. The teacher achieved good results until alcoholism impaired his effectiveness. He accepted the church of the Revolution, and later disappeared into exile. John was then appointed preceptor in French and Latin to Félicité. Too soon! The master was less prepared than predecessors for the ungovernable youth. The first lessons were from Livy and Tacitus, but the rebellious junior resented the elder's assertiveness. Insurrection followed and classes degenerated into civil wars, pupil and teacher slashing with goose quills and recklessly setting up barricades. The master was forced to leave, his legitimacy slighted; Felicite triumphed, raising his cap on a discarded pole planted between overturned stools at the center of the room. A few months passed and lessons stopped.[5]

The intriguing and jovial Uncle Des Saudrais then took over the education of his nephews. A liberal disillusioned by the brutality of the Revolution, a reader of philosophers and a disciple of Rousseau, he is alternatively described as orthodox and reactionary. He received his two nephews in his home of Saint-Servan, opened his sizable private library to them, supervised their work, charmed them by his lessons and incited them to inquire on, though he forbade them to read certain authors.[6] He managed to obtain some settled study from his spirited younger nephew. Félicité once wrote at the foot of a notebook page: *"My uncle gets angry at me because I do not read my grammar rules before doing my assignment."*[7] Considering the known character of the youngster, the uncle wisely left the two adolescents to themselves for extended periods, perhaps remembering Rousseau's *Émile;* he was known to have punished Félicité by locking him in his library.

The uncle's lessons transformed the young rebel into an indisciplined reader who recalled bending over his books for hours in his room at night. The libraries of the time often placed disallowed books in controlled sections called *inferno:* no zoning could keep Félicité from foraging at will through the pages of forbidden authors. Lockup was a reward more than a punishment for him; John read and studied with finer discernment. Even at an early age, John's catechism of the Diocese of Saint Malo had become a companion book to which he held until death. The two brothers remained ever grateful to the tutor of their adolescent years, the lovable uncle Des Saudrais.

Trench-dark streets, wide-open world

There were other windows to the world. The island life of Saint-Malo taught more lessons than the children of the citadel could ever absorb. Ange Blaize writes of a *"sad and dark"* Saint-Malo with *"very tall"* buildings which *"overhang narrow winding streets"*[8] Observers standing on city walls have sometimes referred to those streets as trenches, but only foul weather and war could hold occupants in their shadows. All streets quickly led to the ramparts and up to the light. Are there stronger temptations for children than to escape and to climb?

The La Mennais children did not have to discover fortresses in storybooks; they lived in one. Their image of fortress walls was hard stone under their steps. The ramparts fascinated them, inbuilt winding stairs challenged them, raising their vision of the world from turrets and lookouts along a wall wide enough for promenades and play space. The view from the heights was an artist's dream: shades of perennial green draped the land to the edge of the sea, while restless winds spun gristmill sails spinning near Saint-Servan. Over the causeway, *le sillon,* and along the eastern shoreline towards Paramé, the restless waters challenged the rugged coast, while the islands of the bay reflected the matchless blue of the sky mirrored in the waters at the foot of gray walls.

The back-bay can no longer be seen as John de La Mennais saw it. Félicité complained about developments: *"my old Saint-Malo is being spoiled for me. It is no longer that of my childhood."* He inquired about the basin from prison in 1841.[9] And indeed the digging of docking basins was transforming the bay. During John's childhood, the young family watched ships float in from boundless ocean to receptive harbor, before the breakwaters and docks of later years modified the scenery.

The sea was the life of Saint-Malo, the sea, open, mysterious, impulsive, unpredictable. It lured the imagination of the La Mennais children away from the walls to freedom and fantasy. Its inspiration was never lost whether it came from sunlit blue seas or the threat of rumbling storms! The sea was a power to reckon with. They saw it come forth to embrace the city with tidal punctuality, and stood through its darker moods when it beat at the gates with compulsive fury. The children soon realized that its power made of their walled city a city of the world. A constant flow of ships, cargoes, sailors and travelers fed avid youngsters with an unmatched variety of human drama and sea lore. No mere spectacle! Saint-Malo went to the world, and much of the world came to it. The openness of the Saint-Malo society was a healthy experience for John who would later embrace so much of the world in his readings, and ponder the life of the Church universal and the needs of foreign missions from the heartland of Brittany!

The countryside taught what the city and the sea did not. The family and its in-laws were land owners; they kept secondary homes, expanded their holdings, benefited from rented property and planned for the future. The children spent leisure time on several of their estates. They were welcome at *Val-Ernoul in Saint-Méloir*, ten kilometers east of the port and even Mount *Saint-Michel* was visible in the distance. It was the favorite vacation home of grandfather Louis-François; its town cemetery would become his final resting place in 1804. During the years of its occupancy by the family, *Les Corbières in Saint-Servan* provided regular opportunities for quiet rural living along the banks of the Rance. The Lorins provided an alternative; they loved to take their grandchildren to La Chesnaie where Pierre Lorin built a comfortable manor. That estate would later have special meaning for John and his brother.

"Noblesse oblige!"

Pierre-Louis presided over the destiny of his young family, managed a large commercial enterprise and found time to serve as one of 62 sub-delegates to de Bertrand de Molleville, the last royal Intendant for the province of Brittany with domicile at Rennes.[10] Nobility has its obligations. The nobility of Pierre-Louis was one of character, but it almost became one of title. As Sub-delegate for Saint-Malo, he gave work time and provided reports and advice.

The economic life of his district interested him and he reported on its social and moral implications. He passed severe judgment on the excessive number of mendicant religious who drained needed resources from local charities. He was concerned about children abandoned by destitute mothers, and he reacted to the inadequacy of public charity by seeking to render it more effective, as his father-in-law had done. Hard times periodically revived his concern for the needy.

Lean years came to Brittany in 1785. Mr. de La Mennais saw the obligation of public authority to protect the poor and provide them with means of survival, and he recommended controls to guarantee that assistance would reach them. When the harvests of flax and hemp failed, the home spinning and weaving industry lost its basic raw materials, and peasants lost their basic income. Re-supplying prime quality seed of the preceding year became critical, but the assistance was self-defeating when merchants bought reserves of high-yield seed to speculate, leaving the older lower yield stock to the poor. To protect vital remunerated labor, the sub-delegate proposed to channel prime quality seed at low cost for the poor through parish or charity representatives; if necessary, he accepted deferred reimbursement until the next harvest.

Home industry was an important base of family income. In 1787, Mr. de La Mennais supported the Sisters of the Cross of Saint-Servan in their request for an expansion of their building. They were teaching some 300 children when the Bishop asked them to include a free spinning school. Mr. de La Mennais had suggested the innovation because spinning was essential for weaving export fabrics, a source of income for the poor at the time. He not only favored the permit, but made his own contribution, requesting a measure of public financing and began to supply raw hemp.

Failing harvests, steep grain prices, and bread rationing periodically afflicted the poor. Emergency grain and flour imports offered at reasonable cost were essential to force local prices back to normal, as was the case in 1785. The alternative was misery, even famine. Mr. de La Mennais was a grain importer with a heart larger than the tonnage of his ships. He met the emergencies in the region of Saint-Malo and Saint-Brieuc with imports sold at basic rates, often at cost or at personal loss, for which he never requested reimbursement. At the request of the Intendant, he sent cargoes to ports supplying other regions of the province, and brought in fodder on the same terms. His superiors highly appreciated his liberality, but the public had little knowledge of his personal commitment. He served as Subdelegate until the Revolution ended the royal government.

In September 1786, Mr. de La Mennais requested patents of nobility, (*lettres de noblesse*). The document was granted with the signature of Louis XVI, May 13, 1788, but only after sponsors bypassed the bureaucracy and appealed directly to the monarch. Misfortune struck the family at the time. Gratienne died on Sept. 22, 1787, and severe illness visited three of her children. A major contribution to the royal treasury, the Golden Mark (*le Marc d'*-*or*), was required for the registration of such titles. In view of heavy losses recently incurred for the public good, the candidate requested an exemption. Unrest paralyzed the government and the unattended plea vanished in the revolutionary fever. His ennoblement had not been recorded at the Audit Office of Nantes. Mr. de La Mennais was never officially titled, a deferral which may have saved his life during the Revolution.[11]

Émile Forgues who published the posthumous works of Félicité, described the family members as *"staunch individuals, energetic; a race of resolute men, steadfast,"* sometimes *"driven to strange extremes"*[12] by an *"intractable nature."* The friend who wrote these observations after witnessing the last days of Félicité, failed to notice the generosity and civic responsibility flowing through the family history. John was too young to fully understand the accomplishments of his elders and he was still grieving over the loss of his mother. The events which followed 1789 would test his adolescence before he could fully appreciate his father's generosity.

---

[1] **Lav**, vol. I, pp. 3-10.

[2] Ange Blaize, Oeuvres inédites de F. Lamennais, Paris: E. Dentu, 1866. 2 vols., vol. 1, p. 4.

[3] **Lav**, vol. 1, p.5.

[4] Segments selected from Christian Marechal, *La Famille de La Mennais sous l'Ancien régime & la Révolution,* Paris: Perrin, 1913. Pp. 202¬-224.

[5] Account based on the author, who wrote after conversing with Félicité. [Hippolyte Barbier], *Biographie* du *Clergé contemporain par un Solitaire*, tome premier, Paris: A. Appert, 1841, pp. 152-153. The chapter on "M. de La Mennais" is from pages 145-180.

[6] Before the rediscovery of the La Mennais occupancy of **Les Corbières** in Saint-Servan near Saint-Malo, biographers locate the library of Des Saudrais at **La Chesnaie**, almost 30 kilometers away and better known by its subsequent history. See H.C. Rulon, **Chron**, nos. 213 (January 1958):73-80 and 214 (April 1958): 146-152. In fact, three authors simply give "the country" as the site. See **Chron**, no. 214, p. 152.

[7] Ange Blaize, *Oeuvres inédites de F. Lamennais*, Paris: E. Dentu, 1866. vol. 1, p.14.

[8] Ibid., Vol. I, p. 2.

[9] Letters to Marion, Nov. 21, 1839 and March 3, 1841. **Cor gén F**, vols. VIII, pp. 443-444; VII, pp. 41-42.

[10] Antoine-François de Bertrand de Molleville (1746-1818), at this time royal Intendant overseeing Brittany from Rennes.

[11] Marechal, op. cit., pp. 58-201, 330-333.

[12] Émile D. Forgues, *Oeuvres posthumes de F. Lamennais*, Paris: Paulin et Le Chevalier, 1859, 2 vols. Tome I, p. IV.

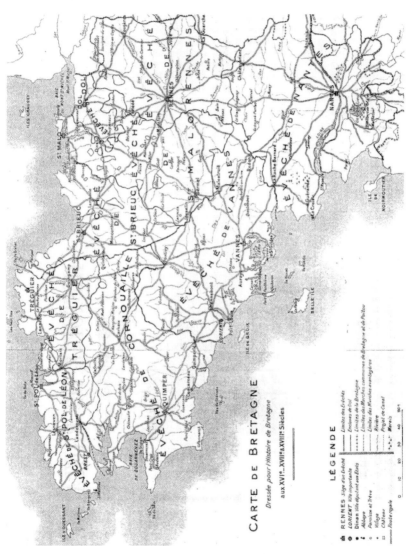

CARTE DE BRETAGNE

Dressée pour l'Histoire de Bretagne

aux XVIe...XVIIe&XVIIIe Siècles

LÉGENDE

RENNES *Siège d'un Evêché*
LORIENT *Ville importante*
Dinan *Ville où siégeaient aux Etats*
Abbaye
Paroisse et Trêve
Village
Château
Route royale

Limites des Evêchés
Enclaves de Dol
Limites de la Bretagne
Limites des Marches communes de Bretagne et de Poitou
Limites des Marches avoisinantes
Rivière
Projet de Canal
Marais

Map of Brittany during the 17th Century

Chapter 3

A DECADE OF VIOLENCE

Who will serve the Bishop's mass?

The Parisians who stormed the Bastille on July 14, 1789, could not anticipate the magnitude of their revolt. The French Revolution began as a justified plea for long needed reforms; it quickly turned into a nightmare which shattered the existing regime and shook the thrones of Europe. In Saint-Malo, it incited the rabble, unseated the Bishop, and changed the life of the young John de La Mennais in unexpected ways.

Louis XVI convened the States General on May 1, 1789, in the hope that it would approve new taxes to solve the financial crisis of the kingdom. The monarch and the nobility were squandering the people's earnings faster than the nation could replenish the royal coffers. The Third Estate, the delegates representing the common people, pleaded for reform. On July 9, 1789, it broke the resistance of the other two estates by unilaterally declaring itself the National Constituent Assembly.

By August 4, the new Assembly was briskly eradicating all titles of nobility, all privileges and all traces of feudalism. Administratively and financially, the French Church was tightly bound with the royal government and the feudal system. It supported itself and funded charities, hospitals and schools with benefices and revenues from extensive, often private land endowments. Each diocese was both a religious and a political entity. As head of a diocese, each bishop served as a spiritual guide and as a duly constituted lord, levying tithes and exercising the responsibilities and privileges of lords. In times of hardship, the people found it difficult to dissociate the pastor of souls from the *seigneur* benefiting from the fruits of their labor.

Church administrators bore the fate of the royal regime when on July 12, 1790 legislators brashly created a government church by enacting the *Civil Constitution of the Clergy*. The measure violated the Concordat of 1516 by severing the official French Church from the authority of the Pope, by modifying diocesan boundaries, by electing bishops by popular vote and by requiring priests to become civil employees appointed and salaried by civil authority. Louis XVI signed the law under duress on August 24, but Pope Pius VI rejected it as its enforcement subverted the Church of France.

Bishop Cortois de Pressigny abruptly lost his diocese. The law cut the number of dioceses from 134 to 83, thereby suppressing 51, including St Briuc. As subjects of a Lord Bishop, the people of Saint-Malo welcomed relief from traditional taxes, not necessarily the destruction of their Church. The people met the demands of the royal administration with difficulty. When hardship revisited the land and the price of bread rose, they understandably resented the additional tithes and feudal rights of their Lord Bishop. The coarser citizenry celebrated the suppression of the diocese with a riot as a howling mob broke onto the grounds of the Episcopal palace on October 11, 1790; the National Guard forced it back and closed the gate.[1]

At ten in the morning of Thursday, October 14, a city commission entered the Cathedral choir after the office and ordered the Bishop and the Chapter to terminate their functions immediately; though churchmen did not deserve such treatment, so ended the Diocese of Saint-Malo. Realizing that his city had nothing for him but prospects of harassment, aggression, loss of freedom or worse, the Bishop quietly fled.

De Pressigny was neighbor and friend to the La Mennais family. He kept a residence at the minor seminary of Saint-Servan where he could rest from administrative duties. A gated stone wall was the only separation between the seminary and *Les Corbières*. Father François Manet, a contemporary of these events who spent the Revolution hiding in the region, writes simply that the Bishop slept at the seminary of Saint-Servan on October 15, and left for Paris the next morning.[2]

John de La Mennais would neither forget the evening of the fifteenth, nor the departure of his Bishop on the sixteenth. Bishop Cortois de Pressigny spent his last evening in the Diocese with the family of Mr. de La Mennais in Saint-Servan. Before retiring to his residence, he proposed to celebrate a last Mass and asked who would serve it. *"I will,"* replied John. *"So, you can serve Mass!"* replied the surprised prelate. *"Do you know your catechism?"* John could answer *"Yes"* and his understanding of the text satisfied his visitor. *"The times are evil,"* said the Bishop. *"I have to leave without knowing if I will ever be allowed to return. Tomorrow, you may receive your first communion and confirmation."* After Mass in the bishop's chapel on the morning of October 16, 1790, John received his Lord in holy communion and the sacrament of confirmation.

John was nowhere in sight when Cortois de Pressigny parted with a farewell blessing. Everyone stared when John suddenly reappeared cane in hand, necessities bundled in a shoulder sack. *"Where are you going my son?"* asked the father in surprise. The resolute traveler turned to the Bishop in reply. *"My Lord, you are my Bishop, I want to be a priest and I am following you."* The fugitive explained the impossibility of John's coming, blessed him, and promised to ordain him in due time. He left John to the emotions of his first communion, disappointed but not resourceless. The youngster was a lad of ten at the time, though one with a keen sense of the unfolding drama.[3]

The exile was silent about his plans because indiscretion could be fatal. Rumors sent him north across the Channel, to the French *émigrés* on the Island of Jersey. The assumption led John to comment: *"The Bishop is going among the Protestants, and he will need someone to serve his mass."* De Pressigny slipped through Paris, skipped past the French border into neighboring Savoy and beyond, where he lived the life of a fugitive until the end of the crisis.

In Paris, extremists gained control of the Revolution and the Assembly quickly turned against religion. On November 2, 1789, the

Assembly decreed the confiscation of Church property; on February 13, 1790, it outlawed religious orders by prohibiting religious vows. The Civil Constitution of the Clergy of July 12 enlisted priests to the constitutional church much too slowly, so by November 27, the Assembly required from every priest an oath of compliance. On November 29, it declared "suspect" all nonjuring priests, those who refused to take the oath of allegiance.

City of chilling fear

Revolutionary fever fed on feasts and parades. Before the departure of Bishop Cortois de Pressigny, Saint-Malo held a review of the National Guard followed by a mass for the military. The Assembly was then requiring a loyalty oath from all citizens. The National Assembly ordered all churchmen to swear public acceptance of the new church, but few priests yielded to intimidation regardless of the tight surveillance. On February 6, 1791, the city demanded the signature of an official oath, without reservations. On February 12, when Le Saout, Parish Priest of the Cathedral, refused to read publicly the new instructions of the National Assembly, two guards escorted a city official who read them from the pulpit. On May 29, the city abolished the old worship; on June 5, the mayor installed a constitutional priest at the Cathedral; priests who rejected the new church were banished from the city. Only the clergy of the government church could legally worship from then on, confusing events for the conscience of a ten-year-old.

Status, social pride and a sense of civic responsibility moved Pierre-Louis de La Mennais to participate in patriotic celebrations. He once had a formal uniform tailored to prepare John for a military and religious parade. The youngster eagerly awaited the event until he learned that constitutional priests would preside. He questioned aunt Des Saudrais on the eve of the feast: *"Will the government priests be there?"* *"Yes,"* answered the aunt. *"Then, it would be a sin to assist,"* continued the young nephew. *"I'm afraid so; indeed it seems forbidden,"* replied the Aunt. John needed to hear no more. When called the next morning, he had disappeared, not to be seen till he returned hungry in the evening, regretting the displeasure caused to his father, but at peace with his conscience.[4]

The experience was a prelude to more difficult choices. In June 1791, the revolutionaries thwarted the attempt of Louis XVI to flee, declared war on Austria, suspended royal powers after the invasion of the Tuileries, abolished the Monarchy and installed the Convention on September 21. They jailed the King on December 3, and guillotined him publicly on January 21, 1793. In March, the Vendean uprising stirred rebellion in the west; domestic resistance, armed insurrection at home, and the movements of foreign armies revealed the fragility of the new regime. Nervous revolutionaries singled out internal enemies for rigorous repression, a list that included nobles, the non-constitutional clergy and members of religious orders, citizens faithful to the old Church, families of *émigrés*, and untrustworthy officers.

Loyalty to the 'old Church' soon become treason to the nation. The Assembly ordered the deportation of all "non-juring" priests on May 27, 1792. Those who stayed behind became the hunted priests, outlaws who slipped into hiding. On November 17, 1793, the Convention quickly created a Committee of Public Safety, legitimizing a Reign of Terror and giving Robespierre, the 'monster' control over the Committee. Arbitrary imprisonments and public executions at the guillotine became routine. (It is estimated that 300,000 victims were imprisoned, and between 35,000 to 40,000 executed, at least 17,000 of them after trial, 20,000 on mere accusation).[5]

An armed insurrection in the west preoccupied the Convention. It commissioned the Proconsul Jean-Baptiste Le Carpentier to crush all resistance in Normandy and in the region of Saint-Malo. Le Carpentier arrived on the evening of December 15, 1793, and ruled the port city with unsparing rigor during eight months. At the request of citizen Baize, the City Council met him as a body and Mayor Perruchot delivered a welcoming speech. Le Carpentier jailed the mayor on short order and sent him to the guillotine in Paris for lack of revolutionary zeal. A friend and business associate of Mr. de La Mennais, Louis Blaize de Maisonneuve thought it prudent to offer hospitality to the agent of the Convention. There seemed no better protection, nor quicker source of information than the Proconsul in residence; hospitality thus brought the "Terror" perilously close to John's family.

During the term of this Jacobin's rule, the adolescent eyes of John de La Mennais saw Saint-Malo change from an exuberant community of merchants, to a city of chilling fear. Le Carpentier asserted that 3,000 good citizens would be enough in the city. To reach that goal, 9,000 heads in the district would have to fall. He shocked the population by the brutality of his intentions and horrified it by the cruelty of his decrees. He quickly jailed 500 "suspects" and executed 120 of them. Annoyed by a declining arrest rate, he proposed to set up more prisons after filling all available space.

He boasted of his effectiveness to the Convention, stating that non-juring priests would have to use *"ocean currents"* to *"deport themselves to the next world,"* for they are *"vigorously pursued in ours."* He preferred brisk action to time-wasting interrogations: *"Name, profession, a shove, and the trial is over!"* The thrust of a victim's neck under the fatal blade impassively closed proceedings. His executioners operated an active guillotine in front of the city hall a few streets from the La Mennais residence. He ordered prisoners shot on the beach and followed such deeds with public festivities at the scene of his crimes. Unsatisfied with executions in his city, he sent cartloads of victims to the public guillotine in Paris as samples of his purge. His last victims were freed in transit when the Convention abruptly ended his rule.[6]

Le Carpentier overstocked metal gates, ramps and railings requisitioned from churches and stately homes and plundered roofing all to provide lead for bullets. Plaintiffs accused him of taking three quarters of the wealth of the La Mennais and other enterprising families. Extortion had impoverished the merchant Louis Blaize de Maisonneuve, the host who later petitioned the Convention to restore his wealth stolen by Le Carpentier. Blaize complained to the Convention that the tyrant had intimidated the wealthy by extortion: *"Your money or your life!"*

The coup d'état that overturned Robespierre, ended the Reign of Terror for the nation on July 28, 1794, and the mandate of Le Carpentier for Saint-Malo. The Paris Convention recalled the Proconsul responsible for some 600 local executions and hundreds of arbitrary prison terms. John was not yet fourteen when the fanatic sheepishly left a victimized population for Paris on August 11, 1794.[7]

Citizen Des Saudrais, Citizen La Mennais

Wealth and influence were heavy liabilities after 1789, and for John's father and uncle Des Saudrais, there was no way to hide. Denys Des Saudrais served in active public administration on the City Council from December 5, 1790, until he resigned after his third term in 1792. During his tenure, he voted, signed and occasionally suggested decisions against his Church. The Saint-Malo revolutionaries did not hesitate to confiscate Church property, evict the Brothers of the Christian Schools along with other religious, intimidate priests into signing the clergy oath, install constitutional priests, prohibit the old worship, close churches, and jail or expel "non-juring" priests.

On April 5, 1792, Bishop Cortois de Pressigny informed his former diocesans by letter from exile that Pope Pius VI had rejected the Civil Constitution of the Clergy. The Revolutionists had disillusioned Denys, an active liberal until it became impossible for him to accept the senseless violence. He resigned from office after his third term December 6, 1792, and turned to the education of his nephews. Arrogance and brutality had converted John's uncle to Christian views and the wisdom of his later years. Fortunately, Denys Des Saudrais had left the scene before the arrival of Le Carpentier. [8]

Experience with a tyrant also tested the liberal leanings of John's father. True to character, the former Subdelegate faced the hardships of 1789 with unmitigated generosity. He became a "voluntary" contributor to various revolutionary funds, and provided wheat and flour to stave off famine. When called upon, he advised about public charity, dispatched emergency shipments to Grandville during Le Carpentier's merciless Norman campaign, served as Assistant Police Commissioner, President of the Commercial Court and Treasurer of the Hospital. Ruinous giving and cumulated unrequited services failed to shield him from attack. At one point, he confounded his accusers by requesting and obtaining an official certificate of good citizenship; he lived to see the demise of Le Carpentier.

Young outlaw

Saint-Malo and Saint-Servan were never short of loyal Christians to shelter hunted priests. Non-juring priests hiding in attics, basements, sheds or farms could celebrate secret masses in the city, in suburban Saint-Servan, or in the secluded farmsteads of the vicinity. Mr. de La Mennais' philosophical rationalism was known, but intimate friends were also aware of his willingness to hide persecuted priests even during frantic tracking activity. John shared the risks of his father's vulnerable hospitality with adolescent finesse. He once accosted a carefree "American sailor" at the port with the words: *"Come with me, a room is waiting for you at my father's house." "Who are you?"* replied the astonished stranger. *"I am the son of Mr. de La Mennais, and you are a priest,"* replied John, as the pair slinked away.[9]

The sailor was indeed a priest in disguise. Mass with the family would occasionally follow. Ange Blaize reports a family experience: *"To adore God was to risk one's head. Now and then, in the evening, a non-juring priest, the disguised Father Vielle, slipped into the paternal home. The family assembled in a garret at midnight. The dear maid Villemain watched outside. Two candles burned on a table transformed into an altar. Father Vielle, assisted by my uncle John de La Mennais, then thirteen, celebrated mass."*[10]

The lad of thirteen knew the whereabouts of other hunted priests and managed to assist them, sometimes with the complicity of Amélie Sauvage, a girl about his age who lived in Saint Servan. The youthful cunning of the conniving pair kept prudent bonds between secluded heroes. John served their masses and led them to the bedside of the dying. Having witnessed executions in Saint-Malo, he knew that he was tempting fate, but ruthless men failed to subdue his buoyant zeal. He was hurrying to the hideout of Father Engerran on a winter moonlit night when a patrol guard's bursting *"Halt!" (qui vive !)* abruptly called him to a trembling stop. The child's cool reflex bridged the pause. *"Friend, what time is it?"* *"One o'clock!"* John gratefully skipped home with a crisp *"Thank you, citizen!"* and bouncing steps.

The example of a brother's wily courage was not lost for Marie when the Reign of Terror ended. After Le Carpentier's departure, and after aunt Félicité's death, neighbors organized a simple neighborhood dance and Mr. de La Mennais promised to send his only daughter. The prospect of a republican ball intrigued the child. In the absence of her aunt, John had become a refuge and a guide and she turned to him for advice. The budding theologian suggested that it would be prudent not to attend. It was easy for an eleven-year-old lad to vex a quick-tempered father with a refusal. The expected response came without surprise: *"Sir, doctor must have decided that also!"* With the back of his hand, he made the meddling counselor atone for his inflexibility. The scene ended between an irate father, a stoic offender and his tearful sister who still told the story with emotion half a century later.[11]

Quiet call

Father Engerran was a priest from the Cathedral parish. Hunted through the Revolution, he was among the better-known hidden clergy whose ingenious courage inspired hope. He had been confessor and spiritual guide to the young de La Mennais before the latter met his "sailor" on the *Sillon*. The "sailor," was Father Louis Vielle,[12] a priest from the city of Noyon who fled to Paris to engage in secret ministry when friends informed him that "insubordinates" in Saint- Malo were seeking the illegal ministry of a non-juring priest. The port offered opportunities to escape into exile, but Vielle stayed to share the fate of his new friends, changing hideout whenever his secret was at risk. He was seeking new cover when John identified him; the new friendship transformed the fugitive into a secret home tutor. The sly youngster could not anticipate that his uneasy guest would soon guide him along the ways of learning and virtue while the Revolution tore through his city.

No lesson could equal the living examples of heroic faith given by Engerran and Vielle who combined heroic lives with solid instruction. Engerran, who had guided John's first experience of church life, remained a trusted adviser even while the Revolution outlawed his ministry. When Vielle came, the youngster was ready for decisions of adolescence which often set the course of a lifetime. Home and parish had played their roles, juvenile impressions had developed into adolescent understanding, early-life options were now evolving in a winter of incredulity. Hard choices had become part of John's life by this time. The hunted Vielle began John's intellectual and spiritual preparation for a priesthood which remained outlawed by the Revolution.

A third influence enriched John's spiritual life at this time. Father de Clorivière[13] had been a Jesuit until the Church suppressed his society in 1773. A native of Saint-Malo, he had become the Parish priest of Paramé, eastern neighbor to his home city, and after 1789, he had lived a clandestine existence. Religious life was then officially outlawed, but during the Terror, he had planned the foundation of two secret religious orders, one for women and one for men. Their members would profess vows, live by a flexible rule under a religious superior, wear no distinctive dress, reside wherever their lives required, meet whenever possible in times of crisis, but assemble regularly when freedom prevailed.

The de Cloriviere priests would become the short-lived Society of the Sacred Heart, the women, the Daughters of the Heart of Mary. John was then temporarily ineligible for membership in the priest's Society of the Sacred Heart, but the Founder's advice and example inspired his life. With Engerran and Vielle, de Clorivière guided the youngster's response to the quiet inner voice calling ever more clearly through the shambles of a shattered world.

John had survived persecution, but the abuses of Le Carpentier had cruelly traumatized his very dear aunt. The tyrant left Saint-Malo on August 11, 1794: Aunt Félicité Des Saudrais passed away on September 27. Her death certificate specifies that she died in her home in Port-Solider, the name of Saint-Servan during the Revolution. Ange Blaize reports: *"My Uncle John assisted his aunt at her last moments. Overwhelmed with tears, he exhorted her to a holy death."*[14] After his mother Gratienne, Aunt Félicité had been a source of advice and comfort. The guillotine had touched no one directly in the family; however, the abominations of Le Carpentier had weakened the endurance of John's second mother and hastened her death.

[1] Jean Baptiste Ogée, *Dictionnaire historique et géographique de la Bretagne*, Nouvelle édition par A. Marteville et P. Varin, Rennes: Deniel, 1853. 2 vols., v. 1, p. 813.

[2] François Manet, *Biographie des Malouins célèbres*, Saint-Malo: Chez l'Auteur et H. Rottier, 1824. pp. 380-383.

[3] **Lav**, v. l, pp. l4-15. The event occurred at Saint-Servan near Les Corbières, not at La Chesnaie as earlier writers state. See H. C. Rulon, **Chron**, No. 214 (April 1958), pp 146-152. Jean Baptiste Ogée, Dictionnaire historique et géographique de la Bretagne, Nouvelle édition par A. Marteville et P. Varin, Rennes: Deniel, 1853. 2 vols., v. 1, p. 813.

[4] **Lav**, v. 1, p.22.

[5] Bertier de Sauvigny, *Histoire de France,* Paris: Flammarion, 1977. P. 290. L. J. Rogier (et autres), ed. *Siècle des Lumières, Révolutions, Restaurations. Nouvelle Histoire de l'Église, Vol. 4,)* Paris: Éditions du Seuil [1966]. Pp. 176-182.

[6] Letter to the Convention, March 22, 1794. Vicomte de Brachet, *La Terreur dans l'Ouest, Le Conventionnel J.-B. Le Carpentier (1759-1829),* Paris: Perrin, 1912. Pp. 190-191, passim.

[7] See also Eugene Herpin, *Saint-Malo sous la Révolution,* 1789-1800, Saint-Malo: Maurice Guérin, éditeur, 1931. Jules Haize, *Une Commune bretonne pendant la Révolution, Histoire de Saint-Servan (Ille-et-Vilaine) de 1789 à 1800,* Saint-Servan: J. Haize; Paris: Honoré Champion, 1907. **Lav.** v. l, pp.15-18. Ogée, op. cit., note 1, above, pp. 813-817.

[8] Christian Marechal, *La Famille de La Mennais sous l'Ancien régime et la Révolution,* Paris: Perrin, 1913, pp.225-333.

[9] **Lav.** v.1, pp. 18-21.

[10] Ange Blaize, Essai biographique sur M. F. de La Mennais, Paris: Grenier 1858. pp. 18-19.

[11] Lav. v. 1, pp. 22-25.

[12] Étienne Pierre Engerran (1727?-1806) and Louis Vielle, (1765-1856).

[13] Pierre Picot de Clorivière, (1735-1820).

[14] Ange Blaize, Oeuvres inédites de F. Lamennais, Paris: E. Dentu, 1866. v. 1, "Introduction" p. 11. H. C. Rulon, **Chron**, No.213 (January 1958), p.75. **Lav.** v. 1, p. 23.

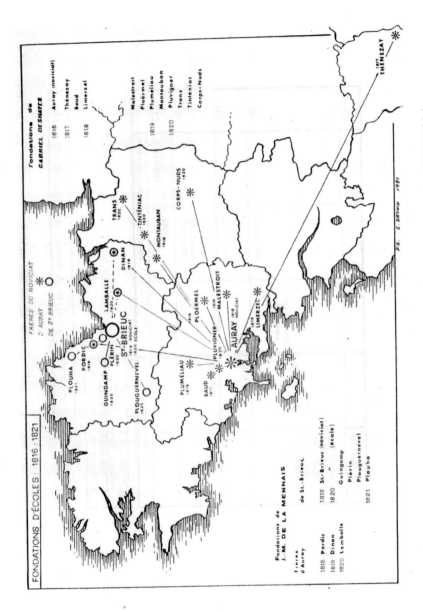

Foundations of Father Deshayes and de La Mennais, 1816-1821

Chapter 4

A YOUNG MAN'S CALLING

A general's peace

A sense of freedom returned to John's life at the fall of Robespierre and the departure of Le Carpentier, domestic peace coming with the boom of cannons. A short Corsican general known as Bonaparte saved the Convention from a coup d'état, gave it time to draft a new constitution and install its short-lived successor, the Directorate. French armies were vulnerable abroad and the new regime quickly appointed the Corsican to salvage conquests. Bonaparte triumphed in northern Italy, failed in Egypt but miraculously slipped past the English frigates and reached Paris on time to pacify the quarreling men of the **Directorate.**

The need for authority was obvious. General Bonaparte stunned rivals and scattered pretenders with a whiff of grapeshot, unseated the Directors and seized power. A confused nation suddenly found itself staring at a resolute general. On December 25, 1799, Bonaparte was ready with a new constitution. By February 1800, the Revolution and the aspirations of the Republic had ended. The nation ratified his **Consulate** by plebiscite. Order and reconciliation would begin under the **First Consul;** during fifteen years France would be the France of Bonaparte.

The first blessings of reconstruction came with the peace of the Consulate. From Paris, Louis-Marie would write to John: *"I saw Bonaparte in a parade yesterday. The First Consul was on a most beautiful, richly harnessed white horse.... He is yellow and quite small, but I bid you to tell papa Mennais that the bust on his chimney is a resemblance."* [1] John did not share his grandfather Louis-Francois' esteem for the general.

"You are my bishop"

The La Mennais family would never be the same without Gratienne and her sister. Marie was outgrowing her childhood in Normandy, and shortly after aunt Felicite's death, she moved to Avranche with her Lorin grandparents, away from the worries of Saint Malo. Though the men struggled to rebuild a lost business, a decade of Revolution had shriveled the family enterprise now kept afloat only by native resourcefulness. John was part of the administrative team though his aspirations were other than commercial. In his country home of Saint-Servan, uncle des Saudrais continued lessons to his two nephews.

John was resolutely setting the course of his own life with increasing assurance, while father and uncle were reorienting theirs. At seventeen, he received the following letter from Father de Clorivière: *"From the deepest feelings of my heart, I bless the Author of all gifts for granting you the grace to give yourself entirely to him and consecrate yourself irrevocably to his service. Do not hesitate to believe that his grace points to others which he will give you in the future, 'in tempore opportune,'* [at the proper time]." [2]

Social peace came with the new ruler. Outlawed churchmen emerged from hiding and the exiled began to find their way home. Bishop Cortois de Pressigny settled in Paris, his friendship unforgotten in John's family. Des Saudrais petitioned for the reopening of the church of Saint-Servan, and joined his brother in a request for the restoration of the bishopric of Saint-Malo and the restoration of its prelate. Parisian executives presented Mr. de La Mennais' letter to the Bishop who acknowledged the reality of changed times and the unlikelihood of his return. [3] John decided to go to the Bishop who could not come to him.

In December 1801, John was in Paris, but it was only years later that he disclosed to a bosom friend the preoccupations which followed him there: *"Father did not want me to enter the clerical state. On the day of St.*

Francis Xavier 1800, I renewed my plea and he agreed that I could receive the sub-deaconate in Paris. Given that circumstances were very difficult, I attributed this unforeseeable reversal to the intercession of the Apostle of India, and I will never be able to thank him adequately. If only I had his charity, his zeal! If I understood the value of a soul as he did!"[4] He left Saint-Malo bearing letters of recommendation from his father and his uncle, and settled at the Foreign Missions Seminary, rue du Bac, where Cortois de Pressigny was known. One morning, the voice of a celebrant at mass ended his search; John stepped forward, identified himself and opened his soul to his Bishop.

The letter of his father has not been preserved, but Saudrais' recommendation describes John as someone in whom virtue shone naturally. The uncle left no doubt about the respect which the young man's character commanded: *"I love John as though he were my son. John was born with a strong inclination to anger, which he has so thoroughly mastered that the disposition has changed to gentleness; such matters always surprise us, people of the world."*[5] Ten years earlier, the same John stood before the same prelate in Saint-Servan and said: "You are my Bishop and I want to be a priest. I am following you." How could a Bishop not appreciate a young man capable of surviving a decade of chaos with such clear vision? John had persevered in study and lived by the advice of Engerran, Vielle and de Clorivière through the madness of the Revolution.

Men without jurisdiction in the matter had suppressed the Diocese of Saint-Malo, but the Pope had not deposed Cortois de Pressigny. Pius VII had appointed John's Bishop provisional diocesan administrator of Saint-Malo before the Concordat of 1801. The Bishop's term would be short, but he was no longer the resourceless fugitive of 1790; he still had authority to rule in matters of ordination and he invited John without hesitation: *"Prepare for tomorrow and I will make you a sub-deacon."*

The experience of the next morning reads like a page from the acts of the early martyrs. The Bishop led his candidate to an abandoned Carmelite church. They were both meditating in a Chapel where the fracas of recent carnage still echoed in the memory of an outraged neighborhood. Here, visible blood stains recalled the work of executioners during the

September massacres of 1792. The Bishop reminded his young friend that the persecutors could strike again at any time. John had witnessed executions in his neighborhood during his adolescence in Saint-Malo, so it was easy for him to explain how the example of martyrs had confirmed his faith and inspired his resolution

The quiet ceremony took place a short distance away in a convent chapel of the Ursuline nuns. Unexpected as it may seem, the episode of October 16, 1790, at the Bishop's departure from Saint-Servan, ended in Paris on December 21, 1801. Now, father and Bishop had both lifted the last obstacles to John's ordination to the priesthood.

Seminary at home

The subdeacon's involvement with family life in Saint-Malo continued with little change. The Revolution had mellowed the father's attitude. Bishop Cortois de Pressigny observed that for some years, Mr. de La Mennais had been *"more mindful of religion than at any time when I knew him,"* (October 3, 1813). [6] Napoleon's fragile Peace of Amiens between France and England, March 25, 1802, was expected to restore the freedom of the seas. On September 5, the merchant father left with his eldest son to reestablish trade with Cadiz, Spain. By then, Marie had returned from Normandy, grandfather Lorin had passed away in 1799, and grandmother Lorin followed in 1803. The children now enjoyed the freedom of Les Corbières.

Letters written during the long absence reveal an affectionate father carefully reporting to appreciative children. From Cadiz, Mr. de La Mennais wrote, Dec. 24, 1802: *"Féli* (familiar name of Félicité) *invites me to continue my observations about Spain,"* and the correspondence abounds in travel episodes and comparisons between life in France and Spain. He wrote with a mind hovering over *Les Corbières,* and a heart lingering with his children. Ever the practical executive, he even provided directives about farming.

The basic order of life had been set, but he nevertheless advised, even prescribed, with the precision of an executive. He mobilized the entire family to exploit the land with the help of domestics. John and Félicité became responsible for sowing, harvesting fodder and managing straw, hay and fertilizer. Some letters show them as overseers helping with the pruning of trees, the planting of potatoes, the transfer of orange trees into the sunlight. Instructions occasionally become very specific. Thus: half of the large lot is to be sown in peas and beans; potatoes must be planted in the remaining space. Seed ordered jointly must be shared generously with a partner; we will use what he does not choose. What should be planted in the enclosure? Is the lucerne sprouting? Fertilizer must not be wasted: control the use of compost and manure. I intend to purchase a pig to fatten during the summer and kill around Christmas. Sterile cows must be sold. Hold the milk bearers while they yield. Let Marie decide which animals to keep. Marie manages the chicken yard and is reminded to spare the straw. Nothing seems to escape this father's interest. The letters show John and Félicité in rustic roles not usually described by John's biographers. The experience will later serve them well at La Chesnaie.[7]

The life of the Church entered the correspondence. There was concern about the conversion of the constitutional clergy, and a genuine interest in the local parish and the diocese of Rennes, now enlarged to incorporate Saint-Malo. John's intensive preparation for ordination transforms such matters into family affairs. The letters reveal a paternal intimacy long eclipsed by the overbearing preoccupations and the madness of revolutionary years. Mr. de La Mennais is not fully converted to his traditional faith, but the Revolution has shaken his liberal convictions; he is soul-searching and probing options.

John understood the gradual transformation. His example was influencing the fretful *Felicité* with whom ten months of undisturbed intimacy filled the void left by the absence of Louis and his father. The most diligent biographers of the rebel point out that part of John's studies at the time centered on answers to the rationalism of philosophers, while Felicite's mind was still running the philosophical crossways of Rousseau's contemporaries.[8] Study eventually led Félicité to accept the teachings of the Church, but years of undisciplined reading matched the habits of an undisciplined life. Even if his new convictions remained in his head, the spell of Rousseau prevailed

The alienation of Félicité from the Church did not antagonize the father; the country gentleman's interests and his children's lives were one. He was acutely aware of Félicité's tormented soul, but he pleased him with answers to his requests. He treated Marie as a trustworthy young woman on the verge of marriage. He responded to the common concerns of John and his junior when he wrote to them jointly. He reminded them that trust in Providence must not lull anyone into sterile indifference. The letters did not close the dialog: *"We will consider all this in front of the hearth at Les Corbières where we will have a great deal to share,"* (April 3, 1803). [9] The Peace of Amiens failed, the seas would not open, thus the Spanish voyage lost its purpose. Mr. de La Mennais left Spain and came home with his eldest, July 26, 1803. Soon the family assembled around the hearth; his heart had never left it.

Meanwhile, the Church kept a different agenda than that of the La Mennais family as the Pope consecrated a new Bishop for the Diocese of Rennes. A Napoleonic decree allowed dioceses to open ecclesiastical schools and the Bishop came to inaugurate one in Saint-Malo late in September, 1802. The school was to open in October and John was asked to help.

"The value of a soul; The Priesthood"

The priesthood Spiritual anxiety gripped the young man who yearned to understand "the value of a soul," as Francis Xavier did. As he moved resolutely through the last steps to ordination, John wrote to his former Bishop from Saint-Malo, thanked him for the grace of the sub-deaconate, and pledged fidelity to his calling. The prelate responded with advice: *"You must be like the bee which produces honey from the substance it finds in each plant. . . . I still believe that it would be useful for you to spend a year in an ecclesiastical community. . . . I urge you to set aside one year to spend with Mr. Duclaux at Saint-Sulpice."* Circumstances made a year at the Sulpician seminary impossible at the moment, but the first letters opened a continuing relationship between the subdeacon and the Bishop.

Bishop de Pressigny and John de La Mennais both took their commitment seriously. Saint John Chrysostom's Treatise on the Priesthood generated in the subdeacon a "holy fear" which prompted his new adviser to reassure him: *"My friend, I will be the one to answer to God for your ordination and I do not fear that it will be cause for condemnation for me. I tell you truthfully that no human motive has determined me to ordain you; I decided only on the testimony of persons deserving respect and trust, who judged that you could be useful to the Church; I have judged likewise. Have no misgivings about embracing the ecclesiastical state. Your vocation is sound; it is now a matter of responding to it. . . . When the Bishop of Rennes calls you to the deaconate, later to the priesthood, then to service in the ministry, obey without hesitation,"* (December 10, 1802). John stayed the course as a deeper understanding of priestly responsibilities motivated him to intensify his preparation rather than hasten the date of his ordination.

Msgr. Jean-Baptiste De Maillé, [10] the new Bishop of Rennes, had lived in a Parisian hideout during most of the Revolution, and survived a year in prison after having been taken in chains to the Island of Ré. He conferred the deaconate on John, September 24, 1803, then called him to the priesthood and ordained him five months later, February 25, 1804. The candidate was slightly under canonical age, but the scarcity of priests was so critical and the qualifications of the candidate so favorable, that. ordination proceeded by dispensation.

The letters of Bishop de Pressigny followed the progress of the young priest: *"You are quite right, my friend, in worrying about your own insufficiency; but when we recall that Jesus Christ promised to be every day with those whom he sent forth, justified self-distrust changes into perfect trust that we will .not be abandoned, as long as we follow the teachings of the Church and the principles of conduct it laid out."*

Personal progress remained a concern: It was my wish that you spend some time here [in Paris] *under the direction of Mr. Duclaux . . . God, who does not allow it, will supplement that in other ways."* When John's work led to a friendship with the young Mr. Hay, Bishop de Pressigny approved, and advised: *"Friends must not be chosen lightly, but it is useful to have some who can help us in our work, encourage us and* *above all warn us of our faults; render that mutual service to each other; such is the mark of true friendship," (*October 12, 1803).

Encouragement followed ordination to the priesthood: *"You have all the signs of a sound vocation: you never solicited admission to Holy Orders and you proceeded with fear because your superiors were ordering you to. Trust then in the grace of the Lord; never entertain any misgivings about your acceptance of the priesthood . . .The two virtues most necessary for all Christians, but particularly for priests, are a total and perfect trust in God and a profound distrust of self,"* (April 17, 1804). [11]

Letters between the two men reveal a concern for study, virtue and service. John studied Tertullian's *Treatise on Prescriptions,* Nicole's little Treatises, Eusebius' Ecclesiastical History, Saint John Chrysostom's *Treatise on the Priesthood.* The lessons of Engerran, Vielle, de Clorivière and Des Saudrais were bearing fruit. The Bishop congratulated him for discernment, advised him against unsound authors and suggested new readings: the *Pastoral* of Saint Gregory, the *Treatise on Consideration* of Saint Bernard, the *Ecclesiastical History* of M. Fleury. John quickly perceived the Gallicanism of Fleury and set out on a lifelong battle to defend the rights of the Holy See against French rulers who meddled in Church affairs. His first biographer, Sigismond Ropartz, wondered how a young man of 22 could proceed with such sound discernment, unaided in the study of Church doctrine, as even Bishop de Pressigny stood in the Gallican camp. [12]

---

[1] Thermidor, Year 10; August 4, 1801. C. Merechal, La Jeunnesse de la Mennais... Paris; Perrin, 1913.
[2] Letter, Dec. 28, 1797. Manuscript. **AFIC**, Quoted in **Lav,** vol.1, p.29+.
[3] Sept. 27, 1801.
[4] Letter to Bruté de Rémur, Dec. 3, 1809. **Cor gén J,** v. 1, pp. 79-80.
[5] Copy without mention of source, **AFIC**, 01-7.
[6] Letter. Quoted in **Lav.** v.1, p.138.
[7] As excerpted from letters in **AFIC**, 5 (12). Marechal, op. cit., pp. 47-57.
H. C. Rulon., Chron, No. 213, (January 1958), p.79.

[8] Marechal, op. cit., p.65+.

[9] Letter. **AFIC,** 04. Excerpts quoted in Marechal, op. cit. p.56.

[10] (1743-1804).

[11] **AFIC,** 17. These letters and those which follow are filed in sequence though some are undated. All available dates are given.

[12] **Rop,** P.35.

City of Auray, Favorite Parish of Father Gabriel Deshayes.

Chapter 5

ECCLESIASTICAL SCHOOL AND CATHEDRAL PARISH

The Emperor's Church

John de LaMennais lived under the two Bonapartes: he was ordained under the First Consul, and he was exercising his ministry under the Emperor ten months late. Bonaparte brashly cut his own way to the imperial throne, the First Consul becoming **First Consul for life** on August 2, 1802, and prescribing a new order in his **Code** of March 21, 1804. Though Napoleon invited Pope Pius VII to crown him in Paris, he ceremoniously crowned himself **Emperor** of the French nation in the Pope's presence. Consul Bonaparte had become **Emperor Napoleon I.**

In Italy, General Bonaparte affirmed that a nation without religion was ungovernable; however as Consul, he set out early to fashion the Church of France into an instrument of his government. The Concordat approved by Pius VII, July 17. 1801, had restored a provisional peace with the Church, but before its official implementation, the First Consul duped the nation with his own reinterpretation. On April 8, 1802, he had the Assembly vote the 77 provisions of the **Organic Articles,** a tactic which legalized the arbitrary manipulation of church life.

There was little mystery about the Emperor's motives. During his Italian campaign, General Bonaparte had decreed that Pius VI must be the **Last** Pope. His soldiers seized the pontiff in Florence, May 28, 1799, and domiciled him a captive in Valence, July 14. The sick Pope died and was solemnly laid to rest in that French city, January 31, 1800. Bonaparte ordered his army to prevent the election of a successor. The Cardinals having anticipated the move, assembled a secret conclave in the monastery of Saint George on an island in the lagoon of Venice, and elected Pius VII within three months, on March 14, 1800. The thwarted General would deal with the consequences; the fate of Pius VI foreshadowed what could be that of his successor should he ever frustrate the Emperor.

Engerran's ecclesiastical school

Father Engerran had directed the cathedral school of Saint-Malo during two decades when the Revolution broke out. Confronted with spiritual desolation, he resumed his teaching with humble faith. He was in his seventies when he began to prepare a new generation of priests for his diocese. As the number of recruits exceeded his means, he enlisted Father Vielle who was privately tutoring a few students. The two priests had asked John to assist them to teach in a common seminary. John became part of the team in the audacity and privations of the beginnings. He was then preparing for his own ordination at home; however, his life changed as he moved to a school where his duties included preparing lesson plans in an understaffed institution lacking essential textbooks; thus began the ecclesiastical school and minor seminary of Saint Malo.[1] Engerran administered it and taught theology while serving at the cathedral parish. Vielle taught Latin, and John, still a deacon preparing for ordination, taught philosophy.

Their school was a private ecclesiastical secondary school referred to in local terminology as a *collège*.[2] It opened late in October, 1802 soon after a Napoleonic decree authorized dioceses to open such institutions. A few teachers eventually supplemented the three founders. Given the makeshift lodging, Engerran's school lacked almost everything except students and loyal teachers. The early years tested the willingness of professors to bear discomfort, cumulate functions and extend service time. John later became responsible for theology at a time when the theological knowledge of students was so diversified that it became necessary for him to organize three different sessions daily. The young teacher met the challenge with lesson plans, notebooks from the works of accepted authors, and supplemental study material from current publications.

Holy mass opened the day, low mass on week days, chanted high mass with sermon on Sunday. The young de La Mennais soon gained a reputation for his ability to inspire young listeners. He occasionally allowed the more advanced students to question him, sermons becoming a dialog provoking the most incisive responses from the speaker. The discourse was sometimes planned with one alert student prepared to challenge the homilist with objections. The preacher in turn understood the limits of young listeners, managing to complete his message in twenty minutes at a time when churchgoers were generally subjected to hour long sermons.

Cathedral parish, changing relationships

The year 1804 brought important changes in John's personal life. His Bishop called him to the priesthood and ordained him at Rennes on February 25. Marie married Ange Blaize de Maisonneuve on April 5, thus giving him a brother-in-law and a new family to love. On May 7, the beloved *Papa Mennais,* grandfather Louis-Francois, died at 88, and was laid to rest at *Val Ernoul* across the bay from *Mount Saint-Michel.* The ailing Bishop de Maillé appointed him to assist Father Engerran at the Cathedral Parish on September 3, and dies three weeks later in Paris. Étienne Célestin Énoch,[3] an exile in Italy during the Revolution, became his Bishop a few months later.

In 1804, Félicité de La Mennais found his way back to religious practice. John helped him by example and advice, but the neophyte still lacked the essential act of faith. Then, at the age of 22, the convert received his first communion.[4] The two brothers would henceforth travel a common journey from 1804 to 1814. Since the ecclesiastical school was short of teachers, Félicité was invited to teach mathematics; the intemperate reader of adolescent years now became known at the school for his passionate study habits.

When Engerran's diminishing capacity required intervention, John accepted parish responsibilities despite heavy teaching duties and changing relationships. The homilist at school began to accept his turn as monthly homilist at the cathedral where a seasoned audience soon discovered the quality homilist already appreciated by the students at the ecclesiastical school. Confessions, teaching, the preparation of classroom material, homilies and all the unavoidable workday preoccupations of educators filled his time. His letters reveal that he did not spare his time when sought for spiritual advice; and with the death of Father Engerran, [5] John even assumed additional responsibilities.

The limits of zeal

Father Vielle worried about the health of his young assistant so in December, 1805, he reduced John's three theology classes to one. However, John's condition continued to deteriorate, rest becoming a necessity. Before accepting a leave of absence, John saw to it that the five finishing students of the year emerged successful from their official examinations. He then withdrew, but only after preaching his scheduled parish mission at Plouer. The health of Félicité had also deteriorated and the two brothers settled at La Chesnaie, the teachers of Saint-Malo obliged to cope without the two severely exhausted colleagues. [6]

Death in the La Mennais family aggravated matters. Louis-Marie, the eldest, died unexpectedly of a chest condition in Saint-Malo on December 17, 1805. His sudden disappearance traumatized Félicité to the point of destroying his ability to teach, causing grave concern among the family. A short period of rest at La Chesnaie was insufficient as Felicite fell into spells which frightened the family and led it to seek relief for him in Paris. John could not remain aloof from the tragedy. He requested Father de Grandclos, the local diocesan representative, to explain the circumstances to the Bishop. *"Father de La Mennais, who lost his oldest brother more than a month ago, finds himself obliged to accompany his younger brother to Paris for medical treatment. His father and his uncle wanted him to profit of the same opportunity for his own recovery,"* (January 25, 1806).

Two months later, he wrote: *"Mr. De La Mennais is better. . . Nevertheless, the doctors believe that he must abstain from all stressful work until his strength is restored. He will spend the spring in Paris because of his brother's illness which is graver than his own. On his return, he will no longer prepare notebooks for his students. We now have them study in one of the theology manuals used in seminaries today," (March 29, 1806)* [7]. The letters revealed both John's slow recovery and his involvement in the church life of his native city. His return relieved Father Vielle who had written, *"I find myself compelled by the illness of our dear La Mennais to accept the responsibilities of theology teacher and assistant vicar."* [8] Félicité had delayed his treatment until his condition had seriously deteriorated, a reason for the extended stay of the two brothers in Paris.

---

[1] A *collège* usually a public municipal (or regional) secondary school. Ecclesiastical secondary schools could exist only with government authorization. Students moved from a major seminary on to ordination. Young men preparing for other professions often studied at their side. Under Napoleon's *Concordat*, the education of future priests was under the authority of the bishop, but the government interfered by regulating ecclesiastical schools. Napoleon used the subterfuge even to limit the number of schools, students and ordinations.

[2] On the history of the school, see E. Herpin and others, *Histoire du collège de Saint-Malo,* Ploërmel: Imprimerie Saint Yves, 1902. Pp. 1-82. **Rop,** 69-125. **Lav,** v. 1, pp. 42-57, 95-131.

[3] (1742-1825).

[4] The exact date is unknown—According to the traditional account, John told Félicité, *"Confesse-toi."* Compare **Lav** v. 1, pp. 47-48, with Delpuits de Grandmaison, *La Congrégation* (1801-1830), Paris: Plon, 1889, pp. 43-44.

[5] On December 4, 1806 (at 78/79?).

[6] Ange Blaize, Œuvres inédites de F. Lamennais, Paris :E. Dentu, 1866. V. 1, p. 22. **Lav**, v. 1, p. 57.

[7] Letters, **AFIC**, dossier 27/17. The theology text was that of Bailly.

[8] Undated letter to Father de Clorivière in Paris. Quoted in Jacques Terrien, Histoire du R. P. de Clorivière de la Compagnie de Jésus,Paris : Pousielgue, 1892. P. 418.

Father John Mary Robert de La Mennais,
Co-Founder of the Brothers of Christian Instruction,
1780-1860.

Church of St. Brieuc.

Father Gabriel Deshayes, Co-Founder of the Brothers of Christian Instruction, 1767-1841.

City of Auray, Favorite Parish of Father Gabriel Deshayes.

Chapel of St. Ann, City of Auray, France.

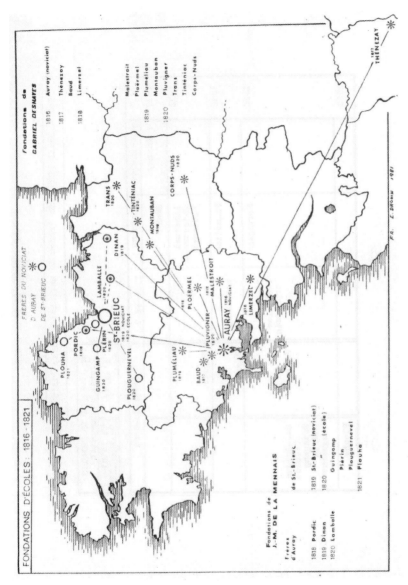

Foundations of Father Deshayes and de La Mennais between 1816 and 1821.

Chapter 6

PARIS, LA CHESNAIE AND A FOILED MINISTRY

The Sulpician Seminary Paris, the incomparable intellectual hub at the heart of the nation, was clambering its way out of confusion, its radiance obscured by the legacy of rebellion and war. But the confusion of the flustered city mattered little to the two brothers whose immediate objective was to visit a specialist of nervous disorders. They traveled three-to-four winter days in an uncomfortable coach, and established residence at the Foreign Missions Seminary, *rue du Bac.* Félicité suffered strange nervous spasms followed by fainting spells, severe depressions, periods of dark brooding broken by sudden fits of anger and prolonged intervals of listlessness and mental void. The physician, Doctor Philippe Pinel, was reputed to be the most caring and the most respected specialist of the nation for patients of that category.[1]

Pinel prescribed milk, moderate exercise in open air and abstention from prolonged intensive intellectual work. The two brothers submitted to the milk regime immediately, the opportunities for exercise more limited at first. Félicité began to attend the lectures of the Hellenist, Jean Baptiste Gail,[2] at the *Collège de France.* The teacher befriended the newcomer and John occasionally accompanied his brother to Gail's lessons until his own priorities moved him to the Sulpician Seminary on *rue de Babylone,* where theology and church life were taken seriously.

John was duty-bound to rest and his first opportunity had finally come to follow the advice received earlier from Bishop de Pressigny. He had responded to the immediate needs of ministry in his native parish, he had opened his heart to the spiritual needs of the nation, but the work had robbed him of reflection time. With a mind brimming over with questions and a heart impatient for service, John found Pinel's limits on study difficult to keep.

In the freedom of the moment, he investigated the needs of the Church with insatiable intellectual hunger, and reassessed his understanding of priestly service with a keen sense of pastoral responsibility. His Sulpician guides challenged his mind and refined his discernment. De Pressigny had urged him to spend time with Father Duclaux; John owes to this master of the spiritual life a complement of priestly formation for which he sensed a need. He met him in Paris and John treasured a relationship which continued through the few remaining years of the Sulpician's life.

Father Jacques Émery,[3] the superior of the seminary was respected as the oracle of the Parisian clergy. The scholarly priest quickly appreciated the intellectual vigor of his new disciple and respected his driving zeal. He did not hesitate to challenge his mind with the most demanding inquiries and invited him to prolong his stay to avail him of the serious books rarely found outside Paris. The Church and its restoration in France after the Revolution remained foremost in John's priorities, but never separated from the life and the struggles of the Universal Church.

Among the younger priests at the seminary, Father Paul-Émile Teysseyre, later influential upon Félicité, attracted John's attention. This new friend had given up studies at the *Institut Polytechnique* for the priesthood, and until his untimely death, he remained one of John's correspondents. Two seminarians appeared in this circle of friends: one of them the young Hyacinthe de Quélen from Saint-Brieuc would reappear as Bishop of Rennes, the other Simon Gabriel Bruté de Rémur. Bruté (Pronounce *Brütay*), as he was to be referred to, had come to study for the priesthood and had joined the Sulpicians after completing a degree in medicine. The letters which flowed between the two brothers and this zealous seminarian reveal the intimate aspirations of the three men. A maturing friendship lasted even after Bruté de Rémur left France for the

Sulpician missions of Maryland in 1810, and even after Brute became the first bishop of Vincennes, Indiana in 1834.[4]

Rest, study and new relationships sustained the two brothers in Paris for over five months. Though the desire to stay longer was strong, fatigue worried them and Pinel's advice prevailed. The immediate necessity was exercise under the open sky. Paris was soon behind them as their coach wheeled westward. The work started in Paris would never really stop, and only death would end some of the new friendships. The sheltered peace of a familiar farmstead in windswept Brittany provided the untroubled setting recommended by Pinel better than Paris ever could. Their journey ended about twenty-eight kilometers (eighteen miles) south of Saint Malo, at La Chesnaie. Colleagues at the ecclesiastical school, and a dwindling but close-knit family awaited their return.

La Chesnaie, gift of the Lorin grandparents

John and Félicité were at home at La Chesnaie. Purchased by their maternal great-grandfather Roce in 1730, the estate was given to his daughter Bertranne at her marriage with Pierre Lorin. The legacy of Grandmother Bertranne Lorin linked them as the third family owners of the property. Félicité once wrote of large and lovely lakes without which *"no landscape, no countryside, picturesque though it be, is complete for me."*.[5] La Chesnaie provided him with a home-size green pond set in a live oak grove where he could relax and reflect in its shade only a few hundred steps from his room. The Lorins left more than a pond to the two brothers. Pierre Lorin had restored La Chesnaie as an escape from the restless pace of life in Saint Malo, and a refuge from the burdens of public service.

The estate was complete with prairies, farmstead, rustic garden, service sheds and a private wood stand. In 1778, two years before John's birth, grandfather Lorin built an ideal secondary residence, a little two-story white chateau topped with a high-pitched gabled roof in the local style, popularly called *malouinières,* for *malouins,* the citizens of Saint-Malo. The little manor became a haven of togetherness where the family could relax in subdued elegance in the rural serenity of the Breton countryside. It was a setting away from the port and Les Corbières where the two brothers had frolicked during childhood. In 1806 and 1807, it became their temporary convalescent retreat.

Years later, a disciple of Félicité wrote that the forest cover was such that "a house was not visible within a hundred steps." As a resident he felt *"surrounded, trapped, pressed and somewhat stifled by the woods,"* and the rare clearings revealed an *"immense uniformity showing the expanse of the forests"* with *"gray trees blending with the gray sky"* in the distance. The manor relieved the bleakness, but for him, La Chesnaie remained *"a solitude amidst solitudes,"* where nothing was heard but the birds and *"the whispering wind in the woods."* One could not understand how *"so much solitude could exist... Work was a need, an indispensable necessity"* in such stillness.[6]

In an interlude of forsakenness and anxiety, John once wrote of La Chesnaie to a friend as *"the only place on earth where one could live, considering that only trees could be seen and no other noise heard but that of frogs croaking at the end of the pond,"* (February 16, 1815).[7] The light-hearted irony reflects a personal fondness for the place. The estate could not escape the moods of Brittany with its low-hung clouds and dank drizzle, blanketing fog and saline breeze, brooding skies and shifting sunlight. But when spring cut through the gray, and new life broke through the bleakness, Breton vigor revived the land. Melancholy could invade the winter stillness, but it could never stifle the life it touched nor smother the breath of spring.

Healing was the top priority for the two brothers in Brittany. On March 29, 1806, Father Meslé de Grandclos wrote to John's Bishop: *"Mr. de la Mennais is better ... The doctors believe that he must avoid all burdensome work until his condition improves."*[8] Five months of Paris had roused a native restlessness. Once settled at La Chesnaie, they would have to reconcile an innate sense of enterprise with the hush of undisturbed isolation.

John would not resume his work at the ecclesiastical school of Saint Malo until the end of December, 1807. Meanwhile, solitude tested his patience and his resourcefulness. On August 16, he wrote to a bosom friend: *"... for almost ten months, we have been living as genuine hermits in deep solitude. We have prohibited boredom from invading us, and it has not yet dared, even once, to approach our door. Good health has not been as compliant, and though we invite it wholeheartedly, it seems that we may not count upon it for a long stretch.... What is certain is that the best remedy is to rest calmly in the will of God, who thinks only thoughts of peace for us, conjuring thoughts of love for our miserable hearts."[9]*

The doctors had ordered rest and moderate exercise under the open sky; a solicitous uncle Des Saudrais unfailingly reminded them of this priority even before they left Paris. He urged Félicité not to read for long uninterrupted intervals; (*cut after fifteen minutes, then resume.*). The password was **rest**. *"Rest, rest! Have you managed to rest, then you have accomplished more than the conqueror of empires and cities!"* (April 23, 1806).[10] He recommended leisurely promenades and horsemanship. Both were good hikers while the saddle extended their roving range. Félicité, who was not known for moderation, took to the latter with the zeal of a sportsman, even momentarily forgetting his passion for study. Winter wore his patience as he languished housebound through the hostile chills of a passive season. Come spring, he dashed from the fireside to catch a glimpse of the first swallows.

The two hermits awaited the lagging return of health in thankless patience. They kept "company" through correspondence with family, colleagues and friends in Saint Malo a few leagues away. Without magic footwear, distance precluded frequent home visits, but their father was not beyond reach and Marie was affectionately involved with her family. Uncle Des Saudrais played father, mother and intellectual associate through his letters, and their interest in the ecclesiastical school sent their thoughts to the north shores.

Hoof tracks, bracing air, adventurous mind and a "Torrent of Ideas"

John claimed a right to *"laziness,"* but mindful of his uncle's advice, he prudently harmonized rest, study and recreation. Hoof tracks marked his ventures across the Breton moors; as his restless mind scanned the landscape, his thoughts instinctively returned to the themes of his Parisian studies. Nothing ever made him forget the Church and the concerns of his ministry. The French capital had stirred his creative capacities, rest and the native air were restoring his stamina. The two brothers naturally began to flip through the leaves of their books after treading the leaves of the forest floor. John, for whom *"ten letters did not amount to one hour of conversation,"* wrote from his solitude to his Sulpician friend: *"We feel how important it is to study Church issues; nothing is more essential today.... We do not like general judgments which avail to nothing."*[11] Study, meditation and inspiration opened new levels of understanding.

The first fruits of their thinking was a synthesis of their dreams for a revitalized Church. John set it to paper on November 13, 1807, between four and five thirty in the afternoon. He scribbled in a marginal note how insights flooded his mind in a rush of fresh thoughts after reading lines from an article on the Jacobites in the theological dictionary of Bergier. The text, 13 pages of clear tight orderly script, outlines an amazingly thorough summary of the major Church issues of the day in concise, segmented, incompletely phrased statements. The notes reveal his intellectual activity through his readings, studies and consultations of recent months.

He described the summary as a *torrent of ideas, more precisely, of vague ideas* (new thoughts to be explored). They were indeed spontaneous and unrefined concepts, ideas to be reexamined, clarified and amplified, but they were anything but vague. *The torrent drives* the mind through a numbered sequence of glowing insights, an array of 33 assets, difficulties and initiatives.[12] Its raw expression is the work of a neophyte -- he was then early in his twenty-seventh year, but it reads like the initial sketch of a professional, revealing intellectual finesse, breadth of vision, depth of understanding, a capacity for synthesis; it forecasts the writer's boldness in the face of challenge. John could outline his thinking on that November evening, but he could not predict its impact on his life, for his thoughts did not die on paper.[13]

Insights from this *torrent of vague ideas* propelled John's mind from his native soil towards the outposts of contemporary Christian missionary work around the globe, from the maxims of unbelievers, to the disputes of feuding European Christians, from the smugness of complacent clerics, to the outreaches of enterprising zeal. *The torrent of ideas,* vague and unrefined, flowed through his experiences gaining in breadth and precision to the end of his days, challenging his mind, inspiring his prayer, firing his zeal.

In the church of his native France, he identified the tensions between the Empire and the Church, the scarcity of priests and the need for the renewal of the clergy, the estranged masses disoriented by the Revolution, and the necessity of personal Christian renewal. He was confined to a rest haven, but the life of the Church throbbed in his heart; there was no gloom in the soul of this convalescent priest, and seemingly no limits to his aspirations.

From "Torrent" to "Réflexions"

John's return to Saint-Malo late in December 1807 *was premature;* the password was still rest. Letters from Félicité reminded him of it: *"I urge you not to tire yourself too much. To speak little and think even less is the remedy for our illness; a little stupidity would serve us well,"* (1807).[14] The advice was well taken, the prescription of their doctor still in *effect, and the estate of Les Corbières easily accessible. In the spring, John wrote to his Sulpician friend: "We will be going to our country estate in Saint-Servan for a milk cure,"* (April 26, 1808), but the same letter reveals that the shared studies of the two brothers had not ceased.[15] The months at La Chesnaie had been a time of physical rest, though a period of relentless intellectual activity.

Religion had not preoccupied Félicité until his recent return to religious observance, yet he had come to share the enthusiasm of his elder for the church issues of the day, with a will to write about them. When John left La Chesnaie, they were both organizing notes on the state of the Church in France. From this cooperation, Félicité drafted a first book which John sent in manuscript to Bruté de Rémur for review by the Sulpicians of Paris. Consultations proceeded on a strict mandate of discretion: no one, not even the Sulpicians, must know the names of the authors as the bold little essay that would upset the complacent and displease the government.

The manuscript was ready on February 18, 1809. Félicité had written from his reading notes and from studies shared with John, making generous use of the latter's **"torrent"** of November 13, 1807. The text broke into print anonymously as reflections on the state of the Church in France during the 18th century and on its current situation. *(Réflexions sur l'état de l'Église en France au XVIIIe siècle et sur sa situation actuelle).* The publisher dated it by its composition in 1808, though it was printed in the spring of 1809 and released in June. Napoleon's police seized the book soon after its publication;[16] Félicité would reissue it in 1814, and later in revised editions.

Before the end of 1809, the two brothers reappeared again in print without frustrating Napoleon. John was then deeply interested in the spiritual life and was translating with Félicité the Latin sixteenth-century guide to the spiritual life, *(the Speculum religiosorum* of Louis de Blois). The French version appeared under the title of *Le Guide spirituel ou Miroir des âmes religieuses*, without the names of the translators.[17] The activities of the two brothers continued unimpeded through the political vulnerabilities of the moment, despite the seizure of the *Réflexions*. Ongoing study of Church life refined their understanding and stimulated Félicité to new works in defense of the Church.

"We now have 80 students"

Late in December 1807, John returned to Saint-Malo mindful of his health restraints. He wrote to his Sulpician friend: *"My health has improved during the last three months, though I am not fully healed."*[18] The ecclesiastical school had outgrown its living space at a time when the Emperor's men peered over the shoulders of French seminary teachers and fretted over the growing number of ordinations. Space, not government regimentation, was the easier problem to solve. After abandoning plans to purchase adjoining houses, the administration decided to relocate the school in a spacious building given to the diocese. John and two other priests pledged to guarantee an annuity of 2,500 francs to the 72-year-old benefactor. The students crammed into the old quarters soon moved into the new space though John could not join them at the time: *"Only in the spring will I be able to restore my miserable health perfectly.... I sometimes find myself wishing to recover my strength to resume my former work; however, it seems preferable to long for nothing and await in peace whatever it pleases the Good Lord to ordain,"* (February 2, 1808).[19]

Napoleon's institutions were essentially centralizing. The *Université* created by the decree of March 17, 1808, tightened controls on French schools. John frequently commented on the consequences for Saint-Malo. The Concordat kept the education of the clergy under the authority of bishops, but the inclusive language of the decree now swept minor seminaries into an ambiguous category. The ecclesiastical school had been founded before the creation of the new monopoly and had lost its title of minor seminary even before the decree on the *Université;* it regained its listing as a seminary without recovering its lost freedoms.

Imperial authority now exercised obnoxious controls. The teachers of a private seminary had to promise in writing that they would abide by state regulations. Eventually, the director, the saintly Father Vielle, had to be approved by the *Université* and listed with its members. John's school temporarily lost authorization to receive students other than those preparing for the priesthood. The bishop could declare that all students were in that category, but the government eventually required parents to certify in writing that their sons were clerical students.

The needs of the school were increasing with growing student numbers: *"We now have about 80 students,"* wrote John. Over 60 of these students were candidates for the priesthood. He would soon observe symbolically that their number increases *"daily."* In 1809, he would count *"ten teachers and one hundred and sixty seven students."* [20] Illness had forced John to leave before the creation of the *Université*. The Emperor's control was interfering with the education of priests as was the government's decision to limit the number of ordinations; despite the interference, the ecclesiastical school and minor seminary of Saint-Malo was a success story through the zeal of its founders.[21]

At one juncture, success could have threatened the distinctive character of the school *"as a seminary."* The city supported its own secondary school which lost most of its students through mismanagement and lack of dedication from its staff. Alarmed parents began to transfer their sons to the ecclesiastical school. Not to deprive local students of a secondary education, *Université* inspectors approved these exceptions despite the objections of city officials. There was even question of transforming the ecclesiastical school into the municipal *collège,* the secondary school of the city of Saint Malo. John moved to avert that possibility; he had struggled through his own preparation for the priesthood and understood their difficulties; he was totally committed to the education of desperately needed priests. John insisted that the only way to prepare enlightened and zealous priests was to educate seminarians without government intrusion.

John defended his school with his pen and served its mission with his life.[22] John's search for a library was merely one of his preoccupations. He first gathered all the books remaining at the suppressed bishopric, and obtained from the prefect 6,000 volumes confiscated from religious houses during the Revolution and now decaying in storage. Despite the damaged works and incomplete sets, the gift included practically all the Fathers of the Church and various writings of early theologians.[23]

The inevitable struggle for the material survival of his school never detracted him from his spiritual priorities. Early in his teaching career, we find him caring for the religious progress of his students by founding the "Congregation of the Holy Angels."[24] He provided student retreats at the beginning and at the end of the school year, and organized weekly religious conferences to discuss matters of faith. Without neglecting his own spiritual and intellectual progress, he discharged his parish ministry, preached at the cathedral, heard confessions and provided spiritual guidance. References to works on devotional and theological themes filled his letters. At the invitation of his friend, Bruté de Rémur, he spent part of the summer of 1809 at the Sulpician Seminary in Paris meeting his spiritual advisors and studying the life of the Church.

Pius VII responded to the Emperor's May 16 annexation of the Papal States by excommunicating him on June 10. The Emperor did not want the decree to be known in France, but the superior of the Sulpician seminary clandestinely procured the text and the seminarians provided copies for volunteers to carry past the imperial police. Father Émery asked the young Eugène de Mazenod[25] to prepare a copy for John and his companion; Bruté de Rémur hid the document in the hollow of his hat and the text was released on arrival at Vitré.[26]

After the publication of *Réflexions* and the translation of the *Guide Spirituel*, John needed time to rest and to renew himself before the start of the new academic year. He was then assembling documents on the tradition of the Church concerning the selection of bishops, while teaching or convalescing from illness. In addition, he was performing parish duties, working to provide the necessities of a growing school and defending the freedom of education with personal interventions and letters. His services did not pass unnoticed. Father Émery offered him a chair of theology at Rennes; John declined the offer through loyalty to his school. His Bishop recognized his talents and his zeal by naming him Honorary Canon at the Cathedral of Rennes, insisting that he was not granting a favor, only acknowledging a right and performing a duty.[27]

Pruned vine, bursting life (1812-1814)

By all standards but those of the Emperor, the founders of a thriving school with an undisputable record of service had earned the right to continue their work. Napoleon now excluded that possibility. The imperial decree of November 11, 1811, limited dioceses to one minor seminary per diocese, and prohibited ecclesiastical schools in cities lacking a secondary school approved by the *Université*. As was expected, Bishop Enoch kept the minor seminary of his episcopal city; Saint-Malo continued as the sole functioning minor seminary of the diocese until the bishop reorganized his own. One August morning in 1812, a clerk of court served notice to Father Vielle that the government had closed his school. On August 19, Father de La Mennais assumed the debts of the institution in exchange for ownership of the furniture.[28]

John's separation from his seminarians was a heart-rending experience, cruelly ending a decade of seminary teaching. The season had changed, a painful isolation settled over him, though feelings of privation could not defeat a young priest with a heart yearning for the salvation of souls. As a pruned vine sprouts new offshoots, John sought new ministries to fill the void. He devoted more time to parish ministry, pursued studies and literary activities undertaken with Félicité, and maintained an active commitment to the spiritual progress of those who called on him

He remained close to his family. While the two brothers cooperated actively in the study and writing for their early publications, Napoleon's continental blockade against England simultaneously hurt British trade and crippled French shipping, ruining the La Mennais family. By 1813, bankruptcy forced John's father to close his business and default with creditors. The two brothers and business partner, he abandoned all his possessions to cover his losses. Pierre-Louis was then old and ill-suited for the complex liquidation proceedings. John skillfully carried out this task with business sense, fairness and honor.[29] In the inevitable property sales which followed, *Les Corbières*, the cherished family country estate in Saint-Servan, passed out of the La Mennais ownership. With Marie, and his two brothers, Félicité and Gratien, John arranged to provide a suitable retirement income for his father and for uncle Des Saudrais.

The closure of the seminary dispersed his close associates and the challenge of shared responsibilities. Vielle retired provisionally at Saint-Servan, and Bruté de Rémur left for the American missions of Maryland, entrusting his aging mother to John's care.

John's early intellectual partnership with Félicité prepared the way for a more ambitious work. Preoccupations with the intrusions of the State in the life of the Church led John to assemble historical notes on the tradition of the Church concerning the nomination of bishops. He reported progress to his Sulpician friend: *"The small notes which you saw before your departure, increase daily and have become or will soon become three volumes,"* (June 8, 1812).[30] The three-volume treatise first appeared anonymously in 1814 as *Tradition de l'Église sur l'institution des Évêques;* John had already taken new commitments then.

Father de Clorivière, the former Jesuit who had once planned to follow Father John Carroll to Maryland had stayed in France. Fathers Vielle and Engerran were among the first members of his priest's Society of the Sacred Heart, and John's membership followed theirs after ordination. Father Vielle was superior and spiritual director of the Daughters of the Heart of Mary of the reunion of Saint-Servan. John de La Mennais succeeded him in that position when Vielle left for Saint-Brieuc.[31]

Several friends in Saint-Malo shared his apostolic commitments. Friends, like Querret and Langrez, made it possible for him to keep a link with the students he was compelled to leave.[32] At his departure, Querret held during eleven years the position of principal of the reorganized public secondary school of the city of Saint-Malo.[33] He had taught mathematics to John and Félicité in exchange for lessons in literature. The intellectual relationship which followed matured into a friendship of the heart. John guided his mathematician along the ways of Christian commitment and the challenge of mature spirituality. The only secondary school left in Saint-Malo after the closing of the ecclesiastical college was secular, but John's influence on the life of its students continued for several years through the influence of the new principal.

Father Langrez, a young priest from Saint Servan who had studied under him [34]at the suppressed minor seminary of Saint-Malo, accepted to teach at Querret's municipal secondary school. In that capacity, he paid special attention to students planning to attend the seminary. John followed their progress through him, and the bond with his former students and members of the student Congregation of the Holy Angels remained emotional. He wrote to Father Langrez: *"I carry them all in my heart, and, though unable to speak to them, I speak to God of that little family which he had given me, and which I will ever love dearly,"* (August 5,1814)[35]. What he could no longer achieve in the city of his birth, he would resume elsewhere by responding to new challenges.

---

[1] Doctor Philippe Pinel (1745-1826).
[2] (1755-1829).

[3] 1732-1811.

[4] Father Paul-Émile Teysseyre (1785-1818), Hyacinthe de Quélen (1778-1835), Simon Gabriel Bruté de Rémur (1779-1839).

[5] Letter to the Baron de Vitrolles, September 29, 1844. **Cor gén F**, v. 8, p. 341.

[6] The quoted expressions are gathered from *Maurice de Guérin, Journal, Lettres et Poésies*, Paris: Librairie Académique, Didier et Cie, 1868. Pages 170-177.

[7] Letter to Querret, February 16, 1815. **Cor gén J**, v.1, p. 265.

[8] **AFIC**, 17 (9).

[9] **Cor gén J**, v. 1, p. 28.

[10] A.Roussel, *Lamennais et ses correspondants inconnus*. Paris: Téqui, 1912, p. 18.

[11] To S. Gabriel Bruté de Rémur, July 4, 1807. Cor gén J, v.1, p. 25.

[12] Textually, *Torrent d'idées vagues:* torrent of vague thoughts (first thoughts, to be reexamined and clarified).

[13] Text in **ÉM**, No. 2 (April 1988), pp. 25-29.

[14] **Cor gén F,** v. 1, pp.33, 58.

[15] **Cor gén J**, v. 1, pp. 41-42.

[16] See Brother Paul Cueff, **ÉM**, No. 2 (April 1988), pp. 52-56, and Marechal, Jeunesse de La Mennais, pages 199¬-250.

[17] **Lav**, vol. 1, pp. 80-82, and Marechal, *Jeunesse de La Mennais,* pp. 251-278.

[18] To S. G. Bruté de Rémur, February 2 and April 22, 1808. **Cor gén J**, v. 1, pp. 38-40. Tight quarters remained a constant concern. There were several acquisitions and adjustments in the use of space over the years.

[19] To S. G. Bruté de Rémur, **Cor gén J**, v. 1, pp. 38-40.

[20] February 2, 1808, and June 10, 1809. **Cor gén J**, v.1, pp. 38-40 and 66-67.

[21] See particularly E. Herpin (and others), *Histoire du Collège de Saint-Malo,* Ploërmel: Imprimerie Saint--Yves, 1902. Pages 32-82. On the history of the school see also letters to S. G. Bruté de Rémur for 1808 and 1809 in **Cor gén J**, v. 1; **Rop**, pp. 69-125; **Lav.** vol.1, pp. 114-131.

[22] E. Herpin, op. cit., pp. 54-57. At one point he and Félicité donated 10,000 francs. Ibid., p. 56.

[23] To S. G. Bruté de Rémur, February 2 and April 26, 1808. **Cor gén J,** v.1, pp. 41-42. E. Herpin, op. cit., pp. 54-55.

■

[24] On this and similar sodalities (or lay congrégations), see E. Herpin, *Histoire du Collège de Saint¬-Malo,* Ploërmel: Imprimerie Saint-Yves, 1902, p.44, and *L'Abbé Jean-Marie* de La Mennais ..., Ploërmel: Imprimerie Saint-Yves, [1898], pages 237-246.

[25] Eugène de Mazenod (1782-1861), future founder of the Oblates of Mary Immaculate, was volunteering time in the emergency "scriptorium" of the seminary.

[26] Jean Leflon, Eugène de Mazenod ... (3 vols.), Paris: Plon, 1957-1965. Vol. 1, pp. 384-385. **Lav.** vol. 1, p. 120.

[27] Quoted in E. Herpin, *Histoire du Collège de Saint-Malo,* p. 72.

[28] **Lav.** pp.128-131. **Rop,** pp.69-125. Herpin, *Histoire du Collège de Saint-Malo,* pp.81-92. Marechal, *Jeunesse de La Mennais,* pp. 372-381.

[29] **Lav.** pp. 136-139. Marechal, La *Jeunesse de La Mennais,* pp. 442-446.

[30] Post scriptum to a letter of Félicité to Bruté de Rémur, **Cor gén J,** v. 1, pp. 122-123.

[31] See André Rayez, "Lettres de direction de Jean-Marie de la Mennais," *Revue d'Ascétique et de Mystique,* vol. 33, no.133 (October-December 1957), pp. 422-450.

[32] Jean-Joseph Querret (1783-1839), Father François Langrez (1787-1862).

[33] See E. Herpin, *Histoire du collège de Saint-Malo,* pp. 83-109. **Lav.** vol. 1, pp.132-134.

[34] L. Kerbiriou, Au service des Orphelines et Face au Tabernacle, La Congrégation de l'Adoration Perpétuelle, Brest: Imprimerie Le Grand, 1936. P.21.

[35] Ibid., p. 24 and **Cor gén J,** pp. 183-184.

Marchais Lith.

Paris. Imp par Auguste Bry. 141. r. du Bac

Bishop John Baptist Marie Caffarelli, 1763-1815

092.i

Chapter 7

A DIOCESE CALLS

Bishop Caffarelli in a restructured diocese

On 18 March 1814, Bishop Caffarelli wrote in the account book of his diocese: "On this day, *Mr. de La Mennais accepted the responsibility for the accounts which I entrusted to him.*" [1] For the moment, John would sit at a desk in a diocesan office along the northern shores of Brittany, 75 kilometers (some 50 miles) west of his native Saint-Malo. Doors had closed and another door had opened; John had lost a school and a parish in a walled city, and now called to a new diocese.

The Revolution had not bypassed Saint-Brieuc. Under the new statesmen, a juring bishop supplanted the legitimate prelate, while a revolutionary court harangued suspects and travestied justice in the chapel of Saint Peter. [2] A national batallion subdued resistance fighters and patrolled the city. The revolutionaries temporarily housed the guillotine in a chapel, occasionally parading it through the countryside to intimidate the defiant and the laggard. The fatal blade severed a few heads, but the ordeal ended without the excesses which disgraced Saint-Malo and Nantes. Saint-Brieuc was spared a bloodbath, but not the hell of social and moral chaos. [3]

John came to bring spiritual relief to Saint-Brieuc without realizing that his father had once assisted the region with low cost grain in a time of famine. In 1813, Father Renault, [4] then interim secretary to Bishop Caffarelli, informed his superior that Father Vielle had recently retired in Saint-Servan after the closure of his school. Sensing the availability of a seminary director, Bishop Caffarelli commissioned Father Renault to invite him to Saint-Brieuc. [5] Through Vielle, John became acquainted with a Bishop in need of assistants. Visits blossomed into friendship, and the invitation to accept secretarial responsibilities in the diocese followed. John shared the office with Father Renault until the latter assumed other duties. [6] His first mission had been in his home city; he would now address the needs of a diocese under Bishop Caffarelli, his mind and heart opening ever more widely to the universal Church.

Proposed by Napoleon, Bishop Caffarelli[7] came to the see of Saint-Brieuc in May 1802, hardly five months after John's ordination to the sub-diaconate. He had lived in Spain during the Revolution after refusing to serve the constitutional church. He remained consistently loyal to the Emperor in matters of civil rule, without neglecting his pastoral responsibilities. His brother, one of Napoleon's officers, had been killed during the Egyptian campaign. [8]

The diocese which he inherited was a creation of the Revolution. The state church established under the *Civil Constitution of the Clergy* of July 12, 1790 had suppressed 50 dioceses now dropping to 85 with diocesan boundaries identical to those of the newly created administrative departments. *The Concordat* of July 17, 1801 cut the diocesan total down to 60, an ecclesiastical map drawn by civil authority because the Pope felt obliged to approve Bonaparte's reorganization. Bishop Caffarelli would administer Church matters in the department of Côtes-du-Nord, a diocese with additions clipped from the fringes of prerevolutionary neighbors. His jurisdiction included all the original parishes and parcels from the dioceses of Quimper and Vannes, and fragments from the suppressed dioceses of Tréguier, Dol and John's home diocese of Saint-Malo.

The deplorable legacy of the Revolution created perplexing problems for an inexperienced bishop along with adjustments to regional and linguistic diversities[9] Bishop Caffarelli faced the irksome challenge of reorganizing pastoral services in a ruined diocese, with remnants of a depleted clergy wearied by a decade of mistreatment. The task seemed hopeless under an Emperor prone to marshal the clergy as a moral gendarmerie commissioned to guarantee popular submission. Brutal revolutionary innovations, a divided clergy, and traditions of **Gallicanism** weakened the prospects of curbing Napoleon's insolence.

The Four Gallican Articles of 1682

Gallicanism in France, like Josephism in Austria, was one of several doctrines advocated in Europe to exclude the Holy See from the management of state affairs, and to limit its role in local Church administration. Its historical roots plunge beyond the Council of Constance, (1409) to the early Christian emperors. [10]

The version of Gallicanism revived during the Empire had been drafted into four articles by a national assembly of the clergy convened during the reign of Louis XIV. It is known as the "Declaration of the Clergy of France on Ecclesiastical Power," dated March 19, 1682. Louis XIV promulgated a royal decree forbidding the teaching of any contrary doctrine.

After immediate objections from the Pope and prolonged difficulties with church authorities, Louis XIV recanted in a letter to Pope Innocent III: *"I have given the necessary orders that my edict of March 22, 1682 . . . need no longer be observed,"* (September 14. 1693). It nevertheless survived in the theology of the Gallican clergy and was frequently referred to as the "Four Articles of 1682." Napoleon wielded it to manipulate Church life. Those who recognized the primacy of the Pope were referred to as **ultramontane** because they recognized authority from beyond the Alps. The term **gallican** applied to those who presumed "privileges" for the French Church. [11]

John de La Mennais came well prepared to associate with Bishop Caffarelli. The Emperor demanded the teaching of the four Gallican articles in seminaries, and John's school had not been exempt from harassment on that account. Since his Paris experience, and particularly during the interim following the closure of his school in Saint-Malo, he had persistently compiled historical proof of the primacy of Peter's successor in Church tradition. Félicité had written the fruits of this research in a three-volume treatise, partly in Saint-Brieuc, partly in Paris, and prepared it for the publisher by July 1814. The confiscation of the *Réflexions* of 1809 had not been forgotten: the publisher deceptively gave *Liège,* Belgium, as the city of publication for a book printed and released anonymously in Paris in August 1814 as *Tradition de l'Église sur l'Institution des Évêques,* (Tradition of the Church on the institution of bishops). [12]

Without the Emperor's downfall, reprisal was certain; however, the allies forced a first abdication on Napoleon, April 4, 1814, and speedily exiled him to the Island of Elba, April 20. When he escaped Paris-bound on March 1, 1815, Félicité fled to London to divert attention from his brother's role in the book. Waterloo and the second exile ended the likelihood of sanctions. Félicité wrote about *La Tradition* to their common friend and frequent collaborator then living in the United States: *"It is indeed my work, having done it entirely from texts that he [John] had assembled,"* (April 25, 1815). [13]

Félicité does not state that John had written a few sections of the treatise and assisted with revision. A number of observations and text inserts are in the hand of the elder who had been collecting and studying the material for nearly a decade. [14] The introduction states that the Pope exercises his primacy through many channels; the authors had chosen to demonstrate this authority through the doctrine of the Church on the selection of bishops. [15] The intrusion of Napoleon's ministers into the seminary affairs of Saint-Malo had prepared the young secretary to deal with arrogant statesmen; neither he nor his Bishop was inclined to surrender Church functions to the Emperor, or to any government administrator.

Pathways to reconstruction

While Napoleon brooded on Elba, John de La Mennais recalled the belligerent attitude of Bishop Caffarelli during the Emperor's years of power: *"When crowned pride resolved to strangle the Church of Jesus Christ in its steel embrace, the Bishop of Saint-Brieuc submitted to only one fear, that of God."* [16] After attempting to prevent the election of a successor to Pius VI, the reigning Emperor allowed a successor on his terms and dealt with Pius VII by evading the terms of the *Concordat* of July 16, 1801. The chronicle of his reign is thickset with accounts of violations, beginning with the seventy-seven *Organic Articles.* [17]

Caffarelli was grateful for the favors granted by Napoleon to his family. He owed his diocese to him, but in church affairs, he lived his loyalty without servility, the Emperor resenting his political independence. When Napoleon called the national council of 1811 to prevail against the Pope's authority in the selection of bishops, Caffarelli drew a sharp remonstrance for his objections: *"You know,"* said the Emperor, *"that I can take your bishopric from you and put you in jail."* *"That,"* is reputed to have replied the Bishop, *"would be much easier to do than to give me back my brother who died for you."* Napoleon later acknowledged the prelate's services by adding his name to the rolls of the Legion of Honor. [18]

The Emperor's manipulation of Church affairs vexed churchmen. Twelve bishops and half of the clergy had taken the constitutional oath to the church of the Revolution. Persecution, exile, even execution had been the lot of those who had refused to serve under the *Civil Constitution of the Clergy* causing tension with parishes loyal to the Pope. Napoleon protected the priests of the revolutionary church, but soon these men would have to retract to restore unity of pastoral service. The Emperor demanded that a percentage of *"constitutional"* priests be kept in office; he prevailed temporarily, but moral loyalty guided some bishops to demand from dissidents a formal expression of fidelity to the Holy See.

On June 20, 1802, Saint-Brieuc celebrated Caffarelli's installation with solemn rites and festive illumination of streets at night, but an official rigidity chilled his first encounters with public administrators. Prefect Boullé, [19] had advised the prelate to respect the constitutional clergy, and other officials had defined the "civic" attitude expected of him. [20] The Prefect repeatedly interfered with the new Bishop's work to support the church of the Revolution, but the people disregarded his directives and returned to the Church of their fathers. By 1800, the revolutionary cult had lost its following and the constitutional church died before the Concordat voided the *Civil Constitution of the Clergy.*

Caffarelli administered his diocese with two Vicars General. The first, Father Manoir, [21] assistant to his prerevolutionary predecessor, the other, Father Jacques Depagne, was an unrepentant constitutional priest. Forced to include one priest from the church of the Revolution among his vicars, Caffarelli chose him since he was insignificant and harmless. The un-reconciled constitutional clergy of the diocese numbered at most 150, the priests loyal to the Pope, about 800. Napoleon's government required a fair apportionment of parishes between the two clergies. Boullé insisted on the attribution of one third of them to the constitutionals, but the Bishop refused to allow more than one fourth.

Caffarelli reclaimed unsold church property confiscated during the Revolution, liturgical ornaments, sacred vessels, even buildings, and the Bishop also reorganized his diocesan seminary. Napoleon's refusal to reinstate most religious orders of men kept their active members in clandestinity, but Caffarelli managed to obtain legal authorization for several religious orders of women. When the Emperor re-authorized the Brothers of the Christian Schools, Caffarelli pleaded unsuccessfully with their superiors to reopen the school which the revolutionaries had closed a few streets from his cathedral; the lack of brothers made that request impossible at that time. [22]

John de La Mennais had been called to Saint-Brieuc by a zealous executive willing to reorganize his diocese according to the directives of the Holy See, against the claims of the Emperor. When ill health interfered with his work, John de La Mennais stood ready to battle at his side. Bishop Caffarelli and John de La Mennais resisted Gallican presumptions as twin souls.

A fallen Emperor, a funeral, grave responsibilities

Bishop Caffarelli invited John de La Mennais with openhearted fellowship: "We will live as two brothers helping and encouraging one another to bear the burdens of the episcopate, which you kindly accept to share with me," (October 19, 1813). [23] The biographer of Father Renaud recalls how the Bishop shared the day with his two assistants: *"Every morning after breakfast, Father de La Mennais and Father Renaud met around a table in the office of Msgr. Caffarelli. The prelate opened his portfolio and assigned to each his share of correspondence, recommending promptness in order to save time for conversation afterwards."*[24] The sharing which followed lingered on into the treasured memories of later life.

John had been assisting his new superior for less than one month when the European allies twice forced Napoleon to abdicate, April 4 and 6, 1814. The defeated Emperor left for exile on the Island of Elba, April 20; Louis XVIII entered Paris, May 2. The Empire had collapsed and the heir of the Bourbons was attempting a first royal *Restoration.* On June 17, 1814, the new secretary delivered in the pulpit of the cathedral the funeral oration of the ill-fated Louis XVI guillotined on January 21, 1793. [25]

Caffarelli found it embarrassing to hail the Monarchy after a decade of manifest loyalty to the Emperor. He assigned the solemn oration to John who asked to be exempt in favor of more prestigious orators. Caffarelli insisted, and continued to involve his secretary closely in his administration. Assignments followed briskly as John progressively became Vicar General without the title. The young assistant wrote administrative correspondence, episcopal letters and proclamations, and traveled with his superior when needed. He prepared a formal request for the release of Pope Pius VII then held captive by invading Austrians in Italy. Towards the end of 1814, Bishop Dubourg consulted the Bishop of Saint-Brieuc about a revision of the Concordat with the Holy See. John drafted the text for his superior, objecting to Gallicanism and warning against lingering Jansenism.

The year 1814 was filled with a deepening commitment to diocesan administration, deepening bonds of friendship with former associates in Saint-Malo, and personal plans for the future. For John, Saint-Malo was no further than his heart. Through rare visits and a loyal correspondence, he kept relationships with the associates of his first decade of service. [26] He realized that plans for the restoration of his home diocese had not been abandoned, and that he might be invited to assist its bishop.

His studies during his convalescence in Paris and La Chesnaie had opened new avenues of service. The first fruits of his work with Félicité led to the publication of *Les Réflexions* in 1809, the *Guide Spirituel* of Louis de Blois in French translation in 1809, and *La Tradition* in 1814. He planned other publications, but the closing of the ecclesiastical school of Saint-Malo disorganized his apostolate until the call to Saint-Brieuc changed his life. Contradictions tested his ability to cut through obstacles, while his cooperation with Bishop Caffarelli challenged his ability to cope with the unexpected.

His work on the *Institutions* of Bishops had appeared in print by dint of perseverance, thus explained to a friend: *"I need your advice, particularly in my studies. During several months, I have somewhat abandoned them; perhaps you might revive my smoldering enthusiasm. If the work from which you have read a few pages is useful to the Church, the credit reverts to you. I have several times reached the point of stopping, exhausted with fatigue, falling asleep like travelers brought down in the snow by mortal cold. However, the hand of God lifted me, thrust me forward, supported me, and we two brothers assisted one another allowing us to reach our goal."*[27]

In 1814, Félicité was in Paris busily preparing the treatise on the institution of bishops for publication, while John was preoccupied with endless planning, concerned for his and Felicite's health and financial woes. The two men shared interests ranging from church history to journalism. John was uncertain about his future and thought of writing a church history, while both brothers dreamed of founding a religious periodical. Félicité hung his hopes on John's interests, and proposed a study center and a printing press at La Chesnaie where both might join forces. Futile dreams! Prudence and responsibility more than ever called John at the side of a bishop afflicted with the gout, and relying on his services. The dream of a printing press faded into oblivion, while plans for a church history vanished in the hustle of diocesan affairs.

On January 11, 1815, Bishop Caffarelli experienced acute head and chest pains while resting in his armchair facing the hearth. He was taken to bed, but died unexpectedly between ten and eleven the next morning, leaving speechless associates and a heartbroken John de La Mennais. The diocesan chapter assembled on the same day to provide leadership during the vacancy. It chose a trio with a single valid member: the respected Father Manoir, the only candidate with administrative experience, with Fathers Floyd, aged 82, and Bollard, almost totally deaf, to assist him. Before adjourning, the chapter voted unanimously to add the young Father de La Mennais to the team. The young "outsider" was in tears by the side of the deceased Caffarelli when a messenger broke the news of his election to him.

He first shared his grief with a trusted priest of Saint-Malo: *"My sorrow is extreme, and why would it not be? Death snatched a friend, a brother from me, and what a brother! Every time we met, he greeted me with as much joy as if we had been separated for six months. He acted as if he were interested only in me, and in everything likely to interest or please me, never opening his mouth but to speak kind things that rejoice the heart, bearing in his own only the love of good, the purest and keenest zeal. He was a pastor, a true father, the kind of bishop no longer to be found. He passed away in my arms, and I had the sad consolation of bringing the last consolations of religion to him. But, my good friend, I find consolation in the thought that the will of God is accomplished in me. His hand led me here and his hand still keeps me here. I find myself entrusted with the administration of a diocese, the object of unlimited trust; I hope to continue part of the good accomplished by the worthy Bishop who remained the object of my grief,"* (January 16, 1815). [28]

John was asked to liquidate his friend's estate. He had closed intricate business affairs at the joint bankruptcy of his father and uncle Des Saudrais before coming to Saint Brieuc; executing the will of an impecunious Bishop was a minor inconvenience after the loss of an irreplaceable friend.

Advanced age and waning capacity led the three elderly vicars to rely on the energy of the fourth and youngest, then approaching 35. John understood the gravity of his new status under Father Manoir's authority. The first statements and the first official documents of the diocese were from his hand, as henceforth others would so often be. The diocese of Saint-Brieuc was calling John for the second time.

───────────────────

[1] Archives of the Diocese of Saint-Brieuc, Account book (March 1814-January 1815). The Bishop added: *"without giving him the unexpended balance which I kept."*

[2] The sanctuary of *Notre Dame de l'Espérance* now occupies the site. The Chapel of Saint Peter has been demolished.

[3] Jules Lamarre, Histoire *de la Ville de Saint-Brieuc,* Saint-Brieuc: Imprimerie Francisque Guyon, (Société d'Émulation des Côtes du Nord, Comptes rendus et mémoires, Tome XXII (1884). J. B. Ilio, *Histoire de Saint Brieuc,* 1931.

[4] François J. Renault (1788-1860).

[5] Achille Guidée, *Notice historique sur le P. François Renault,* Paris: Charles Douniol, 1864. Pages 246¬-251. The young Father (later Bishop) de Quélen had introduced Father de La Mennais to the Bishop.

[6] **Lav.** pp. 145-148. **Rop,** pp.129-132. Father Renault joined the Society of Jesus a few years later.

[7] Jean-Baptiste-Marie Caffarelli, (1763-1815).

[8] F. Le Douarec, *Le Concordat dans un diocèse de l'ouest,* Paris: Éditions Alsatia, [1958], pp. 33-41. **Lav.** pp. 145-174.

[9] René Durand, *Le département des Côtes-du-Nord sous le Consulat et l'Empire (1800-1815),* Paris: Félix Alcan, 1926. 2 volumes.

[10] It was re-expressed through the centuries in France. Sometimes defined as a form of ecclesiastical home rule in matters traditionally reserved to the Holy See, it has been used to justify the seizure of certain church revenues by the sovereign and the nomination of bishops by him, often in opposition to the pastoral responsibility of the Pope. It has been advocated as a guard against the intrusion of churchmen into the affairs of state On the roots of nineteenth-century Gallicanism, see E. Preclin et Eugène Jarry, *Les luttes politiques et doctrinales aux XVIIe et XVIIIe siècles,* Paris: Bloud & Gay 1955. (Histoire de l'Église depuis les origines jusqu'à nos jours, Vol. 19), pp. 157-161, and for context pp.149-164, 220-233. On the nineteenth century, see Paris et Rome, Paris : Éditions de l'Atelier/Éditions Ouvrières, 1996. (*A translation of his Paris*

and Rome, The Gallican Church and the Ultramontane Campaign, 1848-1853),1986.

[11] A simplified summary of the "Four Articles" could be stated as follows: (1) Saint Peter, his successors and the entire Church have received only spiritual powers from God. Kings are subject to no ecclesiastical power in temporal affairs. --- (2) The fullness of powers exercised over spiritual matters by the Holy See does not supersede the decrees of the Council of Constance (1409) which have ever since been observed by the Gallican Church. --- (3) The laws, customs, and constitutions of the realm and of the Gallican Church invariably retain their full force. --- (4) The Pope has the principal role in deciding questions of faith, but his judgment is not irreformable unless sanctioned by the consent of the church.

[12] *Tradition de l'Église sur l'institution des Évêques,* À Liège, chez Le Marié, Duvivier, Imprimeurs-Libraires, et se trouve à Paris, à la Société Typographique, 1814. 3 vols.

[13] Letter to Bruté de Rémur, **Cor gén F,** v.1, pp. 241-242.

[14] **SA** (1960), table, p. 18, and pp. 15-32. Earlier, less precise accounts are given in Marechal, *La Jeunesse de La Mennais,* pages 299¬-357, 386-436, and **Lav.,** vol. l, pp.71-94.

[15] Introduction, vol. l, p. xiii. The formal term used is: *"institution"* of bishops.

[16] January 13, 1815. Declaration of the Vicars Capitular of Saint-Brieuc written by John de La Mennais. Quoted in **Lav.** vol. 1, p. 175.

[17] Voted on April 8, 1802. Then came the imperial catechism of 1806 with its doctrine of loyalty to his person, the decree on the *University* of 1808 centralizing control over all schools, the annexation of the Papal States to France, May 1809, the captivity of Pius VII in Italy and France, July 6, 1809/May 24, 1814, the attempts to force the acceptance of his second marriage by the Church, 1810, the national council of 1811 to prevail against the Pope in the nomination of bishops, the false concordat of 1813 signed by an intimidated captive Pope at Fontainebleau, and quickly disavowed. A superfluity of executive decrees busied his men with unending interventions.

[18] **Lav.,** vol. 1, pp. 149-150.

[19] Jean Pierre Boullé (1753-1816).

[20] F. *Le Douarec, Le Concordat dans un diocèse de l'ouest, Monseigneur Caffarelli et le Préfet Boullé.* Paris: Alsatia, 1958. On Boullé, see pp. 43-54.

[21] Michel Louis Hugues Manoir (1756-1819).

[22] Durand, op. cit., vol. 1, pp. 365-486. Le Douarec, op. cit., pp. 85-153.

[23] Cited in **Rop.,** p. 132.

[24] Guidée, op. cit. pp. 10, 11.

[25] Episcopal proclamation, **Cor gén J,** v. 1, pp. 163-165. The date of June 9, 1814 appears at the end of the manuscript, the official diocesan announcement sets June 17 as the date of the celebration.

[26] **Rop.,** pp. 127-173. **Lav.,** vol. 1, pp. 154-174. Marechal, *Jeunesse de La Mennais,* pp. 439-446.

[27] June 18, 1815. Letter to Bruté de Rémur at Rennes., **Cor gén J,** v.1, p. 307.

[28] Letter to Father Hay. **Cor gén J,** v. 1, pp. 242-242., p. 166-167.

St. Brieuc

Chapter 8

SHEPHERD WITHOUT STAFF

"Under their daggers"

The Allies confined on the Island of Elba the man who had subverted the governments of Europe. As they were negotiating a new European order in Vienna, the captive slipped past his guards and sailed to southern France. Remnants of his imperial army followed him to Paris where he reorganized his troops, panicking Europe during a "hundred days." Louis XVIII fled to Belgium and waited in Ghent the fugitive's defiance.

Waterloo had already sealed Napoleon's fate when John wrote to his friend Querret in Saint-Malo: *"I no longer fear the man of the Island of Elba, he is worn out, his name recalls irreparable miseries to all Frenchmen, all abhor him."* In Saint-Brieuc, the Emperor's escape had nevertheless rekindled hostilities.

A blustering godlessness swept across the land, scattered worshipers and hardened dissidents. John added: *"The Jacobins brazenly prevail, and although they momentarily forbear to act, they nonetheless stand ready to promote their system of universal destruction.... We have lived during three months under their daggers, oppressed by their insults and their threats, and we have witnessed again the scenes of '93. You would not believe how painful my personal situation has been,"* (July 22, 1815)[1]. He had to protect the diocese from anticlerical arrogance while tempering the imprudent zeal of virtuous ecclesiastics.

A first warning came after the death of Bishop Caffarelli. Napoleon's reappearance alarmed the diocese because in the funeral oration, John had scored the Emperor's tyranny. Realistic friends warned him that the outlaw could retaliate: *"Flee, you are lost! The Jacobins have sent your oration to the Emperor."* John's response bared more fighter than fugitive of the little man *"no taller than a Jacobin's boot." "I am not displeased if the Emperor reads it. So be it, what is written is written, my actions will not contradict my words. I could be killed but not vanquished."*[2]

Bonaparte was rising to power as John answered the call to the priesthood; when the diocesan Chapter of Saint-Brieuc invited him to administrative service, the Emperor's career had ended. Father Manoir, the only experienced member of the interim team had served under the last bishop of the Old Regime, had borne the hardships of hunted priests, and he had survived captivity during the Terror. His years with Bishop Caffarelli had prepared him for emergency service, but age forced him to rely on the young John de La Mennais even in highly sensitive matters. The sudden death of their bishop was a call to administrative service. Neither of them could know that almost five years would elapse before a new bishop would be installed late in 1819. Father Manoir passed away shortly before the arrival of a successor.

Caffarelli's effectiveness in a diocese rising from chaos could not be doubted: *"He disputed every foot of ground against civil authority to draw from the Concordat and the Organic Articles maximum advantage for the Church and 'succeeded almost completely."*[3] His assistants had shared his battles; neither of them was inclined to yield hard-won gains as priorities guided them.

New freedoms, new opportunities, new dilemmas

"The Revolution set out to de-christianize France, casting the country into anarchy. The Empire maneuvered to enlist religion in the service of the state, and degenerated into tyranny."[4] The new monarch represented a dynasty's tradition of service to the Church. John would remain faithful to that legacy, expecting divine protection, support of the

clergy for the throne, and support from the throne. Louis XVIII guaranteed freedom of worship to dissidents, while reinstating the Catholic Church to its prerevolutionary status of state religion. Recovery would be slow after the confusion and violence of a quarter of a century. Parties clashed over policy, while the King, more comfortable with Voltaire than with the works of churchmen, equivocated while the ship of state lurched. Given the ideological rivalries of the times, churchmen could expect interference even in the legitimate exercise of their priestly functions. The Vicar General of Saint-Brieuc would not be spared his share of frustrations.[5]

John would have to deal with heady statesmen for the next five years in the administration of diocesan affairs, and thereafter in the management of his religious congregations and his own priestly initiatives. Interfering Jacobins, (as certain "liberals" were then referred to), could frustrate the most legitimate pastoral initiatives. Strange as it may seem, the foundation of elementary schools and the selection of schoolmasters would eventually create sharp conflicts.

The reins would be held at the Ministry of the Interior in Paris, first by Lainé, then by Decazes. Lainé[6] was a gifted lawyer and a career politician from Bordeaux remembered for the phrase, *"The kings are going,"* but who served the kings as long as they employed him. He had incurred the disgrace of Napoleon for advocating respect for institutions from his seat in the legislature. He came to his cabinet post in 1816, prepared to mend relationships with the Church, but his good will failed to temper his statist politics and doctrinaire extremes. Late in December 1818, he was relieved from his duties for obstinacy, replaced by the more discerning and diplomatic Élie Decazes.[7] Good practical sense and political realism more than personal interest in religion enabled him to restore the peace destroyed by his predecessor.

The horizon was clear for Christian renewal in 1816 as Louis XVIII ended the restrictions which had plagued Bishop Caffarelli. John assessed the needs of the diocese with enterprising zeal, and a heart saddened by the spiritual desolation around him. He marshaled pastors while surveying the faithful, never forgetting the children.

"Woe to me if I do not announce the Gospel!" [8]

The young Vicar General called the clergy and religious of the diocese to spiritual renewal. [9] In July 1816, he invited the priests of Saint-Brieuc to assemble at the major seminary for their first clergy retreat since the Revolution, a span of close to twenty-five years. John reminded them of the Apostle Paul's sense of mission. The retreat started in heartwarming fellowship under the guidance of an effective retreat master. After years of isolation, the elderly fraternized with speechless emotion at the edge of the tomb. The more respected pastors heard the confessions of the group. Renewal in the grace of their priesthood was so encouraging that in September, John convened those who had not been able to attend in July.

John opened the first retreat; he directed the second with simplicity and unpretentious authority. At the renewal of their sacerdotal promises during the closing liturgy, he invited the priests to face the daunting task awaiting them with realistic courage: *"If anything must astonish us, it is not that men still seek the priesthood, but that at the sight of so much terrain overgrown with thorns for lack of laborers, at the cry of so many children pleading for bread as no one steps forward to feed them, so few declare like Saint Paul: 'Woe to me if I do not evangelize!'"* [10] The second retreat repeated the success of the first; all but one of the priests who had weakened during the Revolution retracted publicly.

After the shepherds, the faithful! The population of the city heard the call to follow the example of the clergy without delay. The Jesuits had been reestablished by Pope Pius VII in 1814, after half a century of suppression by the Church. Father de Clorivière had reorganized them in France and had founded a special mission center at Lamballe, about 22 kilometers, (14 miles) east of Saint-Brieuc. From there, missionaries set out to preach throughout the Breton towns to offset the spiritual damage caused by a generation of irreligion. The Jesuits from Lamballe were not given to refined rhetoric: they avoided politics and urged the people to return to the faith of their fathers in direct terms, inviting the persevering faithful to a deeper understanding of their heritage. John called them to lead the spiritual exercises, a mission opened at the Cathedral on October 6, 1816 for the first time in a quarter of a century.

The young vicar's initiative panicked the local Jacobins. They argued that the mission would disturb the conscience of the population, revive the painful memories of recent decades, divide families and rekindle old hostilities. A team of eight men led by Father Gloriot directed the exercises at the Cathedral and in the churches of the city. John left the cathedral pulpit to the missionaries and preached in the local churches. The results exceeded expectations as even the prefect, the mayor, the commanding general of the garrison and the captain of the gendarmerie all attended the retreat at the Cathedral. Their example inspired the population and dispelled false rumors. The missionaries raised a commemorative mission cross in the park facing Saint Peter's chapel, the present sanctuary of Our Lady of Hope. Men carried the cross followed by a large crowd, John joining to plead for repentance.

John would not rest on the successes of 1816. When missionary teams were available, he called on them to reawaken the dormant faith of traditional parishes, and met emergencies personally when they could not come. The memory of saintly preachers like Vincent Ferrer and Louis de Montfort remained alive in the land. As he followed their example, contemporaries wondered how the overworked Vicar General managed to preach so often.

The missions of 1816 had revived Christian life in Saint-Brieuc. The following year, he set out to reaffirm its blessing by mounting the pulpit for the opening sermon. When he saw the capacity audience as an overflow of hundreds stood outside, he announced: *"I am not preaching here. Follow me up Vicairie street to Saint Peter's Square."* He moved through the crowd, led the way uphill to the chapel of Saint Peter where the mission cross recalled the resolutions of 1816, and preached standing on a chair. During the week, an increasing daily attendance heard his invitation to live by its faith, and to persevere in the devotion rediscovered with the help of the Jesuit missionaries.

The retreats of the time generally memorialized the deceased with a session in the cemetery. It was the custom in the old Breton parish burial grounds to gain space for new burials by removing long-term occupants and gathering residual bones in parish ossuaries, sometimes exposed to the public. It was not uncommon for missionaries to preach on eternal destiny by raising a skull in one hand and interrogating the dead on their observance of Christian responsibilities. ("How did you live? Where are you now?") The young Vicar General excelled in this form of examination of conscience.[11]

Hard won spiritual gains can easily be lost. After the missions of 1816, John readily gave generous time to those who asked for confession and spiritual advice. The faithful who took their Christian life seriously came in such numbers that the service had to be divided, Father Vielle confessing the women, John the men.[12]

John founded at the Cathedral a society in honor of the Sacred Heart of Jesus for men and women; the register quickly accumulated 1486 names. The same society was organized in Tréguier with the cooperation of Father Tresvaux, and later in the churches of Loudéac, Lamballe and Quintin. He inspired the formation of a group known as the "society of young women" from the well-to-do elements of the population; their members were to guide and assist their poorer sisters.

Merchants and craftsmen had been meeting regularly in Saint Peter's Chapel as a lay religious society before the Revolution destroyed it. Since the police still held their records, Father de La Mennais claimed them and revived the congregation under the name of "Association of Mary." The objective of the society was to seek personal sanctification through the help of Mary, to spread her devotion and to imitate her virtues.

The spiritual life of the young equally preoccupied him. In November 1816, he founded an association of the Immaculate Conception for young women of the bourgeoisie, and he personally directed it during three years.

The students of the secondary school of Saint Brieuc had a reputation for insubordination and godlessness; to help improve their discipline, Mr. de La Mennais established a student "congregation" similar to the successful one at the college of Saint-Malo a few years earlier and personally directed it as voluntary chaplain during two years. The example of its 40 to 50 members in a school of 300, the dynamic influence of Father de La Mennais, and the work of the priests he had recommended as teachers gradually transformed the institution. A realistic blend of devotional exercises, Christian living and good works characterized the lay religious societies which he founded.

Before founding his student congregation, he wrote to his friend Querret, the headmaster: *"What a riot a collège can be! Reforming that of Saint-Brieuc costs me more care and grief than the words spoken between January 1, and December 31. Everything must be decided in Paris where everything, or just about, is decided wrongly. Then there is the prefect, then the mayor, then the decision of this one, the regulations of that one, the intrigues, the recommendations, and what not? It is endless. It is easier to destroy these schools than to establish discipline in them,"* (January 30, 1816). [13] Capitulation in the face of opposition was against John's character; obstacles sounded a call to arms.

"Come, follow me!"

In the fourteen-year period since 1803, there had been a deficit of 210 priests in the diocese. At the end of 1815, thirty-two parishes were without pastors. Bishop Caffarelli had reclaimed unsold confiscated church belongings, and had reorganized the diocesan seminary now directed by Father Vielle. Though seminary teachers were indispensable to the formation of future priests, they received despairingly low wages; John struggled to improve their lot and to enlarge their living quarters. When assistance from the public treasury fell short of costs, private charity provided the difference needed for the purchase of an adjoining building.

The vital factor in the education of future priests was the ecclesiastical secondary school, the minor seminary. Napoleon had closed many of them to prevent the rise of an effective clergy. The only surviving diocesan institution was in the city of Dinan, too inaccessible for local candidates from the Breton-speaking western districts. It soon became clear to Father de LaMennais that there was a great need to reorganize some schools and to found new ones.

Ecclesiastical schools could not be founded without a royal permit. The dire need for them set John on a struggle with municipal secondary school administrators in a climate of government resistance to religious institutions. Some of the public *collèges* had become ineffective centers of learning, some becoming centers of insubordination and immorality. The reputation of the *collège* of Saint Brieuc was such that the Prefect of the department refused to enroll his son, and asked father Vielle to tutor him. Alert parents hesitated to spend their earnings for tuition in schools likely to turn their children into thieves and rebels.

When John requested permission to open his ecclesiastical school at Tréguier, the officials of the University of Rennes replied that the schools of Brittany were adequate for the region. Because they ignored the local situation, Father de La Mennais pointed out that prisoners came in larger numbers from districts without clergy; this plea prepared the way for a royal permit. John rented an empty building in the vicinity of the seminary and soon more than 120 students came that first year. The administration of the municipal school soon realized the futility of competing, and closed its school leasing the space to the diocese.

Loss of revenue convinced the owner to part with the unsold section of the building. The diocesan chapter patiently waited for the sale, but the local Jacobins conspired to prevent the reacquisition of the confiscated property by the Church. They organized a private auction to conclude the affair before Father de La Mennais could learn about it. The ploy seemed flawless until a citizen from Tréguier traveled through a winter night storm to advise the Vicar General at four in the morning that the sale would take place at ten. The Vicar General immediately tumbled into civilian clothes, saddled his horse, traveled through foul weather, and settled at dawn at the rectory of Tréguier.

At auction time, no one paid serious attention to an unexpected presence in a corner of the room. Several individuals entered, chafing hands against the cold, whispering satisfaction that the cleric from Saint Brieuc had been tricked. The auction opened in earnest and the stranger waited until the bidding weakened and buyers called late bids. John then raised the standing offer by two thousand francs. Whispers and questions floated through the room and someone raised the offer by a few hundred francs. The intruder added fifteen hundred and closed the bidding. But who was the buyer? Father de La Mennais, now owner of the seminary for the diocese, curtly gave his name and left.[14]

The success of the ecclesiastical secondary schools annoyed many public administrators. Realizing that ecclesiastical secondary schools admitted resident and extern students, they revived an old Napoleonic ordinance to exclude externs. The ruling could ruin the schools by depriving them of additional students and survival income. In John's estimate, how could sound discipline, respect for religion and academic soundness be valid reasons for persecuting minor seminaries? He pleaded against those who sought to destroy successful institutions supported by parents; the authorities soon dropped the ordinance.

Early in 1818, the government required seminary teachers to teach the Four Gallican Articles of 1682, and demanded an explicit written promise to comply. Gallicanism, again! After years of resistance to Napoleon's interference with theology teachers in the minor seminary of Saint-Malo, John was not ready to allow Lainé, Minister of the Interior, to meddle in the affairs of Saint-Brieuc.

His first reaction to the Gallican Articles was formal resistance. After prudent consultation, he complied with formalities without compromising principle. He had no objection to the first Gallican article which expressed the independence of secular power from religious authority; however, the three other Articles dealt with the spiritual realm and matters of church administration. John reminded authorities that the Pope had rejected them and that Louis XIV had ceased to enforce them.

He prefaced the promises with the following reservations: (1) The declarations were directed first to the Vicars General of the diocese during the vacancy of the see, because the Bishop was the only authority responsible for the teaching of theology in his diocese. (2) It must be understood that the articles are mere opinions never raised to the level of a dogma by a competent authority. The teachers will therefore teach them as such. (3) The teachers promised to refer to them as opinions, but to uphold official Church doctrine.[15]

Louis XVIII proposed to broaden the freedom of education though keeping the Université as an effective instrument of government; even ecclesiastics serving in the organization sometimes privileged the interests of the system above the needs of society and religion.

Laborers for the harvest

Bishop Caffarelli passed away before completing his plans for the restoration of local religious congregations. Realizing the need for assistance, John worked tirelessly to reinstate religious congregations specializing in the education of youth.[16]

The dispersed Ursulines in Dinan, Lamballe and Lannion were seeking legalization and living space. The municipality had organized a *collège* in an old confiscated convent known as *la Victoire*, but now the institution had closed and Dinan had no interest in a vacant building. In 1816, Father de La Mennais requested the building for the Ursulines. Lainé, Minister of the Interior, might have conceded the building without hesitation, but the *Université* claimed it for the future. John pleaded for the Sisters with the committee of public instruction, and the Ursulines were allowed to reoccupy their home.

The former Ursulines of Lamballe still numbered 58. The institution which once housed the nuns, the boarders and the lay congregation of ladies had become the home of a *collège*. The chapel and recent additions were reserved as the barracks of a future garrison; the garden had become city property. The Vicar General intervened for the release of the property, and after extensive negotiations, the Minister of the Interior allowed the Ursulines to reenter their former home.

Vigilant shepherd

The Vicar General intervened when parishes in the care of negligent clergy slipped into indifference. John used the ecclesiastical sanctions of the time to end scandal, even calling for the suspension from priestly functions in extreme cases. An interdicted priest occasionally sought to evade diocesan sanctions by asking liberal parishioners to address supportive letters to the Minister of the Interior. The government then shielded those who had served in the church of the Revolution.

Repression was John's last resort, patient admonition the rule! When the intemperance of a priest became a scandal, John wrote to him: *"Where is your faith? Are you or are you not a priest, a Christian? If your conscience is blunted, do you believe that the conscience of your superior is dead?"* He proceeded with indulgence, adding: *"Do not constrain us to deprive you of your title. Examine your conscience; return to the Lord. I speak to you in his stead; in his name, I beg you not to lose your soul and those of your brothers."* [17]

Certain parish priests regularly assembled fellow priests for card games lasting far into the night, against the explicit directives of the diocese. Father de La Mennais was aware that such gatherings continued well beyond reasonable hours in a rectory of the vicinity of Saint-Brieuc. One night he mounted his horse, surprised the delinquents and reprimanded: *"Gentlemen, is that the importance you attach to the circulars from the diocese? Well, then, I leave you to your conscience."* With those words, he turned away and disappeared. Local tradition reports that the priest pitched the cards into the fire the next day.

There were more creative interventions. Breton-speaking parishes in the western sector of the diocese were deprived of service when priests refused to cross the language barrier. He resolved part of the dilemma by sending zealous young French-speaking volunteers into Breton territory.

In 1819, John sensed that the results of the missions of 1816-1817 were wearing off. Father Gloriot and his missionaries were then preparing to preach at the port of Brest. He prevailed upon them to set aside two weeks to repeat in Saint-Brieuc the exercises conducted earlier. He then organized similar renewal programs for the parishes of the diocese and readily shared the work of his priests. He preached a message of hope, rallied neighboring clergy and assigned roles for them. By opening retreat activities, his presence filled the church.

He was known to serve even meager audiences. A Mrs. Grandville from Nantes related how John once traveled to a community in dreadful weather to preach a retreat for women. The disappointed sister superior apologized for the empty church. *"Empty,"* responded the retreat master, *"but here is one woman who braved the elements and is waiting alone to hear the word of God."* He preached for the single listener who was moved by the performance; her story attracted a growing attendance and the retreat was an unexpected success. He was said to improvise sermons, but he prepared his preaching with prayerful meditation and written text, often crossed out with revisions.

The Vicar General or Grand vicaire, as he was sometimes called, pursued his mission oblivious of personal fatigue though friends worried about his health. Félicité counseled moderation: *"Spare yourself, everyone says that it is impossible for you to bear the excessive labor which you lay upon yourself,"* (August 23, 1818). [18]

Meddlesome government officials complicated his task; Félicité wrote to a Sulpician friend: *"John is still in his diocese, battling the countless obstacles raised against the Church. You cannot imagine our situation; in comparison we were almost in heaven under Bonaparte. We have orders to give church funerals to duelists, to suicides; prohibition to instruct the people about invalid marriages; prohibition to write to Rome for dispensations through channels other than the Ministry of the Interior, etc., etc. Oppression has no bounds and finally the new concordat is rejected indefinitely,"* (November 30, 1818). John lived by words once written to the same friend: *"Nonetheless, let us not lose heart, and let us work with zeal equal to the difficulties which we must overcome,"* (September 30, 1815). [19]

John was reclaiming ground taken by the ungodly or lost by the uncaring: *"We provide many missions in this land, all of them very successful. When they close in rural parishes or even in cities, the number of persons who have not come to the sacraments can be counted on fingers.*

Faith is still alive, and it manifests itself with miraculous vigor in these days of salvation and grace, when it is preached to the people in a truly apostolic manner... After the mission of Saint-Brieuc, we have founded three congregations, one for young women, one for adult men, a third for young men; I direct the latter," (May 11, 1818). [20]

Discord within the fold is often more daunting to churchmen than hostility from without. John was occasionally a target for peevish retaliation in his dealings with disappointed ambitious clerics. In the Saint-Brieuc of the time, Canon Hervé Le Sage, [21] for all his moral integrity, is remembered for leading a continuing cabal against the Bishop. His written comments provide useful information, but his appreciations are often *"malicious to the point of injustice;"* his pen did not spare John de La Mennais. He could dine as a guest of the Vicar General, then return home to write disparaging remarks against his host and embittered pages about the diocese.

John assumed broad responsibilities in the diocese at an age of peak physical and mental vigor; he was then thirty-five. His biographers agree on his appearance and main character traits. Those who met him saw a tawny relatively short man remembered for the winning friendliness radiating from his person, despite his irregular features and long, prominent nose. Those who came to know him appreciated the mental vigor flashing from deep-set eyes, under a broad high forehead.

John could converse without monopolizing attention and was sought for his fine repartees and the remarkable ease of his joyous laughter. His ways were simple and grave though without stiffness. The kindness of his features invited friendship without opening to familiarity. He was prone to native anger and cynicism, but he had tamed the power of that inheritance. Those who shared his life soon realized that he was gifted with serene common sense, refined tact, and a rare understanding of people and events. A blend of determination and exquisite goodness endowed him to assume major responsibilities.

His personality compelled even the denigrating Le Sage to admit his qualities: *"His mind is sharp, piercing, he is eminently insightful, has an extreme facility for administration. No one is more persistent in his purposes, more resourceful in determining his means, steadier or more untiring in their use."* In various contexts, Le Sage writes about his knowledge and mental qualities recognizing him as a man of wit, fit for management: he settles matters *"somewhat Napoleon style, that is ever moving forward, and with a self-assurance that confounds his adversaries. He does not know retreat. Should an insurmountable obstacle arise, he pauses merely to change course, and always manages to achieve his purpose."*[23]

Without determination and a driving sense of mission, who stood a chance of surviving the confusion without loss of spiritual vision and zeal? There was opposition, sometimes from unexpected quarters, and it would increase when he set out to found Christian schools. Given the demands of his office, he was not expected to provide elementary schools, but he would not neglect the children for they were the future of the nation.

---

[1] **Cor gén J,** v.1, pp. 318-319. "Scenes of '93": Revolutionary scenes of 1793.
[2] **Lav.,** vol. 1, pp. 176-177.
[3] Durand, op. cit., vol. 1, p. 484.
[4] G. De Bertier de Sauvigny, *La Restauration,* Paris: Flammarion, 1955. P. 408. See pages 406-446.
[5] The political forces weighing on the diocesan administrators at the time must be kept in mind. --- Bickering over terms of a new concordat with the Holy See blighted the first hopes of 1815. Pope Pius VII rejected a first draft, ratified a second (1817), created 42 dioceses and named two cardinals and 34 bishops. Under the new agreement, the Church would not recover unsold confiscated property, though the state would compensate for lost resources by paying a some Church expenses from the public purse. The king could propose bishops for approval by the Pope; the acts of the Holy See were subject to review by legislators; the *"franchises, maxims and liberties"* of the Gallican Church were reaffirmed.

After the agreement, legislators unilaterally transformed its spirit and meaning as the Emperor had done. They refused to approve the king's list of new dioceses and the new bishops stood temporally without sees. Pius VII protested while domestic feuds tangled negotiations. (See G. de Bertier de Sauvigny, *La Restauration,* pp. 9-14.).

The number of dioceses did not pass from 50 to 80 until 1822 and the state proposed to apply the *Concordat* only insofar as it did not violate the rights of the Church, and pledged not to interfere with priests who exercised their ministry according to the directives of the Holy See. The limits of religious peace would be tested issue by issue.

[6] Joseph Henri Joachim (Viscount) Lainé (1767-1835).

[7] Élie Decases (1780-1860).

[8] 1 Cor. 9:16.

[9] See generally **Lav.,** vol 1, pp. 175-291; **SA** (1960), pp. 33-53 and **Rop.** pp. 175-254.

[10] As quoted in **Lav.,** vol. 1, pp. 184-185.

[11] **Lav.,** vol. 1, pp. 262-266. On the missions of the Restoration, see Ernest Sevrin, *Les Missions religieuses en France sous la Restauration,* 2 vols. Vol 1, Saint Mandé (Seine): Procure des Pères de la Miséricorde, 1948. Vol. 2, Paris: Vrin, 1959.

[12] See his letter to Querret (February 16, 1818), **Cor gén J,** v. 3, pp. 35-26.

[13] **Cor gén J,** v.1, pp. 377-78.

[14] The account, based on family tradition is from *L 'Abbé Jean-Marie de La Mennais, Fondateur de l'Institut de Ploërmel, par l'auteur des Contemporains* [Eugène de Mirecourt], Paris: Bray et Retaux; Vannes: G. De Lamarzelle, 1876. Pages 56-61. --- The seminary was purchased in two sections, the first, probably in 1819, by Mr. de La Mennais, the second in 1821 by the Bishop of the diocese. See "Achat du Grand Séminaire de Tréguier", by Louis Quéau, **Chron.,** no. 241 (January 1965), pp. 55-58.

[15] See letters to Lainé, Minister of the Interior, February 13 and March 8, 1818 in **Cor gén J,** v. 2, pp. 24, 32.

[16] **Lav.,** vol. 1, pp. 245-255 and memoranda in **Cor gén J,** v. 1, 434-437, 446-448, and v. 2, pp. 123-124.

[17] **Cor gén J,** v. 1, p. 502, (March 17, 1817).

[18] **Cor gén F,** v. 1, p. 433.

[19] To S. G. Bruté de Rémur, from Félicité, **Cor gén F,** v. 1, pp. 458-459. From John **Cor gén J,** v. 1, pp. 346-347. In cases of suicide, canon law did not authorize church funerals.

[20] **Cor gén J,** v. 1, pp. 44-46.

[21] Hervé Julien Le Sage (1754-1832), former Norbertine monk from the Abbey of Beauport (Côtes-du-Nord), outlawed and exiled at the Revolution, incardinated into the diocese after a long exile in monasteries of his order.

[22] Lav., vol. 1, pp.150, 285, 373.

[23] Ibid.. 181, 182.

Paris

Chapter 9

OPENING THE SCHOOL DOOR

The legacy of the Revolution

The Revolution closed most established schools, and Napoleon's government virtually left popular education to private initiative. When citizens later sought to reopen elementary schools, they found the hand of the state by theirs at the door, both to assist and to monitor. When John de La Mennais began his school work during the Restoration, the royal government shadowed his initiatives with encouragement, funding and a persistent supervision which stiffened into regimentation, and later into various forms of harassment.

John lived the early years of his priesthood as a teacher at the ecclesiastical secondary school of Saint-Malo. Circumstances permitting, he promoted schools for the education of future priests to the end of his life. He opened elementary schools as Vicar General, and in the diocese of Saint-Brieuc, he reorganized the schools of teaching sisters. Then in 1818, he opened schools for boys with the Brothers of the Christian Schools and through the Brothers recently-founded by Father Gabriel Deshayes. He pursued that work in the face of difficult realities by founding the Daughters of Providence of Saint-Brieuc with Marie Anne Cartel, and the Brothers of Christian Instruction with Father Gabriel Deshayes.

The men of the Revolution and their followers were more prolific with school plans, laws and control mechanisms than with supportive funding. They kept close watch on the generous citizens who opened schools that public administrators failed to provide. John soon determined to supply badly needed teachers for rural Brittany, his leadership role in the work of his two religious Congregations spanning two-thirds of his active life. Because the government remained a major force in education, John's educational initiatives are difficult to interpret without an understanding of government laws and government controls.[1]

Especially after 1815, many statesmen showed their concern with the general illiteracy of the population by taking initiatives to encourage the establishment of elementary schools. Intervention began under Napoleon; the mixed blessings of legality and controls followed along with very modest funding. By Napoleon's decree of March 17, 1808, and its reinterpretations, all French schools were placed under the wings of an Imperial University: *"No school, no teaching establishment whatever, will be organized outside the Imperial University and without the authorization of its chief, (Article 2)."* A Grand Master would administer the ambitious enterprise; the organization complete, even down to primary schools with the introduction to reading, writing and arithmetic, (Art. 5). The *Université* served the role of a supreme ministry of education. It ruled through thirteen *Académies,* a name designating regional administrative and reporting authorities linking prefects, mayors, committees, inspectors and schools in a web of supervision.

The government opened secondary schools soon after the Revolution. A French secondary school was then referred to as a *collège.* A private secondary school administered by priests was an ecclesiastical school, but could not open without government authorization.[2] *Univerté* executives were instructed to guarantee the integrity and professional qualifications of schoolmasters, and the establishment of normal schools for the preparation of teachers. They were expected to utilize the best teaching methods. A required *brevet* (a teaching permit), would be granted by the authority of the Grand Master; regulations from Paris reached even the lowest levels of education in every hamlet in the country.

The government was promoting monitorial schools when John intensified his school work. The teaching method required in the new government schools was known as mutual instruction, *(l'enseignement mutuel).* The form proposed for France was recent and innovated independently by Andrew Bell (1753-1832) in Madras, India, and Joseph Lancaster (1778-1838) in his Borough Road School, in London.[3]

Genuine humanitarian motives moved the two men to devise inexpensive ways of rescuing poor children from illiteracy. Their schools were referred to as mutual, tutorial or monitorial schools. By training students to teach others as monitors, one skillful schoolmaster could train a team of student leaders to drill three hundred to a thousand children simultaneously. The program was divided into simple units of instruction planned for easy transmission through a series of mechanical commands. The unconventional system had its limits and its abuse exposed some of its procedures to ridicule. However, the system provided basic instruction at little cost to thousands of children at a time when few other systems could respond to the educational needs of poor children.

After 1815, the method was forcefully promoted in France where it became the storm center of national, political and religious controversy.[4] The first attempt to implant it by Lazare Carnot, (1753-1823) Minister of the Interior during the Hundred Days, ended with the downfall of Napoleon. Joseph Lainé, (1767-1835) Minister of the Interior under Louis XVIII, aggressively revived Carnot's campaign. The movement eventually failed after stirring extended rivalries by the way it was used more than for its limited potential.

The system proved useful for drilling children in the basic skills of learning, but could achieve little beyond that. John de La Mennais used it occasionally for such purposes, but opposed its general application. In France, it often served to advance political, ideological, and antireligious causes. Some former revolutionaries promoted the system through their administrative powers, abused its potential, their tactics often offending the religious traditions of the nation.

Unlike Napoleon who did virtually nothing for elementary schools, Louis the XVIII awakened the conscience of the people to a new responsibility for the education of the young with his Royal Ordinance of February 29, 1816. The document is particularly significant in the life of

John de La Mennais because it welcomed the participation of religious congregations, and opened the door to the founders of new societies of teachers.

Basic law: the Royal Ordinance of February 29, 1816

The royal Ordinance signed by Louis XVIII on February 29, 1816, swept like a warm spring wind across the national school scene. The King's rules, laboriously reinterpreted by public administrators, stood as the basic law for elementary schools until the Guizot law of 1833 reorganized the school system.[5] The Ordinance had forty-two articles incorporating and guiding the development of elementary schools, and compelling towns to organize schools and local administration committees. The Ordinance clarified the procedures to obtain a teaching permit, how to organize the curriculum, what teaching methods were encouraged or approved, how to select school inspectors. All regulations were under the control of the *Université* and its regional administrative centers the *Académies;* Brittany was under the *Académie* of Rennes.

Though the document established structures and controls, it provided no regular funding. The Royal Ordinance abandoned the teachers to the maneuvers of preoccupied city councils not inclined to generosity towards schoolteachers. It set aside fifty thousand francs annually, not as a budget subsidy, but as an incentive fund to assist local schools. Father de La Mennais and Father Gabriel Deshayes both obtained assistance from that fund, and from local public budgets.

Contrary to the regimentation of the Empire, certain provisions of the Ordinance revealed the openness of the royal regime to private initiatives, even to new religious orders of men. Legal authorization for lay and religious teaching societies was equivalent to incorporation under civil law. Some measures of government supervision were prescribed, but the document could hardly have suggested a gentler invitation to new societies of teachers than the following articles:

Article 36: *All religious or charitable associations, such as those of the Christian Schools, will be permitted to supply, under predetermined* *conditions, schoolmasters to the towns requesting them, provided that these associations are authorized by us and that their regulations and their methods have been approved by our Commission of Public Instruction.*

Article 37: *These associations, and particularly their novitiates, could be supported in case of need, either by the departments where it might be deemed necessary, or from the funds of public instruction.*

Article 38: *The schools, staffed with schoolmasters by that form of associations, will remain subject, like the others, to the supervision of the authorities established by the present ordinance.*[6]

The Ordinance granted permission to organize, to prepare and supply teachers to the towns, to encourage associations even with occasional public funding. The Ordinance required towns to provide a school, to salary teachers, to set student fees, and to provide schooling without cost for the children of indigent families. It was criticized for not returning the supervision of elementary schools to the Church which controlled them before the Revolution, and for overlooking funding. However, the parish priest was a member of the local school supervising committee and was responsible with the mayor for the approval of local teachers.

Despite its openness to new religious congregations of teachers, the royal government frowned on their property holdings by denying them the right to accept donations and acquire property except through the *Université*. This restriction caused endless vexations to the founders of new teaching congregations. The ordinance required prayer, Bible Study and the teaching of the Catholic catechism; it further provided for Protestants and Jewish leaders to teach their religion to the children of their faith.

Unauthorized schoolmasters continued to teach illegally, but the law gradually reduced their number. The obligations and controls laid upon the towns initially applied only to schools for boys until the ordinance of April 3, 1820 corrected the oversight by extending its provisions to schools for girls. The legislation which followed in the Guizot law of June 28, 1833 deliberately excluded schools for girls from its provisions. The obligation to provide for boys explains the great need to prepare schoolmasters for boys' elementary schools, and the flood of requests which Father de La Mennais never seemed able to satisfy.

Schools for girls, which had prospered without special legislation, gained broad recognition when the Pelet law of June 23, 1836 incorporated them into the national scheme. Notwithstanding its deficiencies, the royal document was a creative response to the school emergency, creating an open climate for local initiatives and encouragement at the national level. Religious orders of teachers fared well under the Ordinance. Their shackles fallen, they reorganized with the vitality of a resurgent people, many new congregations joining their ranks. Between 1816 and 1822, the number of students in French elementary schools almost tripled. It is precisely during that six-year period that John de La Mennais and Father Gabriel Deshayes started to supply teachers for their first schools for boys.

Religious Congregations after the French Revolution

The revolutionary assemblies abolished religious orders by the law of February 19, 1790, but the exclusion of that measure from the Concordat of 1801 eliminated it from the legal system, but Napoleon had no intention of authorizing religious orders on request. As early as 1804, he prohibited *"any congregation or association of men or women to organize, even under the guise of religion, without prior authorization by imperial decree, after examination of the statutes or regulations by which its members proposed to live."* [7] The needs of French society were such that he gave preference to religious congregations devoted to social service, such as education and the care of the sick, over those with exclusively religious objectives. He legalized societies of women more freely than societies of men. Individual members from some 37 pre-revolutionary teaching communities had continued their activities privately during the Revolution. They quickly reorganized when the government of the Empire opened that possibility, and many new local service societies were formed. When Louis XVIII came to power, 942 local groups of religious women were nationally recorded. [8] Legislation entitled authorized societies to function and hold property; as a response, French Catholics founded religious congregations in unprecedented numbers after the downfall of Napoleon.

While treating the service-oriented orders of women liberally, the imperial government authorized men's congregations with deliberate political prudence and wary suspicion. It preferred to authorize congregations recognized by the Holy See before the Revolution, and was inclined to disallow new congregations.[9] The unauthorized traditional groups survived in clandestinity, the Brothers of the Christian Schools an exception. Chaptal refers to their *"admirable"* work in the cities before the Revolution.[10]

Confronted with a severe shortage of capable primary school teachers, Napoleon accepted the suggestion of his nephew, Cardinal Fesch, to restore full legal authorization to their institute in 1804. Their Congregation inspired the school work of Gabriel Deshayes and John de La Mennais, prepared the way for the foundation of new teaching societies, and profoundly influenced elementary schools in France and abroad. Father de La Mennais was founding a new school for girls when he invited them to open a school for boys in Saint-Brieuc.

---

[1] The summary offered in this chapter is supplemented by Appendix I.

[2] Whatever their names, the ecclesiastical schools of the period were minor seminaries which also admitted young men not destined to the priesthood. Such was the ecclesiastical school of Saint-Malo, the site of John's first teaching experience.

[3] Hugh M. Pollard, *Pioneers of Popular Education, 1760-1850.* London: John Murray, 1956. Pp. 214-261.

[4] Raymond Tronchot, *L'Enseignement mutuel en France de 1815 à 1833.* (Privately printed. Multigraphed doctoral thesis, Sorbonne University, 1972).

[5] Raphael Sevrin, Histoire de *l'Enseignement primaire en France, Vol. II, La Restauration,* 1815-1830. Paris: Vrin, 1933. Pp.14-28.

[6] Octave Gréard, La *Législation de l'Instruction primaire en France depuis 1789 jusqu'à nos jours* [1900], Paris: Delalain Frères, (Not dated). 7 vols. --- Vol. 1, pp. 240-248, particularly pp. 244-247.

[7] Decree of June 22, 1804 (4 Messidor year XII).

[8] Summary from Tronchot, vol. 1 part 1, pp. 42 ff. Note 8, above.

[9] F. Le Douarec, Le Concordat dans un Diocese de l'Ouest. Paris, Éditions Alsatia, 1958. Pp.149-153.

[10] Jean Antoine Chaptal (1756-1832), Minister of the Interior for the Consulate. Report of 18 brumaire, year IX (November 8, 1800), *le Moniteur, No. 49, Year IX.*

Chapter 10

THE DAUGHTERS OF PROVIDENCE

The heart of a young woman

John de La Mennais began to provide for the education of the young by reestablishing Congregations teaching sisters, then by inviting the Brothers of the Christian Schools to teach the boys in his diocese. He founded those schools without expressing any intention of founding his own religious congregations. He did not open his schools until a woman thoroughly devoted to social charities came to him with a friend for guidance. Her example inspired him to encourage and support the humble services which became his first school; neither he, nor she, could foresee what would follow. The beginnings were simple, the sequel changed the course of their lives.

The puzzled onlookers who might have wondered about the activities of a young woman rambling discreetly through the neighborhoods of Saint-Brieuc during the early years of the nineteenth century, would soon realize that the familiar stroller was deeply concerned about the sufferings of their unfortunate neighbors. Though Marie-Anne Cartel[1] was born with medical problems on the third of June, 1773, she soon became the idol of the family despite the care required by her condition.

Her parents, Doctor Charles-François and Marguerite-Marie Cartel entrusted her education to an overprotective sister. Marie sheltered her so thoroughly that Marie-Anne found it difficult to leave the house or carry on conversations of her own even at the age of twenty. An affection so unconsciously egoistic gradually degenerated into a form of tyranny. The consequence for Marie-Anne was a grave illness to which the doctors found no better immediate relief than exercise and open air. Frequent promenades away from the overbearing attention of her elder sister gave her the freedom to associate with a younger friend.[2]

Miss Poulin de Corbion was from one of the most distinguished families of the city, and was the admiration of Saint-Brieuc for her devout life and her work among the underprivileged. When their needs exceeded her personal resources, she begged for means to relieve their misery. Marie-Anne Cartel decided to assist this servant of the poor as the two friends turned to the cheerless world of the penitentiary together. They understood the despair as the source of the degradation which saddened them, and they learned to bear the coarse ways, the quarrelsome temper, the foul speech of the inmates.

Three times a week, they came as messengers of hope from nine to twelve, teaching catechism to the women, introducing them to prayer, inquiring about their personal needs and carrying out legitimate errands requested by them. They supplemented their own means with a monthly collection for this service, a collection which became known for the liberality of the contributors who shared their compassion. The pair thus became the treasurers of wealthy friends who trusted them to distribute their charities.

In her spare time, Miss Cartel assembled children for catechism lessons, and gradually added devotional exercises with the practice of the "interior life." After the loss of her father in 1788, and her mother in 1802, the elder sister attempted to tighten her possessiveness, but Marie-Anne learned to deal kindly with the frustration. Little else is known about her until her fortieth year. A deep sense of loss invaded her soul when Miss Poulin de Corbion died prematurely in 1812, exhausted by her unsparing zeal.

Marie-Anne continued her life of social service with the help of Miss Fanny Chaplain. The two companions were of one mind in prayer and charity, sensing that the Lord was calling them to special work, yet not knowing clearly what that should be. They performed their good works generously, practiced mutual correction, and sought to progress in their spiritual life. Whenever they passed a church, Miss Cartel was in the habit of saying: *"Let us enter to ask God what he wants us to do for him: I feel that he is asking us something."* They consulted Father de La Mennais who offered the beginnings of an answer; their relationship continued for a lifetime.

A first association: the Congregation of Young Women, 1816

After the retreat of 1816, Father de La Mennais founded a diocesan society of young women for the support of charitable works. When the two friends joined the group, its members elected Miss Cartel as their superior. Marie-Anne was devoting her time rescuing neglected children from illiteracy and religious ignorance by gathering them for instruction. Her many years of social service inspired the young society and enabled her to assist new recruits.

Miss Marie Conan came with the desire to teach the young. Her spiritual guide, Father Chantrel, the former director of the seminary, had approved her desire to become a member of a religious congregation, advising her to instruct the young while considering the formation of a teaching group. A fourth member approached the humble associates with a different enterprise. Miss Julie Bagot, daughter of a former mayor of Saint-Brieuc, lived in the adjacent town of Cesson where she cared for the sick and instructed children in her home. At the suggestion of several persons, she decided to join the new group. She longed to found an orphan's home exclusively for abandoned children and associate them to her charity for the children of poor rural families.

Miss Cartel wholeheartedly espoused the project, but neither of them had the personal means to support it and turned to the entire society of young women for assistance. Miss Cartel singled out four lasses chosen for the total forsakenness of their condition; however, the society refused to support them because they were not from the city. On hearing of their disagreement, Father de La Mennais paid their upkeep personally. The

Society then added four young women from fifteen to eighteen years of age living in a promiscuous environment, and found a modest lodging for eight boarders on *rue de la Grenouillère,* October 1, 1817.

The society entrusted the care of the orphans particularly to Miss Bagot as Marie-Anne Cartel and Fanny Chaplain concentrated most of their time to charity and family duties. Miss Cartel continued to gather for religious instruction vagabond children of the neighborhood, and the four associates agreed to accept all the children willing to prepare for their first communion. About thirty girls came, some of them expressing a desire to acquire domestic skills.

Father de La Mennais was then actively seeking help to prepare boys from poor families for their first communion. Since the Brothers of the Christian Schools assigned to Saint-Brieuc would not arrive until the fall, the associates of Miss Cartel were the only teachers available. At the call of Father de La Mennais, eighty boys came to prepare for their first communion. Twelve members of the Society volunteered to help the overwhelmed organizers by instructing the boys in the afternoon, after teaching the girls in the morning.

The small residence of *rue de la Grenouillère* soon proved inadequate. The lessons soon developed into a school which moved nearby in October, 1818. Miss Bagot lodged her orphanage in a section of the former bishopric only a few streets away.[3] After deciding to support orphans, the Society now found itself involved with a second enterprise. Tensions strained relationships, as Miss Bagot insisted that the school was a deviation from the original plan. When the friends asked Father de La Mennais which of the two initiatives he would approve, he laughingly replied: *"It is very simple; I approve them both."*

John de La Mennais was then working to open Christian schools for boys. On April 10, 1817, the city Council of Saint-Brieuc voted to invite the Brothers of the Christian Schools to reopen their school closed during the Revolution. The Brothers agreed, but they could not come immediately. On the sixth of June, 1818, a group of anti-clericals persuaded the city Council to authorize a monitorial school. The sponsors of the second school unsettled the peace of the city, confronting the Vicar General with a dilemma. Since a monitorial school for girls generally followed the foundation of a boys' school, John de La Mennais worked to prevent that by transforming the services of Miss Cartel into a fully organized school.

The small program evolved into a school with all the problems of resourceless beginnings. Children from poor families kept coming, sometimes walking hungry to their lessons. Within a year, the school outgrew the provisional space occupied since October 1818.

Father de La Mennais supported the orphanage from the beginning and had named it "Our Lady of Providence." The school needs redefined his priorities as he sought to provide for the instruction of some two hundred girls. Miss Bagot could not accept the change of priorities and decided to leave the group rather than abandon her orphans. The separation was painful, and Miss Bagot realized with astonishment that she could no longer expect his full participation.

Her biographer later wrote that Father de La Mennais suddenly abandoned her.[4] This was a harsh judgment, as Father de LaMennais was forced to make a difficult choice in a difficult time! The rush of events, not indifference, forced this option. Father was then struggling to provide Christian schools in a tightening contest with militant anti-clericals. Miss Bagot complained that her advisor had forsaken her, however she was able to maintain her work,[5] as benefactors continued to assist the heroic mother of orphans.

A second commitment: the Daughters of the Heart of Mary, 1818

Success blessed the labors of Miss Cartel's Society. Students attended lessons in rising numbers, the trust and assistance of the families comforted the foundresses, the teachers laboring on, wondering how to guarantee the future. How would the school survive without a society to perpetuate its services? Father de La Mennais persuaded the leaders who had expressed a desire for religious life to bond together as members of an existing religious congregation, and he proposed to associate them as Daughters of the Heart of Mary.

When the revolutionaries outlawed religious orders in 1790, Father de Clorivière founded two religious societies, one for diocesan priests and one for women. [6] The members of these religious congregations wore no distinctive habit, lived at home according to their personal circumstances, secretly professed religious vows and observed a rule of life under the guidance of a superior. The groups led a clandestine existence during the Revolution, but met regularly whenever possible.

The flexibility of that association was particularly adapted to the new group. Both Miss Cartel and Miss Chaplain had family duties which they could not readily neglect. The father of Miss Chaplain was an honest man, but a non-practicing Catholic with Voltairian persuasions. He had been elected Vice President of the society organized to promote monitorial schools in the city, a responsibility which allied him with militant opponents of Father de La Mennais. Under the circumstances, indiscretion could readily compromise the school.

Father de La Mennais directed the leaders opting for religious life to follow a novitiate program preparing them for membership in the society of Father de Clorivière. John had become a member of Cloriviere's society of Priests of the Heart of Jesus after ordination, and had provided spiritual assistance to the Daughters of the Heart of Mary of Saint-Servan during his years in Saint-Malo. As superior of religious in the diocese of Saint-Brieuc, he took it upon himself to prepare Miss Cartel and her closest associates for membership in the society of the Daughters of the Heart of Mary. He asked the virtuous Madame Pouhaër, a religious of the society of Saint Thomas of Villeneuve then superior of the hospice, to serve as their mistress of novices. [7]

The new commitment started with a special consecration. On Christmas night, 1818, Misses,Cartel, Conan and Chaplain met secretly in the chapel of Our Lady of Refuge adjacent to the home of Father de La Mennais on *rue Notre Dame,* and inaugurated their novitiate with a special act of consecration. Eight days later, Miss Beauchemin joined them by pronouncing the same consecration. They invoked Saint Ignatius, Founder of the Society of Jesus of which Father de Clorivière had been a member before its suppression by the Church.

The novitiate followed, abridged from twelve months to eight because of circumstances. Members of the Society of young women substituted for them at school during their absence, and popular support kept the enterprise alive until it outgrew its second home even before the return of the foundresses. On March 19, 1819, during the absence of the four novices, the classes moved into larger quarters rented by Father de La Mennais.[8] The Vicar General wrote to Blaize, his brother-in-law: *"At Easter we will have a school of two to three hundred girls,"* (March 11, 1819).[9]

On August 15, 1819, the four novices pronounced their first religious vows as Daughters of the Heart of Mary, and resumed their work in their new home. Father de La Mennais explained the circumstances to Madame de Saisseval, the Superior of the sisters in Paris excusing his unconventional procedure: *"Realizing the good works performed by the Daughters of Mary [sic] where they are established, I have desired to form a few in Saint-Brieuc and fortunately, I have been successful. I long meant to advise you of my actions, but various circumstances have prevented me from doing so."* After mentioning the abridged novitiate and the profession of the new members, he added: *"As diocesan Superior, I believed that I was entitled to receive their vows, with the intention of reporting to you at the first opportunity,"* (September 9, 1819).[10]

The Brothers of the Christian Schools had inaugurated a school for boys a few days before the opening of the monitorial school, but the anti-clericals of the city were not resting. After founding their school for boys, they planned a monitorial school for girls. Father de La Mennais felt obliged to provide space for additional students to counter the new monitorial institutions. The need for dependable teachers was acute. Father de Clorivière knew John de La Mennais and understood the emergency, but he deplored the abridgement of the twelve-month novitiate. Madame de Saisseval asked Father de La Mennais to link his group with that of Miss Amable Chenu, Superior at Saint-Servan, not to leave the new group unattached to her society.

The recently professed Daughters of the Heart of Mary had left an unwieldy enterprise providing catechism lessons, school sessions, day nursery, workroom for needlecraft and domestic skills; they returned to a rapidly changing institution prospering in roomier quarters. The Vicar General could write: *"We have seven classes: three of reading, two of writing, one of embroidery and needlework, and one of sewing. The workers of the latter earn their meals from the income from their work. We have 400 children receiving a Christian education gratuitously; an excellent layman has placed sufficient funds at my disposal to make this possible. The house which we have rented is spacious and convenient; I have established a small interior chapel where the congregation meets twice a month,"* September 9, 1819. [11]

Soon classes outgrew even the new locale, forcing the Vicar General to search for a permanent home as the school population forced the sisters to teach in a shed with sail cloth separating classes. Father de La Mennais ended the classroom migrations with the purchase of the Beuscher Home, a three-story building with attic, two yards, an additional two-story building in one of the yards, and a third building serving as stable and storage. [12] All buildings were slate-roofed. A section of the complex was inhabited, the other sections were begging for repairs. Seeing the place for the first time, Miss Cartel observed: *"We will be happy here, the cross is planted for a long time."*

Father de La Mennais purchased the property on June 19, 1820 for 24 000 F. A friend, Jacques Sébert and his sister Antoinette donated the sum with the proviso that it serve only as the Christian school of Saint-Brieuc, founded under the name of "Providence," for the education of girls. Roofing and other substantial repairs were required to restore the building and soon, two rooms were combined to form a chapel. As Miss Cartel was very ill at the time, she was assigned to an adjoining room, and a window left opened to allow her to follow the religious exercises.

Adjustments were eventually made to receive orphans. One of her brothers had died leaving six orphans, and the care of four little girls made it impossible for her to join her companions. When Father de La Mennais invited her to establish definitive residence at the Providence, she showed him the four lasses. His reply was immediate: *"Bring them with you; they will be your first boarders."*

The Daughters of Providence, March 25, 1821

On November 17, 1819, Father de La Mennais became Vicar General of Bishop Mathias le Groing de La Romagère, the new Bishop of Saint Brieuc. Very soon, conflict between the assistant and his new superior interfered with life at the Providence. The Bishop planned to transfer ownership of the sister's property to the diocese, and to have the papers drawn out to his name. [13] To that end, he demanded accounts, deeds and papers from the sisters.

The annalist of the Providence writes about the relationships with the Bishop: *"He came many times to visit our community, even before our coming to this house [the Providence], and always to blame and threaten. He believed that we were concealing the affairs of the Congregation to him, because he could not believe that we had no funds to subsist, no security to guarantee the permanence of our work. When we explained that Mr. de La Mennais never allowed us to lack necessities, none of us would have dared to ask him if he would still provide for our needs after his death. He considered our statements as specious reasons to conceal what he wanted to know.... When our Mothers visited him, he either refused to admit them or received them merely to mortify them with rebukes. He sometimes came when least expected and threatened to expel us from our house."* [14]

In December 1820, the Vicar General wrote to his bosom friend in the United States: *"I am in the saddest position with respect to my Bishop; he resolutely wants to take my title away from me, and to dismiss me; he has even threatened to interdict me,"* (December 18, 1820) [15]. Félicité supplemented the statement in January: *"Fifteen days ago, my brother established a Christian school at Guingamp to oppose a monitorial school whose students had recently killed one of their classmates. Moreover, he established a Providence, that is a Society of Ladies who care for the sick and teach religion and work skills to young girls from poor families. What do you suppose the Bishop said about that? He threatened him with interdict. You may think that you have misread: no, with interdict,"* (January 5, 1821). [16] The situation deteriorated as Mr. de La Mennais helplessly observed the meddling of his superior with the Providence.

He wrote to Madame de Saisseval describing his embarrassment as *"such that I cannot expect to be able to stand the strain more than one or two months." Survival requires adjustments, even a major change of plans. "The young women directing the house of the Providence, knowing that they might lose me, and desiring to provide more stability to their establishment, believed that it must be transformed into a religious community without delay, with provisions to have it approved legally. That is no longer compatible with the regulations of the Society of the Daughters of the Heart of Mary, and it totally changes my original project; but I believe I see in the external events which obstruct their execution, a special design of Providence and I let it guide me. I will therefore hasten (for the matter is urgent) to save the house which some would invade in view of knocking it down,"* (January 29, 1821). [17] The letter announced that his brother would soon explain the dilemma verbally in Paris.

Reorganization was far from premature! Two days later, on January 31, 1821, the Bishop dismissed him as Vicar General and superior of religious, but left him with the responsibility for primary education. Juridically, he ceased to be the ecclesiastical superior of the Providence. His society could easily collapse without a quick change of status requiring separation from the Daughters of the Heart of Mary. [18] Mr. de La Mennais saw the reorganization as the only way to save the new Society and the institution.

On March 25, 1821, Marie Anne Cartel, Foundress, Marie Conan, first Superior, Fanny Chaplain, Mistress of Novices, and Esther Beauchemin received new Constitutions from Father de La Mennais, and on the same day professed their vows as first members of the new Congregation of the Daughters of Providence of Saint-Brieuc. The second transformation of the Society was as discreet as the first, some would say, as secret. The special role of Founder entitled the former Vicar General to powers distinct from those of his function in the diocese, and made it more difficult for the new diocesan authority to exclude him from the Providence.

The new Bishop's meddling compelled the Founder to clarify the status of the Congregation. He explained to the Bishop that Miss Conan could not comply with his demands concerning finances and records because she did her work in selfless simplicity without inquiring about such matters. He added: "Before I can consider transferring to anyone ownership of the house of Providence, it must first be paid in full, and it is not yet so. What is paid has been paid in part, from my own funds, and I cannot renounce what is due me before knowing what assistance I will obtain for the other establishments for which I am responsible. ... The regulations of the house are provisional; experience will indicate their proper modifications. Once I make their determination, I will submit them to anyone capable of offering me useful suggestions, and among those that I will consider, yours, Monsignor, will be particularly precious to me, and I will receive them with no less respect than gratitude," (September 12, 1821).[19]

The sisters continued to wear secular clothes during two years. When Father de La Mennais was about to leave Saint-Brieuc, they sought to identify their society publicly as a religious congregation and requested a distinctive religious habit as a clear sign. They had already chosen one and had worn it for special religious celebrations in the privacy of community life.

On November 21, 1822, the feast of the Presentation of Mary in the Temple, Father de La Mennais presided at their first vesture ceremony and they began to wear the religious habit publicly. Father de La Mennais had not prescribed a special religious dress probably because public opposition to the religious habit was still strong. The annalist of the house wrote: *"Our Mothers had to bear the complaints of their parents and the mockery of people shocked by that singular habit."* [20] The frustration passed without curbing the vitality of the congregation.

Only the zeal of the Sisters, their trust in the Lord's Providence and the generous support of benefactors guaranteed some chance of success in the challenge of addressing the needs of the poor children in the region. The city approved and supported their work from the beginning. The women of Providence served through privation and hardship, guided, fortified by Father de La Mennais who advised them, making their cause his own. Bishop de La Romagère eventually acknowledged their virtue, and valued their services in his diocese.

The Foundress, Marie-Anne Cartel, could not administer her Congregation beyond its early years. She died on October 21, 1821 after years of sickness and a prolonged agony. Her patience and resignation reflected the selfless charity of her life; her funeral was a triumph. The poor came to thank her, and the clergy of the city was present without convocation. Her virtues had converted Bishop de La Romagère to a more supportive attitude towards Father de La Mennais, to whom he granted the necessary authorizations for the vesture ceremony at the Providence.

The Congregation of the Daughters of Providence was born from the charities of Marie Anne Cartel and her companions, first as independent initiatives, then as the orphanage of Julie Bagot and the support of the diocesan Society of young women founded by Father de La Mennais.

The Vicar General's participation began when the women came to him for advice; it continued as direction and material support, leading to the foundation of a new religious congregation in three steps: (1) the diocesan Society of young women in 1816; (2) membership in the Daughters of the Heart of Mary, beginning on Christmas night, 1818; (3) the Daughters of Providence of Saint-Brieuc, beginning with the religious profession of March 25, 1821.

The work started without plans for the foundation of a religious congregation. The course was uncharted, the transitions abrupt and incongruous, the human means unreliable and ecclesiastical relationships disconcerting. The Lord worked through the zeal of Miss Cartel and her team to transform them into Foundresses. Miss Cartel never premeditated anything of the kind; for Father de La Mennais, the role of Founder would not end with the Providence.

[1] 1773-1821.

[2] See [Aline Hamon], *Notice sur les trois Fondatrices et premières Religieuses de la Providence,* Guingamp: Éditions E. Thomas, 32 pp.

[3] In a street called *Derrière Fardel.*

[4] Blanche de Rosarnou, *"Mademoiselle Julie Bagot."* in *Biographies Bretonnes,* Paris: J. Mollie, 1877. Pages 1-132.

[5] The orphanage of Miss Bagot still exists. Considering the frequent misunderstandings between Bishop de La Romagère and his assistants, it would have been difficult for Mr. de La Mennais to continue advising Miss Bagot while striving to guarantee the survival of Miss Cartel's school.

[6] The role of Marie-Adélaïde de Cicé (1749-1818) in the foundation of the Daughters of the Heart of Mary is told in *Mère de Cicé, Fondatrice de la société des Filles du Coeur de Marie,* Paris: Maison généralice de la société des Filles du Coeur de Marie, 1961.

[7] Earlier accounts sometimes leave the impression that the foundation of the Daughters of Providence was an unbroken progression. New documents have enabled H. C. Rulon to distinguish three different periods. "La Fondation de la Providence d'après des découvertes récentes," **Chron.,** no. 226 (April 1961) pp. 167-176; no. 227 (July) pp. 247-256; no. 228 (October) pp. 333-337.

[8] On *rue Quinquaine, in the building referred to as La Porte Taron.*

[9] **Cor gén J,** v. 2, p. 111.

[10] Letter to Madame de Saisseval. **Cor gén J,** v. 2, pp. 131-132. From the Archives of the Daughters of the Heart of Mary. Copy, **AFIC,** 76 (2).

[11] Ibid.

[12] Located at the corner of *rue du Collège* and *rue du Ruisseau Josse.*

[13] **Lav.,** vol. 1, pp. 302-303.

[14] From the "Annals" of the Providence, as excerpted by Rulon, note 6 above. **Chron.,** 227 (July 1961), p. 251. Rulon supplements and rectifies **Lav.** Vol. 1, pp. 301-304.

[15] To Bruté de Rémur, at the end of a letter of Félicité. **Cor. gén. J,** v. 2, p. 164.

[16] Letter to Saint-Victor. **Cor. Gén. F,** vol. 2, pp. 165-166.

[17] **Cor. Gén. J,** v. 2, p. 170. Copy, **AFIC,** 76 - 2.

[18] The letter to Madame de Saisseval attributes the initiative for the secession to the women at the Providence; in the Annals of the Society, Madame de Saisseval attributes it to Mr. de La Mennais.

[19] **Cor. Gén. J,** v. 2, p. 176.

[20] As quoted by Rulon, note 6 above, **Chron.,** 227 (July 1961), p. 255.

Gabriel Deshayes

Chapter 11

THE BROTHERS OF THE CHRISTIAN SCHOOLS AND GABRIEL DESHAYES

The Brothers of the Christian Schools reorganize in France, 1804

The French Revolution almost destroyed an educational system that was one of the most highly developed in Europe. Though Napoleon and the Revolutionary government made multiple plans to reestablish the system, the lack of qualified teachers and adequate resources stymied most plans. In addition to the lack of professional training, the questionable character of teachers often chosen from the dregs of society further weakened a budding school system.

Serious reformers were aware that only a sound educational system could successfully address the problems resulting from the French Revolution. Father Gabriel Deshayes and his friend Father de La Mennais were among the early reformers who immediately realized that only an education based upon sound Christian principles could effectively correct the situation.

John Baptist de La Salle had founded the Brothers of the Christian Schools in 1684; they too were actively reorganizing at that time providing tuition-free elementary schools for boys. One thousand brothers were serving in French cities in 1789. The revolutionaries soon expelled religious teachers and replaced them with schoolmasters compatible with their ideas concerning the education of the young. The Brothers were left homeless, a few were executed for refusing to accept the *Civil Constitution of the Clergy,* some found employment as independent schoolmasters, many adopted new social roles, some married, others fled into exile.

Need and the mediation of his uncle, Cardinal Fesch, [1] convinced Napoleon to authorize their reorganization. A nucleus (one of several) had regrouped spontaneously in Lyon, and a search for the missing Brother Agathon, the legitimate Superior General, had begun. A revolutionary tribunal had condemned the Superior to prison, but he had vanished into hiding after he was released due to illness. He barely had time to reveal his whereabouts by letter on August 23, 1797, before dying at Tours, September 16, 1798.

Three years earlier, Pope Pius VI had appointed the exiled Brother Frumence interim superior with the title of Vicar General on August 7, 1795. Brother Frumence left Italy with the cortège of Pope Pius VII when the latter traveled to France for the crowning of Napoleon. The Vicar General stopped in Lyon, November 19, 1804, and gradually began to reorganize his institute.[2] Napoleon eventually granted the Brothers a special status in his school plan. Article 109 of the decree of March 17, 1808 which established his *Université* stated: *"The Brothers of the Christian Schools will be certified and encouraged by the Grand Master, who will review their internal statutes, admit them to the [loyalty] oath, prescribe a distinctive costume for them and arrange to have their schools supervised.* ***The superiors of these congregations may become members of the University.*** *"* [3] This privilege would later facilitate the work of new teaching congregations.

After the death of Brother Frumence, January 27, 1810, the brothers elected Brother Gerbaud as Superior General. A flood of requests for teachers from all sections of the nation overwhelmed the superiors; the demands were particularly heavy from the cities where the Institute had served before the Revolution. The Brothers had no choice but to refuse most of these requests for lack of members. Frumence, then Gerbaud, patiently sought out recruits and opened schools according to the successful traditions of their society. Mayors, city councils, bishops, parish priests, all authorities involved with the reorganization of Christian elementary schools for boys would have to deal with the two superiors. So would Fathers Gabriel Deshayes in Auray, and John de La Mennais in Saint-Brieuc as educational needs led them to their door.

The new furrow: The initiative of Gabriel Deshayes, 1816

After the Revolution, the first school opened in Brittany by the Brothers of the Christian Schools was founded at the persistent request of Father Gabriel Deshayes, (pronounced *Day hay*). [4] Father Deshayes began to found schools for the children of his parish of Auray as soon as he could find teachers. The resourceful priest had lived an eventful existence before coming to his parish in 1805.

Born in Beignon, Morbihan, (1767-1841) a shepherd in childhood, he began preparation for the priesthood early under the guidance of a local priest, and later at a seminary staffed by the Vincentians until the French Revolution interrupted his studies. The Bishop of Tréguier, who was then a refugee on the island, ordained him to the priesthood. Dissatisfied with the sterile life of a fugitive, Deshayes secretly returned to his Breton homeland expecting no better welcome than to be tracked as an outlaw. [5] His life as a hunted priest was a tale of narrow escapes from revolutionary patrols.

John de La Mennais was still an adolescent when the young Father Deshayes was outwitting the soldiers of the Revolution. When the violence ended, Fr. Deshayes served during a few years at Paimpont *(Les Forges)*, and at Beignon, his home parish. The area had passed to the neighboring diocese of Vannes after the reorganization which followed the suppression of the diocese of Saint-Malo and *the Concordat* of 1801. His new bishop quickly called upon him for special services, chose him as one of his Vicars General, and appointed him parish priest of Auray. The Revolution had left a dismal trail here as elsewhere.

The sturdy churchman came to his parish with nothing but breviary, haversack and shepherd's staff, and immediately invited his people to a renewal mission which he preached personally. Father Deshayes set to work, cooperating with public officials, visiting families, taking a parish census, instructing his people. In addition, he spent hours hearing confessions, catechizing children, seeking out lapsed Christians, caring for the poor, generally encouraging good works. He sensed the need for revival beyond the limits of his parish and cooperated generously with the renewal work of parish missions; the rectory facing the church of Saint Gildas became a renewal center. To strengthen the Christian life of his people, he invited religious orders to his parish. His bishop readily turned to him for assistance with diocesan responsibilities.

Gabriel Deshayes was so firmly persuaded of the importance of Christian schools that he undertook three initiatives to provide elementary school teachers. With Michelle Guillaume, [6] he laid the base of a new religious society of teaching sisters in his native parish of Beignon in 1807. [7] Since his own sisters were not ready to leave their first home, he called on the recently-founded Sisters of Charity of Saint Louis to open a school for girls in Auray in1808, and he acquired a convent confiscated by the revolutionaries to house them.

The Brothers of the Christian Schools were reorganizing in Lyon at the time. He pleaded with their superior to open a school for boys in 1808. The request came while the Brothers were still rebuilding their numbers, and Brother Frumence who had returned from Italian exile a few months before the arrival of Deshayes in his parish, could only reply that he would be *"unable to send brothers for a long time,"* (June 23,1808). [8] Pastoral responsibility called for action and Father Deshayes asked his bishop to intervene. He repeated the request, promised candidates and the opportunity to open a novitiate for the community, and he prepared to acquire a building. Deshayes acted as if the brothers would come and he had to be told a second time that they would not. Brother Frumence died in the interval, and when Brother Gerbaud was elected Superior General in 1810, the request from Auray received his attention.

Brother Gerbaud assigned three brothers to Auray, a city where the Brothers had not served before the Revolution. The hospitality and parish support was excellent, and the understanding of the Pastor unusual. Father Deshayes had obtained an annual subsidy from the city council to pay the teachers' salaries, and a building was waiting for the teachers. The demands for teachers were so numerous, that they accepted requests only from localities presenting three valid candidates for their community; Father Deshayes did better by preparing the way for the opening of their first novitiate in western France after the Revolution.

The pastoral vision of Father Deshayes reached beyond his parish and his diocese. Before the brothers came, he had asked the Superior General permission to have his men teach the deaf mutes and help prepare the sons of sailors for coastal navigation, as the brothers had done in maritime Brittany before the Revolution. Brother Gerbaud realized that his brothers would have enough to do and advised the superior of the Auray community to refuse any accessory activity. The brothers arrived in Auray in November, and inaugurated their school on the first of January 1811. The success of the school and the example of the brothers attracted candidates for their Institute, as Fr. Deshayes and his Bishop had anticipated, and the brothers opened a novitiate in the city. [9]

Gabriel Deshayes had a compassionate heart for children isolated from the world by hearing and speech disorders. In 1811, he acquired the Charterhouse of Auray *(la Chartreuse)* and invited the Daughters of Wisdom, founded by Louis de Montfort, to care for them. From humble beginnings, the education of deaf-mute children became his lifelong concern, and his association with Father Yves François Duchesne, [10] Superior General of the Sisters, would change the course of his life in unexpected ways.

With two schools in Auray, a home for deaf-mute children nearby, and a growing community of sisters in Beignon, the Pastor of Auray kept a paternal eye on the neglected souls of the diocese. The boys' school prospered, the pastor managed to increase the number of brothers, but he worried about the lack of teachers in the smaller rural towns. By their rules, the brothers would not form communities of less than three brothers. The rural towns were too poor to fund three salaries; however, there were no other communities willing to station only one brother in a school.

Father Deshayes heard a call to action, so where the Brothers of Christian Schools could not go, he would train schoolmasters in a new society to supplement their work. He invited volunteers, and on January 10,

1816, he opened the door of his rectory to Mathurin Provost, his first candidate, a thirty three year old native of Ruffiac. Others soon joined but most left, though by February 1817, he was able to send his first teacher, Brother Joseph-Marie Boyer to open a primary school at Thenezaz, Deux-Sevres, and soon after another to Baud, Morbian.

Hardly a month passed before the Royal Ordinance of February 29, 1816 encouraged such initiatives. Remembering that John Baptist de La Salle had thrice tried and thrice failed to have his brothers train lay schoolmasters for rural France, Father Deshayes modified the concept and proposed to organize a form of third order, called: "The Brothers Associated to the Brothers of Christian Schools," *(Frères Associés aux Frères des Écoles chrétiennes)*.

Wanting to formalize his association with the Christian Brothers, Father Deshayes boldly sent a detailed 13 Article proposal for discussion to the General Chapter of 1816. The members of the General Chapter returned the document with a brief comment that "the plan was not in its competence." Undeterred, Father Deshayes continued his *"little society"* with the formation of his first candidates.

Early in 1818, he was able to respond to the urgent request for a religious teacher from Father de La Mennais, who was then interim administrator of the diocese of Saint Brieuc. Together, they opened a school at Pordic, Cotes-du-Nords staffed by a young man trained by Father Deshayes, Brother Paul, Mathurin Guyot. Since his society was not yet authorized, the Brothers of Christian Schools provided his first teachers with their official appointment from their own institute. The government quickly prohibited the ambiguity; by then, Father de La Mennais entered the scene and the "little society" was about to reorganize. Though Father de La Mennais and Deshayes had met at least three times in 1817, the foundation of the school in Pordic was their first joint educational project.

John de La Mennais and the challenge of Saint-Brieuc, 1817 John de La Mennais had not been a student of the Brothers of the Christian Schools, but the brothers had been in his native city since 1746, though expelled by the Revolution in 1791. In 1808, the year Father Gabriel

Deshayes first requested brothers for his parish, the city of Saint-Malo asked for the return of the Brothers to their city. John, who was then teaching at the ecclesiastical school of Saint-Malo, drafted the mayor's letter. That same year, Bishop Caffarelli made a similar plea for the city of Saint-Brieuc. The three requests failed for lack of sufficient numbers in the brotherhood; Gabriel Deshayes was the first to succeed.

In 1816, at a time when Father Deshayes was receiving his first candidates for his new society of Brothers associated with the Brothers of the Christian Schools, Father de La Mennais was requesting teachers to open a school in Guingamp from Brother Gerbaud, the Superior General of the Brothers in Lyon, (February 6, 1816). Brother Gerbaud's answer was similar to other refusals and for the same reasons.

However, the Brothers of Christian Schools had come to Auray during the quiet years preceding the religious controversies which accompanied the French Lancasterian movement. Militants pressing for the foundation of a monitorial school in Saint-Brieuc created a radically different scenario in 1817. In 1816, English Lancasterian schools caught the fancy of men in the Ministry of the Interior. French prefects had already received circulars recommending the adoption of the new system when Lainé became Minister of the Interior on May 7, 1816, and began zealously promoting the new system. Brittany was slow to respond, but monitorial schools were coming ever closer to the episcopal city: there were seven new-style schools in Brittany in 1817, none of them in the department of Côtes-du-Nord.

Father de La Mennais was aware of their coming when he asked Brother Gerbaud to send him brothers: *"The Prefect is preparing to give us schools of the Lancasterian style which will cost much less, and which will complete the ruin of religion and morals in a diocese where it will be difficult to revive them,"* (February 6, 1816). [11] The text reflects the rush of an overworked administrator; the reasoning sprang from pastoral anguish over the secularization of schools in a traditionally Christian society. For lack of brothers, the request was not more successful than the one by Gabriel Deshayes. Brother Gerbaud sent a prospectus suggesting that he direct recruits to his society.

When the liberals of Saint-Brieuc insisted on a Lancasterian school, Father de La Mennais could not rest until he persuaded the Superior General of the Brothers to send him teachers. [12] He may not have known about the work of Father Deshayes in 1816, but in 1817, he called on him to endorse his second letter to Brother Gerbaud, who was well acquainted with the Pastor of Auray. [13] On May 10, 1817, the two priests signed the same request and Father Deshayes added a postscript recommending the opening of a school in Saint-Brieuc. [14] This simple act of solidarity was the beginning of a friendship which would last until the death of Father Deshayes, December 28, 1841.

At the request of Mr. de La Mennais, Mayor Louis Jean Prud'homme asked and obtained from the city council authorization and 1,200 F to found a school directed by the Brothers of Christian Schools in the city, April 10, 1817. [15] John de La Mennais' letter of May 10 to Brother Gerbaud endorsed by Gabriel Deshayes followed. A group of dissatisfied councilors pleaded to substitute a monitorial school for the school of the Brothers, but the Council voted the sums to add its monitorial school to the one of the Brothers. The Mayor overstepped his personal convictions, approved a monitorial school for those who insisted on one, and appointed a committee of five to prepare the opening of the alternative institution. The dissidents turned the act of conciliation into a political war over the selection of a schoolmaster.

The year 1818 was not a pleasant one for anyone involved with elementary schools in Saint-Brieuc. The Mayor and the Vicar General prepared the coming of the brothers while dealing with their own detractors. The city was providing a school for the brothers, the one earlier confiscated and converted into a hospital; Father de La Mennais prepared their residence at his expense. The Mayor dutifully found a home for the monitorial school and let the committee of five prepare it for the schoolmaster. John de La Mennais urged Brother Gerbaud to hasten the coming of the brothers lest he lose students to the monitorial school. Father Gabriel Deshayes found three recruits for Father de La Mennais and sent them to the novitiate of the Brothers in Auray to assist his overburdened friend; Father de La Mennais paid for their upkeep at the novitiate.

The monitorial schoolmaster arrived on November 12, the Brothers on the 14th; the Brothers started their classes on the 29th. The brothers began with 150 students in two classes their number doubling within a few months, while the Monitorial school enlisted 175 names but counted only 110 students early in January. The two schools were municipal public schools, both prospering in ways reflecting their differences, the choice of parents deciding their fate. Father de La Mennais conscientiously guaranteed space for all students requesting admission at the brothers' school. Brother Gerbaud soon received a request for a fourth teacher, though success in both camps failed to generate peace.

John de La Mennais requests the "Brothers from Auray," 1818, 1819

The Brothers of Christian Schools were now teachers to the boys of Saint-Brieuc, while Father de La Mennais' school for girls was developing through the zeal of Marie-Anne Cartel and the diocesan Society of young women. John realized that failure to anticipate requests from other towns would most likely invite new contests. The delays and relatively heavy costs involved in the coming of the Brothers of Christian Schools had to be avoided. John de La Mennais and his new friend understood that requests for brothers far exceeded Lasallian reserves, and that the only effective way to provide reliable Christian teachers for the poorer towns was to prepare them. In 1818, he asked Father Deshayes to send him one of his teachers to respond to an opportunity to open a Christian school in Pordic, a few kilometers west of Saint-Brieuc.

Gabriel Deshayes contracted with the Parish priest of Pordic and sent Brother Paul (Mathurin Guyot), his second disciple, who opened a one-room school in rented quarters. Since the arrival of his first candidate on January 10, 1816, Father Deshayes had continued to form recruits. He had twice expressed his desire to organize "Brothers" as an "associate" society to the Brothers of the Christian Schools, somewhat in the nature of a confraternity. [16] Despite the refusal of the Brothers of Christian Schools to accept his plan, he had sent members to six parishes before the end of 1818. [17]

His new friend in Saint-Brieuc again needed the help of his burgeoning society in Dinan, the second largest city of the department. After two years of preparation, city administrators were planning a monitorial school and a council vote in favor of the Lancasterian method was imminent. In May, John traveled to Auray to request three brothers from Father Deshayes.

Though the teachers were not due in Dinan until September, Father Deshayes traveled to Saint- Brieuc on June 7 with four brothers, spent a few important days of discussion with Father de La Mennais. [18] He lodged them at the *Hotel de Bretagne* because no preparations had been made to receive them. They were eventually housed in the rectory, but they had to accept provisional space in a seminary where they assembled students until the opening of the school in September. In September 1819, a capacity audience gathered to hear John de La Mennais inaugurate the school from the pulpit of the parish church. Brother André relates how the liberals plastered the town with posters representing a jackass followed by three long-eared colts. [19] The "colts" won the approval of the parents as the report of 1820 lists 200 children in the care of the brothers from Auray.

Father de La Mennais waited a few months before requesting the teaching certificates required by the *Université*. Material assistance came from a generous, loyal pastor. The Brothers from Auray suffered poverty and sporadic persecution, but the parents continued to send their boys to the simple men from the novitiate of Gabriel Deshayes. The September inauguration had deepened John's commitment to Christian schools. He had called on the brothers and they had come three times, but they were brothers from different societies: Saint Brieuc welcomed the Brothers of the Christian Schools, Pordic and Dinan the "brothers" founded in Auray by Gabriel Deshayes.

The harvest was abundant and the "little society" of Father Deshayes was beginning to supplement the Brothers of Christian Schools, though occasionally assimilated to them in the popular mind. John de La Mennais called on Father Deshayes without realizing that the men from Auray would soon be members of his own society of brothers. The sequel followed without planning.

[1].Cardinal Joseph Fesch (1802-1839), Archbishop of Lyon and ambassador to the Holy See for the Empire.

[2].George Rigault, *Histoire generale de l'Institut des Freres des Ecoles Chretiennes. Tome III, La Revolution Francaise. Paris:* Plon, 1940, pp. 498-608.

[3].Ibid. Tome IV, *L'Institut restaure* (1805-1830), pp. 93-157.

[4].Gabriel Deshayes, (1767-1841).

[5] Probably the most useful work in English on the role of Father Gabriel Deshayes in the foundation of the Brothers of Christian Instruction is Br. Marcel Sylvestre's booklet "Deo Soli, Our Patrimony as Brothers of Christian Instruction, No 1, Antecedents and Beginnings, 1816-1820". (1996).The booklet clarifies some of the earlier confusion over the role of Father Deshayes, while showing the great cooperation that existed between the two men who were so instrumental in the success of the Brothers of Christian Instruction. The work is based on the leadership role of Br. C. Paul Cueff in response to a specific resolution of the General Chapter of 1982 and the General Conference of 1985.

[6].Alexis Crosnier, L'Homme de la Divine Providence, Gabriel Deshayes. Paris: Beauchesne, 1917, 2 Vols.

[7].1779-1826.

[8].The society would eventually become the "Sisters of Christian Instruction" (of Saint Gildas des Bois), by the location of the mother house.

[9].Letter book of Brother Frumence, **AFEC**, EE, 273 (19).

[10].The novitiate was moved to Vannes and later to Nantes where the Brothers had been from 1721-1792.

[11]. 1761-1820.

[12].Letter to Brother Gerbaud, **Cor gen J,** v.1, pp.379-380. Manuscript at **AFEC,** En 414 Mr. de La Mennais may not have been known about the beginning novitiate of Father Deshayes when he wrote that request.

[13].A very detailed summary of the controversy in Saint Brieuc has been written by H. C. Rulon. See **REH,** Chapter V, "La bataille mutuelle dans les Cotes-du-Nord," pp. 1-40.

[14].A reporter published a summary of the work of Gabriel Deshayes in 1816, without publishing his name. (*Ami de la Religion et du roi,* Vol. 8, No. 189, pp. 92-96. See Chron., no. 355, July, 1993, pp. 322-323. Mr. de

La Mennais may have known about the school work of Mr. Deshayes before that date.

[15].**Cor gen J,** v. 1, pp. 522-523.

[16].For an account of the local controversy see Edmond G. Drouin, "Le Maire de Saint-Briuec appuie l'oevre scholaire de Jean de La Mennais," **Chron.,** No. 361, (January 1995), pp. 62-73 and "Obstacles a l'Enseignement chretien: Saint Brieuc et Brest," No. 362, (April 1995) pp. 167-180.

[17].Letters of April 16, 1816 and August 16, 1818, **AFEC,** NC 399-2, (Copies, AFIC), 23-2).

[18].In 1817: Thenezay (Deux Sevres), in 1818: Baud, Limerzel, Malestroit, Ploermel.

Father De La Mennais

Chapter 12

THE BROTHERS OF CHRISTIAN INSTRUCTION

Educational Concerns of Father de La Mennais

Early in his role as diocesan leader, Father de La Mennais had determined to open as many schools as possible directed by teachers with sincere religious faith. Since he knew that these men and women were not readily available, he determined to organize his own training centers. With this goal in mind, the Vicar General's quill scratched a resolute letter, a simple request to Father Tresvaux, friend and parish priest of La-Roche-Derrien. The date was March 20, 1819.[1] Since the Brothers of the Christian Schools could not meet the needs of his diocese, Father resolved to prepare the Christian teachers so urgently needed in Brittany.

John had a copy of the recruiting prospectus of the Brothers of Christian Schools and he was asking Father Tresvaux to seek out qualified young men willing to come to the novitiate of a new society of teachers which he had decided to found.[2] Immersed in diocesan administration, he had long sought ways to supply Christian teachers to a land in need of alphabetization. The prospect of losing students to teachers with little or no concern for the religious future of society drove him to emergency action.

Two letters were written on March 20, one by Prefect Saint Aignan, the other by John de La Mennais; the first explains the timing of the second. On that day, the Prefect dispatched a circular letter to the mayors of Côtes-du-Nord inviting them to send candidates for training in a new teaching method; that invitation prompted the appeal of John de La Mennais to Father Tresvaux for recruits. Rémond upgraded his school with a normal school program for the training of monitorial schoolmasters and was preparing to open a school for girls. Saint-Brieuc could become a center of Lancasterians; John de La Mennais would make his a center of Christian education.

In 1818, John had called the Brothers of the Christian Schools to Saint-Brieuc, and the brothers of Gabriel Deshayes to Pordic. The leading members of the Society of young women had made their religious consecration three months earlier and were preparing for their vows as members of the Daughters of the Heart of Mary. While other members of the Society were substituting for them, he had transferred their school to its third home on *rue Quinquaine,* precisely on the eve of his letter to Father Tresvaux. He needed Father Deshayes' brothers from Auray for the city of Dinan, but he had no brothers of his own and no candidate for his novitiate as he penned his request.

From experience in the restoration of the schools of the Ursulines and the Brothers of Christian schools, and from the installation of the first Brothers from Auray in his diocese, John de La Mennais fully realized that his initiatives to organize his own novitiate would have to reckon with government supervision and control. He was beginning his new society when the entire chain of appointees linking his activities to Paris was collapsing. In short order, the Mayor and the Prefect were recalled by the Ministry of the Interior, and the King dismissed Lainé as the head of that ministry. The political instability and decisions of transient officials would affect every aspect of his educational activities.

The year 1819 dawned on strained relationships. Minister of the Interior Lainé dismissed Mayor Prud'homme for conflict with his administration, and support of the school program of John de La Mennais. On January 9, 1819, Prefect Saint Luc was dismissed by the same Minister, and replaced by Athanase Marie Count Conen de Saint Aignan, a militant advocate of the new pedagogy. There would be no peace in national and local politics, and no respite for religious founders.

As members of the *Université,* the Brothers of the Christian Schools with a century of experience in preparing teachers, were not required to request individual permits from the government. On January 19, 1819, Father Deshayes was notified that the training of his new teachers by the Brothers of the Christian Schools would not exempt them from their obligation for personal teaching certificates. The ruling applied to the brothers from Auray in the diocese of Father de La Mennais, and would affect the teachers sent from the novitiate of Saint-Brieuc.

The uncompromising Lainé persecuted the Brothers of the Christian Schools for refusing to adopt the monitorial system. The law allowed them to keep their own proven pedagogical tradition, but the Minister retaliated because they exercised that right against his directives. He disregarded the special status granted to the Congregation, and required each brother to apply for certificates personally. He then proceeded to close some of their schools for noncompliance, and threatened to revoke their exemption from military service.

The King dismissed him for his inflexibility on December 31, 1818, and appointed the more understanding Élie Descazes to succeed him. The new Minister restored peace with a new accord with the Brothers on February 7, shortly before the centennial celebration of the death of John Baptist de La Salle, their Founder. The accord provisionally reinstated the legal validity of direct assignments by the Superior General, preparing the way for similar understandings with new teaching congregations. The shifting political scene brought little peace to the brothers and sisters of John's new societies. On June 6, the Founder signed an agreement for the novitiate he was about to open; in November, a new Bishop assumed authority over the diocese.

A contract between two Founders

On June 6, 1819, less than three months after John's letter to Father Tresvaux, Gabriel Deshayes met John de La Mennais in Saint-Brieuc. The immediate agenda of the meeting was the emergency foundation of a school in Dinan, but the meeting led to a new understanding and a merger.[3] Gabriel Deshayes realized that his host concurred perfectly with his views and with the spirit of his little society. He later wrote of his visit: *"During the eight days which I spent with him, I realized that he concurred perfectly with my views and my plans. I proposed to associate him with the work which I had started. He assumed responsibility for the Brothers assigned to the diocese of Saint-Brieuc.'We administer the Congregation jointly',"* May 13, 1835.[4]

At the beginning of June, Father Deshayes and four of his brothers were with Father de La Mennais in Saint Brieuc. He would accompany three of them to Dinan on the seventh, but on June 6, 1819, the feast of the Holy Trinity, the two priests signed an agreement, a "contract," which would transform the brothers of Auray into a different society on the following terms:

In the name of the Holy Trinity, Father, Son and Holy Spirit; We, Jean Marie de La Mennais, Vicar General of Saint Brieuc, and Gabriel Deshayes, Vicar General of Vannes and Curé of Auray, Moved by the desire to provide reliable Christian teachers to the children of the people, particularly to those of rural Brittany, we have resolved to organize provisionally at Saint Brieuc and at Auray two novitiates of young men who will follow, as far as possible, the rule of the Brothers of the Christian Schools and use their teaching method. Realizing that this newly formed good work would grow and consolidate only with time, and that each one of us could die before it is sufficiently mature to continue on its own, we agree on the following:

1. The two novitiate houses already established, one at Saint Brieuc and the other at Auray, will be directed as follows: the first by Mr. de La Mennais; the second by Mr. Deshayes.

2. The two houses will have the same rule, the same teaching method and will be one.

3. Each of us will take the means at his disposal so that his resources will be transmitted to the survivor, who will add them to his own for the support of the society.

4. When we deem it advisable, we will choose from among the Brothers a superior and two assistants, and we will designate the house in which they are to dwell; should the choices not have been made before the death of one of us, or should the other, for whatever reason, be unable to participate in them, choices and arrangements for the good of the society will be made by one of us.

5. We will attempt to find, as quickly as possible, a central house for the two dioceses, not too distant from a highway, and as much as possible, in the country.

6. Each one of us will take the necessary precautions to guarantee that, at his death, the resources at his disposal will pass on to the survivor, who will add them to his for the support of the society.

Drafted in duplicate at Saint Brieuc, on Trinity Sunday, June 6, 1819.

Signed: Deshayes
Vicar General and Curé of Auray
J.-M. Robert de La Mennais
Vicar General of Saint Brieuc.[5]

With this act, the existing society of Gabriel Deshayes and the projected society of John de La Mennais, then still awaiting its first candidate, became one.[6] John had requested Father Tresvaux to seek candidates for the new society on March 20. The first three, Yves Le Fichant, Allain Coursin and (?) Mindu, arrived at his home from La Roche Derrien in Breton-speaking country between June 6 and July 4. There were only two at the end of September; Mindu had returned home, possibly because he needed to support the family after the death of a brother.[7]

Simple beginnings, quiet assemblies

John de La Mennais wrote about the beginnings of his novitiate: *"I started in my room, in Saint-Brieuc, with two young low-Bretons who could hardly speak French."*[8] As in Auray, the Brothers of the Christian Schools helped with their preparation by teaching them the essentials. Father received them in his simple home on *rue Notre Dame,* and guided their first steps in their new life.

In September 1819, he assembled about ten men for the first annual retreat of his society, the brothers from Auray in his diocese, and the new recruits who had joined the first arrivals. Judging from the recollections of

Brother André Labousse, the retreat master touched the souls of his disciples: *"He preached to us himself, in one of his apartments. [He] spoke to us with such feeling and eloquence that we were impressed and convinced of the truths that he was exposing. From then on, I was drawn to him with an irresistible impulse, and I had for him a deep veneration and such a profound esteem that these feelings have always remained engraved in my heart; how could it have been otherwise? Have I not seen him so moved as he preached the word of God that his face was wet with tears?"*[9]

In September 1820, the novices and the brothers from the diocese of Saint-Brieuc traveled to Auray for the first common retreat of the two groups, in a convent acquired for the school of the Sisters of Charity of Saint Louis by Father Deshayes. The two Founders shared the direction of the exercises; Father de La Mennais preached the sermons, Father Deshayes presided during the meditations and gave the conferences. Father de La Mennais led the opening session, Father Deshayes closed the exercises. Forty to fifty brothers attended this first gathering away from the quarrelsome school politics of Saint-Brieuc.

The retreat, held between September 9 and 15, was a unique community experience for the Brothers. Some came eagerly to meet a Founder and brothers they had not yet seen. The two Founders named them **Brothers of Christian Instruction** and gave them the motto: "God alone," *(Dieu Seul!*[10]*)*. The *Rule* was read solemnly in chapel. Mr. de La Mennais dictated three-to-four large sheets of text to the school directors; these transcriptions were the only available copies until the first printing in 1823. Mr. de La Mennais commented it and explained the vow of obedience. The superiors heard the confessions of the Brothers, and a Breton priest came for the confessions of the Breton-speaking "postulants." The brothers rose at five, spent the day in silence except for the subdued conversation allowed during the recreation which followed meals. One quiet observer, Félicité de La Mennais, remembered that experience with hallowed reverence.

The brothers had been wearing a simple black garb. The Founders presided over the first solemn vesture ceremony during the closing celebration. They symbolized the sacredness of the religious consecration by giving a "religious name" to the postulants who had not been assigned one. The first profession of vows was particularly impressive. Some twenty men made the vow of obedience for one year, kneeling before the Founders who were standing on the steps of the altar.

At the suggestion of Father de La Mennais, the brothers from Auray promised obedience to Father Deshayes, and in the case of his death to Father de La Mennais; those from Saint-Brieuc reversed the formula. Father Deshayes, who thought the parallel ritual unnecessary, insisted that the two houses form a single house *"as you and I, Mr. de La Mennais are one."* The profession was the vow of obedience, the single vow which effectively incorporated the three elements of the religious consecration. The rule prohibited personal funds and celibacy was understood from the start, for none but generous celibates could live the life of the new society. Before parting, the Founders sought the protection of the patroness of Brittany by leading their disciples in pilgrimage to the sanctuary of Saint Anne which Father Deshayes had helped to restore at Auray.

The surprising vitality of the little group rejoiced the Founders. The brothers left the retreat with the sense of belonging to a religious family. The Founders had endowed the simple society with highly motivated service-oriented young men in a structured fraternity. The retreat of 1821 would build on the commitments of 1820, despite the unexpected circumstances which changed the life of Father Deshayes.

The unexpected calling of Father Deshayes, May 1821

A pensive Parish priest rode the coach south from Auray to a forlorn town of rural *Vendée* in November 1820, and several times early in 1821. Gabriel Deshayes had a reputation for understanding religious orders. He invited them to his parish, supported their work, and recruited members for them. He had called the Daughters of Wisdom to the *Chartreuse* of Auray, and in 1811, he had entrusted them with the care of deaf-mute children. As one of the Vicars General of his diocese, he had come to know their Superior General and had worked with him to organize retreats for the faithful. Father François Duchesne[11] was Superior General of the Missionary Company of Mary and of the Daughters of Wisdom, both founded by Saint Louis de Montfort. Duchesne so valued the understanding and zeal of Gabriel Deshayes, that he commissioned him to visit the communities of the Daughters of Wisdom in Brittany when illness held him bedridden.

The Founder of these congregations had died in Saint-Laurent-sur-Sèvre *(Vendée)* in 1716, and his religious families had since centered their administration in the town. In 1820, when poor health restricted Duchesne, grave apprehensions about the future of his company of priests led him to offer Father Deshayes the title and the powers of Assistant to the Superior General. The two men met in a conference in November, and Father Deshayes referred the matter to his Bishop.

On December 21, Father Duchesne asked him to visit the communities of the Daughters of Wisdom in Brittany; heart failure ended his life on December 22. On December 30, the superiors of the two societies wrote asking Father Deshayes to come to Saint Laurent immediately. On January 17, 1821, the missionaries and the General Council of the Daughters of Wisdom elected him Superior General. The Missionary Company of Mary still had seven priests and four coadjutor brothers, the Daughters of Wisdom 778 sisters and 47 novices in 96 communities.

Accepting this call meant leaving Auray. With responsibilities to his parish, to his diocese, to his two religious congregations and to the good works which he was supporting, Father Deshayes could neither assume the role of Assistant, nor that of Superior General, without consulting his superior. Bishop de Bruc knew the priest, valued his services, but he also understood the needs of the Church as well as those of his diocese. When consulted he replied in substance: *"If I consider the interests of my diocese, I must tell you to stay; if I consider the interests of the Church, I must allow you to go."*

Rather than wait until September, the two Founders called the brothers to a second common retreat in Auray in May, before the departure of Father Deshayes. Classes were canceled for fifteen days in the latter part of the month, and about 55 men, including 20 novices, assembled in the convent which had welcomed them eight months earlier. The exercises followed a standard pattern,[12] the work of the preceding September continued with special attention given to the circumstances. Responsibilities had been shared between Founders; cooperation would continue between them, but the absence of Father Deshayes would leave all members under the immediate authority of Father de La Mennais who was little known by the brothers from the diocese of Vannes.

Moreover, the brothers from Auray had to part from ten of their companions. Since his conversations with Father Duchesne in November, Father Deshayes had returned to Saint-Laurent-sur-Sèvre in January, then again after bidding farewell to his parishioners in March. Before his return for the May retreat, he had decided to continue in Vendée the special school apostolate which was progressing so well in Brittany. He was convinced that *"a society which was achieving so many and such remarkable accomplishments in Brittany, could not fail to have equally beneficial results in a land where the same principles of loyalty to Religion and the King are professed."*[13]

Two brothers had followed him to their new home in March. On the day following the May retreat, eight novices were selected to join them; their mission was to repeat in Saint- Laurent the society of teachers founded in Auray.[14] They would form in Vendée a society distinct from that of Brittany, with its own constitution, a separate administration, and a distinct interpretation of service in a land where a few coadjutor brothers of de Montfort's Missionary company of Mary had taught school in the past.[15] They would eventually be known as the Brothers of Christian Instruction of Saint Gabriel.

The novitiate of Auray had been the cradle of two congregations of religious brothers. Gabriel Deshayes and John de La Mennais agreed in 1825 to set the Loire River as a demarcation beyond which neither would found schools; the new society of Father Deshayes would serve south of the river, the society of Brittany governed by Father de La Mennais, north. While governing the two societies of Louis de Montfort, Father Deshayes remained an amazingly active founder of elementary schools until his death in 1841. During the two decades of his activity in Saint-Laurent, his new society founded about a hundred elementary schools, many of them small and a number of them short-lived.[16]

The departure of Father Deshayes alarmed some of the brothers and momentarily confused established relationships within the Congregation. The separation was painful, in some cases tearful, but with the exception of Gabriel Deshayes, no one felt the burden more than John de La Mennais who was assuming full responsibility for all the brothers of Brittany. Father Deshayes would remain an active collaborator to Father de La Mennais, and would keep his promise to meet his brothers at their annual retreat in Brittany. Ill health caused the only abstention.

After the retreat of 1821, John de La Mennais returned to the vicissitudes of Saint-Brieuc. His driving concern remained to provide in his diocese a classroom seat for every child led by its parents to a Christian school.

---

[1] François Marie Tresvaux du Fraval (1782-1862). The letter is known from the reply of Father Tresvaux. See letters, **AFIC**, 24-A.

[2] See chapter 11. J. de La Mennais requests the "Brothers from Auray."

[3] Alexis Crosnier, *L'homme de la divine Providence, Gabriel Deshayes,* Paris: Beauchesne, 1917. Vol. 2, p. 59 note 4. Letter to Mr. Féry (May 13, 1835). On the same page, see also the letter to Father Lamarche, O.P. (January 8, 1837).

[4] As given in **ÉM**, no. 5 (July 1990), pp. 60-61. **Cor.gén. J,** v.2, pp. 122-123. **Lav.,** v. 1, pp. 333-334.

[5] On his passage at Saint Brieuc, Brother André wrote that he had seen no sign of a novitiate in the home of Mr. de La Mennais (**AFIC** 80 (1) - 5). A letter from Félicité to Miss de Lucinière is the only other known document. which sets dates. Félicité wrote: *"We will leave at the end of August [for Paris]. Unfortunately, my brother will not be with the group: a novitiate of little brothers which he is establishing in his own house will not make it possible for him to leave."* (July 4, 1819). **Cor gén F**, vol 1, p. 560.

[6] See Paul Cueff (on the basis of the H. C. Rulon studies), **ÉM**, no. 5 (July 1990), pp. 58-60.

[7] The term "low Bretons" *(bas-bretons)* designates the Breton-speaking population of (maritime) western Brittany. Letter to Father Boucarut at Nîmes (January 12, 1844), AFIC, 115.

[8] Letter (June 24, 1864) in response to Father Houet who requested accounts of souvenirs. **AFIC**, 80.

[9] Abbreviated as "D.S." for the French *Dieu Seul*, from the Latin Deo Soli. It is customarily written with a small cross appended between the two letters.

[10] Father Yves François Duchesne (1761-1820) was Superior General of the Missionary Company of Mary (or Montfort Fathers), composed of priests, coadjutor brothers and Daughters of Wisdom.

[11] Between the eighteenth and twenty-fourth of the month, according to the imprecise records.

[12] The excerpt given here is from the preface to the *Constitutions* of the Brothers of Saint Gabriel published in 1874, as taken verbatim from the introduction to the manuscript *Statutes* signed by Father Deshayes in 1837. Archives of the Brothers of Saint Gabriel, 162, 001. See also Paul Cueff, **ÉM.**, no. 9 (October 1992), p. 70, and **Cros.**, vol 2, p. 195.

[13] See Louis Bauvineau, *History of the Brothers of Saint Gabriel,* (Translated from the French by Adélard Faubert). Rome: [The Brothers of Saint Gabriel], 1994, pp. 11-27.

[14] At the legal authorization of 1823, Father Deshayes named them *Brothers of Christian Instruction of the Holy Spirit*. In his rule of 1837, he gave them the definitive name of *Brothers of Christian Instruction of Saint Gabriel.*

[15] The list established by Brothers René Mary and Michel Vion was revised and published by Brother Louis Bauvineau in the Magazine of the Brothers of Saint Gabriel, no. 102 (June 1991), pp. 30-34.

Chapter 13

LABOR OF PEACE AND THE CONTROVERSIES OF 1819

Prizes, a recognition assembly and a stinging controversy

In 1819, the elementary schools of Saint-Brieuc were prospering, including the Providence which continued to progress as a private institution. The Brothers of the Christian Schools were teaching some 400 boys, and two brothers were added to serve the new students. The monitorial school was reporting an increasing attendance of some 125-150 students. Prosperity and the favors of the city council inspired its sponsors to raise a triumphant banner; they clamored for attention through the formality of a school assembly. The Mayor had generously granted them their own school, the city council had provided funding and parents enjoyed the freedom of choice for their children.

On August 14, 1819, the Prefect Saint Aignan convened 51 subscribers of the monitorial school to organize them into a legal association under an ordinance requiring supervising committees. The founding statement asserted that the children benefited from a truly Christian education at the monitorial school, and that everything in the system inspired true principles of morality and religion, in tacit reference to the Christian schools of Mr. de La Mennais. The proceedings were published and distributed; a public manifestation would soon follow.

On the feast of the King, August 25, less than three months after the contract between Gabriel Deshayes and John de La Mennais, the new association solemnized the success of their school in a public distribution of prizes, with a solemn high mass at the cathedral and a formal convocation in the large hall of the *collège*. Saint Aignan, presiding, awarded prizes, New Testaments from the Paris Society, a non-approved version. The honored students were crowned with laurels, applauded and acclaimed. The celebration proceeded with a leading address expounding the merits of mutual instruction in monitorial schools. The main speaker was none other than the father of Miss Chaplain.

Mr. Chaplain earnestly expounded the humanitarian objectives of the association. He reviewed the introduction of the method in France four years earlier, and rejoiced that the national society had contributed to establishing the system in some twelve thousand French towns. He hailed its success in all the countries of Europe, and observed that it was established in the French colonies and would be a herald of civilization and social order in respect to religion, he observed that the method was practiced in Rome and that the Sisters of Saint Joseph of Cluny had adopted it for their mission schools. He pointed out that a school in which teachers led classes to weekly mass, and the students learned the catechism, recited prayers and were surrounded with maxims from the Gospel and from sound moralists could not be irreligious.

His praise for the method was unrestrained, his admiration for its founders boundless as he echoed the overtones of a national controversy. He affirmed that the system achieved quick results, and proposed it as the *"surest and most infallible"* means ever invented by human reason, and the *"key"* providing access to the sciences, the arts and the laws. Its founders should be honored with statues like the inventors of printing, of the potato, of vaccination. Mr. de La Mennais, the leading opponent to its extension in the diocese, was (intentionally?) absent from Saint Brieuc on that day, but he reacted quickly after reading the published report.

The quill which had raced through a request for novices six months earlier, now labored through an incisive response to the polemic. On September 20, 1819, printer Louis Jean Prud'homme, the former Mayor, filed with the Prefect Saint Aignan a declaration of intent to print 500 copies of a publication on mutual instruction written by Jean-Marie Robert de La Mennais.[1]

The pamphlet, entitled *De L'Enseignement mutuel,* deplored the government imposition of a new teaching method based entirely on the mechanical commands of children tutored by a supervising schoolmaster. It was an analysis of monitorial schools, a defense of the role of the teacher and the classroom method practiced by the Brothers of the Christian Schools.

The 22-page reply came from the desk of a busy diocesan administrator during a confrontation with militants determined to organize their schools. The author wrote it during eight work-days. *"I would have preferred to avoid a discussion in which it will be difficult for me not to offend anyone; but there are circumstances where it is not permissible to remain quiet; in this particular circumstance, silence would disgrace my lips."* The exuberant declarations of Mr. Chaplain reecho through the text, but having followed the movement from the beginning, John offers a sketchy review of its progress in France, and probed far beyond the assertions of the orator.

His argumentation is lucid, firm, informed, at times cutting. He joins other polemists in a tangy unruly national debate. He begins abruptly and proceeds with directness to the end. John writes under constraint of time, reacting to the national controversy and the speech of Mr. Chaplain with occasional flashes of irony, passages lacking reserve.

He rejects certain material aspects of the method as counterproductive, his observations practical. Writing daily on sand and slate deforms the hand which must learn to hold a quill for ink on paper, while the constant rumble, repetitions and group rotations are obstacles to mental concentration and quiet study. He describes the system as mechanical, reducing the teacher to a drill master. He questions the social consequences of a system which reduces learning to basic skills, without allowing the teacher to impart elementary concepts of virtue. He objects to the excessive role delegated to children, when even experienced teachers hardly manage to discern the needs of individual students.

The concessions made to religion preoccupy him. He commented, a child is hardly born and already means are taken to banish religion from its cradle; instead, the young are delivered into the care of a "philosophy" which severs French children from their Christian heritage. Mr. de La Mennais observes that an agenda is not equivalent to a practice, particularly when ill-prepared teachers disinterested in religion. Mere verbalization fails to carry the message of religion into the hearts of the young. The instruction manual specifies that the very nature of the method is *"purely grammatical,"* and that teachers must keep absolute silence concerning matters of religious faith.

John de La Mennais wrote the tract in reply to a published speech; the sponsors of the school rebutted it resoundingly through the masterly pen of Louis René Bienvenue,[2] lawyer at the Parliament, Vice-President of the Civil Tribunal of Saint-Brieuc, member of the Commission for monitorial schools, and orator at the Masonic Lodge; the skillful barrister was the logical candidate for the task.

On October 16, 1819, less than a month after the publication of John's pamphlet, Bienvenue read his twenty-five-page rebuttal to the Commission for monitorial schools in the city hall. The Commission voted to widely distribute the text immediately; it was printed in the October 1819 issue of the *Journal d'Éducation,* to the satisfaction of those who planned a public castigation of the Vicar General. The title was unequivocal: *Réponse à l'Écrit de M. Robert de La Mennais sur l'Enseignement mutual,* (Reply to the essay of M. ... on Mutual Instruction).[3]

Bienvenue writes a point-by-point repartee to the arguments of Mr. de La Mennais in the skillful phrases of pleaders at the bar, with *"a moderation which contrasts with the violent tone of his adversary,"* often deftly turning the arguments of the Vicar General against him, and declaring that he would leave to his insults the author whose clear purpose does not alarm people of common sense, Bienvenue accused John of forgetting all proprieties for the vain prestige of a pamphlet inspired by partisanship.

Opinions were divided on the issue in Saint-Brieuc, in Paris, in the nation. Some received the arguments of Mr. de La Mennais as *"an excellent résumé of the principal difficulties of mutual instruction,"* while others rejected them and rebuked the Breton priest. However, soon the tempest subsided and the competition for students continues.[4] The Vicar General busied with a rebuttal, soon turned to action and left the draft unfinished.[5]

The end of the story

There was a sequel to the controversies of 1819. The students of the Brothers of the Christian Schools soon exceeded the capacity of their school. Desirous of avoiding losses to the monitorial school, Mr. de La Mennais opened classes in his home with brothers from Auray. He continued to open schools in rural parishes, the *"blockade of Saint-Brieuc,"* he would call this phase of his enterprise. To avoid losing students for lack of space, John built two additional classrooms in his courtyard as an annex to the school. The monitorial school never enrolled more than 170 students, an increasing number of parents sending their sons to the brothers' school.

After exalting the value of the monitorial system, Bienvenue had closed his reply to Father de La Mennais with a flourish: *"We shall pursue our career without distraction, without emotion, and we shall reach our goal."* The public administrators of Saint-Brieuc decided otherwise for the city, and posterity judged the system otherwise for the nation. After a change of government in 1821, the Ministry of the Interior began to cut incentive funds. In Saint-Brieuc, the city reduced the monitorial school subsidy and suppressed it completely the following year; the school closed and the spacious hall was placed at the disposal of the Brothers in January 1823.

The Lancasterian system was abandoned in England before it lost ground in France.[6] Gabriel Compayré, historian of education wrote that the system, kept until 1867 in certain Parisian schools, *"had long been regarded with an extraordinary prestige. During the Restoration, its success reached the level of a fashion, of a fury. Mutual instruction had become the banner of the liberal party in matters of instruction."*[7]

In 1837, the philosopher Victor Cousin[8] expressed his personal views to the Dutch educators who explained their rejection of the system to him: *"I must concede that mutual instruction still enjoys a deplorable popularity. A few men, well meaning, but superficial and utterly unacquainted with public instruction ... considered as a masterpiece what was the infancy of the art, and let themselves be dazzled."*[9]

Octave Greard,[10] Director of primary instruction for the department of the Seine, concluded in 1878 that the system imparts merely *"what can be taught mechanically: reading, writing and arithmetic; nothing else."* He refered to monitors turned into *"little despots"* and acknowledged that a misunderstanding of character formation flawed the system. He then pointed out that *"Schools directed by religious congregations had been protected very well by their Constitutions,"* but that *"it had not been thus for those directed by lay schoolmasters and schoolmistresses. Under the constraint of ideas cherished by the liberal party of the Restoration, they had been uniformly pledged to mutual instruction."*[11]

A choice of lights

The leaders of the French "enlightenment" cast a spell over the generation of John de La Mennais, and their disciples confronted Christian educators with a choice between the rationalist heritage of the Revolution, and the religious traditions of the nation. When the Lancasterians used education as a political instrument to promote their agenda, John de La Mennais followed a course enlightened by the values of the Gospel.

The Lancasterian system kept the teaching of religion at a disadvantage. Victor Cousin set the issue clearly: *"Christian instruction was impossible with that method, for no monitor, even at twelve, was capable of teaching religion and morality: thus the consequence of reducing religious instruction to almost nothing."*[12] That is precisely the analysis of Father de La Mennais: *"But behind mutual instruction, hostility against religious influence was hiding."*[13]

The humanitarians who promoted the system do not lose credit for their work. They advocated it at a time when little or nothing was done for popular education, and thus they rescued thousands from illiteracy before the availability of teachers, a sounder pedagogy, and the advent of schools for all children.[14] In France, a controversy over method would have been a very different experience.

Father *de La Mennais explained the beginnings of his brotherhood to Louis de Kergorlay in terms of basic values: "Carnot is the real author of our society." During the Hundred Days, Lazare Carnot submitted to Napoleon a report on the national organization of primary instruction. Father de La Mennais later advised the clergy of his diocese that he perceived "a tiny black spot on the far horizon; but it is the cloud which harbors lightning."* He then observed that elementary school teachers would henceforth influence the minds and the souls of the young, and the teachers proposed by Carnot seemed to offer *"no guarantee of morality."* Father de La Mennais considered it urgent to anticipate events with *"the foundation of religious institutes for primary instruction."*

In 1837, the philosopher Victor Cousin expressed his personal views to the Dutch educators who explained their rejection of the system to him: "I must concede that mutual instruction still enjoys a deplorable popularity. A few men, well meaning, but superficial and utterly unacquainted with public instruction ... considered as a masterpiece what was the infancy of the art, and let themselves be dazzled."

---

[1] The required declaration has recently been discovered in the Prud'homme family papers inherited by Magdeleine (Prud'homme) Boca of Saint-Brieuc. All references are from the printed speech of Chaplain and the response of Father de La Mennais, **AFIC** from the published text.

[2] 1760-1835.

[3] Saint Brieuc: Chez Le Monnier, Libraire, 1819.

[4] Louis Grimaud, Histoire de la Liberté de *l'Enseignement,* Paris: Rousseau, 1944+. Vol. 5, *La Restauration,* pp. 637-639.

[5] Draft notes at **AFIC,** 100.

[6] The religious thrust of the controversy stirred England before dividing France. The Church of England opposed the promotion of a confusing

nondenominational Christianity in the schools. It set up a separate sponsoring society for the schools of Bell, and rejected the directives given by Lancaster to replace its catechism with the reading of Scripture without comment. In England, teachers replaced monitors as soon as they became available.

[7] Gabriel Compayré, *Histoire de la Pédagogie,* Paris: Palu Delaplane, 1884, p. 435.

[8] 1760-1835.

[9] Victor Cousin, *L'Instruction publique en Hollande,* Paris: F.-G. Levrault, 1837, p. 31.

[10] Gréard, op, cit., note 8 above, p. 31.

[11] Eugène Rendu, *M. Ambroise Rendu et I 'Université de France,* Paris: Fourot et Dentu, 1861, p. 113.

[12] Interview with John de La Mennais. Louis de Kergorlay, "De l'Institut des Frères de l'Instruction Chrétienne de l'Abbé J.-M. de Lamennais [sic]," *Revue Provinciale,* Vol. 2 (1849), pp. 81-99. See pages 84-85. Also published in La Vigie de l'Ouest, May 1, 1849. See **Lav.**, v. 1, pp. 228-230.

Pleoermel

Chapter 14

THE NEW BISHOP OF SAINT-BRIEUC

Bishop de La Romagère

On the high ground of Saint-Brieuc, along the road to Brest, the Mathias Cross recalls the memory of Mathias Le Groing de La Romagère,[1] successor to Bishop Caffarelli as Bishop of Saint-Brieuc from 1819 to his death. De La Romagère assumed his functions after commendable administrative experience, and with a good reputation of respect for his services and priestly virtues. Born on December 5, 1756, in a noble family of Saint-Sauveur (Allier), he studied with the Oratorians of Vendôme, with the Sulpicians of Paris, and at the Sorbonne where he became Prior in 1780, the year of John de La Mennais' birth.

Bishop de La Romagere was imprisoned during the Reign of Terror. Before his nomination to Saint-Brieuc in 1817, he served as Vicar General of Bourges and titular Canon of Clermont. A political snag postponed his consecration until 1819. He restored the minor seminary of Plouguernevel and founded several other institutions in his diocese. The mental asylum of Léhon opened by the Brothers of Saint John of God, and a home for deaf-mutes directed by Father Garnier in Lamballe, are both due to his initiative. His compassion for the poor and his generous assistance to the victims of cholera of 1832 at Bréhat and Paimpol lived on in the gratitude of his diocese.

He came to Saint-Brieuc with the distinction and the physical scars of martyrdom. Compelled to hide in the woods for his fidelity to the

Church during the Revolution, he was tracked, imprisoned in 1793 and condemned to deportation. Extreme cruelty on the prison ship *Les Deux Associés* in the port of Roquefort justified a plea for mercy. The captain to whom he turned for redress advised him to draft a petition for the district administration. The administrator rejected the request, severely reprimanded all signers, immediately ordered them riveted in irons and had their chains bolted to the deck. De La Romagère grieved for having unwillingly worsened the fate of his cosigners more than for his personal sufferings. Of the nine priests from his diocese on the ship, he was one of the two survivors freed after the fall of Robespierre, and after seeing his own brother die by his side. He bore the consequences of his wounds for the rest of his life. He was known for his deep sincere piety and is memorialized in the cathedral for a remarkable charity for the suffering and the needy.[2]

His nomination was well received in 1817. When early rumors suggested that he might decline the responsibility, Félicité wrote to Ange Blaize that it would be regrettable if he did *"because much good is generally said of him,"* (October 18, 1817). Within a month, information about the irksome quirks of a virtuous man began to filter through. Félicité wrote that his friend Frayssinous found him to be a man *"of mean intellect, speaking much"* but *"appearing pious."* However, he believed that *"it would be possible to manage with him,"* (December 16, 1817). John read his brother's revised evaluation when de La Romagère visited Félicité in Paris: *"I dread the moment of his entry into his diocese. The matter is not that he is deprived of piety and zeal. But what a poor man! How boring! He writes verses, then readily recites and even sings them. At the mission of Clermont, he persisted in exhibiting his singing talent ... Father Frayssinous, who is not suspect, agrees that he is an appalling eccentric.[3] He nevertheless said flattering things about you,"* (August 14, 1818).[4]

Such information justified prudence. John advised his new superior not to visit prematurely, but on an April evening in 1819, a visitor stepped down from the coach from Vannes and greeted Saint-Brieuc residents *incognito*. The ungainly appearance and nondescript manners of the lanky visitor had nothing of the dignity expected of a Bishop. Félicité wrote that the brief visit made *"against everybody's advice,"* had already *"totally discredited him,"* (September 24, 1819).[5] De La Romagère kept a letter contact with John during two years before his arrival, showing interest in the institutions of the diocese, pledging 2,200 francs for the seminary of Tréguier, and declaring his intention to come as soon as possible. Some feared that John might leave Saint-Brieuc, but the Vicar General could discern treasures of faith and zeal through the triviality of discourse and the banality of appearance.

The two-year interval before the bishop's consecration was the consequence of political bickering over the proposed concordat between France and the Holy See.[6] The object of Napoleon's Concordat of 1817 was to reorganize the Church in France and thwart its influence though the basic terms had already been set in 1816. John was considering his own options when the Concordat of 1817 signed between Pope Pius VII and Louis XVIII opened possible alternatives. Bishop de Pressigny could return to Saint-Malo, and he seriously considered John for the office of Vicar General; Bishop de La Romagère was listed for Saint-Brieuc.

A strong liberal opposition blocked the ratification of the Concordat during two years of wrangling, and reinstated the one of 1801. Saint-Malo would not be restored as a diocese and de La Romagère asked John to stay as Vicar General of Saint-Brieuc. Two years passed between the nomination of de La Romagère and his consecration in Paris on October 19, 1819. It is during the insecurity of that two-year deferral that John requested the Brothers of the Christian Schools for Saint-Brieuc and began to organize two new religious congregations.

Bishop de La Romagère took control of his diocese on November 15, 1819, and governed it for twenty-one years until his death on February 19, 1841, in his 85th year. He quickly demonstrated an exaggerated sense of personal esteem, and wielded authority without discretion. No one denied his generosity and priestly virtues, though no one overlooked his eccentricities. He could preach intemperately, boast of his accomplishments, and intersperse singing and irrelevant comments during worship without realizing that such behavior could provoke ridicule. In his first administrative decision two days after his installation, he appointed John de La Mennais Vicar General.

John was living precarious times at the arrival of de La Romagère; he was sponsoring three schools recently founded by the Brothers of the Christian Schools in Saint-Brieuc, and the Brothers from Auray in Pordic and Dinan. He had signed his contract with Gabriel Deshayes and received his first three novice candidates four months earlier. His Sisters at the Providence had been living under their first vows as Daughters of the Heart of Mary for a mere three months, and hardly three months had passed since the first retreat of his new society of brothers. Public controversy had disrupted his life and the polemic was still seething when de La Romagère assumed responsibility.

Resignations and a "dismissal"

Confronted with serious misunderstandings and a variety of unacceptable decisions, John offered his resignation. In addition to his difficulties with the Bishop, the sessions of the diocesan council utterly disappointed him. He appreciated a clear analysis of difficulties, respect for priorities and an efficient execution of decisions. However, several times a week, he had to bear the tedious digressions of a distracted man, slow to understand, prone to confuse issues. When the Bishop took decisions, he often disregarded the advice of realistic assistants to follow his own lights. John again offered his resignation in September; realizing the futility of his presence at diocesan council meetings, he was no longer attending sessions. When the Bishop insisted that he remain, John deferred his departure and accepted to participate in administrative decisions, but by direct private consultation without intermediaries. De La Romagère dismissed him on January 31, 1821, naming him honorary Canon of the Church of Saint-Brieuc.

When De La Romagère complained to the royal officials overseeing ecclesiastical affairs, he received this response: *"It is truly unfortunate that the differences which have arisen between you and Mr. de La Mennais have reached the point of a separation. It has been brought to my attention from all quarters that this ecclesiastic earned the esteem and the consideration of the entire diocese of Saint Brieuc, and I need no further proof of this than the numerous establishments for good works which exist through the charity of the faithful. These establishments will fall with the departure of Mr. de La Mennais. I really fear that public opinion will hold you responsible for it. It is therefore my duty to advise you, if it is still possible, to try to retain this collaborator. Men of that caliber are too rare for their loss not to be irreparable,"* (March 12, 1821)[7].

John found it difficult to leave, but judged it counterproductive to stay. He wrote of his experience to his friend Querret: *"Rather than attenuating embarrassments, he compounds them with new acts of extravagance, silliness and ridicule; you have never seen or imagined anything of the kind. Not knowing which way to turn, he visited me the day before yesterday, and he stayed on to conjure me in tears to resume my title. I refused ... What frightens him most is the inevitable collapse of my schools which he lacks the means to support,"* (February 20, 1821)[8]. Realizing the impossibility of peaceful collaboration, John reaffirmed his decision. The other Vicar General also resigned and Father Vielle judged it advisable to retire as superior of the seminary. The Bishop was left alone. Father Le Mée,[9] a young priest from Saint Brieuc sponsored at the Sulpician seminary by John de La Mennais, was prevailed upon at the age of 27, to replace his benefactor.

Father Le Mée succeeded de La Romagère as Bishop of Saint Brieuc, and John de La Mennais succeeded Bishop de Quélen as personal Secretary to the High Almoner of the kingdom in Paris. The other priests all found service in good works and ecclesiastical assignments outside the diocese. De La Romagère lacked the essential qualities of an administrator, but his genuine goodness shone through his relationships and compensated for the shocking oddities of his character. His charity for the poor, his simple and courageous dedication gradually led his people to forget his faults.[10]

Ecclesiastical peace and the fate of two religious congregations

John's standing in the diocese was such that discretion could not shield him from the praises of the people who knew him well. He tightened: *"In Saint Brieuc, everyone meddles; prefect, · mayor, administrators, even the liberals, everyone grumbles, never has such confusion existed,"* (September 28, 1820). *"My dear friend, do not scold me; since my destitution I have received so many visitors, I have been the guest of so many dinners, I have had to deal with matters so numerous and so varied, that I have hardly found a few moments to write the most urgent letters. .... You cannot imagine the attachment manifested to me. The city moves to a man without partisanship in my defense; the most ardent liberals, the most resolute Jacobins come forward. I confess that such unanimous feelings make deep impressions on my heart, preventing me from leaving this good land,"* February 20, 1821.[11]

Bishop de La Romagère displayed no greater tact in dealing with John's two religious congregations than in his relationships with clergy and public officials. The brothers' congregation was then a fragile organization without significant property, and sometimes still considered by some as the society of Gabriel Deshayes.

The bishop's interventions were particularly obnoxious for the sisters at the Providence where de La Romagère saw an educational institution in full service. However, despite the bishop's persistent meddling, John managed to save his two religious congregations from clerical misunderstandings.

From Saint-Brieuc to Paris

In November 1822, John de La Mennais was assuming new responsibilities in Paris. No known document fully explains the origin of his invitation to work with the royal administration, and none of the various explanations referred to by his biographers bear scrutiny.[12] Letters to the Count of Senfft reveal that Félicité was aware of the offer made to his brother in June 1822. John hesitated as long as the functions remained poorly defined; he accepted and left after receiving official notification of the King's ordinance appointing him.[13] Félicité insisted that the reason for John's hesitation was the need to strengthen the fledgling congregation of brothers: *"Consider the state of a newly-formed congregation abandoned to itself, and you will agree that it would be risking the destruction of an important work when only a short time is needed to strengthen it,"* (July 7).[14]

Given the tensions, the native fairness of de La Romagèrè shone through the unexpected confidential recommendation which he wrote to John's future superior. *"When you asked me information on the ecclesiastics of my diocese whom I judged apt to occupy positions of distinction, I thought myself compelled to designate Father de La Mennais. ... I stated that he had talents which could render him quite capable of discharging elsewhere the functions entrusted to him. I therefore learned without surprise, Monsignor, that you have called him to your service. ... I owe him the justice of saying that he has shown much prudence, having cared exclusively for the schools of the little brothers which he had recently founded. I believe that he will be worthy of your trust and that he will accomplish all the good that you expect of him,"* (November 18, 1822).[15]

Paris would overwhelm John with new relationships, new responsibilities and new preoccupations, but as his coach rolled on toward the heart of the kingdom, his mind could not help flashing back to the loved ones taken from him in recent years. Three lives had ended in 1818. In May, the beloved maid Villemain who had so dutifully served the La Mennais household and was respected as one of the family was taken to her last abode. In August, Ange Blaize notified the family that the confused existence of Gratien, the youngest of the La Mennais children, had ended. He died of yellow fever in a Caribbean hospital while on his first commercial cruise, after having burdened the family for years with his instability and financial irresponsibility. On August 23, Félicité wrote to John that Father Paul-Émile Teysseyrre, a personal confidant, had passed away after a brief illness.

In addition, John had recently lost the first member of each of his two religious congregations. Marie-Anne Cartel, the Foundress of the Daughters of Providence, died on October 21, 1821, after years of illness and a prolonged agony. Hardly seven months before leaving Saint-Brieuc, the Founder had announced the death of Yves Le Fichant at Guingamp on May 3, 1822. Brother Yves had been the sole survivor of the first three candidates sent to him by Father Tresvaux. Brother Yves died while serving on his first assignment after leaving the novitiate of Saint-Brieuc.

The recent death of Father Guy Carron was of immediate concern to Félicité, John and the hosts who were awaiting him in Paris. This zealous priest had become spiritual director to Félicité during the latter's London exile, had directed him to the priesthood, and had remained a source of comfort and counseling.

John had come to Paris often though never making it part of his world. Father Carron's associates were now awaiting him there, at *54 rue des Postes* where they had relocated after the death of their Founder. John had recently lost one of his own spiritual guides of adolescent years, Father de Clorivière who had passed away in his eighty-fifth year on January 9, 1820. John had been a member of his society of priests during the short life of that association. The heroic Jesuit of revolutionary days had worked to restore the Society of Jesus since its reinstatement by Pope Pius VII in 1814. When the end came, he uncomplainingly suffered the loss of sight, dulled hearing and failing memory.

Recollections from seven years of a wholehearted diocesan apostolate, and memories of friends and associates, living and departed, followed John into the throbbing metropolis. Miss Hélène de Lucinière, leading member of the Carron "family," had prepared a haven to ease the transition from his Breton apostolate to the undefined responsibilities awaiting him. She had written to Félicité: *"Perhaps it would be appropriate for him to withdraw from the crowd, and to slowly rise above the scene before venturing onto this vast stage. I cannot help but giggle at the thought of the Abbè Jean transformed into an abbè of the court"* *(November 18, 1822).*[16]

---

[1] 1756-1841.

[2] **SA** (1960), pp. 173-183, 204-214. **Lav.**, vol. 1, pp. 370-383. **Rop.**, pp. 254-267. Société Bibliographique, *L'Épiscopat français, depuis le Concordat jusqu'à la Séparation (1802-1905),* Paris: Librairie des Saints Pères, 1907, pp. 548-549. *Ami de la Religion,* vol. 108 (February 25, 1841), pp. 377-378.

[3] Denis Antoine comte de Fraussinous, 1765-1841. Later Royal chaplain (1821), Grand Master of the *Université* (1822), Minister for Ecclesiastical Affairs, (1824-1828).

[4] **Cor. Gen. F,** vol.1, pp. 371, 426-427.

[5] Letter to Bruté de Rémur. Ibid. p. 582.

[6] Jean Leflon, *La Crise révolutionnaire,* 1789-1846 (Histoire de l'Église de France depuis les Origines jusqu'à nos jours, vol., 20), Paris: Bloud et Gay, 1949, pp. 331-336.

[7] As cited in **Lav.** vol. 1, pp. 377-378.

[8] **Cor. Gén. J,** v.2, pp. 170-171. (Literally, John's expression is, *"resta pour sept quarts d'heure:"* (stayed seven quarter hours). In Saint-Brieuc, 1,700 children were affected, 700 of them resourceless.

[9] Jacques Jean Pierre Le Mée (1754-1858). He became the next bishop of the diocese.

[10] **Lav.,** vol. 1, pp. 381-382.

[11] Letters **Cor. Gén. J,** v. 2, pp. 155, 170-171.

[12] The various conjectures are summarized by P. Friot, in **ÉM,** no. 10 (July 1993), pp. 2-4. The suggestion that active lay association known as *La Congrégation* had promoted his candidacy remains unsubstantiated, and probably unprovable. Daniel-Rops, *L'Église des Révolutions, 1, En face des nouveaux destins* (Histoire de l'Église du Christ, vol. VI), Paris: Fayard, 1960, pp. 285-287. M. Geoffroy de Grandmaison, *La Congrégation (1801-1830).* Paris: E. Plon, Nourrit et Cie., 1889.

[13] **Cor. Gén. J,** v. 2, p. 197.

[14] **Cor. Gén.,** vol 2, pp. 287-325, especially the letters for June 8 and 23, July 7 and 27, October 12 and November 9 concerning both, the offer made to his brother and conditions in the diocese of Saint Brieuc. The King signed the nomination ordinance on Nov. 9, John received notification on Nov. 16, and left on Nov. 22.

[15] As quoted in Friot in **ÉM,** no. 10 (July 1993), p. 3. This fair assessment follows the letters of Félicité. It is dated a few days before John's departure, but it refers to earlier undated communications.

[16] **Cor. Gén. F,** vol. 2, p. 638.

Felicite de La Mennais, renown, controversial author, (1782-1854).

Port of Saint Malo during the time of the La Mennais brothers.

The Port as seen more recently.

Bishop Mathias de La Romagere, Saintly, Controversial Pastor.

La Chesnais, favorite secluded study area for the two La Mennais brothers.

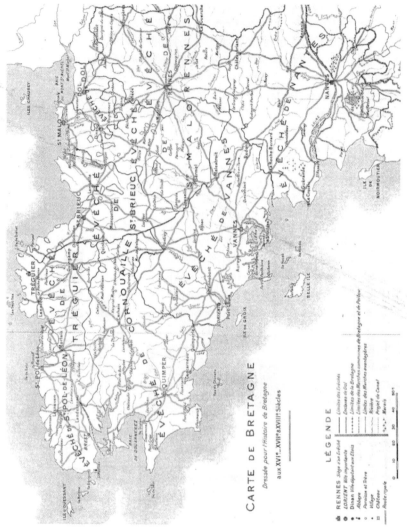

Map of Brittany during the 18ᵗʰ Century.

House of Providence, St. Brieuc, Mother House of the Daughters of Providence.

Chapter 15

From Paris to Ploërmel, 1822-1824

SERVING THE CHURCH OF FRANCE

The High Almoner, Prince de Croÿ-Solre

After more than fifteen years of relationships as an outsider with the administrators of the Empire and the restored Monarchy, John was now called to serve the Church from within the royal administration.[1] He understood the ways of service, but he had never been part of the formalities of court life. He came to court with little instinct for the ways of royalty, and left Saint-Brieuc without upgrading his wardrobe. While nothing had been done to prepare his official residence, convivial friends had prepared a room for him in Paris; the cowl does not make the monk, nor silk the prince, but some circumstances require formal wear.

Fully aware of her friend's carelessness *about dress, Miss de Lucinière called the clothiers to action.[2] She described the performance to Félicité: "Your good brother arrived at nine; at ten, everything was in action for his apparel: tailors, hatters, shoemakers, hosiers. Finally, the metamorphosis was complete at two, and the abbé Jean appeared before us spry, lively, elegant and bursting with laughter. It will be amusing to see him dressed in beautiful silk-lined court attire, French style."* (November 28, 1822).[3]

Gustave Maximilien Just, Prince de Croÿ-Solre, Bishop of Strasbourg[4] had been appointed High Almoner hardly thirteen months before John's arrival.[5] He was the third to occupy that office since the Revolution, having been preceded during the Empire by Napoleon's nephew, Cardinal Fesch, then by Cardinal Talleyrand-Périgord.[6] John would serve under him from November 1822, to the fall of 1824.

The High Almoner's office still functioned essentially as a ministry for ecclesiastical affairs. The services of the office were guaranteed by the High Almoner, titled as High Officer of the Crown, by a first Almoner high Officer of the House of the King, eight Chaplains per quarter of the year, a Vicar General with the rank of Officer of the House, a confessor to the King, eight chaplains for the Royal Chapels, and finally a secretariat administered by a Secretary General.

John had to understand the duties of his new superior because he would be required to substitute for him in a variety of liturgical and protocol functions, and even stand for him in key administrative matters. The High Almoner pledged fidelity directly to the King, and delivered certificates of oaths of fidelity of the Archbishops and Bishops. He served as chaplain to the King and his family.

Among other duties, he baptized and married members of the royal family in the presence of the king, acted as leading celebrant at designated royal liturgies, presided over the Royal Chapter of Saint-Denis, and he administered royal charities. In the temporal government of the clergy, he presented to the King nominations to archbishoprics, bishoprics and other ecclesiastical titles, a major responsibility until August 1824. He appointed to royal chaplaincies, provided spiritual service to royal houses of education, to the schools of the Legion of Honor, and was responsible for the temporal and spiritual administration of the royal hospital. Besides assigning chaplains to the royal chapels, he was responsible for Royal military chaplaincies;[7] a Vicar General, or several, assisted him in the administration of his office.

De Croÿ was gifted with a rare facility to communicate the teachings of the faith to children of his age, but he avoided preaching to adults for lack of ease in the pulpit. He used his wealth to relieve the needy and assist good works. He was not a natural administrator but was wise enough to delegate authority. He valued the administrative skills of his chief Vicar General, trusted his insights, favored effective procedures and relied on his assistant's resourcefulness to establish them.

John soon realized that the transition from Saint-Brieuc to Paris was a leap from confusion and obstruction to trust and cooperation. In 1842, a biographer wrote about de Croÿ's choice of collaborators: *"He chose as vicars general men of proven talent and virtue, among whom Mr. John de La Mennais is prominent. This remarkable priest substituted for him during mandatory absences; he even became the acting administrator, and the clergy had every reason to be satisfied with his extensive influence. I consider the choice of the elder Mr. de La Mennais among the best accomplishments of Mgr. de Croï [sic]."* The High Almoner was now entrusting the most sensitive responsibilities of his office to a priest who was then pledged to supplement with two new religious congregations the work of John Baptist de La Salle's Brothers of the Christian Schools, in Brittany and far beyond.

Duties, cooperation, priestly presence

The official responsibility of the Vicar General was to administer the office of the High Almoner, a role which entitled him to the same honors as the chaplains. He ranked with them immediately after the Chaplains, and assisted the High Almoner as first assistant priest in liturgical celebrations. Delegated authority broadened his responsibilities whenever the duties of the Royal Court or the affairs of the Diocese of Strasbourg required his superior's presence.

Official descriptions aside, John was immediately assigned the reorganization of an office in disarray. The elderly Cardinal Talleyrand-Périgord had left numerous important matters unattended, key assistants had left the office, and a few had followed Archbishop de Quélen his assistant to the Diocese of Paris. John wrote to his friend Querret in Saint Malo: *"You have no idea of the state in which I found the affairs of my administration; I will need time to restore order; on that account I am pleased, because I see the good to be done which I hope to accomplish,"* (December 26, 1822).[8]

John recruited personnel while appraising the various responsibilities assigned to him. Besides official liturgical functions and presence required by necessity, protocol or convenience, he was expected to (1) oversee the secretarial services and administrative functions, (2) suggest recommendations for chaplaincies, manage the correspondence and deal with a variety of incongruous services, and (3) assist his superior in the preparation of lists and recommendations for the nomination of Bishops.

Prince de Croÿ moved his personnel from the cramped quarters available at his arrival to the more spacious setting *2 rue de Bourbon.* John managed the new installation, filled two vacancies and organized the administrative services. Closer bonds soon developed between the Vicar General and his superior as John co-ordinated the secretarial service dealing with a continuous flow of issues. Between December 1822 and August 1824, some 1200 letters kept assistants at their desks. Given the trust between the prelate and the Vicar General, John managed affairs with assurance.

The unavoidable frustrations of administration did not affect John's personal relationships with his superior. We find him seeking rest and distraction with the former assistants of the deceased Father Carron, with Miss de Lucinière, her companions and their guests in an environment where hearts opened, friendship sparked laughter, and questing souls shared insights while refining their thinking. The conviviality was particularly buoyant when Félicité, then concentrating on the sequel to his Essay *on Indifference in Matters of Religion,* came to visit from his La Chesnaie retreat.

John's unaffected ways facilitated friendships across all levels of official Paris. It was widely known that the Duchess of Angoulême, daughter of King Louis XVI, always stood ready to assist him. John met the high and the mighty, but honors did not enthrall him; his priesthood was for everybody. Whatever his associations, whatever the importance of his functions or the demands upon his time, John de La Mennais lived the simple priorities of his priesthood. We find him directing a retreat at the Royal hospital or preaching at the religious profession of a sister at the orphan school of the Legion of Honor.

John complied whenever his brother priests called on him for help, and he presented requests for their assistance from royal charities. He helped to resolve misunderstandings between churchmen, and found time for those who requested spiritual advice. He continued in Paris to work with lay congregations as he had effectively done in Brittany. Father Carron had founded two lay congregations for the spiritual formation of young men and young women; through the duration of his presence in Paris, John accepted to direct the men organized as the Association of the Blessed Virgin.

John had to prepare a report in the jurisdictional conflict between a good friend, Bishop Hyacinthe Louis de Quelen, and Prince de Croy, John's immediate superior. In order to have as accurate a response as possible, he studied the historical roots of the conflict, assessed the validity of the arguments, then searched for documentation that would clarify the legal prerogatives of the High Almoner. The history and the records of recent practices convinced him to support the claims de Croÿ. The report is an excellent example of clear, masterly, logical reasoning –

Shepherds called to account [9]

Under the concordat with the Holy See, John's superior was required to mediate the selection of bishops by proposing to the King a list of candidates for vacant bishoprics. The King submitted his selections for approval by the Pope, but the initial choice of candidates came from the High Almoner who involved his assistant in this sensitive task. Although 122 of the 135 bishops in the Constituent Assembly had voted for the Civil Constitution of the Clergy in 1790, only four of them had sworn the oath to the constitutional church. The others had all been dismissed by the government and gone into hiding.

The new church would be led by constitutional bishops, elected by the people of each diocese, and unrecognized by the Pope. Agreements between Napoleon and Pope Pius VII required the resignation of all Bishops and a fresh start. [10] The Revolution had reduced the 139 dioceses of the Old Regime to 85. Under the Concordat, Napoleon reduced that number down to 60 and ordered the preparation of lists. By mid-August, 1801, Portalis, [11] Director of Cults, had obtained the resignation of all 59 surviving bishops of the schismatic church of 1791.

Pope Pius VII asked all bishops of the Old Regime to step down when he signed the Concordat of August 15, 1801. Of the 83 legitimate survivors from the Old Regime, 36 refused, but on November 29, the Pope deprived them of jurisdiction by abolishing the dioceses of the Old Regime. Nominations started without delay, and the Emperor required the inclusion of twelve prelates from the constitutional church. On July 29, 1802, Napoleon promoted Fesch, his uncle, to the see of Lyon and appointed him High Almoner for the Empire. Episcopal promotions in the Empire were state affairs under the Emperor's iron hand rather than pastoral decisions. Gallican traditions prevailed from the start, but the proportion of Gallican nominees steadily decreased.

Promotions resumed with the coming of Louis XVIII. Talleyrand-Périgord, successor to Fesch as High Almoner, proceeded to fill recent vacancies and prepare lists for the bishoprics proposed during the aborted Concordat of 1817. When the deputies rejected that Concordat, the King froze the lists until the men selected for 1817 [12] had been installed. In the interim, negotiations with the Holy See had opened prospects for 30 to 42 new bishoprics, and the projected jurisdictions had been drawn by October 1822. When John assumed his responsibilities the following month, the need for new candidates was urgent, a responsibility he assumed immediately.

Men like d'Astros under Portalis and Fesch, de Quélen under Fesch, and Talleyrand-Périgord had prepared recommendations before John was called upon to work on the promotion list of 1823. Twenty-six bishops were appointed that year, only six of them from the deferred candidates of 1817. The first nominations did not close the search; sixteen additional posts were filled before John left Paris in November 1824. Brief notes from contemporaries shed light on John's role in this sensitive mission. Father

Le Clerc once surprised him in action: *"I arrived in Paris at the time of [the Vicar General's] rising. He told me, I am rising later because I spent the night making bishops; I named 22, among whom three Bretons; guess who?"*[13]

The listings followed recommendations, inquiries and conferences with de Croÿ, correspondence with individual candidates, a sustained, exhausting research. We find John pursuing direct correspondence with candidates during that period, his hand repeatedly appears on letters as reference notes to his superior.

Forty bishops were appointed during John's term of service, twenty four of them for dioceses that were still without bishops. Ten others filled vacancies opened by death, resignation or transfer. Bishops selected for six other sees complete the list of nominations from November 1822 to August 1824, the period of John's collaboration with the Prince of Croÿ.[14]

Relations with the churchmen of this period often continued through correspondence, consultations, apostolic initiatives or as undying loyalties, across dioceses, even in foreign lands. These men of authority honored with their trust the priest who recommended their consecration, and readily turned to him for advice. Biographer Laveille states that he long remained a most trusted guide for many of them.

John's role in the appointment of Bishops was well known. He recommended, without the power to decide, but his suggestions were often decisive. Canon Le Sage relates that when John went to Tréguier. the parish priest welcomed him, all church bells ringing. When someone observed that such an honor was reserved for the bishop, the old curé replied: *"What are you saying? Is Mr. de La Mennais not the equal of bishops? Hey! He is the one who makes them!"*[15]Brother Hippolyte (Morin) recalls the former assistant to the prince of Croÿ discretely avowing in an assembly of ecclesiastics: *"I gave forty bishops to France, and I believe them all good."*[16] His own name was proposed several times without ever coming to nomination. The same witness relates that John was once pressed to declare that he had refused the honor seventeen times.[17] Pastoral service to the

French Church filled his term of office in Paris without distracting him from the humble work of his disciples in Brittany.

---

1 See Philippe Friot, "Jean-Marie de La Mennais à la Grande Aumônerie de France (1822-1824)," **ÉM**, no. 10 (July, 1993). **Lav,** vol 1, pp. 393-418. **Rop,** pp. 311-329. Jacques Olivier Boudon, L'Épiscopat *Français à l'Époque concordataire* (1802-1905), Paris: Éditions du Cerf, 1996, pp. 285-323.

2 The Society of Saint Joseph directed by Father Lowenbrück assumed the expenses.

3 **Cor gén F,** vol. 2, p. 643.

4 1773-1844; later Bishop of Reims (July 4, 1823), then Cardinal.

5 "High Almoner:" British usage for the French *Grand Aumônier.*

6 Cardinal (Joseph) Fesch (1763-1839). --- Cardinal Alexandre Angélique de Talleyrand-Périgord (1736-1821).

7 The list of duties is long. This summary is based partly on the *Almanach du Clergé de France, pour l'an M. DCCC, XX.* Paris: M.-P. Guyot, Éditeur de l'Almanach royal, 1820.

8 **Cor gén J,** v. 2, p. 205.

9 Ezechiel. 34: 10.

10 L. J. Rogier (et al.) Siècle des *Lumières, Révolutions, Restaurations* (Nouvelle histoire de l'Église, vol. 4), Paris: Éditions du Seuil, [1966], pp. 273-300.

11 Jean Étienne Portalis (1746-1807).

12 Daniel-Rops, L'Église des Révolutions, 1, En Face des nouveaux Destins, (Histoire de l'Église du Christ, vol. VI), Paris: Fayard, 1960, pp. 272-288.

13 As cited in P. Friot, **ÉM,** no. 10 (July, 1993), p. 50. Notes about Mr. John de La Mennais (1861). **AFIC.** The writer's memory is mistaken: the nominee for Nevers was Milaux, not Caro.

14 The list of appointees is given in **ÉM,** no. 10 (July 1993), pp. 70-72) on the basis of a study by Brother Hippolyte Victor (Géreux): "L'abbé Jean-Marie de la Mennais à la Grande Aumônerie de France" (1944). Manuscript, 75 p. **AFIC.**

[15] As reported in **Lav,** vol. 1, p. 413.

[16] **AFIC,** 80 (1). See sources in **ÉM,** no. 10 (July 1993), p. 58, n. 2.

[17] The reference seems to request appointment procedures rather than documented offers from the Holy See.

Port of St. Malo, Birthplace of the La Mennais.

Chapter 16

PARISIAN OFFICE, BRETON HARVEST

The Daughters of Providence

John de La Mennais left Saint-Brieuc in November 1822 with a determination never to abandon his earlier commitments. *"I abandon none of my schools. I keep their direction."* The resolution was firm. He had recently established his residence in Paris when he wrote to his friend Querret about the humble beginnings of his societies: *"It is impossible to be in a better situation than I am, and yet, I dream only of Brittany, of my friends, of the children that I left there."* [1] He accepted new responsibilities with the proviso that he be allowed to revisit his two religious congregations twice a year, and he did, twice in 1823 and twice in 1824. He would not neglect the rising harvest planted by his care. He bared his feelings about his departure in a meeting with his Daughters of Providence: *"I never felt so deeply how dear you were to me and to what extent my happiness was bound to yours. ... I sacrificed my preferences, my affections, my rest."* His consolation was *"the intimate feeling of having fulfilled a sacred duty to the Church."* [2]

He spoke those words before the end of the twentieth month following the profession of the Sisters, as Daughters of Providence, and a mere three months after their vesture ceremony. The Sisters had the stability of a home, their fourth and permanent one. With an increasing family of children, their school was prospering though without financial security. The poverty of the early years never curbed growth at the Providence.

John was planning the construction of badly-needed classrooms as soon as adjoining land became available.[3] He postponed construction and thanked Mr. Sébert for acting on his behalf: *"The purchase of the Porte-Thomasse, [the new acquisition] caused me great pleasure, and if that property had passed into hands other than ours, I would have been inconsolable. My only frustration is the resulting delay in the construction of a new building for classrooms, for I grieve at the sight of teachers in such dank quarters; let us hope that Providence will assist us in another way."*

Soon, John snatched an opportunity for new facilities: *"I have a project in mind which cannot be executed for the moment, but which could be realized in a few years: it would consist in establishing missionaries in that house. An enclosure would be provided for them, and the rest of the land would be reserved for the Providence which would keep ownership of the whole; you realize the advantage for the house to have next to it zealous priests responsible for retreats and instruction, etc... The matter requires mature reflection: whatever the case, today I would not make commitments likely to become an obstacle to that plan,"* (April 27, 1824).[4]

John failed to establish a home for missionary priests and circumstances called for the resale of part of the acquisition in 1826; however, the retreat master, the homilist, the organizer of lay religious congregations lived in the heart and mind of the Vicar General. While the Daughters of Providence labored under one roof, governed by one sister superior, the brothers were dispersed, still awaiting the "central house" of the original plan. They acknowledged two founders, both "absent," both answering calls to yeoman service.

Letters and visits

The rule, still unprinted, required each brother to write to the Superior every other month. John's absence would make that practice the only communication between the Founder and his men between visits. Brother Hippolyte recalls directives: *"He wrote to tell all of us that he was always our Superior General and that we should write to him as usual ... Work was overwhelming at the High Almonry. ... His replies nevertheless were hardly ever long-awaited, for he kept Sundays for personal correspondence with his children. We addressed our letters through the High Almoner; he replied to us via the mail of parish priests; we thus avoided postal fees."* [5] His occupations were such in 1823 that he instructed the brothers to leave half of the sheet blank so that he could reply quickly on the letter.

The immediate need was basic literacy. His men were elementary schoolmasters at a time when preparation and support for the professions was lacking. After a modicum of instruction under the Brothers of Christian Schools, the first contingent of Brothers of Christian Instruction marched on to serve the forgotten children of rural parishes. He later found his own tutors, delegated authority, counseled his first assistants to direct small communities wherever possible, but he often advised directly isolated men in single-classroom schools.

John decided transfers between schools, [6] and his letters cover matters ranging from recruiting and lodging, classroom method and the material needs of penniless neophytes. [7] He also was concerned with their religious duties and the Christian atmosphere in the schools. He managed a meager common purse ever in need of replenishment. We find him providing bedding, requesting the repair of floors, approving food supplies and guiding directors of communities in their administration. He anticipated needs, planned school and classroom organization, expedited routine chores. He could deal with the unexpected and the trivia of life while pursuing matters of high consequence. Thus, he requested his friend, the mathematician Querret, to compose an arithmetic textbook for his teachers, and advised teachers on the use of goose quills, the standard writing instrument of the time, and how to sharpen them.

His correspondence provides practical directives: *"It is unwise to assign too many children at a time to Brother Jerome, children under six must not be admitted in his class. If there are incorrigible children in your classroom and in that of Brother Jerome, do not hesitate to exclude the more unruly until my return. Brother "H" makes little progress, why is it so? If a child resists, never punish while you are upset, and never with force. I do not like violence in correction."* He insisted on regular penmanship exercises for his brothers because handwriting was important at a time of widespread illiteracy; he verified progress but readily abridged practice time in case of poor health. He frowned on supplementary activities because of the fatigue caused by long hours in overflow schoolrooms.

In 1823, he unified basic practices of community life with the first printed edition of the rule. Directives and visits eased the burden of isolated men often lodged in rectories and serving in single-teacher schools. Regularity and fraternity bonded the membership, but he sensed that years of generous service would soon end without real spiritual motivation. His letters supplemented the work started in personal encounters. He insisted on fidelity to the rule, but his basic doctrine was prayer, attention to the presence of God, fidelity to the sacraments, and the basic virtues of Christian life.

His words were simple and direct: "Observe exactly all the points of the rule," (To Bro. Laurent, letter of Feb.23,1823). *"All religious exercises must be in common ; the Brothers must be together for prayer and work; dispensations must be as few as possible,"* (To Bro. Ambroise, Dec. 26, 1823). He recommends *"Obedience and humility,"* (To Bro. Hippolyte, Jan. 3, 1823). Obedience must be "of mind and heart, not merely of action," (To Bro Ambroise, May 13, 1824). He counsels Bro. Marcel against *"Vain worries about your vocation,"* (Oct. 16, 1823). He writes to Br. Ambrose against discouragement: *"The temptations which you experience must humiliate, not discourage you;"* (May 13, 1824); *"Do not grieve; infirmity improves virtue,"* (Nov. 7). He recommends to Bro. André *"Continuous attention to the presence of God, frequent confession."* And long before the days of daily communion, he prescribes communion *"as often as possible, as it is a grave misfortune to miss a single one,"* (Oct. 17, 1823).[8]

In his letters, Father de La Mennais blends austerity and respect for persons, directing his little society with fondness for its members without sacrificing the essentials of community life. He repudiates violence in school and rigor in the community. He advises Brother Ambroise (Director) not to *"insist too strongly"* when a Brother resists, and to guard against *"forcing matters to extremes,"* (May 17, 1824). He strives to measure assignments to the capacity of each individual, and follows personal improvement attentively. He could not withdraw Brother René from the kitchen and he writes: *"He must wait; we will see at the retreat what should be done for him,"* (May 6, 1824).

His methods meet the frail and the untutored with special consideration. He respects poor health and weakness; a fragile individual who finds long writing practice too tiresome after hours in the classroom "must not be inconvenienced," (May 17, 1824). He writes to Brother Marcel: *"Observe faithfully the advice given to you by the doctor to walk every day,"* (June 9, 1824). He requires punctuality at community prayer, but counsels the conscientious Brother Ambroise: *"You must not attempt to make up the exercises which you have been compelled to omit, you would thereby confuse everything."* To the same, prone to voluntary penance, he prohibits *"additional mortifications,"* (May 13, 1824). The times are hard, the revenues sparse; he allows no wasteful spending, but he does not want the Brothers *"to lack necessities."* He wished that directors take their administrative decisions *"for the best, without worry,"* (April 1, 1824). The unpretentious generosity of the Founder and his men shines through the bare language of this forthright correspondence.

Visits provided the founder opportunities for personal action. He wrote in advance to rally his men: *"I have but a moment to inform you that I will be in Quintin, Friday afternoon on the 27th of this month, (February, 1824). I have notified the Brothers from Plouguernevel to come,"* and he requested that the five Brothers from the smaller schools of the region be invited to join the group, (Letters to Brother Laurent, Jan. 19 and Feb. 18). He thus convened his "States of Brittany," as he occasionally referred to these assemblies.

Visits across Brittany were not mere whimsical excursions. Félicité was awaiting him at La Chesnaie when he wrote: *"My brother is now travelling through maritime Brittany to visit his schools and to found new ones; that requires a little time, time that is well spent,"* (February 9, 1823). [9] Whenever it was possible, he would meet the students. A close friend of later years recalled a visit: *"I was one of the first students of the Brothers established in Lamballe in 1824; when Mr. de La Mennais came to visit the school wearing his court apparel and his cross as Canon of Saint Denis. His presence impressed the hundred or so students in the class; his casual simplicity charmed all hearts and left a deep impression on them."* [10]

His commitment to Breton schools lived through a heavy official Parisian agenda. He kept a steady correspondence with his young disciples for he understood the importance of forming his little company into a brotherhood. He was still the only unifying bond between its members, the beating heart at the center of its life. The absence of the two Founders was unplanned and the projected "central house" had not yet materialized.

"Your friend for life" (Gabriel Deshayes)

In 1822, the novices of Father Deshayes were living in the rectory of Auray and those of Saint-Brieuc still occupied the house of Father de La Mennais. Twenty-four brothers served 2,000 students in nineteen little schools. The need for Christian teachers was critical, but the Founder could not send teachers without recruits. He printed and distributed a prospectus inviting them and asking others to promote his crusade. The parish priests were his best recruiters; even public inspectors for the *Université,* and the Rector of the *Académie* of Rennes, a priest, recommended his Congregation. He worried about lodging the young recruits who knocked at his door; meanwhile, he organized provisional novitiates in Dinan, Quintin and Tréguier, communities with space to lodge a few candidates. [11]

The extremists of Saint-Brieuc could not halt the development of the young society. Under John's direction, it gained acceptance as a public service. Public administrators encouraged it and the central government in Paris granted financial assistance even before the formal authorization of the Congregation, at a time when incentive grants were reserved for authorized societies.

John de La Mennais did not act alone. Gabriel Deshayes, now Superior General of the two Congregations of Louis de Montfort, was assembling the elements of a new regional teaching brotherhood at Saint-Laurent-sur-Sèvre in the heartland of rural Vendea without forsaking his disciples in Brittany. Public administrators in Paris and Brittany feared that his little Congregation founded in Auray might not survive the founder's departure. Corbière, President of the Royal Council of Public Instruction eyed its beginnings with interest, and recommended its official approval to the Rector of the *Académie* of Rennes. The Founders submitted no immediate written requests, but while visiting the communities of the Daughters of Wisdom, Father Deshayes stopped in Paris in July 1821.

He spent three weeks seeking legal authorization for his Breton brotherhood. The intervention was personal and effective. Father de La Mennais found such openness when he joined him in August, that he pursued his friend's initiative by submitting the statutes through the Rector of the *Académie* of Rennes. The ordinance dated May 1, 1822, six months before his departure from Saint-Brieuc, authorized the Brothers of Christian Instruction for the five departments of ancient Brittany, and granted them the privilege of the Brothers of the Christian Schools: it empowered the Superior to assign teachers from his novitiate without individual government permits. The provision, which was not conceded to all new teaching societies, ended the obligatory request for the government *brevet*, until a new ordinance suppressed this privilege. [12]

The search for a "central house" continued. A Chateaux in Josselin and Guémené offered by the Rohan family appeared impractical. The Bishop of Quimper invited Father de La Mennais to open a novitiate in his city and planned the acquisition of a building for that purpose. His sudden death left the matter in the care of a successor who opted to substitute the Brothers of the Christian Schools for the less-experienced young Congregation.

The loyal pastoral involvement of Father Deshayes unexpectedly prepared the way for the purchase of a sorely needed common novitiate. From the early years of his ministry in Auray, Father Deshayes worked to provide private retreats for the faithful. As one of the Vicars General of Vannes, he assisted his bishop in the purchase of an old Carmelite monastery in Josselin. In 1828, the Daughters of Wisdom opened a retreat house and a school for girls of poor families in the building. The following year, the diocese acquired an adjoining property for the Sisters. When

Father Deshayes became Superior of the Daughters of Wisdom in 1821, the facilities of the retreat house were under the control of his Sisters. By then, the growing community of brothers needed larger quarters for their annual summer retreat; the Daughters of Wisdom hosted them in Josselin for the retreats of 1822, 1823 and 1824.

Before the retreat of 1823, two adjacent buildings purchased for the retreat house a few years earlier, became the property of the two Founders. [13] The retreat of 1822 was hardly ended when Gabriel Deshayes and John de La Mennais signed an agreement. On September 1, 1822, Father de La Mennais provided six thousand francs to Father Deshayes for the acquisition of two houses and a garden, the required furniture, and funding for the necessary repairs to one of the buildings. Gabriel Deshayes in turn matched the contributions of his friend and pledged to purchase, repair and furnish the buildings.

The novices from Auray moved to Saint-Brieuc during the summer of 1823, and during the first days of August the modest group of 6 or 7 novices and 2 or 3 Brothers traveled to Josselin, their new home and the first common novitiate of the Congregation. Some of the Brothers remembered it as a narrow, gloomy abode. A grant of public funds encouraged Mr. de La Mennais to prepare this new teacher-training center, but he did not have the time to repaid the center in Josselin; this first "central house," proved to be but a brief halt along the way to a permanent home.

The new occupants were hardly settled before the retreat of 1823 when Gabriel Deshayes visited them and later wrote to John de La Mennais from Auray: *"Our brothers of Josselin seem to be doing well. I have been there to taste their first soup. It was excellent."* He continues with unexpected information. *"I have just found a person who will donate 8,000 francs to buy the enclosure of the Ursulines of Ploërmel to make a residence for our brothers."* He closed the letter: *"Your friend for life,"* (August 22, 1823). [14]

The city of Ploërmel was known territory to Gabriel Deshayes. In 1818, he had founded a school there with one of his brothers from the novitiate of Auray, the year he had founded a school in the town of Pordic for Mr. de La Mennais. The city had previously acquired part of the confiscated Ursuline convent; Gabriel Deshayes contracted to acquire the remaining segments of the buildings and the enclosure. On March 6, 1824, he purchased the property from Mr. Alfred Marie Alexis Dollé for the sum of 18,000 francs. He specified that he was acting in the name of the Congregation of the Daughters of Wisdom. The document of the sisters state that he had not determined the precise nature of the institution he hoped to found.

The agreement of August 30 modified that proposal. On that day, the city ceded its share of the buildings on the following terms: (1) Mr. Deshayes will deed the building acquired from Mr. Dollé to the Brothers of Christian Instruction, and will use it to establish a novitiate for the society. (2) Mr. Deshayes and Mr. de La Mennais assume the obligation to provide two brothers to teach gratuitously, and the city will pay 600 francs annually, and the congregation will not be entitled to anything more. (3) After January 1, 1825, the congregation will assume all financial liabilities linked to the property. (4) Should instruction ever cease, the owners assume the obligation within six months to pay the city the sum of 12,000 francs. In case of default, the city would repossess the portion of the buildings it had ceded.

The transaction complete, Gabriel Deshayes would transfer ownership neither to the sisters nor later to the brothers. The law allowed the Daughters of Wisdom to acquire property, as a hospital society, but not without government authorization. That was requested and denied. Tighter restrictions prohibited teaching societies of men from accepting real estate, as the law established only the *Université* as beneficiary of gifts given to congregations for educational use. Father Deshayes avoided the risk of government intrusion by delegating his powers to Mr. de La Mennais, personally. Before his death, he deeded the property to him personally and to a group of brothers, because the law still disallowed corporate ownership by the Congregation.

By August 30, 1824, the Founders of the Brothers of Christian Instruction owned a permanent "central house" for their brothers. John would return the interim novitiate of Josselin to the Daughters of Wisdom who reimbursed him for it. [15] He was still living in Paris in August 1824, but he anticipated that the national elections would prompt his departure and the new acquisition would soon become his home.

Elections in Brittany, reorganization in Paris

On Christmas eve 1823, the Villèle government dissolved the Chamber of Deputies and convened the local electoral college for February 26, 1824. The two La Mennais brothers were known opponents of the regime, mainly for its tolerance of violent enemies of religion, and its laxity in the face of an abusive press. The calumnious *Le Constitutionel and the Courrier Français* routinely insulted the French clergy with impunity, while a flood of negative press soured relationships between Catholics and their government. [16] Félicité complains in his letters: *"Everything unchristian is daily currency among the revolutionaries. There are a number of striking examples here and the Dufougeray family is one of the more notorious. They recently ranted against me and against my brother, by saying that his schools tend to return the countryside to the influence of the priestly rabble, ("la prêtraille"),"* (November 9, 1823). [17]

Outraged, John publicly denounced the stratagem and wrote to Father Hay: *"I considered it my duty to lay aside all occupations in Paris to attend to this one, which I consider of the highest importance. I came to Saint-Brieuc to fight against the prefect and defeat the ministerial candidate. I have managed to rally independent men in favor of a respectable man, Mr. Sébert. As for the people linked to the present ministry, 'with full knowledge of the facts', I consider them to be the most dangerous enemies of religion and the monarchy. In writing as I do, I believe I am discharging an obligation of conscience; I would not otherwise intervene,"* (February 24, 1824). [18]

The two brothers actively campaigned against two official candidates. As a resident of La Chesnaie, Félicité promoted Ange Blaize, his brother-in-law in Saint-Malo. Residence in Saint-Brieuc entitled John to act as "elector." He paid the required poll tax of 300 francs; however, both candidates lost badly. A letter of dismissal awaited John in Paris for intervening in ways which displeased the governing party. The High Almoner immediately appointed him Vicar General for his diocese and kept him by his side in Paris. John wrote to Querret that he had become *"Vicar General to Msgr. the Archbishop of Rouen, High Almoner of France,"* instead of serving in the same capacity *"to Msgr. the High Almoner of France, Archbishop of Rouen,"* (April 10, 1824).[19]

Government reorganization followed in short order. By the ordinance of August 26, 1824, the king created a Ministry for Ecclesiastical Affairs and Public Instruction and appointed Msgr. Frayssinous, the acting Grand Master of the *Université,* to direct it. John's reason for service in Paris disappeared when the reorganization stripped the High Almoner of his most important functions. John met his brothers at their third and last annual retreat in Josselin in August before returning to Paris for his last days with the Prince of Croÿ. Louis XVIII died on September 16; his funeral was celebrated on September 23. John was in Paris on October 13 to take official leave from the Prince of Croÿ. When John left the capital, France had chosen Charles X as its new King.

John's role in the elections of 1824 had apparently caused his dismissal, but Church authorities understood the incident differently. A few weeks after the destitution of John de La Mennais, the Apostolic Nuncio in Paris, Mgr. Macchi, presented his observations about the work of the High Almoner's office. Noting the increasing proportion of bishops supporting Papal authority, he commented: *"The general system of "Roman" doctrines are more widely affirmed and spreading every day, arousing jealousy and a fear that bishops would abandon Gallican maxims. The government took offense and feared that it risked the loss of authority."*

Fortunately, the High Almoner replaced him by Father Perreau, an ecclesiastic whose maxims and principles were similar to those of Father de La Mennais".[20] John would henceforth deal with the government as an outsider, often in the vexatious circumstances which he had so often experienced before coming to Paris. John left Paris without realizing that unexpected forms of service awaited him in Brittany.

[1] Letters to his friend Querret, November 22 and December 26, 1822 respectively. **Cor gén J,** v. 2, pp. 198, 205.

[2] Sermon to the Daughters of Providence during a visit, February 2, 1823. **AFIC,** 75-1.

[3] The property was known as *La Porte Thomasse.*

[4] Letter to Mr. Sébert, April 27, 1824. **Cor gén J,** v. 2, p. 285.

[5] Some categories of official mail were postage free, Notes of Brother Hippolyte. **AFIC,** 80-1, 6.

[6] These letters to the Brothers have been published as *Jean-Marie de La Mennais, Lettres et circulaires aux Frères, [Saint-Brieuc, Frère* Louis Balanant, 1993].

[7] Edmond G.Drouin, "Les Relations de Jean de La Mennais avec ses Frères, de 1822 à 1824", **ÉM,** no, 11 (December 1993), pp. 57-69. Most of this correspondence has been lost. Thirty-four salvaged autographed letters help us to understand the relationships between the brothers and their Founder during this period.

[8] Unless otherwise stated, quotes are from the **Cor gén J,** at the dates given.

[9] Letter to the Count of Senfft. **Cor gén F,** vol. 2, p. 380.

[10] Mgr. François L. Maupied. "Notice sur la vie et les oeuvres de Monsieur Jean-Marie Robert de La Mennais," (Copie dactylographiée), 1895. **AFIC,** 16-3.

[11] See Cueff and Friot, **ÉM,** no. 14, p. 7 ff.

[12] H. C. Rulon, **REH,** Chapter 8, pages 23-34, unpublished. **Cros,** vol 2, p. 59. The exemption was withdrawn for all boys' schools in 1828 but continued for religious teaching institutes of women until into the nineteenth century.

[13] Edmond G. Drouin, "Gabriel Deshayes achète pour Jean de La Mennais," **Chron,** no. 368 (October, 1996), pp. 351-361.

[14] **Cor gén J,** v. 2, pp. 609-610. From **AN,** F 19 939.

[15] **Chron,** no. 368 (October 1996), p. 356.

[16] **Lav,** vol. 1, pp. 410-413. Friot, **ÉM,** no. 10, pp. 59-67.

[17] **Cor Gén F,** vol. 2, p. 419.

[18] As quoted from **Rop,** pp. 321-322.

[19] **Cor gén J,** v. 2, pp. 282-283.

[20] Correspondence of Nuncio Macchi in Paris. Message no.

657,translated and quoted by P. Friot, from the Italian in the Vatican Archives, **ÉM,** no. 10, (July 1993) p. 69 See also letter (March 30),and note 1, **Cor gén J,** v. 2, p. 279.

Chapter 17

THE "CENTRAL HOUSE": PLOËRMEL, 1824 - 1828

A home to build

On November 3, 1824, three or four adults and about ten young men paused at the square in front of the town hall of Ploërmel, faced the entrance of a tumbledown Ursuline convent and entered the gate after dragging their belongings in handcarts the twelve kilometers from Josselin. The construction of the ancient monastery dated back to 1629. In 1792, the revolutionaries ousted fifty-four nuns from their cloister for refusing the required oath to the new government church. [1] They jailed a few religious, confiscated their property and used part of the monastery as a prison. The neglect of 32 years left the entire compound in a deplorable state. Sections of the existing buildings had been sold, others occupied by the city, some units rented out.

The weary company entered the gate without knowing what to expect. Father Deshayes had founded a school here in 1818, one now closed for repairs because the classroom was unfit for occupation, as were most of the constructions. Before moving in, the Founders had asked the Ursulines if they chose to reclaim their former home; the nuns were touched by the request, but they would have found it difficult to leave the former convent of the Carmelite nuns, *rue des Forges,* ceded to them under Napoleon. [2] A tour of Ploermel would have discouraged any one tempted to return.

Crannied walls needed steadying. The chapel held a baker's firewood, the nun's choir served as a hay storage, a farmer having installed his cows there for some time. The living room served as a wine cellar, the east rooms rented out for storage, and the ground floor rooms were more like stables or cellars than human abodes. The flooring was missing, plaster had fallen from the walls, mould had weakened the beams, doors and windows had been carried away. Pieces of marble in the rubble of the chapel memorialized the altar destroyed during the Revolution.

Three rooms in the northern quarter offered the only space fit for humans; the brothers set one up for Father Deshayes, one for Father de La Mennais, the other as a provisional kitchen and refectory. They reserved a lean-to as a temporary prayer room while an attic open to all winds became the first dormitory. The brothers settled in with the novices and awaited Father de La Mennais. The Founders knew that they had purchased a ruin, but they also knew what they planned to do with it. [3]

"To live with them and like them" [3]

John wrote to his Sulpician friend from Paris: *"My only regret is not to live near them [the brothers], or with them and like them; that would make me too happy, that is why the Lord does not want it; the more I try to break the bonds which hold me here, the more they tighten,"* (May 23, 1824). [4] Providence soon severed these bonds with the administrative reorganization in Paris. On November 16, a fortnight after the arrival of the first contingent of brothers, a coach rolled into town bringing the Founder to the little community. Until his death thirty-six years later, Ploërmel would be his home and his personal "central house."

Father de La Mennais lived with his disciples, shared their privations, guided their spiritual life, heard their confessions, gained their affection. Restoration of Ploermel began without delay: walls were knocked down, the façade restored, government funds utilized for repairs. The baker's unexpired lease and the storage of hay in the choir delayed the renovations. The desecration of the house of God was evident here as in many other French sanctuaries. Everything sacred had been stripped from the room; the brothers removed accumulated rubble and dried excrement from the days when stable animals had been sheltered there; the old chapel was restored for his community.

Father de La Mennais began to invite candidates as soon as he could provide suitable living space for them. He doubled the number of novices, prepared the more capable among them to serve as schoolmasters. The following year, he was able to provide additional teachers to a number of growing schools. He personally managed their training, giving instruction and dispensing personal advice with winsome simplicity. The brothers had survived two long years under two absent founders, but the "absent" priests had never forsaken their disciples. The long seasonal transits from the capital ended with his return. The plan of June 6, 1819, envisioned a "central house" near a main highway. Ploërmel was at the crossroads of two highways to the west opening unto the Breton peninsula, and two highways opening eastward to the heart of France.

Father de La Mennais left Saint-Brieuc in November 1822 as the superior of 24 professed brothers. During his absence, the number in the Community had grown to 75, without counting the increasing number of novices. The two "absent" founders had been blessed with generous disciples filled with pastoral zeal guided by the wisdom and the dedication of two highly involved founders.

Life in the capital had not isolated John from his teachers. Besides keeping personal letter contact with them, he had met them annually, founded new schools, planned lodging for new recruits and met every brother at the retreat; Ploërmel would intensify this service. Félicité wrote: *"My brother spends half of his life visiting his schools and founding new ones. ... He is indeed the second providence of little children,"* (June 13, 1825). [5] When Louis XVIII died in 1824, John was on a round of school visits in Brittany, and Félicité was still in Rome.

Life was changing for both of them; Félicité would live the experience with priorities different from his brother. John's association with princes and statesmen ended as he reentered the society of commoners in Brittany. The grace of his priesthood which had steadied his course through Saint-Malo, Saint-Brieuc and Paris now challenged him through the uncertainties of new beginnings.

"My strength, my fortress, my refuge" [6]

What kind of man is this priest who leaves the company of statesmen to live with young apprentices, rural primary schoolmasters still struggling with the elements of learning? What kind of priest is this who recommends candidates as bishops, then preaches retreats to rural folk and school children? Twice dismissed from high ecclesiastical office, he accepted simple ministries with a rare sense of open availability and a total disregard for personal convenience. After conferring with princes and prelates, he mixes with peasants and their children with ease and simplicity. An adolescent when he heard his call to ministry during the Reign of Terror, his first guides were outlaws, hunted for their loyalty to the Church, risking death to live their priesthood.

The orientation of John's early priesthood was a matter of deliberate choice inspired by the soundest spiritual traditions. The times were difficult, the obstacles often overwhelming as he shared the anxieties of his ministry with his Sulpician friend, Bruté de Rémur: *"Yesterday, I said to my imagination: 'Go, I will follow you; let us venture into the future together'. We proceeded for five minutes; my head was spinning, I lost my bearings. Nevertheless, my poor mind, stunned and trembling, had sufficient strength to tell me this: 'John, in one hour you may no longer be here below; why then do you want to know what will happen tomorrow? Wait in profound peace; trust the One who can do everything and who never deceives. You have His word; that word has created a world, and you would fear that the world can be more powerful than His word! You would fear, man of little faith? No, my God, I fear nothing. You are with us, who could be against us?"* (July 18, 1807). [7]

To the same Sulpician who shared his interest in Scripture, he wrote the inspired words that were the source of his strength: *"To know Jesus Christ well, we must probe Scripture, and he personally gave us that advice. Above all, we must read and reread the divine Gospel of the beloved apostle with a soul aflame with faith and love. Each word must be meditated, appreciated, delighted in. Have not our fathers set the example for us? ... Like them, let us feed with a blessed eagerness upon this bread of the elect; in humble and continuous prayer, let us ask God to grant us the understanding of heart that will help us understand and penetrate these mysteries,"* (March 2, 1809). [8]

He had written in his notes of November 13, 1807 that the time had come to return to piety directly, *"in its most beautiful sources, Holy Scripture, Saint Francis de Sales, etc."* [9] The Imitation of Christ inspired his prayer. With Félicité, he translated and published (1809) the long forgotten spiritual guide (the Guide Spirituel of Louis de Blois), thereby sharing with his contemporaries the texts which fed his own spirituality. The comments and letters of his early priesthood persistently reaffirmed the goals of his spiritual journey.

The accents of his prayer rise through his memoranda. *"Pray to the Lord, pray Him every day to be with us at all times, to be in us, to enlighten us, to inspire us, to check the unguarded words which could escape Consult Him often, and in uncertainty about a decision, pray Him with renewed earnestness to be the light of our heart.....Think frequently of God while conversing with men; withdraw within to pray in secret, but freely, without strain, in the great simplicity of love. Listen to God in meditation; open the ears of the heart to His Holy word".* [10]

From the Lord came *"the light and the life"* promised in the Gospel (John 8:12), providing him with the strength to deal with adversity. At the loss of Bishop Caffarelli, he had written to an advisee: *"See how everything passes, escapes us, vanishes; how brief and fragile are the joys of this world? I had found another friend in my misfortune, we lived as brothers, we had but one soul, and behold, that poor soul is suddenly torn away, and mine is of sorts, nothing but a torn and bleeding wound. ... Would that I profit from this grave lesson, and from the ruins which surround me, raise to heaven all my thoughts, all my desires, all my affections. ... remember me often before the Lord: I need His lights and graces more than ever,"* (Feb. 4, 1815). [11]

He voiced his own priorities when he invited others to belong entirely to God. Selflessness was a blessing to implore and he begged his Sulpician friend to join in his prayer: *"Please ask God to create in me a pure heart, a heart which loves Him! Ask Him to grant me the grace of being entirely His, His alone, and forever. Fiat, fiat!"* (June 22, 1809). [12]

During his troubling relationship with Bishop de La Romagère, he invited the same friend to pray with him: *"Mr. Olier used to say that crucified charity was the purest; ask God to render me faithful to my vocation. . . . pray for me, for this poor John whose needs are so great,"* (December 18, 1820). [13]

Intense pastoral involvement subdued the undertones of melancholy running through the repeated transitions reshaping his life. His brother worried about him: *"My brother's work pace has long preoccupied me; he is visibly wearing away. I have spoken to him several times, always in vain. I will speak to him about it again, but without hope of success. That pains me beyond words,"* (November 2, 1825). [14] John was neither spared the hardships of his ministry, nor did he spare himself in the face of adversity. Illness brought him down in 1805; he recovered and worked unabated until age compelled moderation.

He bore the tribulations of the Church and withstood the vexations of his ministry without emotional collapse. He was a young priest of 27 when he wrote to his Sulpician friend: *"Ceasing to do good is a strange way of preventing evil,"* (July 4, 1807). He pursued the theme the following summer: *"When, my dear friend, was it more necessary to join intimately together, and to tighten ranks of sorts? Is not our mother, the Holy Church, attacked from all quarters, and if its enemies combine their talents, their means, their hatred, their boldness, why not together oppose our efforts to theirs, and why not mutually incite ourselves to combat and to victory?"* (February 2, 1808). [15] Extended conflicts kept him battling repeated assaults along a shifting battle zone. It was Christian warfare on the social front in circumstances likely to discourage the hardiest. In defeat, this Breton priest heard the clarion call to new offensives. He came to Ploërmel with the experience of conflict and the spiritual insights needed in times of transition.

With his associates in the ministry, he reaffirmed the goals determined during the early years of his priesthood: *"The main purpose of this retreat is to strengthen the resolution which we have already taken to dedicate ourselves fully to this eminently great task, and to lay the first foundations [of our work] despite the aversion, the worries, the contradictions and the obstacles awaiting us,"* (September 1825).[16] He was then standing in the restored chapel of Ploërmel, preaching a retreat to a few priests from the diocese of Rennes in circumstances calling for leadership. At 45, he was responding to a special call from his brothers in the priesthood, and from his Bishop.

---

[1] On the Ursulines of Ploërmel see, Marquis de Bellevüe, *Ploërmel, Ville et Sénéchaussée,* Paris: Honoré Champion, Éditeur, 1915. Pages131-147.

[2] In 1810/1811.

[3] Souvenirs du F. Hippolyte (Morin), **AFIC,** 80. H. C. Rulon, **Chron,** no. 199 (July, 1954), pp. 1-63. Friot, **ÉM,** No. 14 (July 1995), pp. 116-120.

[4] Letter to Bruté de Rémur, **Cor gén J,** v. 2, pp.290-291.

[5] Letter to his cousin, Madame de Champy. **Cor gén F,** vol. 3, p. 59.

[6] *Jer* 17:19.

[7] **Cor gén J,** v. 1, pp. 27-28.

[8] **Cor gén J,** v. 1, pp 58-59.

[9] The Torrent d'Idées, item 33. **ÉM,** No. 2 (April 1988), pp. 25-29.

[10] Le Mémorial, items 4:1, 15:1, 18:2-3, respectively. **AFIC.** Published text in **ÉM,** No. 15 (December 1995). The *Memorial* is a personal notebook, not to be confused with the *Mémorial catholique,* a newspaper published by the friends of Félicité de La Mennais from 1824 to 1830.

[11] **Cor gén J,** v. 1, pp. 256-257. Also, letter to Amable Chenu, published in André Rayez, "Lettres de Direction de Jean-Marie de La Mennais," Revue d'Ascétique et de Mystique (Toulouse), Vol. 33 (October-December, 1957): p. 440.

[12] Letter to Bruté de Rémur, **Cor gén J,** v. 1, pp. 67-68.

[13] In a postscript to a letter from Félicité, **Cor gén J,** v. 2, p. 154.

[14] Letter from Félicité de La Mennais to the Abbé de Salinis. Ladoue, *Monseigneur Gerbet, Sa vie, ses Oeuvres et l'École Mennaisienne,* Paris:

Librairie Saint Joseph, Tolra, 1872. 2 vols., vol. 1, p. 326. It is Félicité, not John, who generally needs assistance in illness.

[15] **Cor gén J,** v. 1, pp. 38-40.

[16] **SA (1960),** p. 464.

Chapter 18

THE RAINS, THE FLOODS, THE WINDS AND A COMPANY OF COURAGEOUS MEN

Félicité, from Breton seaport to the Rome of Pope Leo XII

John had a brother to meet in 1825 as Félicité had recently returned from Rome with options to set. They had both gone their separate ways after teaching and studying the needs of the Church in fraternal closeness from 1804 to 1814. The years following John's return to Brittany in 1824 were mortifying years for French Catholics. The rains, the floods and the winds, (Matt. 7:25) tested the faith of believers. A souring of national politics provoked conflicts which challenged the two priests as they lived soul-searching transitions. Neither of them could know that they would soon be sharing vital aspects of their ministry. A re-acquaintance with Félicité is indispensable before turning to the circumstances which would call the two brothers to travel a second common journey from 1826 to 1836.

John was involved with Félicité to varying degrees of closeness during twenty years, one third of his adult life. The first decade spanned the years from Félicité's conversion in 1804, to John's arrival in Saint-Brieuc and the publication of the three-volume treatise on the tradition of the Church on the institution of bishops in 1814. The second decade began in 1826 with events leading to the foundation of the Congregation of Saint Peter. Until 1836, the bonds between the two brothers would be such that it would be virtually impossible to understand John's experience without a careful account of his brother's activities and tragic decisions.

When John was preparing to leave Paris in 1824, Félicité was in Rome after wielding a triumphant quill during a decade. The road traveled by the unruly lad of Saint-Malo to the Rome of Pope Leo XII, had been nothing less than a stunning and thoroughly unexpected ascension.

Félicité de La Mennais was born prematurely at seven months, June 19, 1782, with malformations of the stomach, a misfortune which plagued him with a lifetime of nagging discomfort. He lived a melancholic, agitated childhood and suffered fits of anger followed by fainting spells. He refused to study except to please maid Villemain whom he worshiped; she spoke in his defense when he was reprimanded: *"He is quick-tempered, but has a heart of gold."* He missed the loving attention of a mother who, before dying, entrusted him to the kindly maid. He later said to his friend Sainte-Beuve: *"There are men who are born with a wounded heart."* He acknowledged the sadness lingering in his soul: *"It was born with me."* Only a mother could have lifted the gloom from this child's youth; he was five when she passed away.

The imagery of the Breton landscape never left his mind. The Breton fog cuddled his moods, the restless ocean entranced his soul. Who better than he could later describe its rhythm with *"a hum and a roll that rock like a dream?"[1]* Who could better pierce the secrets of its whims? He recalled a particularly violent tempest during which he spoke of *"seeing infinity and sensing God,"* and he characterized the spectators around him: *"They look at what I observe, but they do not see what I see."* His nephew Ange Blaize writes of uncle Félicité's reactions at the thought of this experience: *"Every time my memory turns to those times long past, such a thought of pride in a child of eight still gives me the shivers."[2]*

Companions seem to have respected this scrawny irritable fellow; teachers knew not how to keep him still. One of them despairingly tied him to his seat and restrained him with a turnspit stone. He was expelled from several schools for insubordination. Uncle des Saudrais who tutored the two brothers after the Revolution, was one of the few who had the knack of interesting Feli in study. He was a passionate undisciplined student, an erratic, voracious reader, too often of the less commendable authors for his age. He could easily move from book to music, everything of interest to him.

What does a family do with a child who sees through the mysteries of storms at eight, reads Rousseau at ten, sits for hours before the Blessed Sacrament in neighborhood chapels, prays at length before a statue of the Blessed Virgin? Yet this is a child who abhors catechism lessons, raises serious objections to religion from the *Dictionnaire philosophique,* writes compositions to improve his style, reads Latin and studies Greek alone at 12, without returning to school? Self-taught genius and embarrassing rebel in one weave!

Study became a passion no better disciplined than behavior. He eventually acknowledged that he did little to control his compulsions. He feverishly insisted on understanding everything, drove teachers to despair with his unshakable objections, even affected a hopeless incredulity at thirteen. He suffered extended periods of loneliness and boredom, filled long hours reading pagan Latin authors, preferably with his carefree cousin Pitot from the West Indies, the only company he accepted while the young man lived in France. He shared frivolous conversations with him, and proposed to follow him to the Caribbean but changed his mind the following year 1801. Felicite fell in love with an unnamed young woman of the family entourage, and lightly wounded an adversary in a duel for an unrecorded cause. The literary critic and friend, Sainte-Beuve, recalls the extremes of his early years. Félicité then climbed trees like a squirrel, swam to exhaustion, and was an untiring horseman. A passion for weapons drove him to fencing, sometimes for entire days. His father failed to interest him in the family business and despaired of ever reforming him. We lose track of him during the turbulent years to which he exaggeratingly refers to as years of crime; however, he had indeed lost his Christian faith.

After the grinding oppression of the Revolution, religious renaissance swept the land and a new spring reawakened the faith of Félicité. In 1802, Chateaubriand planted seeds of renewal with his *Génie du Christianisme.* The examples and conversations of John, then preparing for the priesthood at home, widened his mental and emotional horizons far beyond the bounds of his early clandestine readings.

After his conversion and first communion in 1804, the elder enlisted him to teach mathematics at the ecclesiastical school of Saint-Malo. Félicité returned to religious practice and Church affairs, and both brothers responded to the challenges confronting the Church. Grave nervous disorders forced him to rest in 1805-1806, but the two brothers nevertheless traveled a common journey in health and in illness through the first decade of John's priesthood, a decade marked by intellectual and literary cooperation, and the first published writings of Félicité.[3]

Félicité began to speak of the priesthood late in 1808, or early in 1809. He received the tonsure, March 16 in Rennes. On June 19, the two brothers joined in a signed consecration to the Blessed Virgin Mary. The text is from the hand of Félicité who added "tonsured cleric" to his signature.[4] Felicite received minor orders, on December 23; however, the quest for the priesthood ceased when he failed to answer the call to the diaconate. Confused about options, he spoke of monastic seclusion, of missionary life in America, of becoming a Jesuit, then a Trappist, all after the fantasy of following his cousin Pitot to the Caribbean a few years earlier.

Extreme sensitivity marks his letters to Bruté de Rémur[5]. Advice from this common friend and from his brother helped him through an interlude of melancholy and indecision. He wrote to John: *"The primary cause of all my ills is far from recent; I was carrying their germ in that arid and gloomy melancholy, in that dark distaste for life, which, by gradually invading my soul finally filled it entirely....I was holding on to life only by the desire of leaving it,"* (1809)[6]. Friends worried about him, but frequent intellectual consultations with John continued and his craving for books seemed insatiable. The solitude of La Chesnaie was never empty for him, though a protective friend, the young Father Teyseyrre insisted that he not live there alone during spells of destructive brooding.

In 1815, the improbable occurred in London when Father Carron became his spiritual guide and Féli resumed his preparation for the priesthood. John suffered deep anxiety about the decision; the course set, he encouraged him, but not without apprehension about the consequences of his brother's bizarre character. Félicité received the subdiaconate at Saint Sulpice in Paris, December 23, 1815, the diaconate at Saint- Brieuc, February 18, 1816, and the priesthood at Vannes, on March 9, 1816. Before receiving minor orders, he had published *Réflexions* in 1809, while still a recent convert, and the three-volume *Tradition* in 1814, before the sub-diaconate.

His ordination was an ordeal for the two brothers. John expressed grave misgivings to Querret as Father Carron guided Félicité to ordination: *"I pray wholeheartedly that God may enlighten them mutually, but I am delighted to take no part in that decision,"* (August 10, 1815)[7]. Félicité in turn confided to John: *"I am quite pleased to remain near my good father [Carron], and certainly nothing less than his advice and his authority is required to overcome the extreme repugnance which I experience in reaching the decision which he wants me to come to,"* (December 4, 1815).[8]

John never took the matter lightly; he wrote about it to his Sulpician friend: *"It cost him singularly to reach his final resolution. ... My poor soul is still shaken from the shock,"* (June 8, 1816) [9]. Félicité soon sank into deep nervous depression in June 1816. He blamed his brother for not having opposed Carron's direction, then declared: *"If I had been less trusting or less weak, my situation would be altogether different. ... All that remains for me is to make the best of it, and, if possible, to fall asleep at the foot of the stake to which my chain has been riveted,"* (June 25, 1816). He insisted on July 9 that it would be preferable never to recall the matter again. [10]

During the emotional collapse that followed, correspondence became *"a burden,"* and writing generated *"mortal boredom"* until the cause of religion brought on a surge of excitement. The boredom vanished, the priest never stopped writing letters. It was soon apparent that the quill of Father Félicité de La Mennais would not, could not lie idle. Driven by native vigor, the newly-ordained cleric fired the hope of his generation. Félicité achieved fame in one leap with his first volume of *Essay on*

Indifference in Matters of Religion, (Essai sur l'Indifférence en matière de Religion).

The book appeared anonymously in November 1817; the first edition was sold out the following May, and translations soon began to multiply. Its vibrant language and formidable dialectic established the author. He was exalted among the great, and celebrated as a genius: *"no one writes like that."* The reaction of Lamartine reflects the mood: *"I have finally fallen upon something good, even something beautiful, even something sublime. ... It is splendid, thought through like Mr. de Maistre, written like Rousseau, strong, true, lofty, picturesque, conclusive; in a word new, everything."* [11] The impact was unmistakable. There were references to him as "Pascal resurrected," and "the new Bossuet." Félicité knew how to speak to his century. Frayssinous, who considered the author's theology *"mediocre,"* and who would later battle his accusations, said: *"This book would resurrect a corpse."* For Victor Hugo, it would have an *"extraordinary future," (livre effrayant d'avenir).*

The *Essai* filled a void, and sent a clarion call in the first offensive against incredulity since the *Génie du Christianisme* of Chateaubriand fifteen years earlier. The philosophy of the author divided opinions even among early admirers; a bewitching style seducing unwary readers. There were those who perceived a lack of measure in both style and reasoning as the weak side of the writer's genius. They judged the language and the imagery sometimes overdone, and understood that a blend of arrogant logic and facile irony would invite scrutiny and stiffen opposition. The power of the text nevertheless redeemed the faults rooted in the personality of the author, and while the well-deserved ovation comforted the author, he continued to wrestle resolutely with his vision. [12]

Before the completion of the second volume, Gratien, the youngest La Mennais, died of yellow fever in the Caribbean, news that plunged Félicité into deep depression. John wrote to Ange Blaize, *"Féli suffered fits of hysteria at the news of the death of poor Gratien",* August 13, 1818). [13] His brother's condition alarmed him to the point that John thought of rushing to his side in Paris. Félicité stabilized as he acknowledged the sudden emotional collapse: *"sadness weakens me and drains all my energy.*

... I am disgusted with everything, it is a very painful experience," (August 14, 1818). [14]

Felicite momentarily lost the will to write and could not foresee when he would finish the second volume, but he eventually did. [15] Controversy followed its publication in July 1820, and provoked the writer to respond with temperamental vigor and unsparing logic, more likely to alienate than to convince. Father Carron, his spiritual guide, wondered why he had released the work without submitting it to his elder, and pleaded that he not publish on sensitive matters of doctrine again, without consulting with men of sure understanding and dispassionate opinion.

Lamartine introduced Félicité to Joseph De Maistre who valued his talent, urged him to pursue his work without worrying about the quibbling of lesser minds; *("Let the sparrows chirp,")* and to avoid wasting his gift on critics, *("Let them say what they wish,").* De Maistre also observed that the author should not expect logic to easily subdue human pride. Shortly before dying, De Maistre counseled him against extremes, and invited him to temper his vehemence: *"Let us be careful ... let us move softly, I am frightened, and that is all I can say,"* (February 24, 1821). [16] Félicité rebutted his critics in his *Défense de l'Essai* in November 1821, the month his mentor who led him to the priesthood passed away; he completed the Essai series with volumes to three and four in 1823.

After the second volume, the controversy focused on the author's interpretation of *sensus communis,* a theory which interpreted universal consensus as the common perception of truth. The consensus argument affirmed that the fallible private intellect found sure truth in the collective intellect of mankind. French writers refer to it as *le sens commun.* The doctrine is now abandoned, but then it occupied philosophers and theologians. It was subject to several formulations; some observers detected a weak philosophical base and unwieldy theological implications in the sweeping version under scrutiny. [17] Félicité wrote a *Défense* to vindicate his work and demonstrate that his doctrine was not at variance with Church doctrine.

Critics nevertheless injected a measure of caution in this phase of his work. He revised his first volume several times, and presented an eighth edition as definitive in 1825. It is a matter of record that Church authorities had reviewed the disputed *Essai sur l'Indifférence* in 1822, without detecting doctrinal errors in it. [18] As a following rallied around Félicité, *"adventurous principles had alarmed other minds, who at the heart of so many truths, discovered the first traces of a path which could induce into error those who let it lead them down its slope."* [19] The mennaisian agenda was still in its infancy; others would soon scrutinize its evolution.

Around 1820, Félicité accepted an invitation to publish ascetical works from the editor of the *Bibliothèque des Dames chrétiennes,* a "library" for Christian women. His contributions to the series include his translation of the *Imitation of Christ* in 1824, his most widely sold publication, for which he wrote his celebrated *"réflexions."*[20] In addition, he wrote *Guide spirituel,* a reissue of a work originally translated and published with John in 1809; the *Journée du Chrétien, the Dialogue sur les dangers du monde dans le premier âge,* an essay on the dangers awaiting youth in the world. The latter treatise was based in part on notes written earlier by his brother. He later reissued it as the *Guide du premier âge,* (a guide for the young) with five chapters added at John's insistence. [21]

A fragile prosperity based on income from his writings enabled him to invest in property after 1820. He bought a chateau and estate in Trémigon near Combourg and held it for three years until his publisher's failure forced him to resell. His sister Marie and Ange Blaize bought it from him in 1823. It became the home inherited by their children, and a second family vacation retreat for Félicité during the latter years of his isolation in Paris. [22]

Sound finances and devotional writings did not divert him from controversy. He wielded a forceful pen, rebutted criticism with an intensity which stunned readers and increased his acerbic opposition, the *sensus communis* living on in his doctrine, often the focus of opposition. He uncompromisingly defended the cause of the Church, vindicated the supremacy of the Holy See in matters of doctrine and discipline, and stood firm against the government meddling with religion and Church affairs.

His blazing rhetoric won a widening readership; by the end of 1823, he was contributing to several publications. An annoying presence for public authority, a thorn in the sides of Gallican churchmen, and a source of malaise for the advocates of prudence, he battled with an intensity likely to close hearts. He felt the growing solidarity of a resentful Gallican clergy which resisted his ultramontane convictions, occasionally rallying with his political opposition. Félicité was both, loved and hated, respected and disputed, a dauntless militant in good health and a dispirited victim in illness and depression.

Rome! The unplanned pilgrimage of 1824

John's advice started Félicité on the way to Geneva in 1824. As he had so often done in the past, John worried about his brother because of his depressive moods. He wrote to Querret: *"I have persuaded Féli to travel to Switzerland, because a unique opportunity to do so occurred: he reached Geneva in good form, though he is tired of the road; I am convinced that he will soon feel infinitely better,"* (April 10, 1824). [23] He had broken his brother's resistance to an invitation from a friend, a parish priest in Geneva. Félicité revealed his state of mind to the Count of Senfft shortly before leaving: *"Personally, I do not have the strength to continue what I have started. My soul bears the full burden of a dying society. I see the evil, I feel it, and I waste away in the throes of sterile pain and indignation. This condition is violent; it cannot be long lasting. But how will I pull out of it?"* (March 3, 1824).

Once on the road, he visited about and followed his busy host to Rome, keeping in constant letter contact with John, grateful for his concern. [24] He did not like the austere Geneva of the day, but before leaving for Rome he conceded: *"What matters is that I have learned many things here,"* (April 25). He thought the voyage *"more useful than expected,"* and realized the gains, *"ten years of study would have served me less than what I have seen."* arrival to Benoît d'Azy, a common friend: *"Our traveler reached Rome (May 9). On June 27, my dear friend, very tired from his voyage, the rudest penance that God could have laid on him. Whatever, his health is excellent, and he has been welcomed most splendidly everywhere; he stays at the Roman College, in a room prepared for him at the Pope's request; you well understand that all these honors annoy him more than they flatter him,"* (July 20).[25]

To the Baroness Cottu, Félicité wrote, *"Travel is not very amusing in itself, but much learning may be derived from it, and in that respect, I strive to profit from mine. It is likely to be the last that I will make, providing that the views of Providence coincide with mine,"* (May 9). Félicité would see Rome again under unexpected and thoroughly altered circumstances.

At the visitor's arrival, Pope Leo XII reportedly commented to his entourage: *"He is a man who must be led by the heart."* [26] Rome was good to Félicité. He was provided with lodging at the Jesuit *Collegio Romano*.[27] He reported papal receptions to his brother: *"The Holy Father whom I have seen twice and who has overwhelmed me with kindness, wishes to see me again to converse, more at leisure. ... If I have adversaries here, (and they are very few, if any), none dares express himself publicly against me. All personalities of any note, have declared themselves for [me],"* (July 16, 1824).

From Paris, he wrote to a cousin, Madame de Champy: *"I prefer Italy a thousand times for the climate, but above all for the people. That nation has been strangely calumniated, I assure you. They wanted to keep me in Rome, and I would certainly have stayed there if a sense of duty had not overcome my feelings. It seemed to me that I could perform some good in France, and I returned to be the butt of insult, hatred and persecution,"* (October 19).[28]

Félicité was indeed offered a room at the Vatican, and there was unofficial and unrecorded talk of a cardinal's hat for him.[29] There is little mention of conflict in the Roman correspondence of the time, but the controversy about his understanding of the *sensus communis* as the basis for certitude followed him to Rome, the philosophical arguments of the Jesuit Rosaven weighing in opposition. He returned from Italy with more support and encouragement than scrutiny and questioning, and stood by his convictions without responding to the written observations sent to him by Rosaven in France.[30]

Controversy aside, the Roman pilgrimage of 1824 was an inspiring experience for the "recluse of La Chesnaie." as Félicité often styled himself. [31] He was still in Rome when John was preparing to leave Paris. The elder's return to Brittany revived his hopes for the renewal of a partnership with the brother whose influence had inspired his early writings. John was then reorienting his life in ways likely to shatter his brother's hopes, but unexpected circumstances would abridge the transition and bond their lives again.

Ill winds sweep the land!

"Faith is now on the wane, subtly undermined by a subdued and clever persecution; you would hardly recognize this miserable land, and you would tremble at the thought of the sinister future threatening it," (October 8, 1823). [32] Even before leaving for Italy, Félicité was not exaggerating when he penned such observations to Bruté de Rémur. The early years of the Restoration had opened a springtime of Christian renewal, exasperating the enemies of religion. Their reprisal appalled the nation as an undertow of incredulity swept the land with each changing political fortune.

Father Antoine de Salinis, chaplain of the *Lycée Henry IV* in Paris, and future friend of Félicité, observed that in his school as elsewhere, the impious books of the eighteenth century led the faithlessness of most young men. The pockets of a student in rhetoric or philosophy were more likely to hold the *Ruins* of Volney or the book of Dupuy on the origin of cults than the Imitation of Christ. [33] Book dealers and reading rooms offered an alarming flow of controversial works. The *"undefinable torment"* which followed was inescapable: *"man is up against the most terrible interior conflict; he doubts everything of the eternal truths once taught to him."* [34]

The diffusion of impious works reached unprecedented levels since the Revolution. *"It would be a mistake ... to minimize the influence of the materialist trend of thought, deist or atheist, on the spirit of the times. Even without new works, all were provided with innumerable editions of XVIIIth century authors."* Between 1817 and 1824, 1,598, 000 volumes of the works of Voltaire, and 492,000 of those of Rousseau were published. Once

Charles X succeeded to Louis XVIII and the elections of 1824 defeated the liberals, *"the only resource left to the opposition was to appeal to the French love of freedom of thought and expression, and to raise the specter of a clerical domination bent on oppressing both conscience and intelligence."*

The campaign which followed was both political and antireligious. It utilized all the means likely to influence public opinion: *"caricatures, songs, satirical poems, pamphlets, theater, newspapers, coffeehouse talk, and public demonstrations."* [35] Some city governments tolerated the parody of liturgical celebrations, even on religious holidays with demoralizing consequences. In 1826, Macchi, the Apostolic Nuncio in Paris reported: *"More than half of the nation is in total ignorance of the duties of a Christian, and is steeped in indifference. In Paris, one eighth of the population is practicing, and we may wonder if 10,000 men practice in the capital."* [36] The number of illegitimate births increased and in less than eight years, Paris recorded 2,808 suicides.

It was difficult to defeat the royalists with attacks on the successor of Louis XVIII. Prosperity had returned to France with the Bourbons; the "pious" Charles X exasperated the liberals with his Church leanings, but he had also abolished censorship of the press. After losing the elections to the Royalists, discrediting the clergy was an indirect way for the opposition to strike at the administration, maneuvering it into confusing decisions. [37] Discrediting defenseless churchmen became common sport, though ironically, the unruly season followed years of successful re-christianization. These were rascal winds, intruders knocking about the harvest, shuffling storm clouds. The tempest had not yet broken, but there was no reason for confidence in the accelerating turbulence as the two La Mennais brothers meditated on the needs of the Church.

The Priests of Saint-Méen, 1825-1828

Was John de La Mennais destined to found a third religious congregation? In January 1825, Msgr. Claude Louis de Lesquen, Bishop of Beauvais, was appointed Bishop of Rennes. He came to his new diocese with a deep interest in the formation of the clergy at a time when two groups of priests sensed the need for reorganization. Bishop Mannay had united the diocesan missionaries into a society without vows; the priests assigned to the minor seminary of Saint-Méen in turn were hoping to gain solidarity in some form of association. [38] Missionaries for retreats in the diocese had been organized in 1821, and seminary teachers felt the need for solidarity.

Father Dubreil had consulted John about organizing the teachers of the minor seminary before the new Bishop took the matter in hand. Soon after assuming office late in June 1825, de Lesquen appointed John de La Mennais Vicar General with extended faculties and asked him to bond his seminary teachers into a viable society. The Bishop's request rang through John's soul as the call of Christ to Peter: *"Strengthen your brothers,"* (Lk. 22:32). In July 1825, John was the Founder and Superior General of the Congregation of the Priests of Saint-Méen, (Pronounce: Main). [39]

Reorganization began with the teachers at the diocesan seminary of Saint-Méen. Father Pierre François Coëdro, director of the missionaries, immediately requested personal membership in the seminary society and invited his companions to join him. Fathers Dubreuil and Bouteloup (treasurer of the seminary), and some of their colleagues expressed misgivings lest the interests of Coëdro and his missionaries create substantial problems of unity for the new Congregation. Nevertheless, the Bishop and Father de La Mennais associated the two groups in the new Congregation.

The foundation radically transformed John's personal relationships. He later admitted to its members: *"I always had the intention of contributing to the establishment of a congregation similar to this one ... but I did not intend to be part of it."* [40] He meant to limit his attention to the work of his two Congregations of elementary school teachers without undertaking another of a different nature, but he became a member of the new religious congregation at the request of his Bishop. He denied that he planned to merge his Congregation of brothers with the new Congregation of priests: *"Nothing is more contrary to my thinking. .... I want one to be distinct from the other, but the first will have as major superior the superior of the second,"* (June 4, 1826). [41] The Congregation of Saint-Méen evolved into a different society before he could realize that plan.

In 1825, besides overseeing the work of his Daughters of Providence, John de La Mennais was restoring Ploërmel as the center of the Congregation of the Brothers of Christian Instruction. He was coordinating the academic work of the brothers, and issuing the second edition of their printed *Constitutions*. He had recently renovated and refurnished the chapel where he would invite his brother priests to answer the call of their Bishop; John assumed his new responsibilities without delay.

By early July, the statutes were drafted and Bishop de Lesquen signed the initial agreement on July 8, 1825. Father de La Mennais convened the five founding members at Ploërmel for September 8. De Lesquen named Father de La Mennais Superior General, who in turn chose Father Coëdro as first assistant and superior of the missionaries, Father Dubreuil as second assistant and superior of the minor seminary, and Father Bouteloup as treasurer of the same seminary. On November 4, 1825, the first members established common ownership of funds and property, clarified their civil status and defined their relationship with the diocese. The legal entity entitled *Société Universelle des Biens* set the terms of ownership under civil law. [42]

The *Statutes* include seventeen articles, the Rules fifteen. The Founder proposed them as very incomplete; he later explained to a friend and advisee: *"You will remember that I need several years to guarantee the success of my enterprise; but what enduring institution can be improvised? We expect to reap the day after sowing. Note that our charter is very incomplete, though it is a folly to attempt to solve everything in advance,"* (June 4, 1826). [43] John de La Mennais had no such pretensions.

The statutes gave structure and direction to the new Congregation. It defined essential responsibilities, regulated the use of common funds, established the authority of the General Council with respect to the foundation of new houses, and attributed voting rights for the election of the superior general. John reduced directives to a minimum with the understanding that experience would inspire adjustments. He regarded the continuing personal development of its members too important to leave to chance. He accordingly urged them to take study seriously and prescribed two weekly conferences, one on spirituality, the other on theology. He invited each member to prepare the latter with a written reply to a question proposed by the superior. In study and preaching he advised personal alertness. He insisted on adequate preparation for all public talks to offset the sterile glibness so routinely generated by the habit of the rostrum.

The statement of objectives and retreat sermons reveal his soul. The call for service rings through his retreat sermons of September 1825: *"Profoundly afflicted by the ills of the Church, and in the inability of healing them all, we would like to alleviate them to the limit of our strength; we see the divine spouse of Jesus Christ attacked from all quarters, and we see no one assuming the defense of that illustrious forsaken one,"* (September 1825). [44]

The Congregation chose the formation of enlightened, virtuous and capable priests at the minor seminary of Saint-Méen as its primary goal, but without closing off additional realistic options. John supervised the new Congregation in the details of its operation, with special attention to the minor seminary. At Saint-Méen, he organized a lay congregation of the Blessed Virgin to motivate the more dedicated students.

The mission apostolate, the second objective of the Congregation, was not neglected. During the first year, the missionaries conducted retreats in Fougeray, la Fontenelle, Bain and Cancale. When members met for their second annual retreat in September 1826, Father de La Mennais reminded them that the mission apostolate was *"not less important"* than seminary formation, that solidarity and mutual assistance was essential to the work of its members. The Missionaries presided over the observance of the special jubilee proclaimed by Pope Leo XII; the Diocese of Rennes celebrated it in the fall of 1826 with retreats, processions and special liturgies.

John described a procession with three hundred ecclesiastics and eighteen thousand participants. Three thousand men were present every night at the men's retreat in the church of Saint Germain. Retreat exercises were attended by men and women in numbers that left no place empty. At the cathedral celebration all six-to-seven thousand seats were filled at four; the other churches holding the celebration simultaneously were also filled to capacity. [45] After Rennes, the missionaries worked during six months organizing jubilee exercises in Saint-Malo, Saint-Méen, Fougères and Redon. By his own participation, Father de La Mennais revealed that he had not lost his zeal for the retreat apostolate.

The society of 1825 was manifesting its potential. The retreat of 1827 began its transformation *"from a small diocesan institute with modest objectives, into a congregation with a spirit and works that sustain its mission."* [46]Receptive men opened to the vision of an enterprising founder began to think of service wherever Providence led them. The goal: all good works which could be realistically undertaken to further the glory of God and the cause of truth. The limit: the capacity of individuals, the number of laborers, and the invincible obstacles.

Seven recruits joined the founders in 1826, two came in 1827, three in 1828. In 1826, Father de La Mennais wrote that the society counted eighteen members. He hoped to double that number within two years and estimated its minimum needs at about forty: one superior general, one master of novices and two teachers, twelve missionaries, twelve to fifteen teachers in all fields, and eight to ten young novices.

In his written insights of November 13, 1807, (the *Torrent d'idées*), John had acknowledged the necessity of reforming seminary studies. He considered the promotion of religious orders and the restoration of the Jesuits as vital factors in the life of the Church. Félicité was a recent convert to religious practice, and both were involved in the education of future priests in Saint-Malo. John's ideas reappeared in print under the pen of Félicité in the anonymous Réflexions of 1809: *"It would be desirable to establish one or several religious congregations, assigned especially to the administration of seminaries.... It is not only priests, but rather good priests, zealous and enlightened that we need,"* (pages 139-140). [47] Félicité wrote as a recent convert, but his earlier publications reflect a close association with the interests of his elder. After sharing his brother's inspiration, his pen had lost none of its power In 1824, he returned from

Rome with reexamined insights, revived motivation, quickened incentives, and a desire to work with his brother without abdicating his autonomy.

Félicité and his disciples of La Chesnaie

While John was founding the Congregation of Saint-Méen, Félicité was rallying militants, Fathers de Salinis and Gerbet, chaplains at the *Lycée Henry IV*. [48] The school where they had been serving since 1822 ranked as the Oxford and Cambridge of France. De Salinis was the first assistant chaplain, Gerbet the second. The loss of faith among students and in the general population disturbed the two active priests. De Salinis reacted by organizing conferences on the leading religious issues of the day, talks which drew a swelling attendance.

The defamation of the Church so shocked the two priests that in January 1824, they founded the weekly *Mémorial catholique* before Félicité's departure for Italy. [49] Realizing the difficulty of opposing the misrepresentation of Church teaching, they asked John to encourage their beginnings by lending his name as a director. His responsibilities prevented him from serving as an active contributor, but he accepted supervisory directorship and remained a distant guide and a sometimes critical advisor through the short life of the paper. He also convinced his brother to write a letter of support for its first issue. Félicité doubted the possibility of extended success, but admitted that a publication of the kind was *"absolutely"* lacking. The *Mémorial catholique* appeared from 1824 to 1830, when *l'Avenir* superseded it under a reorganized group of sponsors.

The example of his two friends inspired Félicité to plunge into aggressive polemics. In April 1825, he published the first part of an essay on the relation of religion to the political and social order, *(De la Religion considérée dans ses rapports avec l'Ordre politique et social)*; a second part followed in February of the following year. [50] Experience should have taught him to avoid riling his opponents; it did not and on April 22, 1826, his trenchant rhetoric earned him a condemnation in the courts. The Gallican clergy joined in the fray. On April 3, 1826, Msgr. Frayssinous, Minister for Ecclesiastical Affairs and fourteen bishops signed and published a joint declaration against him, appealing to the King and suggesting papal intervention. They pursued their denunciation in *Le Moniteur*, the official government journal. [51]

Referring to Jesuits as *"grenadiers of folly"* and characterizing public administrators by name as *"successors of Henry VIII,"* did not improve relationships. [52] The temperamental violence which broke through his correspondence typified his attitude: *"I would choose the Mémorial to express my thoughts if I wrote in a periodical publication at this time. The time for vain deference is over, we must express ourselves clearly in all things, and I have often observed that in our time, what is not frank, whole and resolute, is without impact on minds. The world can no longer stop at in-betweens; hence there is war against Christianity in France,"* (January 3, 1825). [53]

Félicité assiduously analyzed the state of affairs during his frequent visits with Fathers De Salinis and Gerbet in Paris. The spectacle of a defenseless Church with ministers unprepared to face challengers pained the three friends. John had envisioned *"the reorganization of a learned theological team in France"* in *His Torrent d'idées*, private notes written on November 13, 1807 John and Félicité jointly pressed for action in the anonymous Réflexions of 1809: *"It is essential that we act to conserve the ecclesiastical sciences, the study of which was never so neglected and so necessary. ... Could it be that we do not realize the importance of forming defenders of the faith?"* [54] The cause resurfaced in Félicité's agenda.

By 1824, experience and controversy had convinced Félicité that the solidarity of a working group was urgent. He wrote to John from Geneva: *"It is obvious that a great deal needs to be done everywhere, and it is obvious that nothing is done. Good men seem unaware that only evil men act and accomplish their work. The world relapses into chaos, and darkness lies on the face of the abyss. I do not know whether your situation will be settled at my return. It is probably best for it to remain undecided for a while still. Yet, I will personally have to decide on a course of action next fall,"* (May 16, 1824).

After his return from Italy, he outlined his preliminary planning: *"You know that we plan to assemble here* [at La Chesnaie], *a few friends to live and to work together. That seems to be working out even better than we expected. Persons in whom I have taken interest desire to dedicate themselves to the education of the young, and they might take charge of the Collège of Juilly, which is in an advanced state of decline. They would be very pleased to receive your advice, and insofar as I am concerned, I have an extreme desire that we both meet. Reflect on this, and answer me as soon as possible,"* (Late February, early March 1826). [55]

Through extended conversations with Gerbet and de Salinis, Félicité had won their admiration. Late in 1824, in the salon of Father de Salinis at the *Lycée Henri IV,* he suggested the formation of a society of learned men associated in the defense of the faith. The biographer of Gerbet expresses *"the spirit"* of the discussions. Gerbet cautioned against Félicité's assertiveness: *"Do you not fear to irritate reason rather than influence it by that categorical procedure? Would it not be preferable to reconcile the soul with religion by showing the harmony between its dogmas, precepts, institutions with the deepest aspirations of humanity?"* After claiming that his approach and the observations of Gerbet were complementary, Félicité invited his friends to unite with him in a common enterprise; the thinking which came to be known as "the school of La Chesnaie," was born here. [56]

Gerbet was the first to establish residence at La Chesnaie. He resigned from his chaplaincy and followed Félicité to Brittany in the middle of January, 1825. He quickly wrote to de Salinis: *"In his [Félicité's] reflections on his project for a society of priests, about which he has so often spoken, he thought that we could start by assembling four or five of us to study and write a suitable location would be available in Brittany. The income from the works of that society would be of great assistance to the establishment. The name of Mr. de La Mennais, the character of that society would immediately attract public attention and contribute to their distribution."* Then followed observations on the possibility of initial funding: *"Once properly organized, a few young men could be successively received. Mr. de La Mennais attaches the highest importance to all* (January 16, 1825). [57] De Salinis held back, judging the project too this,"' ambitious and in need of rethinking, but he set out to seek funding, though with little success.

Félicité worked at La Chesnaie until February 1826, then returned to Paris where ill health slowed his pace. He confessed to his brother: *"I have fallen ill several times, and I must observe great caution and take much rest, without which my indisposition would likely degenerate into heart disease,"(* March 11, 1826) [58]. He referred to this condition in his letters until the end of the year though he did not consider the condition serious. In August, he yielded to medical advice, announced that writing was forbidden to him, and he prepared to spend a month at the spa of Saint-Sauveur in the Pyrenees with Father de Salinis.

Felicite left Paris on August 26, and returned on October 15. He describes the experience in a letter to the Countess of Senfft: *"My voyage has been a sort of continual agony. A few leagues from Montauban, near Moissac, they needed to take me from the coach and to lay me to bed in a farmhouse. Then, from stop to stop, and from seizure to seizure, I finally arrived here,"* (September 28, 1826). He wrote to John on his return to Paris: *"My illness is exclusively nervous; no organ is attacked. I expected much from the journey, but the jostling of the coach proved to be quite incompatible with my condition. Finally, I am back, and I very much long to see you,"* (October 7, 1826). He sometimes described his case as a heart condition with choking and fainting seizures.

Felicite was back at work in October. His little following began to assemble while the government kept close watch on his activities, and the Gallican clergy tightened ranks against his defense of Papal authority. In 1826, René François Rohrbacher,[59] a priest from Lorraine, joined the group after reading *Essai sur l'Indifférence*. Others were showing interest; the writer observed the progress of his disciples without losing hope that his brother would join them.

Call to arms, shadow of death

Félicité often commented that he rarely saw his brother at La Chesnaie or Paris, then only briefly or for a few days whenever he did. After his return from the spa of Saint-Sauveur, he asked for serious conversations in Paris: *"I urge you to come in February to have more time, for we have much to say to each other,"* (October 20, 1826). *"Father Le T,* [for Le Tourneur] *will acquaint you with the gist of what I wish to converse with you,"* (November 2, 1826). He insisted: *"I will have a great deal to say,"* (November 15, 1826). [60]

Signs of anxiety surfaced in his correspondence before John's visit. He wrote to the Count of Senfft: *"I have already mentioned to you what holds me here: duty, a grave duty. I am ashamed to say so, but I do not believe to be moved by self-interest, I find myself at the center of those who love and defend religion in this country. Should I go, everything would dissolve. I work so that the good that I attempt to do may survive me, and I hope to succeed despite innumerable obstacles. If I gave up the work, it would collapse instantly. Would I then not be responsible to God?"* (December 22, 1826).

In less than two months, he wrote to the Countess of Senfft: *"Pray, pray for a poor priest, reminded of his inadequacy by everything, and who in that state, may have a grave and important decision to make,"* (February 14, 1827). [61] The projected conversations began when John visited on March 17. John quickly realized that Félicité needed rest. He wrote to the Count: *"I came to meet my brother and to take him to Brittany: though his health is better, I did not want to expose him to travel non-stop alone,"* (April 9, 1827) [62]. They travelled short journeys and stopped to sleep every night. Neighbors who thought Félicité dé ad hailed him as a resurrected man in the peace of La Chesnaie. As Superior General of the priests of Saint-Méen, John left immediately to join his missionaries for the jubilee celebrations in Redon.

Agony forced Félicité to bed on July 15. Gerbet began to write his letters as his condition deteriorated. Ange Blaize, his brother-in-law, was so concerned that he notified the elder. It would hardly be possible to give a better report of events than the account written by Father Gerbet to the Baroness Cottu: *"I arrived at La Chesnaie on the day before he fell ill. Fever seized him on Sunday, July 15 towards ten o'clock at night ... he twice fainted in my arms: I thought him dead! ... 'My friend', said he, 'I have a desire to leave, I have quite enough of this world'. He had asked for the last rites early. His reception of the Holy Viaticum was a very beautiful day for his radiant faith . ... His brother administered the last rites [July*

26]. When that poor brother arrived, he said to him after a few moments of conversation: 'I hand over to you the most beautiful thing in the world, truth to defend.' I recall also on a night when he felt better; I was telling him by way of distraction, that it was a superb moonlit night. He tried to raise himself to catch a glimpse of it through the window, and told me on falling back: 'For my peace, if it pleased God, it would be my last!' All the signs of the end came on Sunday, July 25, from five to eleven in the evening. His poor brother begged me to repeat the absolution of the dying. A change for the better began at eleven." (September 8, 1827). [63]

Insecure steps and signs of healing followed before Félicité could write to De Salinis: *"I am in fair health, but very weak; work fatigues me and the principle of life is worn out: I must hurry. If I finish what I have in mind, and if God still grants me a few years, I will consecrate them to occupations of another type; you will understand what I intend to say,"* (November 5, 1827). [64] The writer's last night had not yet come; surviving convalescence sharpened his quill with an eye to the battlefront. Where would truth and religion find a more resolute champion?

Félicité and his early followers associated more closely with the Congregation of Saint-Méen at this time in 1827. On June 21, Félicité instructed Gerbet to stop at the house of the missionaries in Rennes on the way from Paris to La Chesnaie. Rohrbacher was then working with the *Mémorial catholique;* he sent him to John on June 6 in view of preparing him for a deeper involvement with the work at hand. John agreed, invited Rohrbacher to the September retreat in Rennes, and admitted him to the novitiate. [65]

The quiet transformations of Félicité's work did not originate in a void. A few months before John began to organize the Congregation of Saint-Méen, Félicité was pondering the possibility of rallying a few laymen and priests to work for the cause of religion. By 1827, he was seriously planning a clerical religious congregation. Félicité and his disciples were evolving as he assembled new disciples, Father Combalot and Rohrbacher at the novitiate. [66] Félicité was meditating the future of his society while drafting a plan of action meant for Pope Leo XII. He was pursuing new goals, but not alone.

∎

Historians have written different scenarios about this phase of his life. [67] Whatever their sources and their assessment, two facts stand out as undeniable: (1) The unpublicized thinking of Félicité was quietly changing and (2) the two brothers were working closely together. F. Duine states it as follows: *"In his projects, Félicité was singularly assisted by his brother, who admired him and shared all his ideas. Moreover, Father John, had an aptitude for religious foundations, with an understanding of organizations, and a capacity for action which vitalizes his life."* [68]

John was then directing a well-organized society. At the end of 1827, the Congregation of Saint-Méen had two residences: the minor seminary administered by Father Dubreuil at Saint-Méen, and the home of the missionaries administered by Father Coëdro in Rennes, in a residence too small to house the novices. The Congregation of Saint-Méen and the little group of Félicité were both changing: a wider opening to church ministries was transforming the Congregation of Saint-Méen while Félicité was leading his disciples into a closer relationship with it. There was litttle promise of national peace in the crescendo of irreligion or in the disputes of feuding churchmen. The two brothers were toiling in foul weather with generous disciples; mischievous winds and rumbles of brewing storms called for readiness and resolution.

---

[1] On the childhood and youth of Félicité, see Anatole Feugère, Lamennais avant l'*"Essai sur l'Indifférence"* ... (1782-1817), Paris: Bloud, 1906, pages 15-43. Christian Marechal, *La Jeunesse de LaMennais* ... Paris: Perrin, 1913. Pages 9-87. Jean Lebrun, Lamennaisou l'Inquiétude de la Liberté, Paris: Fayard, 1981, pages 11-29. CharlespAugustin Sainte-Beuve, *Critiques et Portraits Littéraires,* Paris : Eugène Renduel, 1836.

[2] *Oeuvres inédites de F. Lamennais,* publiées par Ange Blaize, Paris: Dentu, 1866. Vol. 1, Introduction, p. 8.

[3] As narrated in chapters 5-7.

[4] **AFIC** 030-05-002.

[5] On this period of his life, see Anatole Feugère, *Lamennais avantl'Essai sur l'Indifférence, d'après des documents inédits* (1782-1817), Paris:

Bloud, 1906. Pp. 104-148. Christian Marechal, *La Jeunesse deLa Mennais,* Paris: Perrin, 1913, pages 251-298.

[6] (1809, undated) **Cor gén F,** vol 1, pp 77-78.

[7] **Cor gén J,** v. 1, pp. 323-324. See also the following letter toBruté de Rémur.

[8] **Cor gén F,** vol. 1, p. 278.

[9] **Cor gén J,** v. 1, p. 413. See **SA (1960),** pages 55-56, 64-65, 87-89.

[10] From a postscript to a letter of Father Carron to John. **Cor gén F,** vol. 1, pp. 310, 311. See the letters from February to July, pp. 303-312.

[11] As quoted in F. Duine, *La Mennais, sa Vie, ses Idées, ses Ouvrages,* Paris: Garnier, 1922, page 61. See pages 59-66, 84-91. CharlesBoutard, *Lamennais, sa Vie et ses Doctrines.* Vol. 1, *La Renaissance del'Ultramontisme,* 1782-1828, Paris: Perrin, 1905, pp. 132-148. AlfredNettement, *Histoire de la Littérature française sous la Restauration,* quatrième édition. Paris: Victor Lecoffre, 1888. 2 vols., Vol 2, pp. 213-239.

[12] Jean Lebrun, *La Mennais ou l'Inquiétude de la Liberté,* Paris: Fayard-Mame, 1981, pages 49-67, the chapter on *"L'Essai: critique et reconstruction,"* and pp. 70-93, *"L impatience de l'universel."*

[13] **Cor gén J,** v. 2, p. 64.

[14] Letter to John, **Cor gén F,** v. 1, pp. 436-427.

[15] **Cor gén F,** yol 1, p. 426. The death of Louis-Marie, the elder, had broken him (See chapters 5-6).

[16] Ibid., vol. 2, pp. 578-579, 595, (See letters from De Maistre, pp. 538, 565, 577).

[17] On the controversy which followed the *Essai,* see Jean Lebrun, *Lamennais ou l'Inquiétude de la Liberté,* Paris: Fayard-Mame, 1981, pp. 73-84. F. Duine, *La Mennais, Sa Vie, ses Idées, ses Ouvrages.* Paris: Garnier, 1922, pp. 84-91.

[18] Charles Boutard, *Lamennais, Sa Vie et ses Doctrines,* Paris: Librairie Académique Didier Perrin, 1905-1913. 3 vols. Vol 1, *La Renaissance de l'Ultramontisme,* 1782-1828, pp. 216, 381-385. Other authors had discussed the doctrine and two of the friends of Félicité wrote about *sensus communis (le sens commun)* without incurring church doctrinal objections.

[19] Alfred Nettement, *Histoire de la Littérature française sous la Restauration,* Paris: Lecoffre, 1888. Vol. 2, pp. 222-223.

[20] Such commentaries were expected by readers of this classic in the editions of the time.

[21] On the ascetical works see: Charles Boutard, *Lamennais, sa Vie etses Doctrines,* Vol 1, "La Renaissance de l'Ultramontisme, 1782-1828," Paris: Librairie académique Didier, Perrin, 1905, pages 273-285.
Antoine Ricard, *Lamennais et son École,* Paris: Librairie académique Didier, 1881, pp. 165-193.

[22] In **Cor gén** see letters to Ange Blaize, March 28, 1819 in v. 1, pp. 520-521, to Marion, March 4, 20; April 13 and May 13, 1821, v. 2, pp. 171, 172, 176, 180; to Benoit d'Azy and Baron de Vitrolles, both on February 4, 1823, v. 2, pp. 375-377.

[23] **Cor gén J,** v. 2, pp. 282-283. See Philippe Friot, **ÉM,** No. 10 (July1993), pp. 65-66. Louis Le Guillou, *L'Évolution de la Pensée religieuse de Félicité Lamennais,* Paris: Armand Colin, 1966, pp. 131-138. Some writers conjecture that he was seeking a Roman declaration in support of his writings, but his letters and the documents of the time do not support that assumption.

[24] **Cor gén F,** vol. 2, pp. 454 and following. See his letters to John and to friends, at the dates given.

[25] **Cor gén J,** v. 2, p. 304.

[26] Literally, *"la main dans le coeur:"* hand in the heart.

[27] See Boutard, op. cit., vol. 1, pp. 256-272.

[28] **Cor gén F,** vol 2, pp. 495, 510. The special conversation did not occur and Félicité left for Naples. After his return, he visited with the Pope briefly then left Rome.

[29] Evidence of conversations on the subject appear in John's correspondence. See Boutard, op. cit., V. 1, pp. 256-272. Paul Dudon, *Lamennais et le Saint-Siège,* 1820-1854, Paris: Librairie Académique Perrin, 1911, pp. 17-32. Louis Le Guillou, "Lamennais fut-il créé Cardinal par Léon XII?" *Cahiers mennaisiens* (Brest), No. 9 (1978), pp. 1-8. After studying the biographers, it seems impossible to conclude the matter beyond the honest acceptance of probability.

[30] **Cor gén F,** vol. 2, pp. 685-688.

[31] His expression was, *"Solitaire de La Chesnaie."*

[32] **Cor gén F,** v. 2, p. 412.

[33] Antoine Ricard, *Gerbet, Salinis et Rohrbacher. L'Écolemennaisienne,* Paris: Plon, 1886. P. 174

[34] Vicomte de Guichen, *La France morale et religieuse à la fin de la Restauration,* Paris: Émile-Paul, 1912, p. 104; see also pages 103-104, 158-159.

[35] G. De Bertier de Sauvigny, *La Restauration, Troisième édition revue et augmentée,* Paris: Flammarion, 1955, pages 344, 282, 383.

[36] L.-J. Rogier, and others, *Nouvelle Histoire de l'Église, vol. 4, Siècle des Lumières, Révolutions, Restaurations,* Paris, Seuil, 1966. Vol 4, p. 320. See 324-325.

[37] Georges Bordonove, *Charles X, Dernier Roi de France et de Navarre,* Paris: Pygmalion / Gérard Watelet, 1990, p. 188.

[38] Charles Mannay (1745-1824), bishop of Rennes from 1821 to his death, December 5, 1824.

[39] See generally Philippe Friot, "Jean-Marie de La Mennais et la Congrégation des prêtres de Saint-Méen, (1825-1828)," **ÉM,** no. 16, (April, 1996). André Dargis, "La Congrégation de Saint-Pierre," Louvain (Belgium): Université catholique de Louvain, Faculté det héologie, 1971. Mimeographed copy of unpublished doctoral dissertation, pages 54-122. **SA (1960),** pages 184-197, 399-404, 421-426. Symphorien-Auguste, *À Travers la Correspondance de L'abbé J. M. de la Mennais,* Deuxième série. Vannes: Lafolye et de Lamarzellle, 1938, pages 1-20. **Lav,** vol. 1, pages 418-433.

[40] Sermon preached to the priests of Saint-Méen in 1826. Symphorien-Auguste, *À Travers la Correspondance de L'abbé J. M. de la Mennais* ,Deuxième série. Vannes:Lafolye et de Lamarzellle, 1938, p. 5.

[41] Letter to Father Mazelier, **Cor gén J,** v. 2, p. 362.

[42] **Cor gén J,** v. 2, p. 346.

[43] Ibid.

[44] Retreat sermon to the founders of the priests of the Congregation of Saint-Méen. **AFIC,** Sermons, 54-564. Text in Dargis, op. cit., Annex volume, pp. 14-16, excerpt in **ÉM,** 16 (April 1996), page 21.

[45] **Lav,** vol. 1, p. 432, note 1. **EM,** no. 16 (April 1996), p. 39.

[46] Dargis, op. cit., p. 108.

[47] See chapter 6 on the *Torrent d'idées* (torrent of ideas) **ÉM,** No. 2 (April, 1988) and *Réflexions.*

[48] Louis Antoine de Salinis (1798-1861), and Philippe Olymphe Gerbet (1798-1864).

[49] Jean René Derré, *Lamennais, ses amis et le mouvement des idées à l'Époque romantique* (1824-1834), Paris: Klincksieck, 1962, pages 169-225, *"Luttes et doctrines du Mémorial catholique."*

[50] Charles Boutard, *Lamennais, sa Vie et ses Doctrines,* Vol. 1, "La Renaissance de l'Ultramontisme, 1782-1828," Paris: Librairie académique Didier, Perrin, 1905, pages 287-324. **Cor gén F,** vol. 3, pp. 166-171, *"Rapport judiciaire ..."* See the letter (April 14, 1826) of Msgr. Frayssinous requesting the signature of additional bishops, v. 3, p. 186.

[51] In writings from 1825 to 1829.

[52] See Derré, op. cit., p. 282. Jean Leflon, *La Crise révolutionnaire,* 1789-1846, ("Histoire de l'Église depuis les Origines jusqu'à nos Jours" sous la direction de A. Fliche et V. Martin, vol. 20), Paris: Bloud et Gay, 1949, pp. 397-398.

[53] Letter to Father Baraldi. **Cor gén F,** v. 3, p.12.

[54] From page 141 of the *Réflexions* (referred to in chapter 6), and Article 23 of the *Torrent d'idées,* ÉM, No. 2, (April 1988), pp. 25-29.

[55] **Cor gén F,** vol. 2, p. 474, and vol. 3, p. 161. In postscript to the second letter, Gerbet expresses his support for the plans of Félicité other letters cited are at the date given.

[56] De Ladoue, *Monseigneur Gerbet, sa vie et ses oeuvres et l'École mennaisienne:* Paris, Librairie Saint-Joseph, Torla, 1872, 2 vols, v. 1, pp. 63-64. Certain authors have dated these conversations, giving December 1824 (Laveille, v. I, p. 423), 1826 (Ricard, p. 134). Ladoue, wrote about the *"spirit (l'esprit)"* of the conversations, without specifying the month, but Gerbet followed Félicité at La Chesnaie early in January 1825. See **Lav,** v. 1, pp. 422-424. Antoine Ricard, *Lamennais et son École,* Paris: Librairie académique Didier, 1881, pp. 133-164.

[57] De Ladoue, *Monseigneur Gerbet, Sa vie, ses oeuvres et l'École mennaisiene,* Paris: Librairie Saint-Joseph, Tolra, 2 v. V. 1, pp. 66-67. See pp. 52-73.

[58] **Cor gén F,** vol 3, p. 162. See letters in the following pages 260 for comments on his health.

[59] René François Rohrbacher (1789-1856).

[60] Letters to John. **Cor gén F,** v. 3, pp. 235, 239, 242.

[61] **Cor gén F,** v. 3, pp. 255-256, 276. He had written earlier to Father Ventura: *"Do not worry that persecution might frighten me and deter me*

from my obligations. With the grace of God, I will fulfill them to the end," (May 14, 1826), ibid., p. 200.

[62] Letters to the Count and Countess of Senfft, March 18 and 27. **Corgén F**, v. 3, pp. 299, 301, 305 note 1 (John's letter to Senfft, alsoin **Cor gén J**, v. 2, p. 384).

[63] **Lav,** v. 1, pp. 439-441, **Cor gén F**, v. 3, pp. 361-367. Boutard, op. cit., v. 1, pp. 373-379.

[64] Letter from Félicité to Rohrbacher. **Cor gén F,** v. 3, p. 334.

[65] Dargis, op. cit., p. 170.

[66] Théodore Combalot, (1797-1873).

[67] Clues from the letters of Félicité and from his activities reveal evolution in his planning. The lack of more precise documentation makes it difficult to reconcile statements of historians.

[68] F. Duine, *La Mennais, Sa Vie, ses Idées, ses Ouvrages.* Paris: Garnier, 1922, p. 118.

Chapter 19

THE CONGREGATION OF SAINT PETER, 1828-1834

The Ordinances of June 16, 1828

In 1828, the Martignac government adapted one of Napoleon's finely crafted expedients to weaken the influence of bishops, and used it against the Society of Jesus and minor seminaries. The government manipulation of education and church life never left John and Félicité de La Mennais indifferent. [1] The Jesuits were active seminary teachers who had reorganized under Church rule despite the proscriptions of civil law against their society; they soon realized the futility of seeking reconciliation with hostile public administrators. On December 27, 1827, the government announced that it would take legal action against the schools of religious orders that were unauthorized under civil law. [2]

The Ordinances of June 1828 dealt with secondary schools exclusively. The Ordinance of October 5, 1814, had given the bishops full authority over their minor seminaries, until the creation of a Ministry for Ecclesiastical Affairs and Public Instruction on August 26, 1824. [3] The new authority seized control of elementary and secondary schools, and in June, the government legalized control over the education of future priests by classifying minor seminaries as *colleges,* then regimenting them accordingly. An outrageous propagation of untruth had paved the way for such procedures before the electoral victory of the liberals in 1827. The extended campaign systematically vilified the role of the clergy in education and public life, discredited the association known as la *Congrégation* and the Jesuits, [4] Montlosier and others denounced the political misdeeds attributed to the "priest party."

The government requested an inquiry of secondary schools. A commission headed by Portalis[5] prepared a report whose recommendations failed to convince the leading committee of the need for additional controls; nevertheless, the men of the ministry pursued their objectives. Portalis drafted ordinances, presented them as necessary measures to restore "legality" in the administration of secondary schools, and pressured the King to sign them. The King yielded after painful hesitations. [6] Félicité had written to his friend, the lawyer Berryer, *"It is Catholicism that it seeks to destroy, only it."* He called the report: *"a declaration of war against the Church and the beginning of persecution."* [7]

But exactly how serious was the decried Jesuit menace? Reports listed 126 legally authorized minor seminaries, and 53 unauthorized schools of the same category. Of the 53, eight were Jesuit schools. [8] The Jesuits lived their religious commitment discretely, discharging their ministry, preaching missions. They also taught in diocesan minor seminaries at the request of bishops, sometimes in personal capacity rather than as members of a religious order. Some were serving in the eight Jesuit institutions mentioned in the report. The insidious domination attributed to them never existed. While the government spoke of restoring "legality," the officious plan was to strike at the Jesuits as a way of influencing the education of future priests in all minor seminaries.

Two ordinances were signed on June 16, 1828. The first transferred to the *Université* control over all secondary schools belonging to a religious congregation not approved by the government. The eight Jesuit schools were summarily taken by the government, and teachers were required to declare that they were not members of an "unauthorized" religious order. The second ordinance set student quotas, and required government permits to open new ecclesiastical schools. [9]

Taken together, these ordinances scored the most complete triumph of the anti-religious party since the Restoration. It was a double victory, one for anti-clerical, one for Gallicanism. By siding with the Gallicans, the party divided the clergy and exploited rivalries between Gallicans and defenders of Papal authority. Clerical skirmishing diverted attention from the new policies, while government ordinances reduced the number of seminary students, invalidating the degrees of those leaving the seminaries, and harassed administrators with confusing rules. Thus, a government presuming to protect the state against interference from the Church did not hesitate to interfere with the education of seminarians.

The coup alarmed John and Félicité de La Mennais. [10] The closure of Jesuit schools and the secularization of a number of minor seminaries confronted them with a Church crisis closely related to their ministry. John's congregation could not solve the problem, but his men would not abandon the education of future priests to poorly motivated teachers ruled by the *Université*. The government allowed the reopening of Lesquen's minor seminary because his teachers certified that they were not vowed members of a religious Congregation. He made it possible for them to meet the formal requirements by dispensing them from their vows for the duration of their teaching. [11]

Two brothers at work, two religious societies in transition

Would the bishops comply in the government's attempt to control their minor seminaries? Less than a month after the passage of the ordinances, John wrote to the Count of Senfft: *"I expect a better future. The Church will undoubtedly be subjected to new trials; they will be painful, they will be bloody, but we will overcome; only a violent crisis could rescue us. ... Let us have faith and courage. Is it not wonderful to see the French episcopate, which we believed to be so weak, rise as one in the face of danger and turn its eyes toward Rome!* (July 14, 1828). [12] Vain expectation! The Bishops reacted weakly and Roman objections were ineffective.

In 1828, John was serving his third year as Superior General of the Congregation of Saint-Méen. The missionaries of *rue de Fougères* in Rennes were increasing under the leadership of Father Coëdro, while the seminary of Saint-Méen was an active center of theological study under

Father Dubreil. During the retreat of 1827, he had persuaded the Congregation to broaden its objectives. The initial goals had not changed, but the society now widened its vision to consider all good works required for the promotion of Christian life, within or without the diocese. Until 1828, members pronounced only the vow of obedience which incorporated the two others. The home of the missionaries in Rennes was filled beyond capacity. An attempt to acquire a separate home in Rillé near the city of Fougères failed, but at the proclamation of the ordinances, within weeks, John acquired a new novitiate and a house of studies.

The attack on minor seminaries surprised neither John nor Félicité; Félicité had even predicted persecution in 1826. He was still in Italy at the signing of the ordinances, writing his essay on the progress of the revolution and of the war against the Church, published in February 1829. [13] He was reviving interest in his little company and seeking financial support when ill health overtook him. After rising from the "agony" of July 1827, he resumed work with his disciples at La Chesnaie. [14]

His men had rented a provisional study center in Paris, *(rue d'Enfer)* and kept a close association with the office of the *Mémorial catholique*. The early members had changed little, with Gerbet at La Chesnaie since January 1825, and Rohrbacher in action since April 1826. Father Combalot who followed him in 1827, helped as financial administrator. The circle widened as Félicité kept active relationships with a number of interested correspondents. His letters to Miss de Lucinière and Berryer reveal that financial embarrassment increased with membership. [15] Felicite needed to strengthen the *Association pour la Défense de la Religion catholique* which supported activities with annual contributions.

Anxiety over trail-blazing decisions shadowed all the activities of that period. In 1827, Félicité began to advise the Holy See about his personal views on religious and political events. He had been sending copies of his new writings to the Apostolic Nuncio in Paris. Early that year, he addressed a long confidential memorandum to Pope Leo XII on the situation of the Church in France. [16] Representatives of the Vatican were approvingly aware of his activities. The Marquis of Coriolis wrote from Paris that the Apostolic Nuncio would like him to reside in Paris: *"He would like you to be directing a political and religious journal that would be widely accessible and able to neutralize the venom of evil. He says that there is leverage only in journals, and that books are not read by those who are the most seriously ill,"* (Paris, January 19, 1828). [17] There was need to address a wider public than that of the monthly *Mémorial catholique,* published since 1824. Events would provide that opportunity in 1830.

Felicite was still in Italy when he sent to Countess Riccini a project intended for the Pope, proposing the foundation of a new religious order to defend the Church. The plan, dated June 21, 1828, a few days after the Ordinances of June 16, was an outline rather than a fully developed constitution. It was normal for the ailing Leo XII to send a word of encouragement and defer consideration, possibly until the completion of a more mature draft. [18] Félicité referred to his group as existing and numbering about forty members, a preemptive number which was real without being the result of his work. The primary education which he included in his statement of objectives was the work of the Brothers of Christian Instruction, and most of the forty priests counted in the project were Priests of Saint-Méen through the initiative of John.

Rennes: the retreat of September 1828

Two innovations converged before the September retreat. In August 1828, John began the reorganization of the Congregation of Saint-Méen. He wrote to his brother: *"Coëdro shares our designs; we must perform the fundamental act as soon as possible, for I cannot say anything to the others before; we must offer them something clear and firm,"* (August 10, 1828). A few lines further, he wrote about visiting the parish priest of Malestroit for information about a house: *"I will probably learn its asking price."* [19] Félicité informed Miss de Lucinière about a coming *"reunion;" "We are in the process of purchasing a house a short distance from Ploërmel. It is necessary to achieve our reunion as soon as possible,"* (August 18, 1828). He reported the acquisition to the same correspondent ten days later: *"We just bought at Malestroit, an ancient community residence to assemble our young colony which increases daily,"* (August 28, 1828) [20]. Félicité did not state that he had contributed over 15,000 francs in revenues from writings and gifts. Political and religious conflict hastened the fusion of Félicité's disciples of La Chesnaie with John's Congregation of Sain-Méen.

The retreat of September 1828 was the fourth and last for the Congregation of the Priests of Saint-Méen, and the first for the Congregation of Saint Peter. John directed it in the residence of the missionaries and later summarized its outcome: *"In 1828, the religious society known as of Saint-Méen, by the consent of its members, transformed itself into another society known as of Saint Peter, of which M. F. de La Mennais was named the head by unanimous vote. New statutes were promulgated during the retreat of September 1828."* [21] Félicité was not present. The change seemed sudden, but the Congregation had been evolving from the date of its foundation. John had planned the reorganization of 1828 with Félicite, and he consulted its members before taking any decision. He had prepared with Father Coëdro drafts of the new constitution for the professed members to discuss and accept privately. The proposition to adopt the change was *"accepted unanimously"* by the professed members on September 7. [22]

John then announced that Félicité intended to become part of the group, and he proposed that he be elected Superior General; the approval was unanimous. Félicité was at La Chesnaie at the time. He was informed immediately of his election and came to Rennes the next day; after he accepted the nomination, he recommended that his election be kept secret pending further directives. Father Coëdro later observed that John had required secrecy concerning the new constitutions and the election of his brother, as a responsibility equivalent to the *"seal of confession."* [23] John however took it upon himself to inform Bishop de Lesquen under whose authority the Congregation existed. [24]

There was no fail-safe course through the interplay of hostilities weighing on these developments. Evasive terminology and cryptic language float like wisps of rumpled fog through the correspondence of the period. Félicité had been condemned by a court of justice two years earlier. He knew that the government was keeping him under close surveillance and that investigators were opening his letters. [25] The only way to keep confidentiality on matters likely to invite interference, was to use elusive language such as: *"'the topic to which you refer,' 'you will understand what I mean,' ' X will inform you about the matter,' 'the subjects which interests us.'"* The Congregation had no legal authorization and the legal weapons wielded against the Jesuits could be lethal to a new society born under an oppressive government. The founders accordingly did not announce their plans and organizational details, and prudently withheld publicity about the choice of Félicité as founding Superior General. [26] Lingering forms of persecution and ecclesiastical rivalries even before the ordinances of June 16, 1828 explain the hushed proceedings.

The members welcomed Félicité de La Mennais as he had the advantage of established relationships with Vatican officials, and his proposal for a new religious order had obtained a personal encouragement from Pope Leo XII. The men attracted to him proved his capacity to rally exceptional talent despite his personal character flaws. Félicité had often been cautioned about his lack of self-control. The tension in his relationships with political authority and with a growing number of French bishops, particularly those in the Gallican camp, marked him for supervision. He would have to deal with unpleasant realities in his new role. [27] The Congregation of Saint Peter was broader than Félicité; it was important to guarantee its success, despite its association with a name entangled in controversy.

The Congregation of Saint Peter, 1828-1834

Félicité redrafted the first outlines of the Constitutions into the official version. [28] After his election, he delegated major responsibilities of the Superior General to John. Félicité, John, and Father Coëdro formed the Council of the new Congregation. The initial form of government was hierarchical; the organization was planned for efficiency. The Congregation would be governed by a Superior General appointed for life by the delegates of the General Congregation, by a Vicar General elected for ten years with the possibility of a renewable term, and a High Council composed of the preceding members with four elected Councilors.

A general chapter known as a "Decennial Congregation" would elect the superiors; necessity could require interim elections. The electors were the superior General, the the members of the council, the Provincial Vicars and four participants invited by the Superior General from among the Visitors and Directors of houses. The dispersal of members would make daily community presence at religious exercises difficult. Except for a brief community evening prayer, prescribed religious exercises were accordingly performed privately. Members would recite the Roman breviary, rather than one of the diocesan breviaries.

The objectives of the Congregation of Saint-Méen were included in those of the new society, members would work together to propagate sound doctrine and counteract error. To that end, the Congregation could undertake all categories of good works in the service of religion and the salvation of souls, but would not depend on any one in particular. Three groups of activities were specified: (1) writing in all categories, (2) education, clerical and lay, (3) missions, retreats, spiritual direction, the direction of lay congregations and academies for the young.

Opportunities for the exercise of personal talent and personal initiative were not lacking in that plan, but the rule stated that the Congregation would guide and coordinate activities in a spirit of freedom and unity, of respect, harmony and cooperation in dealing with the work of others. The membership was varied from the start and it quickly diversified further. The Constitutions were still unfinished though its provisions allowed sufficient flexibility to deal with an unstable social order. The text often reflects the teachings heard from John during the retreats of 1827 and 1828. John insisted that the virtues of religious life must prevail through all activities, and he reminded all members that community life must not be sacrificed to studies. He never thought it wise to decide everything in advance, and relied on experience to adjust rules. He would hold the office of Vicar General from 1828 to the crisis of 1833. [29]

The directives of Félicité confirmed the teachings of his brother. The Congregation must never stray from the fundamental doctrines of the Church and the leadership of the Pope. Congregation members must keep their distance from political authority to safeguard doctrine and freedom. Study was a grave responsibility and activities that support the spiritual mission of the Church should be given priority. Each member must strive to live in a spirit of humility, obedience, zeal and charity.

The new rule required the three vows of religion instead of the single vow of obedience; twenty members made the profession at the ceremony of September 14. After the retreat, 26 men, novices included, turned to broader horizons of service. Their activities were centered in five distinct communities: (1) the minor seminary of Saint Méen, (2) the missionaries of Rennes, (3) the new house of Malestroit, (4) the students at La Chesnaie, (5) the transient group at Juilly soon to be reorganized as the short-lived community of Paris. [30] The existing communities continued their activities, the new ones innovated.

The **minor Seminary of Saint-Méen** was the successor of two earlier ecclesiastical schools, one of which was John's minor seminary of Saint Malo closed by a Napoleonic ordinance in 1811. Its immediate diocesan successor survived until Bishop Mannay obtained the declining municipal *collège* of rural Saint-Méen from the government. In 1822, after its foundation as a seminary in a former Benedictine abbey, the number of students gradually rose to 250. John de La Mennais had organized the priests of the seminary as the Congregation of Saint-Méen in 1825. They were now administering the institution, and Bishop de Lesquen asked them to continue in that trust.

Eleven members of the new Congregation of Saint Peter formed the community in September 1828. Félicité reappointed Clément Haran, director, and François Xavier Énoch, religious superior. Few of the teachers had previously been members of the Congregation, but the proportion of religious kept increasing after 1828. The seminary also admitted a number of students from seminaries closed by the ordinances of June 26, 1828, the College of Saint-Anne founded by Gabriel Deshayes at Auray among them. Father Pierre Ruault came after the closure of his *collège* at Vitré and became a member of the new Congregation; he later served in Ploërmel as confidential assistant to John de La Mennais in the administration of the Brothers of Christian Instruction.

Félicité took an active interest in the life of the Congregation. In 1829, he began to send pedagogical advice to the directors, recommending the memorization of Latin and Greek texts, the teaching of mathematics, weekly teachers' meetings to improve methodology. At the Lenten season of 1830, he wrote spiritual advice to Father Énoch for his religious. [31]

The parish church of the town was incorporated into the *college* building, Father Corvaisier, a member of the Congregation of Saint Peter serving as pastor. When one of his two diocesan assistants passed away in June 1829, Bishop de Lesquen replaced both with priests from the Congregation and assigned the other assistant to another parish. The decision was based on the location of the church, but it generated criticism and lingering resentment among diocesan clergy.

Father Coëdro directed the **community of missionaries of rue de Fougères** in Rennes. The little family of six lived in harmony, zealously directing parish missions and religious gatherings in all sectors of the diocese and sharing the hopes and anxieties of the diocesan clergy. John visited them frequently and welcomed their assistance for retreats in his schools. He held Father Coëdro in sincere affection. On October 25, 1830, he wrote to Father Ruault: *"After having directed so many retreats for others, I am now making mine with Father Coëdro,"* [32]

John established and supervised the new community of **Malestroit,** while Félicité was the living soul of the community of **La Chesnaie.**

Malestroit: novitiate and house of studies, 1829 – 1835

Félicité referred to Malestroit as *"an establishment organized by my brother,"* (May 3, 1829). [33] John acquired the half ruined former Ursuline convent for the Congregation of Saint Peter in August 1828. Through his initiatives and the assistance of Brother Ignace from Ploërmel, the tumbled down structure was raised from the rubble and ready for occupation on January 12, 1829. Once a walled city, Malestroit was a small tightly planned town with winding somber streets in the heart of undisturbed moors 18 kilometers south of Ploërmel. The new home was located in the diocese of Vannes, but passed under the authority of the

Bishop of Rennes on the basis of reluctant concessions from the local bishop. [34]

Father Simon Blanc, a recent arrival, governed as superior of the community and Father Rohrbacher directed studies. Beginnings were slow. Since the role of Félicité had not been publicized, John's influence offset clerical opposition to the controversial writer. Malestroit received novices for the congregation and admitted other ecclesiastical candidates. There were eleven students in May 1829, fifteen to twenty more the following year, their numbers increasing from then on. Limited resources guaranteed hardships, the price for independence to teach Roman doctrines without interference from public officials and the Gallican clergy.

Félicité shared authority on policy decisions for Malestroit, but left operating initiatives to John, who actively promoted the spiritual and intellectual progress of the students; John ruled on admissions, shepherding candidates through tonsure, minor orders, the novitiate, and the vows. [35] The men of Malestroit welcomed his insights and his ability to stimulate the zeal of its members. They heard him speak of their responsibility to enlighten minds against misleading doctrines, to counteract degenerate teaching, even to revitalize the content of the sciences. He challenged them to live by the generous faith to which they were called.

The community rose at five; a half-hour meditation, mass, breakfast and morning chores followed. The program opened a wide intellectual spectrum. The private study of theology prepared minds for the conference on theology presided by Father Rohrbacher. A brief "examination of conscience" followed by the midday meal closed the forenoon. Open time from one to two allowed leisure for conversation, promenade, bowling (on the green) and other recreational options. Personal prayer and the recitation of the rosary before the Blessed Sacrament preceded the afternoon study devoted exclusively to languages and literature. John wrote that the students study *"theology, philosophy, Greek, Hebrew, Arab and most of the living languages; we try to form them to speak and to write,"* (April 20, 1830). [36]

Students chose fields of study with maximum freedom though teachers guided, encouraged, and challenged them. They were required to read pen in hand, to organize notes in preparation for conferences, especially in theology. They were expected to abide by Church doctrine and to respect the philosophy of Félicité de La Mennais, but were allowed freedom of expression. The intensity of the group characterized the school. Father Blanc wrote to Félicité: *"Despite lacking part of our books which are still at St-Méen, the daily conferences on theology and Greek, on Holy Scripture and ecclesiastical history are highly appreciated. In morals, we have followed the advice of Father John, and every Thursday morning at 10:45, we hold a conference on the treatise on human freedom prepared by those who expect to receive the sacred orders soon. --- They present their analysis of prepared material and we make appropriate observations,"* (February 18, 1829). [37] Blanc and Rohrbacher were the regular teachers, while the clear-minded and gentle Gerbet came to teach whenever his occupations made it possible. Rohrbacher, the future Church historian, was the star teacher.

Eloi Jourdain, who came from La Chesnaie in the spring of 1829, describes the library, most of which originally came from Saint-Méen: *"The library was assembled with the broadest and loftiest vision. Only mediocre and bad material was excluded. It included all the main works of the enemies of the Church, which must often be consulted in refuting error. All books were shelved around the room in unlocked cases, where we could always reach them."* [38] It was the only heated room in the school during winter. Teachers supervised, guided and encouraged the use of the library.

The role of prayer impressed him: *"A few people may believe that a heartfelt fervent piety was incompatible with such intensive study ... Excluding myself from the matter, I must truthfully declare that I have never known in my community life a more sincere and vivid piety, a warmer and more devoted charity. Everybody came to the Eucharistic table at least once a week, and several were worthy of approaching it every day."* [39] Jourdain remembered the friendliness which prevailed during recreations and outings about the countryside.

John de La Mennais, founder of two congregations of teachers, was never far from the work of his brothers in the priesthood. He visited them at La Chesnaie, Rennes, Saint Méen, and Malestroit. He was loved and greeted with jovial appreciation everywhere. The responsibility for Malestroit rested with him. He frequently insisted on the primary importance of prayer, humility and the blessings of religious life. He reaffirmed the intellectual responsibilities of the Congregation, while cautioning against pride, often prevalent among men of letters. He valued knowledge as a weapon in the service of truth, rather than as a vain ornament of the mind. Wherever he intervened as Vicar General, he acted without interfering with the Superior General.

Félicité corresponded with the Superior of Malestroit. At one point he seemed to consider establishing residence with the novices, but he rarely came. Blanc reports that during the six years of the school, he stopped for two meals, as though he were in transit, arriving after eleven o'clock and leaving before four. The local pastor, his assistant and two or three known lay royalist friends from the city shared those meals. *"I need not add, wrote Blanc, that in two visits of the kind, and with such company, that the community has not been united at the feet of the great man."* [40] On the advice of John and others, it seems that Félicité was cautioned against intervening too visibly in the life of the school, lest his controversies compromise its existence. The demands on his time were more than sufficient to occupy him otherwise.

La Chesnaie, Juilly, Paris: 1825 to 1834

The genius of Félicité de La Mennais, the timeliness of his crusade and the fascination of his discourse attracted alert young disciples to join Gerbet, Rohrbacher and Combalot at La Chesnaie. Félicité lodged them there and lived with them as the soul of their youthful enthusiasm. While John was stabilizing Malestroit, Félicité was continuing his writing as he guided an increasing family of recruits. [41] The community lived brief years of intense intellectual activity under his guidance. The thinking that evolved in the group is referred to as "the school of La Chesnaie."

The men of La Chesnaie centered their lives on the master, his heartbeat paced theirs, their thoughts moved around his as did the common activities of the group. [42] Prayers and meals were common, but, writes Eloi Jourdain, *"beyond meals and the daily conferences of Misters La Mennais and Gerbet, there were no common exercises. Each one worked as he saw fit, rose and retired at will, in every way following his preferences and the bent of his mind. Though the method had serious flaws, it also had many advantages. It provided leeway for various aptitudes to manifest themselves and follow a natural course of development. Several of us owe to that liberty the opportunity to select the most appropriate line of study and to excel in it."*

Each one worked conscientiously in his room, mindful of the direction and the advice of the master who relaxed in their youthful laughter and shared their recreations, refreshed by their simplicity as he heard their grave observations without ever losing his reputation as a passionate backgammon player. [43] At the end of the day, the group met in the living room for friendly conversation. Philosophy, politics, anecdotes, everything flowed in the most original form in those spontaneous chats led by a master with the gift of eliciting participation.

Félicité actively recruited members, selected them diligently and welcomed them with unforgettable hospitality. Gerbet and Combalot both attracted a few men to the group. Jourdain described his first personal encounter with Félicité de La Mennais: *"During the evening, he led me to his room. For the first time, I found myself alone in the presence of the genius, admitted into his intimacy. He was charming, spiritual, gay, fully uninhibited and trustful, fascinating as he could be when nothing contradicted him, affectionate to a point of tenderness, friendly to the point of familiarity. However, I believe I sensed something overdone in that expansion. ... Under the influence of the very force of that admiration which bent my soul before the genius of that man, I sensed the weakness of his character."* [44] In his embarrassment, Jourdain chose the gentle even-tempered Gerbet as a more appropriate spiritual and intellectual guide.

The house filled with eager young men preparing to defend religion. The author lived among them, quickly earning their affection by his goodness and winning charm, occasionally irritating them with his melancholy and haughtiness. The contrasts of the master's character did not distract from intensive study. Talents flourished, personalities individualized, loyalty to the master intensified. In time, the men learned with Jourdain, that Félicité could ruthlessly reject the most loyal friends who dared seek freedom from his intellectual hold. But as long as he lived with Mr. de La Mennais, Jourdain declared that he never saw or heard anything likely to weaken the respect, the trust and esteem inspired by reading his works.

The master's character did not match his genius. He lived intensely, one hour in one minute or lose weeks in sterile depression. Félicité in print, and Félicité in person was not the same person, but he stood out as the superior intellect, the untiring defender of the Church, ranking with the foremost French writers of his generation, despite the unmanageable extremes of his personality. He spared no pains in his devotion to the intellectual and religious needs of his followers. He wrote to Benoit d'Azy: *"Ill often, then obliged to teach Italian, Hebrew, English, philosophy, theology, to counsel, to hear confessions, to mind the material necessities of the house, guess what time remains available?"* (December 21, 1828). [45] Later, loyal disciples found separation from the man difficult, sometimes even tearful. He led them with the gift of clarifying objectives and uplifting souls.

The first disciples of Félicité came to La Chesnaie before the foundation of the Congregation of Saint Peter. The decision to transform the Congregation of Saint Peter into a society of priests forced the lay members to reexamine their objectives. In the fall of 1829, La Chesnaie became a preparation for the novitiate of Malestroit, and residents without a call to the priesthood left. Some provisionally relocated to Malestroit and deferred their decision. Félicité realized that Paris offered the best intellectual resources to his men, though he lacked the means to found a Parisian house of studies. The foundation of the *collège of Juilly* at Meaux, site of the cathedral of the former diocese of Bossuet and of the tomb of Jean-Jacques Olier, provided an opportunity to move his men close to Paris as a transition to life at the heart of the Capital.

The school, established in an old abbey by the Oratorians in 1638, served as the spiritual and intellectual center, and principal *college* of that order in France for a century-and-a-half before the Revolution. The Oratorians attempted to reorganize it after the conflict, but the government raised so many obstructions that they sought new owners and ceded it to Fathers de Scorbiac, [46] de Salinis and Caire on July 12, 1828. The three priests obtained government authorization and prepared to open their first school in October.

Though the Revolution of 1830 reduced half of its students, several teachers of the old Juilly could not adjust to the new situation and left. The three directors decided to guarantee its stability by associating it with a teaching congregation, thus inviting the Congregation of Saint Peter then expecting approval from Rome. Félicité came to study the situation and his disciples followed towards the end of September, 1830. A few of them participated in the life of the school, but Félicité and the others continued at Meaux the life lived at La Chesnaie. [47] He was often seen draped in a long black coat, pacing during long hours in the park, sometimes encircled with disciples, but generally alone, meditating his daily newspaper articles and his lessons in philosophy. The personal notes of his students made it possible to recapture the text of his lessons, sometimes referred to as "an essay on a system of Catholic philosophy," *(Essai d'un système de philosophie catholique)* [48]. Sainte-Beuve attended these lectures in May, 1831, Montalembert became part of the group, and men like Victor Hugo and Jules Michelet came to meet the teacher.

The old Oratorian *college* had a national reputation and its hospitality provided the men from La Chesnaie an opportunity to work at the doors of Paris before Félicité could provide a residence for them in that city. Félicité stayed at Juilly until the violence of his politics, and the extremes of his journalism drove the directors of the school to seek association with a different group.

Meager finances delayed the opening of a Parisian study center. In 1830 when his funding group announced that it would support the foundation of a daily newspaper, Félicité independently reserved provisional lodging from a Mrs. Martin during the summer of 1831, filled it with some of the men from the Juilly community, and sent the others to La Chesnaie. Realizing that the space was inadequate, he rented for one year until more appropriate quarters became available. He wrote to John a few months before leaving Juilly: *"We are initially 22 persons in the house of Paris ... I do not have the means to bring the others from Brittany, unless you manage to find the resources to pay their expenses in Paris ... The first interest of the Congregation is to support the house in Paris,"* (August 27, 1831). [49] Unforeseen obstacles shattered the dream the following summer.

Félicité cared for the spiritual progress of his disciples despite the material preoccupations which interfered with his work. As Superior General, he shared insights with the superiors of Saint-Méen and Malestroit, and wrote directives to them, but he gave the example of a model priest as he guided their spiritual destiny. [50] His modest chapel was the devotional center of La Chesnaie. In this peaceful Breton sanctuary, he celebrated daily mass, recited the Roman breviary, and preached occasional friendly timid homilies.

His men sang hymns and solemnized holy days, the Bible and the Fathers of the Church providing material for spiritual reading. The retreat comments of disciples reveal a thorough understanding of the sources of Christian spirituality. [51] The community of La Chesnaie lived a brief migratory and fragmented existence from Brittany to Meaux and Paris, its duration and impact barely sufficient to become the object of appreciation and regret; its journey lasting only a few years, though unforgettable years in the experience of its members and in the life of the French Church.

Until his second visit to Rome, Félicité de La Mennais was the insightful and dedicated superior of the Congregation of Saint Peter, but in his writings, he remained the prophet and the soldier risking personal security for the cause of social and religious reform. Rare indeed were the interludes of peace in his life, but Roussel rightly observes that the discreet five years of his leadership in the Congregation of Saint Peter were *"the most productive and the most beautiful"* of his life. [52] He may have lived with the fatigues of a soldier during those years, but he never experienced greater peace and harmony than with his disciples.

Doors opened to the young Congregation early in its brief history. In 1830, Bishop John Dubois[53] of New York was fundraising in Europe for the support of his diocese. Information about the new Congregation and the reputation of Félicité led him to request members of the Congregation to found a seminary in his young diocese. [54] Lacordaire prepared to leave for America with three other priests, but the project miscarried.

The Revolution of 1830 erupted in July and the controversies of *l'Avenir interfered* with the expansion of the Congregation. John de La Mennais later commented to a friend: *"We then planned to found various establishments in the diocese of New York, according to a plan which I had presented to Msgr. Dubois, who named me his Vicar General at the time, a title which I still hold,"* (December 20, 1838). [55] Felicite's controversies also prevented the Congregation of Saint Peter from responding to other invitations from abroad. Even during the summer of 1832, John wrote to de Salinis: *"I expect that my brother will return to Belgium in autumn, and that we will found a house there,"* (July 3, 1832). [56]

Bold words, bitter fruits: controversy in 1829

Félicité's work with his disciples did not deter him from polemics. Early in February 1829, he published his work "on the progress of the revolution and of the war against the Church," *(Des Progrès de la Révolution et de la Guerre contre l'Église).* [57] The essay was his response to the public campaign against the Church, and to the Ordinances of June 16, 1828, but it reached far beyond the ordinances. *"Authority was oppressing the Church; Lamennais separated himself from it and turned towards liberty,"* wrote Mercier. He accordingly *"dealt unsparingly with government. The book no doubt had a generous purpose, to unveil to French Catholics the projects formed by the impious against religion, and their plans to prepare its ruin."* [58]

In nine loosely connected chapters, the author exposed the evil of the day, reacted against Gallicanism as he had so persistently done, and reprimanded the government. He called for liberty of conscience and freedom for all religions, insistently demanding freedom of education. He urged the clergy, from Roman leaders to parish priests, to be fearless in defense of religion, and reproved passive churchmen for cowering under government repression. While public authority was failing and defenders of the faith faltering, Félicité raised the standard of liberty and invited the people to transform society.

The basic flaw in the constitutional *Charter* of the restoration had been the link between the fate of the monarchy and the Catholic religion. Félicité seemed to forget as he advised the clergy to stay away from politics, that the Church was being attacked along many political fronts. *"Be priests"* and *"only priests" and leave rulers and populations to their disputes. "No wiser counsel could be given to the clergy than to back away from political struggles. But that advice Lamennais has so poorly practiced it himself,"* observes Boutard, *"that we are inclined to wonder if he did not merely intend to detach the Church of France from a monarchy whose days were numbered."* [59] His statements were honest, insightful, bold and at times cutting to the point of being offensive. The government, the Gallican bishops and the Jesuits resented his approach. Do we not realize, he wrote, that *"the war that we avoid today will be inevitable tomorrow; that no concession will satisfy the anti-Christian party? ... Woe, woe to the one who, charged with this holy trust, would demean his mind with thoughts of the earth, would fear man and not fear God."* [60]

The bold honesty of the text *"honored the courage of Lamennais more than his prudence. It would have been preferable for him to limit himself to giving useful advice on ecclesiastical studies. In that field, at least,* writes Charles Boutard, *his competency and the superiority of his views were beyond challenge."* [61] His remarks now characterized him as a self-appointed reformer leading his crusade as though Church and society should move at his beat. Church authorities resented his admonitions. After having long linked the cause of religion with royalty, he now abandoned the kings and turned to the people for power, expecting a purified liberalism to supplant both monarchy and Gallicanism. He asked readers who feared liberalism to "Catholicize" it; he proposed novel forms of political action with the first elements of a social and religious agenda still in the making.

This was hardly the time for the founder of a fragile unauthorized religious congregation to hold the center of heated national controversy in the face of a government that had not recognized the Congregation of Saint Peter. There was more agreement about the writer's literary genius than about the contents of his book, and still less about his attitude towards those who disagreed with him. The Gallicans rejected the criticism of their doctrines, while the "ultramontanes" resented his new alliance with religious liberalism. The Apostolic Nuncio judged the book untimely, to say the least. Many, even among friends, found it unrestrained. Benoit d'Azy had seen the proofs and had advised him to soften a number of passages; Félicité rewrote but a few passages at the suggestion of d'Azy and Berryer. [62]

The chanceries and the courts of Europe were watching this feisty cleric who was shaking the columns of the temple. Recourse to the power of "the people" in times of social unrest was bound to alienate public authority. The government instructed its ambassador to voice displeasure in Rome and the French bishops asked the Pope to intervene in the interest of peace. Archbishop de Quélen of Paris, who had abstained from joining fourteen Gallican bishops in the condemnation of April 3, 1826, publicly condemned his theories in his Lenten pastoral letter. De Quélen did not forgive Félicité's attacks on Gallicanism, deploring the internal church war provoked by his writings.

Félicité would not be silenced by a prelate. Miss de Lucinière was aware of his decision to reply in print and pleaded for restraint: *"Oh if, as we indeed expect, you decide to reply, we conjure you on our knees to do it with moderation and in a tone befitting the accuser and the accused. If bitterness and sarcasm are present, it will unfailingly be said that so wrote Luther and the leaders of sects,"* (February 20, 1829). [63] The Parisian friend later conceded that Félicité might be right in his thinking; unfortunately, she did not have to wait long for the extremes against which she cautioned.

Félicité replied to the Archbishop in two letters of 60 and 74 published pages respectively. Taken together they were a defense of his work "on the progress of revolution and of the war against the Church."

The "letters" have been cited as models of polemics, but equally as *"a caustic pamphlet against liberalism and Gallicanism,"* revealing *"an impatience with all authority."* [64] Mercier commented that Félicité wrote lines boiling with anger: *"No longer master of himself, the writer encroaches all limits, ignores all proprieties. When it is not aggressive, even his tone carries elements of haughtiness which reveals an offensive disposition toward anyone who contradicts him."* [65] Félicité challenged Gallicans and denounced them to the Pope; Msgr. de Quélen, on the other hand, called for his condemnation as an insolent and troublesome polemist.

Pope Leo XII passed away on February 20, 1829, a few days after the publication of "The progress of the revolution and the war against the Church." De Quélen preferred peace to wasteful controversy and let the affront rest with the letters. The Roman cardinals who reviewed reports during the vacancy of the papacy, judged the case of La Mennais *"grave."* The breach widened between himself and Nuncio Lambruschini who had befriended him. The Nuncio now reported: *"On my arrival in Paris, I became aware that the Abbé de La Mennais intended not only to influence my way of acting, but to control it and use me to make the Holy See speak openly against the French clergy according to his personal views, particularly regarding his system of universal consensus,"* (September 7, 1829). [66]

Pius VIII, elected on March 31, 1829, would be confronted with the controversies, but neither the Archbishop nor Félicité obtained declarations from him. The first months of Félicité's new journalism fanned widening controversies. Caught between striking the defender of papal authority and the risk of offending a declining monarchy, Pius VIII chose the wisdom of silence; he passed away on October 30, 1830. Gregory XVI who succeeded him February 2, 1831, would break the silence of the Holy See, not by planned intervention, but in response to the widely publicized request of Félicité de La Mennais, Henri de Lacordaire and Charles de Montalembert. John de La Mennais shared the ideals of the team, but would be allowed little more than the role of observer through the unfolding controversies.

"L'Avenir": October 17, 1830 - November 15, 1831

In 1830, opposition to royalty climaxed in France and across Europe. In the spring, the deputies respectfully asked the king to change his ministers. Convinced that he must act to safeguard his constitutional privileges, Charles X dissolved the Chamber of Deputies. Elections returned a majority hostile to the monarchy. On July 25, the King published four ordinances reorganizing the electoral system and severely limiting the freedom of the press.

While Charles X was out hunting, riots broke out in Paris on July 27 at the estate of Rambouillet. Rebels raised barricades and the fighting continued through July 27, 28 and 29, called the three glorious days. On August 9, the Chamber proclaimed Louis Philippe, Duke of Orleans, King. The revolution was not kind to royalists, even less to churchmen. The constitutional Charter remained substantially the same, though the nation, not the King became sovereign by divine right, and Catholicism ceased to be the state religion. Félicité was jubilant, the monarchy was dead, the new king a nominal transition, the Church and the people standing at the dawn of a new era.

Félicité saw the oppression of Religion as an opportunity to educate the clergy to its new understanding of its responsibilities, and the time to launch a daily newspaper. [67] Gerbet ironed out the legalities, published a prospectus in the *Revue Catholique* of August 14, distributed a limited number of copies, and on September 8, founded the society for the publication of *l'Avenir* with his associates. Félicité rejoiced at the news and urged his friend to forge ahead: *"Gaining a day is important!"* He left La Chesnaie to establish residence at the *Collège of Juilly*. On September 28, he ratified the act of foundation in which Gerbet had acted as proxy for him. The present was grim, the future held glowing promises, the time for action had come! The team would work to bring the future into the present.

The first number of *l'Avenir* (the future) appeared on October 16, 1830, bearing the slogan: "God and Liberty." John was closely allied to the ideals of the founders and was an alert observer of their initiatives. [68] The two foremost writers of the journal came to Félicité early. Gerbet had been attempting in vain to persuade Father Henri de Lacordaire, lawyer, priest and young chaplain at the *Lycée Henri IV,* to join the community of La Chesnaie. The absolutist politics of Félicité initially displeased the young priest, but the writer's political evolution melted his resistance. Lacordaire was visiting family in Burgundy prior to departure for the United States, when Gerbet's prospectus offered him an opportunity to engage in active journalism. He cancelled his voyage, came to work with Félicité and learned to appreciate him. Alone, or almost, he assumed the composition of *l'Avenir* for two months, until a brother in arms unexpectedly came to battle by his side.

Information about *l'Avenir* reached the young Charles de Montalembert in Ireland. Montalembert, the son of a peer of France, had traveled to Dublin to study the Catholic emancipation movement of William O'Connell. Gerbet's prospectus fired his enthusiasm, and on November 26, he wrote from London to offer his services. True to his word, he rushed to Paris; the first encounter between La Mennais and this young man of twenty was decisive for both. The personality and the views of La Mennais overwhelmed the new disciple; the master in turn loved the talented newcomer for his intelligence, his charm, his loyalty and youthful vitality. A new team of La Mennais, Gerbet, Lacordaire and Montalembert formed the spearhead of a reform movement.

As he prepared the first issues of *L'Avenir, Gerbet* insisted that the lead article be from the master. La Mennais explained the slogan of the paper. Briefly, two principles still stand: God and Liberty, and the union of the two satisfies the needs of the soul. Applications to politics and religion would fill the paper. *L'Avenir* had a prodigious impact, not only in France, but throughout Europe. Its pages challenged the nation with a controversial agenda which rallied militants, despite the fact that subscribers never exceeded 3, 000, half clergy, half lay.

The incisiveness of the first issues offended friends. Father Vuarin, the companion of Félicité's Roman voyage, read the early issues and advised: *"I would avoid aggravating the disappointments or the hopes of a large number of righteous and zealous souls on what has happened* [i. e., the fall of the monarchy]. *All do not have the capacity to grasp the full scope of your views, nor the ability to rise to the requisite heights to understand and implement them."* (November 19, 1830).

On the following day, Combalot wrote to de Salinis, then director of the Collège of Juilly: *"Persuade our friend that l'Avenir has the possibility of providing great benefits to France and to all of Europe; however, the entire copy must be **strictly supervised**. Insults, personalities, all matters which do not further the work of God, must be avoided."* (November 20, 1830). [69] The advice was timely, but wrote Charles Boutard, *"prudence was not the dominant virtue of La Mennais."* [70] John quickly experienced the consequence of hasty reporting when a copy of *L'Avenir* arrived in town with a *"very inexact account"* of an affair, [71] and the mayor had been *"awkwardly attacked"* in an article; John asked Gerbet to correct the statement of the journal.

The government seized two issues of the paper on November 25 and 26. The first article by Lacordaire was addressed to the bishops of France, the second was a statement by La Mennais "on the oppression of Catholics." The court acquitted the accused on January 31, 1831, but the seizure outraged La Mennais. With his friends, he decided to reorganize the society for the support of *l'Avenir*. De Salinis took the initiative and on December 18, the Society became the "general agency for the defense of religious liberty," *(L'Agence générale pour la défense de la Liberté religieuse).*

The original *Société* had a single goal: to defend religion against the Revolution; the Agence added a second: to defend the freedom of the Church against the power of the government. La Mennais kept challenging his co-religionists to understand and defend their rights. *L'Agence* set out to alert the public and seek redress in the courts. Not only did it triumph in a number of instances, but it opened a private elementary school without government approval to challenge the limits on freedom of education. Though it lost in the courts, it exposed the government monopoly which prevailed until 1850. [72]

Félicité and his team led the battle, inspiring disciples, alerting the uninformed, scandalizing the royalists, censuring the government, scorching the Gallicans. The royalists scorned his vision, the government spied on him, the Gallicans leagued against him. The new religious politics confused the Catholics who did not understand the importance of new alliances to deal with new political forces. The mennaisian team was young and inexperienced; its intransigence reinforced the master's imprudence and provoked reprisals. The government shadowed the paper.

La Mennais and his colleagues aggressively argued the cause of Catholic liberalism with an unfortunate disregard for the essential theological difference between religious and political freedom, and a gross misunderstanding of the meaning of "the kingdom of God," too often understood as a human entity. Bishops increasingly banned *l'Avenir,* and unsympathetic theologians ferreted out questionable statements from Félicité's writings. The chances of continuing publication decreased with the loss of subscribers and the specter of impending bankruptcy. The three leading writers met in emergency session and unanimously decided to deal with reality. The last issue, the 395th in thirteen months, appeared on November 15, 1831.

Ill-advised pilgrimage: November 1831-July 1832

Early on the morning which followed the decision to cease publication, Lacordaire rushed to the room of Félicité with a proposal which he later acknowledged as an error: *"I thought it out, we must not end that way. We must go to Rome to justify our intentions, submit our thoughts to the Holy Father. Whatever the outcome, this public gesture, proof of sincerity and orthodoxy, will be a blessing for us and a weapon taken from the hands of our enemies."* The proposition revived the hope for papal approval. The youngest member, Montalembert, objected: *"What if we are condemned? "Impossible!"* replied La Mennais. Had he reflected, he would have avoided the theatrics of his appeal.

The last issue of *l'Avenir* carried the following declaration: *"The publication of l'Avenir will be suspended as of to-day until it pleases the Sovereign Pontiff to declare himself on our writings which we have submitted to him in deepest humility and ardent love of our heart,* (November 15, 1831). If condemned, the editors declared themselves ready to vindicate themselves by their *"obedience,"* more than they would in the case of *"total approval."* In the hope of hastening a ruling, they announced that three of the editors, La Mennais, Lacordaire and Montalembert, would travel to the Eternal City to meet the Pope. They styled themselves the pilgrims of liberty and left Paris on November 22. John characterized the suspension of *L'Avenir* in some respects *"distressing,"* but otherwise *"fortunate"* for the opportunity it provided for the *"courageous writers"* to demonstrate their submission to the Church. [73]

On November 19, they spent two hours with Archbishop de Quélen. The advice they heard fell on deaf ears: *"If you had simply furthered the true interests of religion, to defend its dogmas, its discipline, its ministers, you would have won on your side all the bishops and well-meaning persons. But you set your mind to overturn the system of ecclesiastical administration established in France, and replace it by another neither useful, nor possible. You have mixed strange and absurd political principles with religious principles, you have adopted the most demagogic language of the press, you have praised and preached revolution, and you then complain of having been blamed by the bishops, the clergy and good Catholics."* [74] The Archbishop suggested that a quiet request for advice and enlightenment would be more effective in Rome than resounding publicity.

The pilgrims of liberty left to vindicate the agenda of *l'Avenir* and the writings of La Mennais. Adrien Dansette observed that the pilgrimage was based on a poor reading of the signs of the times by Félicité de La Mennais: *"His immense capacity for illusion, and the inexperience of Lacordaire and Montalembert were required to conclude that the Holy See, even should it approve of their doctrine, except in matters relating to ultramontanism, would support them against the entire ecclesiastical hierarchy."* [75] The Pope was not intruding; the appeal was the initiative of Félicité de La Mennais and his team.

Admonition and acclaim followed them along. In Lyon where the recent revolt of the silk workers had been harshly repressed, its memory cautioned against popular uprisings. There were friends along the way to Rome, but none of them surpassed Eugène de Mazenod. His congregation, the Oblates of Mary Immaculate, had proscribed *l'Avenir* from its houses, but its Founder who was also Vicar General of Marseilles could distinguish between principles and persons. He disapproved elements of La Mennais' doctrine, but he had helped to uncover the source of a fraudulent letter circulated to discredit him.

Mazenod nevertheless acknowledged the potential value of his movement, met the tormented writer and his two companions with a rare degree of understanding, and organized an ovation for his team. Marseilles was ready for the three travelers. A gathering of sympathizers cheered them at the city gate, and the priests of the city assembled spontaneously for the mass celebrated the following morning. The Bishop of Marseilles greeted them, and at the suggestion of Father de Mazenod invited the team to a reception at the episcopal residence. De Mazenod even wondered if he should have joined the group to help interpret their message in Rome. [76]

Though *l'Avenir* was not an enterprise of the Congregation of Saint Peter but an activity of Félicité de La Mennais, the outcome in Rome was nevertheless bound to concern its members, as it was destined to affect the life of John de La Mennais, the schools of his religious, and the life of family and friends.

Life was changing for John and Félicité. Mourning touched their lives in 1828 and 1829. Pierre Louis de La Mennais, their father, passed away at Rennes on January 28, 1828 at eighty-five. *"I consider him fortunate for leaving on the eve of the evils soon to befall us,"* wrote Félicité to Gerbet, a few days before his father's death. Denys-François, uncle Des Saudrais, the father's brother, *"who had been for us a second father,"* passed away in Saint Malo during the early days of the following June. [77] The only natural family left to the two brothers after 1829 was Marie, her husband and their living children. One of the boys, Louis-Marie Blaize, a nephew remembered by John as a devoted member of the Congregation of the Blessed Virgin at the Collège of Saint- Méen, had passed away, April 16, 1829.

John and Félicité each had families of a different nature in the religious congregations they had founded. Félicité realized that he had lost a listening ear in Rome with the death of Leo XII. His appeal would now come to Pope Gregory XVI, a person with more conservative dispositions. *L'Avenir* had been founded eight-and-a-half months after his election, and had flared out of existence after thirteen months of controversy. John had urged Félicité on to his first trip to Rome in 1824; he hoped that the second, which was not of his making, would bring peace, though no one could predict the sequel of his brother's appeal.

---

[1] See chapter 9 about secondary schools as minor seminaries.

[2] The Jesuits had been suppressed by civil authority in France in 1762. The European sovereigns forced their suppression by Pope Clement XIV on June 8, 1773, but Pope Pius VII annulled that decision on July 31, 1814, and restored them on August 7. Father de Clorivière immediately began their reorganization in France. The bishops frequently resorted to their services because most were learned and zealous. NOTES. (a) See Louis-René de Caradeuc de La Chalotais (1761-1785), *Comptes Rendus des Constitutions des Jésuites, (1761).* (b) Joseph Burnichon, *La Compagnie de Jésus en France, Histoire d'un siècle,* 1814-1914. Paris: Gabriel Beauchesne, 1914. 4 vols. Vol. 1, 1814-1830, pp. 346-402.

[3] The same ordinance redefined the duties of the High Almoner thereby rendering John's service in Paris virtually useless.

[4] Vicomte de Guichen, *La France morale et religieuse à la fin de la Restauration,* Paris: Émile-Paul, éditeurs, 1912, pages 135-180, "Les Jésuites, la Congrégation et Montlosier."

[5] Joseph Marie Portalis (1778-1858), son of Jean Étienne Portalis (1743-1807), Minister of Cults under Napoleon.

[6] Vicomte de Guichen, *La France morale et religieuse à la fin de la Restauration,* Paris: Émile-Paul, éditeurs, 1912, pages 219-292, "Les Ordonnances."

[7] **Cor gén F,** v. 3, p. 412 (November 30, 1827) and letter to the Countess of Senfft p. 462 (January 28, 1828).

[8] These were specifically identified at Aix, Billom, Bordeaux, Dôle, Forcalquier, Montmorillon, Saint Acheul and Sainte Anne d'Auray.

[9] Adrien Garnier, *Les Ordonnances du 16 juin* 1828, Paris: J. De Gigord, 1929.

[10] See "Une préoccupation des frères La Mennais: la formation du clergé," Pierre Perrin, "Félicité, Jean-Marie de La Mennais et l'Université, Leurs idées pédagogiques pour la defense de la liberté de l'ensrignement, de 1806 à1860." Brest: Université de Betagne occidentale, 1988, pages 43-56. (Unpublished doctoral thesis, copy **AFIC**). Published adaptation: *Les idées pédagogiques de Jean-Marie de la Mennais,* 1780-1860: Presses Universitaires de Rennes, 2000, pages 97-102, ff.

[11] The dispensation was granted with the understanding that formal vows would be renewed after serving as teachers. **SA 1960**, pp. 185, 186, 390, on the basis of documents from the archives of the Diocese of Rennes.

[12] **Cor gén J,** v. 2, p. 422 and **Cor gén F,** v. 4, p.16.

[13] *Des Progrès de la Révolution et de la Guerre contre l'Eglise.*

[14] On the foundation of the Congregation of Saint Peter see, André Dargis, "La Congrégation de Saint-Pierre," Louvain, 1971. Mimeographed, (Doctoral thesis, The Catholic University of Louvain, Faculty of theology).

[15] **Cor gén F,** vol. 3, p. 34 to de Lucinière, February 14, 1825; p. 116 to Berryer, Nov. 18, 1825.

[16] Dargis, op cit., p. 166 ff. **Cor gén F,** v. 3, pp. 277-291, Text of memorandum, late 1826 early 1827).

[17] Letter from Paris, **Cor gén F,** v. 3, p. 714.

[18] **Cor gén F,** v. 3, pp. 502-503. Dargis, op. cit., pp. 192-199. Jean René Derré, *Lamennais, ses Amis et le Mouvement des Idées à l'Époque romantique,* Paris: Klincksieck, 1962, pages 282-284.

[19] **Cor gén J,** v.2 p. 425. Cited in Dargis, op. cit., p. 205.

[20] **Cor gén F,** v. 4, pp. 25, 37.

[21] Symphorien-Auguste, *À Travers la correspondance de l'Abbé J. M. de la Mennais,* Vannes: Lafolye et de Lamarzelle, v. 2, 1938. p. 348, from a memoir written February 5-6, 1835, pp. 347-374.

[22] From the notes of Father Houet who was present. Quoted in Dargis, op. cit., p. 212. (On the profession of Félicité, see 217-218).

[23] Letter Father Coëdro to John de La Mennais, September 4, 1834. **SA (1960),** p. 386, (transcription et manuscrit, pp. 380, planche VII hors texte après 384).

[24] Father Émile Feildel reports that John took it upon himself to notify Bishop de Lesquen. However, Fathers Pierre Louis François Coedro and

Pierre Charles Persehais accused him of withholding the information from the Bishop; the facts contradict the accusers. **SA (1960),** pp. 185-186 and 405.

[25] Letter to the Baroness Cottu, (March 25, 1825). **Cor gén F,** v. 3, p. 40.

[26] The story of the first reform convent of Saint Teresa of Avila shows the need for discretion even in the performance of good works.

[27] **Cor gén J,** v. 2, p. 384, and **Cor gén F,** v. 3, p. 305, (John's letter of April 9 1827, and Félicité's letter of April 14).

[28] On the cooperation of John and Félicité, see Dargis, op. cit., pp. 220-230.

[29] On the Congregation of Saint Peter, see Philippe Friot, **ÉM,** 20, (April 1998) and 23, (July 1999).

[30] Dargis, op. cit., pp. 262-464.

[31] Ibid., p. 419.

[32] **Cor gén J,** v. 2, p. 485.

[33] Letter to the Baron de Vitrolles, **Cor gén F,** vol 4, p. 134.

[34] Dargis, op. cit., pp. 313-371.

[35] Ibid., pp. 339-342.

[36] **Cor gén J,** v. 2, p. 474, Letter to Father Frère.

[37] **Cor gén F,** v. 4, pp. 516, 517.

[38] Charles Sainte-Foi [pseudonym of Éloi Jourdain], *Souvenirs de jeunesse, 1828-1835. Publiés avec une introduction et des notes par Camille Latreille,* Paris: Perrin, 1911, pages 98-99, note.

[39] Sainte-Foi, op. cit., p. 103. Excerpts, **SA (1960),** pp. 516-517.

[40] From a memorandum written in 1835. Quoted in Dargis, op. cit., p. 346, note 2.

[41] Dargis, op. cit., pp. 267-312. **Lav,** v. 1, pp. 442-447. Charles Sainte-Foi, *Souvenirs de Jeunesse,* 1828-1835, Paris: Perrin, 1911, pages 37-89.

[42] Dargis, p. 280, ff.

[43] The game is referred to as *trictrac* in French.

[44] Charles Sainte-Foi, op. cit., pp. 41- 42.

[45] **Cor gén F,** v. 4, p. 73. He kept that pace. See p. 250, Letter to the Count of Senfft, February 19, 1830.

[46] Bruno Casimir de Scorbiac.

[47] Charles Hamel, *Histoire de l'Abbaye et du collège de Juilly,* Paris: Charles Douniol, 1868, pages. 492-495. J. R. Derré, *Lamennais, ses Amis et le mouvement des idées à l'époque romantique* (1824-1834), Paris:

Klincksieck, 1962, pages 328-342. F. Duine, *La Mennais, sa vie, ses idées, ses ouvrages*, Paris: Garnier, 1922, pages 137-145.

[48] Christian Marechal, *Essai d'un système de Philosophie catholique* (1830-1831) Paris: Bloud, 1906. The text is from unpublished notes of students. These lectures served as first version to the *Esquisse d'une Philosophie* published in four volumes ten years later.

[49] **Cor gén F**, v. 5, pp. 23-24.

[50] Boutard, v. 2, pp. 96 ff. Sainte-Foi pp. 60 ff, 103. Dargis, pages 291, 401-405. Alfred Roussel, *Lamennais d'après des Documents inédits,* Rennes: Hyacinthe Caillère, 1892. V. 2, pp. 67-143 "A retreat at La Chesnaie."

[51] For 1831-1832 particularly. See notes in Alfred Roussel, *Lamennais d'après des documents inédits.* Rennes: Hiacinthe Caillère, 1893. 2 v. Vol. 2, pp. 3-77.

[52] Alfred Roussel, *La Mennais à La Chênaie,* Paris: Pierre Téqui, 1909. P. x. Dargis, page 265.

[53] John Dubois (1764-1842), Bishop of New York.

[54] See **Lav,** v. 1, pp. 449-450, and the letters of Félicité for May 26, June 29, and Oct. 4, 1830, **Cor gén F,** Vol. 4, pp. 290, 299 and 699.

[55] Letter to Mr. Sauveur de la Chapelle, Deputy from the Côtes-du-Nord. **AFIC,** second letter book of J. De La Mennais, 1837-39, p. 165. **Cor gén J,** v. 4, pp. 131-133. According to a reference in a letter of Brother Xiste (August 27, 1837), he considered sending a few brothers along. See the reference of Bro. Donat-Alphonse Caron in **Chron,** No. 144, March 1938, p. 262. The title of Vicar General was conferred verbally by Bishop Dubois, as was the case for a few other titles.

[56] **Cor gén J,** v.2, p. 569.

[57] *Des progrès de la Révolution et de la Guerre contre l'Église,* Paris: À la Librairie classique-élémentaire et catholique de Belin-Mandar et Devaux, 1829.

[58] Mercier, *Lamennais, 1782-1854, d'après sa correspondance et les travaux les plus récents,* Paris: Lecoffre, 1895, p. 137.

[59] Charles Boutard, *Lamennais, sa vie et ses doctrines,* Vol. 2, Paris: Librairie académique Perrin, 1908. Vol. 2, pages 44-45. Also generally, pages 23-49.

[60] Chapter 9 of Félicité's work.

[61] Ibid., p. 46.

[62] **Cor gén F,** v. 4, pp. 514-515, reply, Jan. 14, p. 83. F. Duine, La *Mennais, sa vie, ses idées, ses ouvrages,* Paris: Garnier, 1922, pages 129-132.

[63] **Cor gén F,** v. 4, p. 518-519.

[64] Mercier, op. cit., p. 139.

[65] Ibid., vol. 2, pp. 54-55.

[66] Letter of Mgr. Lambruschini to Cardinal Capellari. **FL Cond,** pp. 33-39.

[67] On *l'Avenir,* see Ruth L. White, *L'Avenir de La Mennais,* Paris: Klincksieck, 1974. C. Boutard, op. cit., v. 2, pp. 107-257. Mercier, op. cit., pp. 149-210.

[68] Letter to Du Clézieux, October 31, 1830. **Cor gén J,** v. 2, pp. 486-487.

[69] Ricard, *L'Abbé Combalot,* Paris: Gaume, 1891, pages 76-77.

[70] The statement is from Charles Boutard, op. cit., v. 2, p. 131.

[71] Letter to Gerbet, June 18, 1831. **Cor gén J,** v. 2, p. 509.

[72] **Cor gén F,** v. 4, p. 707. White, op. cit., pp.51 ff.

[73] Letter to Father de Verdalle, November 28, 1831. **Cor gén J,** v. 2, pp. 533-535.

[74] As reported in a letter of the Abbé Garibaldi to Cardinal Bernetti, Secretary of State, November 21, 1831. **FL Cond,** p. 45. Other friends had also advised prudence and discretion.

[75] Adrien Dansette, *Histoire religieuse de la France contemporaine,* vol. 1, Paris: Flammarion, 1951, (c 1948), page 304.

[76] Jean Leflon, *Eugène de Mazenod,* (3 vols.), Paris: Plon, 1957-1965. Vol. 2, pp. 424-430.

[77] Letters from Félicité to Gerbet (January 23, 1828), and the Countess of Senfft (June 15, 1829). **Cor gén F,** vol. 3, p. 454-455, vol. 4, p. 151.

St. Malo

Chapter 20

MISCALCULATED ZEAL

Pope Gregory XVI and the Europe of 1831

The revolutions of 1830 shook the thrones of Europe and swept insurrection fever south into the Italian peninsula. The day after the election of Maur Capellari as Gregory XVI, February 2, 1831, Modena rebelled and the revolt generalized in the Papal States. [1] In Rome, the three pilgrims would meet a religious leader with the additional responsibilities of a civil ruler, as the unification of Italy did not free the Church from the burdens continental politics until 1870. Religion and politics involved La Mennais and his two companions in overlapping scenarios. The recently elected Pontiff awaited them with a concern for purity of doctrine, peace for the Church, and concern for the needs of the Church in France. As civil ruler of the Papal States, Gregory XVI was also expected to take into consideration the writer's impact on the political unrest in Europe.

The three journalists reached Rome ten months after his election. Some historians have viewed this Pope only a contemplative monk unaware of the affairs of this world and ill-prepared to understand the work of La Mennais and his team; the reality was otherwise. As Cardinal Capellari, he had served as Prefect of the *Propaganda,* in charge of mission lands, and had participated in the affairs of the Low Countries. Before becoming a Cardinal, he had long served as a consultant for several Roman congregations. He may not have been prepared to understand the new Catholic liberalism, but he was not unaware of the restive secular politics of his day.

Félicité de La Mennais preoccupied both statesmen and churchmen. As diplomats reported on the editors of *l'Avenir,* and as the Austrian Chancellor Metternick channeled information about the writer to Rome, the Vatican Secretary of State could respond that the Pope was informed and had analyzed the issues. The purloined letters of the Austrian agents were useful to the Pope, but Gregory XVI was not inclined to share his conclusions even with the devious Metternick; he believed the Church capable of resolving the case as a Church affair without the intervention of statesmen.

By the time the pilgrims reached Rome, revolutions had shaken Europe. Henri Guillemin summarized the French experience: *"No priest could risk wearing a cassock in Paris; Saint Germain l'Auxerrois was sacked, the archbishopric was invaded, plundered and its library cast into the Seine. Seminaries were attacked by the crowd and devastated in Metz, Lille, Conflans, Dijon and Nîmes. Several terrified bishops fled: the Archbishop of Reims sailed to England, the Bishop of Besançon slipped into Italy, the Bishop of Nancy was seeking refuge in America. Crosses standing in town squares or crossroads were struck down by the thousand. On April 17, 1831, Msgr. De Quélen consecrated Msgr. Gaillard, the new Bishop of Meaux, in a humble convent chapel at night."* [2] The lesson was fresh and heads of state could hardly be blamed for guarding against anarchy. Harmonizing rights, religious freedom and orderly government was an on-going challenge for the new religious liberals, as the experience with new democracies would more likely be a confrontation with irreligion than an encounter with genuine democracy.

Prophetic agenda, confusing theology, contrary times

The "pilgrims of liberty" were the leading French champions of Papal authority. They had been defending basic civil liberties while calling for a Church separated from government. *L'Avenir* kept calling for freedom of association, free elections, the liberation of provinces and towns from centralized authority, and freedom for oppressed populations. They came to Rome after publishing in the last issue of *l'Avenir* an agenda drafted in the form of an **Act of Union.**

They referred to the Act of Union as the great charter of the century. [3] The document set goals and called for action. Briefly: I. The spiritual elements of society must be completely liberated from political intervention. Consequently, the group advocated: (1) freedom of conscience and of worship for all religions; (2) freedom of the press, its strongest guarantee; (3) freedom of education, its long-term protection. --- II. The authority of constitutional governments must be limited to matters of material interest, and administered locally in harmony with the various administrations. --- III. Initiatives for the betterment of the less fortunate classes of society must be planned and implemented by Church and State.

It would be difficult to find anything blameworthy in these objectives, but even more unrealistic to expect their implementation in a time of conflict and chaos. These praise-worthy objectives injected international complications in a year of sporadic revolutions. In a period of revolution, they called for a federation of local associations, a form of Catholic international league for the liberation of oppressed and mistreated Catholics, an unrealistic dream at the time. Similar movements were afoot in England, Belgium and Germany; statesmen dealing with revolution would understandably interpret a call to strengthen popular rights as a call to rebellion.

Philosophy and theology as applied to the politics of Church and State are interwoven in the doctrines of Félicité de La Mennais, and in the editorial statements which the three journalists expected the Pope to approve or declare free from doctrinal error. The movement involved dilemmas of religious policy in edgy social contests during a time when political unrest kept European leaders on the defensive. An appeal to the Pope was untimely, to say the least, as France was crushing riots, and the pro-secretary of state in Rome was battling Italian revolutionaries when the editors of *l'Avenir* arrived in Rome.

The editors of *L'Avenir* had addressed a "Declaration" to the Holy See months before the suspension of the paper. [4] Gregory XVI prepared to meet the French journalists by consulting men who had known La Mennais. Early in December 1831, he had requested advice (1) about the priest, his doctrines and his paper, *l'Avenir,* and (2) about the procedure to follow should the visitors come. With Lambruschini, Barakdi, Orioli and Rozaven, we find Lamennais' friend Ventura among the group of advisors. When the three "pilgrims" arrived, the churchmen had done the preliminary work expected of them. [5]

Father Martin de Noirlieu met the "pilgrims" on arrival, December 31, and led them to the monastery of the Theatine Order on behalf of Father Ventura who had assisted La Mennais in Rome ten years earlier. From then on, relationships with Church authorities did not proceed as expected until they left the Eternal City, July 10, 1832. The intervening six months gradually extinguished Lamennais' personal illusions about his own standing in the political world and in the Church. [6]

Three pilgrims in Rome

La Mennais requested an audience with the Pope soon after his arrival. As no response was forthcoming, the team met and Lacordaire renewed the request. [7] Cardinal Pacca responded on behalf of Gregory XVI. With due *"justice"* to the skill and dispositions of La Mennais, the Pope had not concealed his *"discontent because of controversies and opinions which are at least dangerous, and which have sown wide division in the French clergy, offending good and devout Catholics."*

Satisfied with the journalist's submissive attitude, he agreed to have the doctrines of La Mennais "examined," as the writer had "requested." But such an examination *"could not be done so rapidly. A long time will be required before it is completed."* The Cardinal concluded with the advice to leave Rome: *"You may ... return home, and in due time, you will be informed of the result of the matter at hand,"* (February 25, 1832). Determined to pursue his case, La Mennais replied that his two companions would leave, but that he would stay alone, *"to supply indispensable explanations and respond to the questions which it might be thought proper to ask him,"* (February 27). [8]

The prophetic agenda of *l'Avenir* was both brilliant and confusing, a blend of politics and religion, idealistic in concept, inapplicable as a quick remedy for the ills of the century. Jean Leflon judges the proposal: *a doctrine for new times without regard for nuances and indispensable distinctions, and driving headlong into infinitely delicate problems with astounding candor. With the exception of Rohrbacher, they ignored history, or what is graver, they assumed to know, and their good will notwithstanding, they barely have a sense of the positive disciplines. These weaknesses however, do not prevent them from attempting to direct the evolution of society as though the future had no need of enlightenment from the past. They thus get snarled into oratorical generalities."* [9] Their good will and sincerity, their brilliance and apostolic zeal were obvious, but the basis of their doctrine and its application needed restudy; the Pope refused to take the matter lightly.

La Mennais repeated his request for an audience. The Pope yielded, provided the object of the pilgrimage not be discussed while the case was under study. The meeting proceeded as the protocol audience of March 13, managed by an unsympathetic cardinal. The discussion centered on matters unrelated to the concerns of the team, complicated by translators because the guests did not speak Italian. Lacordaire, who had suggested the "pilgrimage," understood the language of the Pope, and left Rome on the sixteenth after vainly attempting to persuade Montalembert to leave. He advised Félicité that he might feel compelled to leave him should he persist in his quest. Félicité stayed and Montalembert refused to abandon his master; John prayed for them and worried about the course of events. [10]

On April 26, they withdrew to a hermitage belonging to the Theatine Order in Frascati. [11] There, the hermit of La Chesnaie lived during a few weeks as the hermit of Frascati. Distance from the city relieved him from the preoccupations of Rome, but the harmonies of nature failed to alter his moods. With the encouragement of Ventura, he started a book on the woes of the Church and society and resumed his correspondence. [12]

He wrote to John, to disciples, to friends, without ever neglecting Gerbet, his gentle and clear-minded companion at La Chesnaie. He continued to advise his disciples in Paris. *"I encourage you to continue persistently the studies which you have started, and above all to work at becoming men of virtue and prayer, men of God. ... Set aside a few hours to practice writing every week. ... Beware of trying to learn too many things at a time,"* (To Eugène Boré, March 14, 1832). *"Above all, may God make you men according to his heart, devoted to his Church, detached from self, poor in spirit, humble, zealous, ready to undertake and to suffer everything to spread his word, to extend his kingdom, and to light that divine fire that Jesus Christ brought,"* (to the group through Élie de Kertanguy, 1832). *"Strive ... to progress in the holy ways of humility and of self denial; it is the way of peace, even in this world, the way of contentment and inner joy,"* (To Eugène Boré, April 28, 1832). Nothing at this time would justify any doubt about his wholehearted dedication to the Church and to the apostolate of the Congregation. [13]

He acquainted John with his activities and shared his thoughts on the Congregation of Saint Peter. He was thinking of modifying the Constitutions to include laymen. He considered the possibility of obtaining papal approval for his Congregation after the conclusion of his appeal. He thought of recruiting: *"We would need a few young men between 15 and 18 years of age to form them as that is what we need the most. I know of none more perfect than those we have in Paris."* He planned to correct acknowledged laxity and bared his thoughts, his worries, his financial concerns, and commented: *"We are building on a sound basis, for we could not build closer to the cross,"* (April 24, 1832).

Brooding on the evils of the times seared his soul. Bitterness burst through his correspondence and his conversation clashed with the serenity of a countryside sprawling on the dormant remnants of volcanic upheaval. Contemptuous letters confirmed his disenchantment and alarmed close friends who worried about his faith. Their advice startled him, for there seemed to be nothing further from his mind than estrangement from the Church. The misleading encouragement of friends who misread the situation in Rome, raised false expectations. He formed plans to resume the publication of *l'Avenir* with renewed financing, ever confident of his analysis of Church and society.

Unfortunately, the foreign diplomacy of the Papal States with the Czar became seriously compromised. As Russian armies invaded Poland to quell insurrections against occupation, the Czar requested a papal statement against the Polish rebels in return for his assistance with Russian troops in the Papal States. Unfortunately, Gregory XVI complied on June 9, 1832, an act he later considered a mistake.

The Pontiff's political diplomacy of 1832 further alienated Félicité who sympathized with the Polish people. When the Pope requested the Polish patriots to cease their fighting and accept Czarist authority, it contravened every principle of freedom advocated by Lamennais. By Feli's own words, this concession to the Czar was one of the major factors in Feli's alienation from the Church. Outraged, the writer dropped his pen, stopped work on his book and prepared to leave Rome. He never completed the book as planned, but would later incorporate sections in his *Affaires de Rome* of 1836. He left the Eternal City with Montalembert on July 10, without waiting for the judgment on which he had so vehemently insisted. Friends commented that Felicite had discerned signs of his condemnation in the unfortunate Papal brief against the Polish insurgents. [14]

Hardly had he left Rome when rumors carried the news of a forthcoming censure prepared and signed by 13 French bishops. The document was mainly the work of Archbishop David d'Astros. Known by the diocese of its origin as the Censure of Toulouse, it inventoried 56 presumably condemnable propositions painstakingly extracted from the writings of Félicité. It was originally dated April 23, but was not ready for dispatch until July 15. Rome acknowledged its reception on July 28. As a superfluous initiative terminated when the Church had concluded its study, it received a cool reception a few weeks before the announcement of the Pope's decision, too late for official consideration. Gregory XVI never espoused the accusations from the censure of Toulouse.

The encyclical "Mirari vos," August 15, 1832

Converging pathways providentially reunited the team of *l'Avenir* in Germany. Montalembert and La Mennais were travelling north in August, the voyage an experience of enthusiastic tourism for Montalembert, a slow brooding journey for the master. After leaving Rome, Lacordaire had spent some of his time assisting the victims of the plague in Paris. Realizing that the suspension of *L'Avenir* had jeopardized his future, he left for Germany determined to make a fresh start abroad.

In Munich, Montalembert learnt from the press that Lacordaire had coincidentally stopped in that city and he immediately set out to meet him. The reunion was cheerful, but forebodings of the Roman misadventure chilled the encounter between Lacordaire and La Mennais. The team painfully considered the future of *l'Avenir* which La Mennais intended to resurrect. Lacordaire persuaded the master that resumption was unrealistic and returned to Paris to found a new *Revue* as a voice of their movement; the *Revue* never saw the light. [15]

On August 30, admirers honored La Mennais with a banquet in Munich. During the music which followed the meal, an attendant notified Félicité that someone was asking for him outside. A messenger from the apostolic nunciature was indeed waiting to hand him a cachet containing the judgment of Gregory XVI against the doctrines of *l'Avenir,* and a letter from Cardinal Pacca. The Pope had responded to La Mennais's request for an evaluation of his works with the encyclical *Mirari vos,* dated August 15.

The writer's searching mind assessed the consequences of the decision as quickly as his eyes scanned the text. He calmly regained his seat, asked the artist to repeat the verses sung during his absence, and applauded as though nothing had happened. Only on rising from the table did he whisper to Lacordaire: *"There is an encyclical of the Pope against us; we have no option but to submit."* The three friends and M. Rio returned to La Mennais' residence where La Mennais read the encyclical with trembling emotion, and commented: *"That is the condemnation of liberty and the abandonment of the Polish nation."* A silent pause followed before he added: *"God has spoken, I have no option but to say: 'Fiat voluntas tua,' and to serve those two causes by my prayer, now that, by the intermediary of his Vicar, he forbids me to serve them with my pen."*

Gregory XVI was fully aware that this condemnation struck at the most outspoken champions of papal authority in France. He had instructed his Secretary of State to acknowledge the services of the men of *l'Avenir,* while underscoring the salient points of the encyclical. The letter of Cardinal Pacca affirmed that the Pope had disapproved the errors of the team, but had deliberately eliminated the name of La Mennais, references to the works to which the Pope objected, the title of the paper, or the names of its editors. Gregory XVI objected to certain views expressed in the unruly politics of the day without necessarily condemning all of them, and he did not press the limits of the case. He avoided ruling on the universal consensus argument, (the *sensus communis* of philosophers) at the heart of Félicité de La Mennais' teachings.

Through Cardinal Pacca, the Pope blamed the editors for publicly advocating imprudent solutions to the most delicate questions reserved to the government of the Church and to its chief; La Mennais had overstepped his role and fostered discord. In *Mirari vos*, the Pope blamed *L'Avenir* for exaggerating the freedom of worship and freedom of the press, beyond the limits set in the teachings of the Church. In matters of civil and political liberty, the Pope condemned the *Act of union* as an incitement to revolution, opposing all doctrines leading to sedition and revolt. The three journalists could not help lamenting the misadventures of the Church with new liberal governments, and they emotionally deplored the papal policy towards the Czar's invasion of Poland.

Cardinal Pacca's letter probably weighed heavily on the immediate turn of events. Félicité de La Mennais resolved to cease all publicity and all church activity immediately. *L'Avenir* and its supporting society, the *Agence générale,* would thereby be dissolved. On the following day, he proposed an immediate return to France and prepared to publish the decision on arrival in Paris. It was an act of total submission. [16] Montalembert left the group at Strasbourgh.

On Sept 6, Lacordaire and La Mennais were travelling alone towards France when La Mennais suddenly exclaimed: *"Lacordaire, what if we added a statement to our declaration, the statement **for the moment?** We would say **they withdraw for the moment** from the battle."* Better silence in that case, believed Lacordaire, for with such a corrective, the declaration, which was already barely adequate, would lose all meaning. [17] The pair reached Paris on the tenth, and the original declaration appeared unaltered in print the next day, but Félicité de La Mennais had revealed the direction of his thinking, and friends heard glib irreverencies in his private criticism of the Pope.

A brother in need

Félicité returned to La Chesnaie socially destroyed, discredited in the ecclesiastical community, and financially ruined, not merely by the failure of his newspaper, but by the bankruptcy of a publisher with whom he had imprudently invested considerable sums. An associate, the irresponsible Saint-Victor, had fled the country leaving him sole responsibility for a common debt and for the extravagant claims of creditors. Félicité, now possibly subject to imprisonment on passing the French frontier, wisely planned to stall in Germany and Belgium, while a tribunal reapportioned liabilities.

John understood the embarrassment. He travelled to Paris after his brother's return, stopped at the residence of *rue de Vaugirard* still occupied by a few disciples, and intervened with government officials to ease the claims against his brother. Eugène Boré, wrote to Félicité about the intervention: *"Mr. John leaves this evening; the Minister* [of the Interior] *finally received him Saturday with really surprising cordiality and kindness. He granted him all his requests, and if I do not tell you more about it, it is because your brother will tell you all about his affairs and yours when he sees you at La Chesnaie. . . . He charmed everyone he met here. He has taken great pain to ease your affairs! He has accomplished in two days more than your lawyers and associates in two years.... Your accuser would certainly have obtained imprisonment for debt against you because no one would have proposed the agreement for which Mr. John laid the first foundations,"* (December 17, 1832). [18] By then, Félicité had received a detailed account of the equitable terms obtained in Paris. [19] John was gifted with business sense and the administrative qualities lacking in Félicité. He lent 25 000 francs to his financially strapped brother, then turned to the bewilderment awaiting him in the Congregation of Saint Peter.

Shades of submission and valid inquiry

Humiliation shattered Félicité's inner world and eventually tested the quality of his submission. Gerbet and Lacordaire heard echoes of disillusionment rumbling in the depths of their friend's soul. Realizing that this was not the time to abandon him, they accompanied him to La Chesnaie. There, outbursts of wrath exploded through his conversations in the hallowed solitude which his voice had filled with prayers and prophetic teachings. Adversity was destroying the master.

Lacordaire, perhaps the least attached of the La Chesnaie team, had learned to love Félicité in the pursuit of a common cause. He soon found it impossible to bear the writer's unpredictable moods and stood by until the differences between them became untenable, then left. Finding separation too painful, he walked away quietly, deserted, on December 11, while Félicité was out walking on the estate.

A parting message expressed the feelings which he could not speak: *"I will leave La Chesnaie this evening. I leave it for a motive of honor, convinced that my life would be useless to you on account of the differences in our thinking on Church and society which increase every day despite my sincere efforts to follow the evolution of your opinions. ... Without repudiating my liberal views, I understand and I believe that the Church had very wise reasons, in the profound corruption of parties, for refusing to move as quickly as we wanted it to. ... Only in heaven will you know how much I have suffered during one year, simply in fear of offending you."* [20] Friends later blamed him, not for leaving, but for leaving the way he did.

John's loyalty to the successor of Peter was proverbial. To satisfy his own conscience, and to guide the priests who turned to him for guidance, he immediately submitted to the papal decision, but pondered its bearing on the theological implications of his brother's philosophy. [21] There was no ambiguity about the *Act of union,* but a certain anxiety about Félicité's philosophy disorienting the members of the Congregation of Saint Peter.

When the writer, still Superior General, inquired about the teaching of his doctrines, John answered: *"No one among us has varied in the doctrines which you have defended and we hold to them more than ever; we have never hesitated to teach them. With respect to your new philosophy, you yourself did not want us to speak about it before its completion; in fact, nothing would be more dangerous, for we would certainly not understand it, and we would attribute to your name many things that you would disavow, if we opened premature discussions,"* (May 18, 1833). [22]

Félicité was indeed still laboring on a revised expression of his philosophy. The Pope had prudently avoided condemning everything in his work. A tranquil mind could have pursued valid inquiry under the circumstances, but the reports of friends to an anguished soul encouraged wishful thinking and imprudent presumptions; Félicité assumed that what was not specifically condemned, was not disapproved.

The encyclical makes difficult reading on the issues of freedom, but it had not explicitly condemned all the leading declarations proposed by the editors in February 1831. [23] There was room for differences of opinion, pending further directives; the problem was to find it. Even the questions mentioned in the encyclical seemed open to interpretation.

John's clarifications for the Congregation of Saint Peter corrected several hasty conclusions. He observed for instance, that in prevailing circumstances, the Pope saw more disadvantages than advantages in the separation of Church and State advocated for post-revolutionary France. He deplored public agitation about the matter, but that did not mean that he condemned the opinion in itself. John observed that the Pope had approved for Belgium, what the editors of *l'Avenir* were advocating for France. [24] The experience of changed circumstances in other times would cast a different light on the same words and open the way to new solutions, though the hostilities of 1832 were not conducive to understanding.

John assumed wider responsibilities in the Congregation of Saint Peter. His most difficult challenge was to maintain a vital bond between disoriented communities. He wrote to Félicité: *"Some seem to be saying that I lack zeal: that does not take into account the difficulties of all sorts which interfere with the good that we mean to perform, and which I must overcome daily, without complaint and without disclosure to anyone; . . . I will add nothing to this brief statement for the moment,"* (May 18, 1833). [25] He worried about community discipline and prepared to offset the toll of persecution on its members.

The objections of Montalembert and La Mennais to the bewildering political Vatican pact with the Czar, would have been sufficient cause for grief without additional misrepresentation in the press. [26] On July 1, 1832, six weeks before *Mirari vos,* and before the first act of submission, Félicité had written the following statement in a letter to Louis de Potter, a militant advocate of the liberation of Belgium: *"It is with the people, the real people that we must identify ourselves; it alone must we see; it, alone must be brought to defend its own cause, to decide and to act. ... I feel as resolved as ever to resume the great combat to which I have dedicated my life. ... But in no case will I remain silent, and you may expect that my statements will be clear. The time has come to say everything."* [27]

The letter was intercepted by Metternich's agents, and a copy was transmitted to the Vatican. On February 19, 1833, six weeks after the Pope's encyclical, a Belgian newspaper, the *Courrier Belge*[28], published a reply of de Potter to one of La Mennais' letters. The writer unthinkingly quoted Félicité, without dating the letter. Since de Potter's letter was dated September 4, 1832, it made it appear that Félicité had broken his recent promise to cease the activities blamed in the encyclical. A copy of the paper was dispatched to the Vatican, and the misinformed Pope later referred to it as evidence of insincerity by Felicite. The outcome of the controversial letter would have been less damaging, if La Mennais' correspondence had not otherwise justified suspicions about his insubordination as Gregory XVI held additional negative information.

Félicité's letters were far from models of reserve and clear thinking. An angry pen moved through his correspondence at the time: *"If I were inclined to reprint the Apostle's Creed at this time, there would be at least ten to twelve heresies in it,"* (to Guéranger, Nov. 30, 1832). He dubbed the Pontiff *"a cowardly and imbecile old man,"* for manifesting discontent with Father Ventura, (To Montalembert, May 8, 1833). He conveyed an irredeemable image of Rome: *"I have gone to Rome and I have seen there the most infamous cesspools that have ever sullied the eyes of men. The gigantic sewers of the Tarquins would be too narrow to allow the passage of so much sewage. There, no other God but interest; one would sell the people, one would sell the human race, one would sell the three persons of the Blessed Trinity each in turn, or all together, for a plot of land, or for a few coins. I saw that and I said to myself: this evil is beyond the powers of man, and I turned my eyes away in disgust and fright,"* (To the Countess of Senfft, November 1, 1832). [29]

Fortunately, Feli's philosophical principles were not clarified or condemned in Mirari vos of August 15, 1832. Félicité did not thoroughly assess its theological implications and he still struggled with elusive solutions. The prudence of the Holy See in times of generalized revolutions should not have surprised him. As guardian of doctrine and as protector of the Church, the Pope had responsibilities beyond those of Félicité.

Church historians observe that *"La Mennais would have needed prudence, training, time to provide a sound analysis of the theological and historical difficulties concealed in the neuralgic confrontation between traditional Church doctrines and liberal principles. This hope was far too elusive to expect that time, the realities of history, and the requirements of doctrine to provide a prophet the wisdom to present acceptable solutions on such controversial matters."* [30]

The clergy of Rennes requested and expected a personal declaration of submission from every member of the Congregation of Saint Peter. The confusion on the matter bedeviled relationships among diocesan priests, and even within the Congregation of St. Pierre. Community members were unfairly distrusted by the diocesan clergy, and the confusion in the proper understanding of the encyclical and the nature of the submission expected of them caused further divisions.

Father Coëdro, Superior of the missionaries in Rennes, wrote to his Superior General, objecting to his public statements on the Polish question, and asked him to relieve tensions by providing the clarification requested by the Pope. Gregory XVI was indeed asking Félicité to dispel doubts about his loyalty. Félicité now saw how precarious his position had become and realized that his personal embarrassment was no longer exclusively personal.

On July 20, 1833, the Pope admitted in a letter to Archbishop d'Astros, that the encyclical was directed at the writers of *l'Avenir*. During the weeks which followed, Félicité wrote several letters about his situation. One of them was a statement of submission to Gregory XVI in which he announced his resolution to withdraw from Church affairs: *"I declare that, for many reasons, but particularly because the judgment of what is proper and useful belongs to the head of the Church, I have taken the resolution to remain totally separate from the affairs which concern it,"* (August 4, 1833). [31] He then sent the letter to the Bishop of Rennes for transmission to the Holy See.

He advised his brother that he had decided to leave the Congregation of Saint Peter: *"I reflected on what I owed to the Congregation, and I believe to be satisfying that duty. Anticipating insofar as it is in my power the internal disturbance likely to compromise its existence, I address to the Sovereign Pontiff a new declaration which I am sending to the Bishop of Rennes and requesting him to address it himself to the Pope. ... Secondly, having recognized the impossibility of achieving any good in the Congregation, because of the attitude of several of its members towards me, I believe that I must separate myself from it, whatever the cost. It is unfortunately evident that I would be a cause of division."* (August 4, 1833).

A personal decision taken a few months earlier signaled the deeper rupture in his soul: he had celebrated his last mass in the presence of friends on Easter, April 7. By the middle of August, Gerbet also severed all ties with the Congregation while continuing personal relationship with Félicité. [32] The Congregation of Saint Peter had lost one of its Founders, its Superior General, and its peace. Its fate now lay with the Bishop, with John de La Mennais, and with its leading members. To rule out all possible doubt about his own loyalty, John sent to his bishop a letter of total submission to the declarations of *Mirari vos*. [33] The gesture would normally have been superfluous, but widespread suspicion of anything and anyone related to Félicité made it necessary.

The confrontations that followed during the ecclesiastical retreats of August and September were not models of ecclesiastical fraternity. Bishop de Lesquen asked Fathers Coëdro and Hoguet to direct the retreat for the priests of the diocese. The opposition to Félicité having intensified,

Coëdro sensed the need to reassure the diocesan clergy with a statement of full acceptance of the encyclical by all members of the Congregation of Saint Peter. He drafted a statement and submitted it to Father de La Mennais; John disagreed with it because it seemed to repudiate the basic doctrines of *l'Avenir* which did not all appear condemned by the encyclical. He opposed a submission broader than the explicit requirements of the text.

On the first day of the retreat, Coëdro apparently satisfied the priests with a statement acceptable to John, though some priests thought it too vague and insisted on a clearer admission of error. On the last day, in the absence of Coëdro, Father de la Guéretterie, cure of Vitré, publicly expressed to the Bishop the dissatisfaction of most priests with the declaration of the preceding week. Caught off guard, Bishop de Lesquen asked the Superior of the Missionaries for a more explicit statement. Coëdro complied in the interests of peace, mentioning *l'Avenir* and confessing that he had "erred in accepting some of its positions." The avowal widened the feud when he read it in a low tone to a displeased clergy.

The controversy did not end by an admission of error. Before the September retreat, Father de La Mennais drafted a careful interpretation of the Papal document to reassure his men that they were in compliance with the teachings of *Mirari vos.* He deplored exaggerations in the understanding of the text, and would not require submission beyond that required by the Pope.[34]

How would peace return to the Congregation? The withdrawal of Félicité forced a change of captains in troubled times. During the retreat, Bishop de Lesquen asked the members of the Congregation to elect a Superior General. Who but John was likely to restore trust and regain stability? He had been the adviser, the organizer, the stabilizer and a major provider of supplementary funds since the beginning. He served as the acting administrator, the common bond between the various communities, and the link between the Congregation of Saint Peter and the Bishop. Once elected, he called Fathers Coëdro, Corvasier, Enoch, Rohrbacher, Blanc and Ruault to form his council. Father Coëdro continued as Superior of the Missionaries of Rennes. It was now John's responsibility to harmonize the life of the communities, to restore stability while dealing with the first departures; unfortunately, peace was not in sight for the priests of the Congregation.

---

[1] Jean Leflon, *La Crise révolutionnaire,* 1789-1846, Paris: Bloud et Gay, 1949. (Histoire de l'Église, publiée sous la direction de Augustin Fliche et Victor Martin, v. 20.), pages 426-471.

[2] Henri Guillemin, *Histoire des Catholiques français au XIXe siècle* (1815-1905), Genève, Paris, Montréal: Éditions du Milieu de Monde, 1947, p. 73.

[3] **FL Cond,** Text, pp. 531-540.

[4] The statement of February 2, 1831. **FL Cond,** pp. 509-530.

[5] See Louis Le Guillou, **FL Cond,** p. 70. "If Lamennais had known of the mountains of paper assembling under his name, and if he had seen the voluminous reports of the Roman consultants, he would no doubt have changed his mind" about their unpreparedness, page 8.

[6] Boutard, op., cit., v. 2, pp. 258-342. Alexander Roper Vidler, *Prophecy and Papacy, A Study of La Mennais, the Church and the Revolution,* London: SCM Press, 1954, pages 184-220.

[7] *The Mémoire* of February 3, 1832. **FL Cond,** pp. 541-592.

[8] **Cor gén F,** v., 5, pp. 93, 579.

[9] Leflon, op., cit., p. 443.

[10] See his letters to Father Ruault, February 12, March 12, April 7, in **Cor gén J,** v. 2, pp. 549. 550-551, 555-556.

[11] Boutard, op. cit., v. 2, pp. 293-317.

[12] *Des maux de l'Église et de la société et des moyens d'y remédier.* He incorporated sections in *Les Affaires de Rome,* of 1836.

[13] Dargis, op. cit., pp.401-405.

[14] See Jean-René Derré, *Metternich and Lamennais,* Paris: Presses Universitaires de France, 1963, page 108.

[15] Among the numerous accounts of this experience, see Boutard, op. cit., v. 2, pp. 318-407.

[16] **Cor gén F,** v. 5, 177-178. The declaration, destined for publishers, was dated September 10, and appeared on Sept. 11, in the *Tribune catholique.*

[17] M. Foisset, *Vie du R. P. Lacordaire,* Paris et Lyon: Librairie Jacques Lecoffre, 1873. V. 1, pp. 213-214.

[18] Alfred Roussel, *Lamennais intime,* Paris: P. Lethielleux, 1897, pages 133-134. **Lav.,** v. 1, pp. 486-490.

[19] Letters, November 23 and December 2, 1832. **Cor gén J,** v. 2, pp. 597-598, 600.

[20] Charles de Montalembert, *Le Père Lacordaire,* Paris: Charles Douniol, 1862, pages 61-64.

[21] Text of submission, June 29, 1832. **Cor gén J,** v. 2, p. 567.

[22] **Cor gén J,** v. 3, pp. 29-30, **Cor gén F,** v. 5, p. 738.

[23] Dargis, op. cit., p. 504 ff.

[24] Declaration to the members of the Congregation of Saint Peter, September 1833, **Cor gén J,** v. 3, pp. 53-54, and **Lav.** v. 1, pp. 548-550.

[25] **Cor gén J,** v. 3, pp. 29-30, and **Cor gén F,** v. 5, p. 738.

[26] See Gaston Bordet, *La Pologne, Lamennais et ses amis,* 1830-1834. Paris:Éditions du dialogue, 1985, pages 106-107. Montalembert participated in the translation of Mickiewicz's *Livre des Pèlerins polonais* (published in May, 1833), and obtained the permission of F. de La Mennais to publish his *Hymne à la Pologne* (Hymn to Poland) in the postscript. (The hymn had been written in Rome in 1832).

[27] **Cor gén F,** v. 5, pp. 147-148. Photostat of letter, article on "La Mennais" in the Italian *Enciclopedia Cattolica,* (Citta del Vaticano), vol. 7, pp. 850-858. Gustave Charlier, "La "Duplicité" de Lamennais", *Revue d'Histoire littéraire de la France,* Vol. 40, pp. 109-114, (January-March, 1933). Jean René Derré, *Metternich et Lamennais,* Paris: Presses universitaires de France, 1963. Lettre, pp. 110-111.

[28] Also, the *Journal de la Haye* on the 22nd.

[29] At the dates given in **Cor gén F,** v. 7 and 8. He discredits Rome and Church authority as he was prone to vilify whatever displeases him. In letters to Marion we read that society is traversing *"a kind of sewer"* (Oct. 8, 1836), that *"France is rotting on dung,"* (April 3, 1838), that Paris is an *"immense sewer,"* (Nov. 10, 1838), and he declares to the Marquis of Coriolis that the men with whom they are living belong to *"an aborted generation,"* (Nov. 8, 1837). On December 15, 1832, he had written to the Countess of Senfft: ("Of disappearing institutions"). *"It is mud flowing in a sewer and nothing else. Let us look at it from a distance, and hold our noses."* Vol. 5, p. 245. Political hierarchy and

ecclesiastical hierarchy in their present state are vanishing like *"two phantoms embracing in a tomb,"* (to Montalembert, Jan. 26, 1833. Ibid., p. 298).

[30] A. Latreille , J.-R. Palanque (etc.), *Histoire du catholicisme en France,* Paris: Spes, 1962. V. 3, p. 287.

[31] **FL Cond,** Document 139, pp. 373-374. **Cor gén F,** v. 5, pp. 446-447. See related letters and documents for the years 1832 - 1834 in each collection.

[32] The developments are complex. Writers have based their accounts on letters, reports, memoirs, official statements many of which suggest unrecorded intervening conversations and controversy. The available documents neither lay out the full record nor do they resolve all contradictions. See Boutard, op. cit., v. 2, pp. 343-407. **Lav.,** v. 1, pp. 490-500. Dargis, op. cit., pp. 465-530.

[33] August 6, 1833. **Cor gén J,** v. 3, p. 43.

[34] See **Cor gén J,** v. 3, pp. 47-52 on the search for a clear expression in the exhortation of August 26, the statement to Coëdro of August 27, and the declarations to de Lesquen and to the Congregation in September.

Chapter 21

"Oak Broken by the Storm"

John de La Mennais at the helm, 1833-1834

With revolution in the wind, religious persecution on the rise and its first Superior General gone, the Congregation of Saint Peter turned to John de La Mennais for leadership. Though he had already been discharging major responsibilities since the beginning of the Congregation, the dissidence of Félicité paralyzed the activities of the Congregation of Saint Peter, forcing John to accept this new leadership role. [1] The community of *rue de Vaugirard* in Paris began to disperse, a few disciples moving to Brittany, those without a calling to the priesthood withdrawing. Early in September, Félicité informed the residents of La Chesnaie about the changed relationships between him and the Congregation and asked them to leave; he kept as his only assistant, Élie de Kertanguy, who would later enter the family by marrying his niece Augustine.

The candidates for the novitiate left to participate in the annual retreat at the minor seminary of Saint Méen. Three weeks later, the Bishop assigned them to begin their novitiate in the home of the Brothers of Christian Instruction in Ploërmel. The crisis tested loyalties, strained relations, drained the courage of some, caused others to lose their vision. Félicité described his dwindling Congregation as *"more insignificant,"* while John struggled to motivate the standing battalion.

Divisions within the diocesan clergy discouraged Bishop de Lesquen. On September 30, 1833, he offered his resignation to the Pope,

who refused it. Felicite's attitude fostered such confusion that the Bishop thought it advisable to ask the members of the community for a new unequivocal declaration of submission to the encyclical. John sent his immediately, (October 23, 1833); the priests from the seminary of Saint Méen, the missionaries of Rennes, and the directors of Malestroit followed.
2

The ecclesiastical community still distrusted Félicité. Unfortunately, the writer did not help his own cause as his dissident correspondence, supervised and methodically spied upon by the diplomatic community, his published criticism of the Pope's unfortunate Polish policy, and various misconceived declarations alarmed his friends and armed his opponents. Lingering equivocations in relationships with his ecclesiastical superiors displeased the Holy See.

A new crisis ruffled relationships when the Pope asked him to dispel doubts about his sincerity. Gregory XVI wrote to Bishop de Lesquen, October 5, requesting a new unequivocal declaration. Félicité received the message as he was about to leave for Paris. Instead of sending his reply to the Bishop for dispatch to the Pope, as requested, he advised his superior that he would forward it directly to the Pope in a few days. De Lesquen had patiently suffered from Feli's resistance and unpredictability; on November 4, he forbad him to exercise all priestly functions in his home diocese. John dreaded the consequence of new humiliations on his hypersensitive brother.

From October 5, to December 10, 1833, ill-timed messages from various sources vexed all parties in a carrousel of frustrations. Before seeing the Bishop's circular, Félicité wrote to the Pope, November 5, repeating that he still fully accepted the doctrines of the encyclical, and that his attitude had never changed, but he again evaded the inconsistencies at issue.

On December 6, he wrote another letter and a memorandum to explain his letter of November 5. Cardinal Pacca informed him, December 10, that the declaration of November 5, did not satisfy the Pope, and that he was expected to conform clearly to the "brief" of November 15. Letters had crossed: The Pope had obviously not seen the statement of December 6. Félicité replied to the new request with his declaration of December 11, the third in less than six weeks. On the same day he sent a copy of the declaration to his Bishop and offered his respects. De Lesquen expressed satisfaction, December 15, and publicly lifted the diocesan interdict. The Pope congratulated Félicité, December 28; relative quiet returned to the diocese, but Félicité had neither mastered his grief, nor resolved the inconsistency of his conduct.

The contradictions between his professions of loyalty and the forthrightness of his correspondence are delicate personal matters about which it is best to let Féli testify for himself. Pierre Sébastien Laurentie reports a conversation about his last act of compliance: *"I signed! I signed! I would have signed that the moon had fallen in China!"* [3] He confessed that he had signed *"to end it all, to have only other concerns to care for,"* (to Marion, administrator of La Chesnaie, December 24, 1833). He expressed it otherwise to Montalembert: *"The issue of truth which had previously preoccupied me until then, the sad affair was seen now only as a question of peace, peace at any price. ... But at the same time, I decided to cease all priestly functions, which I have done,"* (January 1, 1834). To the Countess of Senfft he added: *"I wanted to begin nobly an entirely new life, beyond the storms generated by the most infected vapors emanating from the human heart,"* (January 24, 1834).

He wrote more revealing disclosures. Father Ventura, his ally in Rome, read about the evolution of his thought: *"The doctrines which had been mine, and which I have defended with a total and sincere conviction, for which I have suffered and would have willingly suffered more, those doctrines, today, are very far from me,"* (May 8, 1833). He reaffirmed his stand to Montalembert: *"I renounce practical politics also, which has become henceforth impossible for me, and without exception, to everything which has filled my previous life. I will try, though tardily, to begin a new one.... We will meet above, I hope, but we will walk two different courses on earth,"* (December 13, 1833).

He was officially professing acceptance of the encyclical as he wrote such private correspondence. *"That sort of submission is valueless,"* observed the Church historian Adrien Dansette, admirer of his past accomplishments. *"He merely wanted to free himself to begin a new life consecrated to politics; we wonder to what extent he had not detached himself from Catholicism, or had not ceased to believe in the divine mission of the Church."* He had already written his next book; [4] the course was set, whatever the consequences. He later confessed to Sainte-Beuve, the friend who found him a publisher: *"There is surely in my character, a certain stubborn and blameworthy impetuosity which I have not sufficiently attempted to repress, that my ideas preoccupy me excessively, that I press them forward with too much force,"* (July 30, 1834). [5]

Félicité was sharing his time between Paris and La Chesnaie, while John was coping with explosive tensions in the diocese, with fragile relationships within the Congregation, and with the thorniest personal rapports about his humiliated brother. The truest friends observed the writer with anxiety, and John soon learned that bitterness was driving his brother's pen. Félicité obligingly read excerpts to John from a new manuscript as he had to Gerbet and a few other friends.

The selections which he offered compelled admiration, heavenly echoes rang through the first selections, verses of tender melancholy and pages sparkling with poetic eloquence, but both John and Gerbet soon realized that the pages which they admired had been presented selectively. *"Next to the hymns, there were blasphemies; curses of unparalleled violence were called down successively upon royalty and the Catholic hierarchy; the sequence formed a strange medley of anathemas and prayers, heavenly visions and infernal scenes which amazed, troubled and eventually entranced the reader."* [6]

Before the book appeared, he courteously answered his Bishop's inquiry, *"You have good reason to believe that I will never violate my voluntary commitment not to write on matters of religion. ... In the future, I will write as I have announced, only on matters of philosophy, science and politics. The little book about which you have been told, is of the latter genre,"* April 29, 1834.

The book may not have been originally meant for the public, but Félicité announced its release to Benoit d'Azy a month before publication: *"You will be less satisfied with my decision which I believed to be a duty. ... "The Words of a Believer" is being printed. Whatever follows matters little for me; satisfaction with self is preferable to everything else. I prefer the tempests outside, to those within,"* (March 29, 1834). With this publication, the interior tempest would roar outside. [7]

"The Words of a Believer," April 30, 1834

In April 1834, Félicité was in Paris, at *rue de Vaugirard* with a few disciples. He had invited the literary critic Sainte-Beuve to meet him about an important matter. The visitor crossed the De Quelen, Archbishop of Paris in the courtyard when he came for the rendezvous. Feli started without delay: *"My friend, it is high time for all this to end."* He opened the drawer of a little wooden table, took a thin notebook written in fine script, handed it to him with instructions to have it published *"as soon as possible. I leave in two days. Make arrangements with a publisher quickly, very quickly, I beg you. I do not wish my name on it."* Eugène Renduel, the publisher, accepted the manuscript despite certain misgivings about the subject matter, but deplored the request for anonymity. La Mennais reassured Sainte-Beuve: *"You are the absolute master. You may change what you wish."*

Sainte-Beuve suppressed two lines which *"seemed to violate proprieties concerning the Pope and Catholicism,"* and replaced them with dots. The correspondence suggests that the two men had discussed the matter, and that Félicité had previously suppressed a page, not merely two lines. It will be clear to everyone from now on, wrote Sainte-Beuve, that La Mennais *"had entered full sails into a new ocean."* [8] A few days before the release of Words of a Believer, he had written to the Baron de Vitrolles: *"Of what importance is it to me, old sailor so often knocked by the waves, if I untie my small craft from the shore and launch it on the waves again?"* (April 25, 1834) [9]

Printing was in progress when Félicité came to Ploërmel and informed his brother. John embraced him and insisted: *"I beg you, do not publish that!"* Montalembert had pleaded as much by letter on April 8. Félicité resorted to evasions until remorse triumphed and he asked John to hear his confession. A coach was then waiting for John who was preparing to visit his schools. He advised his brother to ask one of the chaplains of the house for the sacrament, and left.

Preoccupied for not having taken the time to hear his brother's confession, he met him at La Chesnaie the next day and pleaded with him to recall the manuscript. Félicité yielded, handed him a letter ordering the publisher to stop the printing; John dashed to post it at Dinan. The next day, April 30, the bold newspaper headlines informed him that *The Words of a Believer (Les Paroles d'un Croyant)* was in the ·hands of readers. John understood the consequences too well. Before reading the full published version, he denounced it to Guizot, to Father Coëdro, and to his Bishop, and proscribed it from the houses of his religious communities. [10]

Typesetters generally labor unmindful of the lead at their fingertips, but the publisher told Sainte-Beuve how they previewed this book: *"Even my employees cannot set type without being inspired and spellbound; the print shop is all agog."* The public was soon to be. *"One must have seen the magic impact of that book to realize the power of such a stream of thought. It seemed like a flash of lightning illuminating all horizons at once."* [11] The first issue was unsigned, like the *Essai sur l'Indifférence* in 1817, but the author's entourage awaited its appearance. Readers who could not acquire copies read through it on paid time in reading salons.

Hymns and execrations rose from its pages, astounding Paris, entrancing the nation, echoing abroad. The printers could not keep up with requests. Ernest Renan described the book as *"a sublime Apocalypse, a real Sabbath of anger and love... Lamennais intersperses pages burning with hatred, with oases of verdure,"* [12] mixing *"visions of heaven with those of hell."* Some hear alternating accents *"of prayer and blasphemy,"* inspiring pages compelling admiration. The author invokes God in prayer and hope, calling for justice, compassion, peace, freedom, love. The prose was spellbinding, *"a sublime new language, prodigious, incomparable,"* rhythmic prose set in verses resembling those of the Bible. The message left no reader neutral.

By selecting passages, one could present the book either as a breeze from heaven or a blast from hell, as a Gospel for the times, a cry against oppression, a plea for justice and freedom, or as the Apocalypse of Satan, a call to rebellion, a rejection of the Church, a defiance of Gregory XVI, and a repudiation of the author's past. Read separately from the circumstances of its publication, it could stand as a masterpiece of prophetic poetry; however, it could not be severed from the personal conflicts which inspired its power. No one misunderstood the message; his closest friends disavowed his work, while Felicite's biographers have called it his claim to independence.

The little book resounded like a thunder-clap in a frowning sky and spun gale winds despite the labors of peacemakers. The small book revived controversy and persecution around the Congregation of Saint Peter, shattering hope for the author's reconciliation with the Church, and opening new wounds in the heart of his brother. On May 4, 1834, John wrote to Father Coëdro: *"To pray and to hope is all that remains for me now. What I suffer is merely the beginning of what I must suffer... I must prepare my soul for sufferings 'vast as the sea,' I know it too well. Blessed be the Lord!"* [13]

Sainte-Beuve thought that the book had been written in a week, but this text tapped deep, long-festering wellsprings of anger. As early as 1829, observed Boutard, *"do we not seem to have under our eyes the 'Words of a Believer"* in the letters of Félicité to the Countess of Senfft. [14] The same themes reappeared in letters to other correspondents and in private texts intended for future use, parts of which served as the basis for the Discussions critiques, published in 1841. [15] By the admission of the author to Ange Blaize, the work was "the fruit of mature reflection," (April 27, 1834). [16] Silent seething anger had exploded. [17]

John sought peace and reconciliation, otherwise the whirlwind sown by his brother would rip through his course. He wrote to his Bishop de Lesquen: *"You already know how sharp is the pain I experienced on learning through the newspapers of the publication of a book which has so sadly been troubling minds for several days. Alas! Why must a new tempest follow upon other successfully appeased tempests? It alarms me beyond words. I am grief-stricken, and I need to receive from you a few kind words to comfort my broken heart. Moreover, I know this book merely from news reports*[18]. *I do not wish to read it, and I have forbidden its reading in our houses; but whatever the judgment passed upon it by our Holy Father and the bishops, we will never hesitate (and you may be sure, in advance) to accept invariably and uniquely the decisions of those who have been told by Truth itself: 'whoever listens to you listens to me, whoever despises you despises me,'"* (May 10, 1834). [19]

De Lesquen did indeed comfort John, but he also published the letter with his reply in the *Gazette de Bretagne,* without consulting him and without seeming to realize the possible consequences of the negative publicity on the fragile relationships between the two brothers. [20] After requesting confidentiality, John had to live with a *fait accompli.* He wrote to Coëdro: *"I am hurt by the publication of my letter ... Nothing more cruel could have been done to me, more offensive to Félicité and to the Church. I will no longer be able to do anything to save the one, and to spare the other. ... Alas! I dare not continue ... Oh! how burdensome life is,"*(May 21, 1834). [21]

A quivering hope for understanding wavered through his apology to Félicité: *"Yesterday, I was informed of something which caused me infinite pain, because it is likely to cause you a great deal also. Here is the exact truth. The Bishop asked me a fortnight ago ... to write him a letter about your book, which he would keep in his office, and show only to persons who would attack my establishments on account of it. [Follows a summary of the Bishop's letter.] ... Without asking my consent, and without even advising me about it, the letter was published with a reply from the Bishop, which I received only after its publication. Surely, had I suspected that, and had this been done with my approval, I would have told you last Sunday, and I know you too well to fear that you would have blamed me. The result of the preceding explanations may suggest that I seem to have hidden from you the conduct that I believed I must hold.... My letter has been abused by giving it unintended publicity; I am hurt and I suffer, a great deal more than you will, you may be sure: I am heartbroken. I embrace you affectionately,"* (May 23, 1834). [22]

The brother's cutting reply bared deeper anguish, *"If I am offended by that, it is for you and not for myself ... How could one say: I wanted to do this or that secretly and not publicly? That would be aggravating shame. Since we must willy-nilly, always suffer in this world, I personally always prefer the sufferings which leave no regrets, the sufferings which do not stain," (May 28, 1834)* [23]. He understood better than his words, for he later wrote to a friend that his brother was to be more pitied than blamed with his fifty schools under threat of attack from right and left.

The book and the circumstances of John's letter shattered the relative peace settling in after the Pope's first encyclical. With the diocesan clergy in uproar, the press aflame with controversy, and the priests of the Congregation of Saint Peter discredited with their Superior, Pope Gregory XVI intervened a second time.

The encyclical "Singulari nos," June 25, 1834

Gregory XVI added the book to the Index of Prohibited Books and responded with a second encyclical, *Singulari nos* on June 25, 1834. The record shows that it came after patient attempts to avoid the first encyclical, and after repeated requests for clarification of the writer's position. Father Blanc was in Paris before the promulgation of the encyclical. Archbishop de Quélen communicated the essentials of the text to him on July 13. Blanc informed John immediately on his return to Malestroit that the Pope disapproved the philosophy of *sensus communis* that was still taught in their institution. John wrote to Blanc, July 18, analyzed the essentials of the document, expressed a first prudent judgment about the condemned doctrine and assured him that all the religious of Saint Peter would submit without reservation. [24]

The encyclical was a verdict rather than a statement of principles, as *Mirari vos* had largely been. Félicité learned about it on July 15. The Pope described the *"Words of a Believer as "small in volume, but immense in perversity."* He expressed regrets that the hoped for priestly compliance had vanished, blamed the author for promoting disobedience, and advocating a false theory of power, destructive of all authority. He scored the abuse of Scripture in the defense of the author's opinions.

The Pope had not judged the writer's philosophy in *Mirari vos*; he now felt compelled to deal with the theory of *sensus communis,* (the universal consensus argument) the source of unabated controversy since the Essay on Indifference. The new document condemned *The Words of a Believer,* along with the philosophical system expounded by Félicité and his disciples. [25]

On July 19, 1834, Montalembert, astounded by the encyclical, invited Félicité to desist, though in vain. He had so far even deferred his own act of public submission, despite the invitation of Lacordaire to yield openly. Now that Félicité had dispelled his last illusions, he deplored his audacity and his own procrastination. He noted in his journal, that after long deliberate reflection, at the age of twenty-four, he sent an act of categorical submission to Cardinal Pacca on December 8, 1834, the feast of the Immaculate Conception. [26] When the likelihood of convincing his master to desist faded from his mind, the friendship of the heart survived in hope.

John's first thought was for his brother. [27] He could easily renounce his own association with the condemned doctrines, but the journey through confusion had its pitfalls. Grief broke through his most insightful interventions as he confronted the members of the Congregation, Bishop de Lesquen and the diocesan clergy. He handed in his own written submission to the two encyclicals. In deference to the extreme sensibility of his brother, he again requested confidentiality from the Bishop.

John had been a disciple of his brother in matters of philosophy. Along with Rohrbacher, Gerbet and others, he had been persuaded that the universal consensus argument resolved the problem of certitude better than others and had endorsed its teaching at Malestroit. Complexity did not easily defeat him. He now analyzed the encyclical to avoid interpretations broader than the meaning of the text, as he had done after the first encyclical, and sought clarifications in the hope of salvaging the valid elements in his brother's work. He risked misunderstanding and personal discredit as he outlined distinctions worthy of consideration in his correspondence with Bishop de Lesquen, and in explanations to brother priests. Once convinced of his mistakes, he abandoned the search and invited all the members of the Congregation of Saint Peter to repudiate, without reservations, the condemned philosophical and theological positions.[28]

Tensions were high and the times were not open to subtle distinctions. By then, negative attitudes against Félicité were affecting John's personal life. A few friends even questioned his loyalty, randomly accusing him of approving his brother's dissidence. He nevertheless considered requesting new clarifications from Roman authorities, and drafted detailed replies to personal attacks published against him by the *Ami de la Religion* and the *Univers religieux.*[29] In each case, he abided by the request of Bishop de Lesquen who believed that rebuttal would merely sharpen rivalries. Felicite's book had planted the sword of division in the diocese of Rennes, in the Congregation of Saint Peter, and in John's heart. The two brothers were now working at cross purposes.

Ousted!

Bishop de Lesquen explained to John how tensions forced him to dissolve the Congregation of Saint Peter. *"I realize with pain ... that the Congregation is divided and that several members demand a separation. ... Their reasons seem too strong and too well founded to refuse. Consequently, I must notify you that I am taking under my immediate direction those who are separating themselves from you, and that I place them in charge of my minor seminary of Saint-Méen, and of my house of missionaries. I allow those who wish to follow you the full liberty of doing so, but please tell them on my behalf that I consider them dissociated from my diocese where I will offer them no assignment,"* (Sept. 2, 1834).[30] Formal instructions about his role in the forthcoming elections of a new superior followed. The bishop then formally disbarred John from any leadership role in the Congregation of St. Peter: *"I have always spoken to you honestly; for that reason I must tell you that in the present state of minds, and in the prevailing circumstances, you must declare before the election that you may not accept any office in the Congregation,"* (Sept. 12, 1834).

While his bishop was dismissing him outright, he prepared the election with the most loyal of discourses. The advice he spoke to his brother priests from the pulpit could not be simpler, more direct and more trustworthy: *"Remain unshakable in your loyalty and submission to the See of Peter. ... Never hesitate, as I do not personally hesitate, to perform all the sacrifices required for the salvation of souls. May the man who will replace me and who is still unknown to me not be discouraged and have no fear! May he keep a firm hand at the helm of that poor little bark beaten by so many storms. I am convinced that everyone will strive to lighten his burden and to facilitate his task, by lovingly obeying him, by considering his desires as orders, and zealously pursuing his directives,"* (Sept. 7). [31]

The Congregation elected Father Coëdro Superior General, Sept. 14. No one could be more cooperative than John de La Mennais. The Congregation of Saint Peter no longer existed; it once again became the Congregation of the Priests of Saint-Méen, by the name of the seminary. Malestroit was closed; its ecclesiastical students moved to the Seminary of Saint-Méen. Later, the society was reorganized under the name of the Priests of the Immaculate Conception.

John meant to continue in service as a simple member. He had been enlisting the help of the missionaries to preach spiritual retreats in schools, and he was invited to lead the retreat at the *Collège de Saint-Malo*. Without fully realizing the alienation distancing him from the missionaries, he asked Father Coëdro for help. The request embarrassed Coëdro who explained that his men now resented associating with his work: *"I felt obliged to express this to the Bishop who decided that our Community would not go to that retreat. His Excellency has justified this decision by the fact that **you are no longer part of the Congregation**,"* (Oct. 22, 1834).

John had become an outsider without even the benefit of notification; he replied in pain: *"This procedure surprises me, even after the others. ... O my God, forgive my poor Coëdro, as I forgive him. The most deserving of pity is not me."*(Oct. 31, 1834). [32] The confusion was such that even ecclesiastical superiors and close associates in a position to know his mind failed to understand his innocence. Loyalty and merit mattered little to them as discreditors had blurred the differences between the two brothers.

He bore the pain in silence. The defamations which kept destroying his brother's life burdened his own. He pleaded with Archbishop de Quélen of Paris not to forsake the wounded writer. *"As far as I am concerned, I no longer have any influence on him: that possibility has been completely taken from me through acts of imprudence that I could not too forcibly deplore. There are men who seem to have been endowed with the infernal mission of shoving towards the abyss a man, who could have prevented many others from falling into it, had he been more humble,"* (May 21, 1835). [33]

A trusted friend misjudged John's misfortune. Bruté de Rémur, recently appointed missionary bishop of Vincennes, Indiana, had been closely allied with the two brothers during happier times. He was in France in the fall of 1835, during the controversies which followed the condemnation of *The Words of a Believer*. He misinterpreted the differences between the two brothers, and distance had warped the heroic missionary's sense of reality about the personality of Félicité. After an absence of several years, he came to La Chesnaie with blundering zeal while Félicité was struggling with the consequences of his second condemnation. No one could reason with Félicité after the *Words of a Believer*, this Bishop no better than John or the most loving friends. The missionary resolutely bungled through a situation calling for discretion and refined tact; Félicité protested by letter without tempering the prelate's mood.

Bruté de Rémur was as unsparing with John as he had been with the writer, belaboring him with reprimands for his leniency with an offending priest. Surprised by the blame, John tried to explain his situation, but the detractors had done their mischief: the confidant of three decades returned to the United States on a raw misunderstanding: *"You claim that we should strike with all one's might; I fear that by striking open wounds, we would further irritate them and render them incurable. I fear that forceful procedures might press our poor stray friend further along the false ways he has chosen, and become an obstacle to his return rather than means of leading him back. ... On the basis of false and perhaps malicious accounts, you suppose that, in weakness, I have flattered him. Ah! My good friend, believe none of it: I love him too much for having hidden my tears from him and for having ever mitigated, at any time, the truths that I was required to recall,"* (April 19, 1836). [34] Years of friendly correspondence seemed to end when the Bishop set aside the letters in his possession with a note referring to them as a *"literary treasure to be preserved, even after it ceases to be the treasure of friendship."* [35] The revolt of Félicité had cost John the temporary loss of one of his dearest friends.

The last letters stored in this *literary treasure* are dated September 28, 1833, from Félicité, and April 19, 1836 from John. The friendship ended with Félicité, but later resumed with John. In his last known letter to him, Bishop Bruté de Rémur deplored the aberrations of Félicité, but began to write *"with a trembling hand,"* admonishing him *"To pray, to adore and pray still more ... with the resolve to do as much good as possible until death in the Church of God,"* (April 3, 1837). [36] Unfortunately, time for a full return to former years of friendship lacked as Bishop Bruté de Rémur died in Vincennes, Indiana, June 26, 1839.

"The Affairs of Rome," November 5, 1836

On April 17, 1836, Félicité informed Montalembert that he was compelled to sell his books to cancel debts. [37] John, in turn, explained to Father Rohrbacher how little he could salvage from that sale. [38] Before leaving for Paris, Félicité commissioned a Parisian book dealer to catalog the library and he prepared the lot for shipment. The crating was nearly complete late in May when John stopped unexpectedly at La Chesnaie. Intrigued by the large cases, he asked what was happening. He was told that his brother was selling his library and that it was being prepared for shipment to Paris. The information stunned him. *"The library of Félicité! His library? It seems that he could say **our** library. Ah! Félicité is selling my books!"* He entered the living room and began to strike from the catalog the title of books belonging to him. Félicité heard him, locked himself in his office and refused to open. He packed his bags and left for Paris that evening, never to return. Félicité severed all communications with John; [39] the two brothers would never meet again.

News broke out late in 1836 that Félicité was about to publish a personal version of his relationships with Gregory XVI. Miss de Lucinière reported a dinner conversation with Félicité, who never seemed to tire of self-vindication. Friends anticipated a frontal attack on the Church. Félicité explained that no one knew the substance of his work, for he was sending a succession of sheets to the printer, and he would simply let people say whatever they wanted, (Oct 3, 1836). The preceding book justified concern. John sensed the birth of a new scandal: *"I await this book with painful anxiety ... this miserable book."* He waited hoping that his brother's good sense might still prevail: *"Félicité has too much understanding and too much tact to violate certain conventions; everything will be at least partly veiled in the forms of courtesy and style,"* (October 5, 1836). [40]

Félicité writing in anger was prone to exaggeration. In *Affaires de Rome,* [41] he calmly exposed his version of his sad personal experiences with the Pope with moderation, indicating what he believed Gregory XVI could have said and done. The narrative was skillful, the art superb, the purpose concealed to superficial readers. In the middle of his story, he inserted large sections of earlier writings on the ills of the Church, pages previously written with the encouragement of Father Ventura in Rome and Frascatti. He included the integral text of the encyclicals and a selection of related documents.

He could do no less than pose as an innocent victim to validate the role which he attributed to himself. There is a marked tendency among sympathetic writers and readers to accept his statements at face value, though the book is as important for what it does not say, as for what it does. LaMennais reveals himself best in the candor of his correspondence: 42 *"There was little secret for the Vatican as he wrote the Affairs of Rome,"* observes José Cabanis. [42] Eleven months before the second encyclical of June 25, 1834, Montalembert suggested a *"doubling of prudence;"* *"It seems that they know* (in Rome), *day by day, everything that we do, everything that we say, everything that we write . . . The worst of the matter is that copies of several of your letters addressed to imprudent friends have been thrust under the eyes of the Pope . . . In other words the total result of our mission is destroyed in Rome,"* (July 22, 1833). [43] It was no secret that various embassies, particularly Metternich's Austrian secret agents were intercepting mail and sharing transcripts.

Affaires de Rome outraged his closest friends and associates; even his two companions of his Roman pilgrimage rejected his interpretation of the Roman experience. Montalembert, in Rome at the time, disavowed it in an audience with the Pope on December 28, 1836. Lacordaire later bemoaned LaMennais' lack of restraint in exposing the wounds of the Church to a cruel strife-torn world, rather than working to heal them from within. [44]

Sainte-Beuve, friend and recent intermediary with publishers, rejected the contradictions of a priest proposing to champion opposite causes with the same "logic," and wrote: *"If I wanted to give the highest lesson of practical philosophy to a young man of twenty, enthused and proud of absolute doctrines, I would have him read [this book] and immediately after its reading, I would thrust into his hands the book 'On Religion in its relation to Social Order' by the same author."* He believed that the shock would help to caution his mind against the false enthusiasm of disciples. [45]

The *Words of a believer* had been a declaration of independence from ecclesiastical authority; *Affairs of Rome* was the book of his definitive rupture with the Church. After rejecting civil authority, he was now rejecting the Church of Rome. John Henry Newman was still an Anglican when he wrote from England about LaMennais a few years before his conversion: *"He is a powerful, original, and intuitive writer; but there is an ill flavor in his doctrine, which, in spite of all that is excellent in it, reminds one that it is drugged and unwholesome. This realization makes one tremble lest the same spirit, which could lead one to throw off civil authority, may lead him in disappointment to deny the authority of religion itself,"* (October, 1837). [46] Affairs de Rome proved Newman's foresight.

By their deeds

"By their fruit shall you know them," (Matthew 7:20). The disciples of F. de La Mennais and their successors lived by the best examples of their master's militant faith, and achieved some of his goals. Philippe Gerbet, his first and closest associate at La Chesnaie, became bishop of Perpignan in 1854. His friend, Louis Antoine de Salinis who had taken the initiative to organize the financing group of *l'Avenir, (l'Agence générale)* gradually distanced himself from the controversies stirred by the extreme policies of the editors.

De Coux, interpreter of economic and social issues at *l'Avenir,* remained involved with journalism and became professor of political economy at Louvain from 1834 to 1845. Eugène Boré, orientalist and persevering friend, kept close bonds with his master, studied revelation, became professor at the *Collège de France,* and was ordained to the priesthood. He was later elected Superior General of the Priests of the Mission and of the Company of the Daughters of Charity.

René François Rohrbacher, director of studies at Malestroit, had followed his master to the point of publishing a catechism of the *sensus communis, (Catéchisme du sens commun),* but would not approve his revolt. He taught dogma and morals in the seminary of his diocese of Nancy, and completed work on a twenty-nine-volume history of the Church. Father Blanc, spiritual superior at Malestroit, held a position at the Collège Stanislas, and later became director of a religious community in Paris. Guéranger's association with Félicité was brief. After the dissolution of the group, he worked to restore the Benedictine order in France and led the liturgical renewal of his century.

The leading team of *l'Avenir* never abandoned the cause. Henri de Lacordaire deplored Félicité's absence, when the results of his early work would have gained from his participation. After leaving La Chesnaie, he became a Dominican in Rome and restored the Dominican order in France. As early as 1841, he began to preach the Lenten sermons at Notre Dame in Paris, without objections from Gregory XVI. He entered political life, won election as deputy from Marseille, served his term while his former master was also serving in the same assembly. Félicité avoided him when they met in the Chamber. Relationships with Montalembert continued until Félicité stopped answering his letters. Montalembert published several works, was elected member of the *Académie française* in 1851. His career of public service included the struggle for the protection of working children, and leadership roles in the campaign for freedom of education partly won by the Falloux law of 1850. Félicité broke off all relationships with these men, but their friendship with John lived on.

Félicité had not labored in vain. Successors achieved some of his goals, proceeding from a different base than his, and the harvest rose with startling promise even before his death. [47] *"La Mennais predicted everything,"* wrote the Church historian Adrien Dansette: *"he has tilled the old field of Catholicism with a compulsive plough; he has broken through all its sod; and generations have reaped an unexpected harvest. It has rightly been said, that there must be written about the La Chesnaie center, a book that would be for the 19th century what the 'Port Royal' of Sainte-Beuve was for the 17th, its intellectual life, its discipline, its politics, everything renewed by its influence. Before leaving, the relentless plowman saw the first rising blades of the wheat he had sown and he repudiated them: the holy land had become foreign, enemy to him.... But time would gradually teach his heirs how to distinguish between respect for doctrine, and the necessities of politics."* [48]

There were those who applauded Felicite's revolt, others who respected the memory of his early achievements. Louis Veuillot invited a detractor, who asked to publish his affronts in his newspaper, to respect the writer's last days instead: *"We must not forget that M. de Lamennais has rendered immense services to religion: he was the first to express all the ideas which we are defending, he has opened the breach through which we are trying to pass, and while rejecting his faults, we must pray for him rather than abuse him,"* (May 22, 1846). [49]

Beyond suggesting that John abandon the Congregation of Saint Peter, (Sept. 1, 1834) or advising Montalembert to cease trifling with institutions that he considered outworn, Félicité de La Mennais did not attempt to draw followers along his personal journey. [50] The time for which

Félicité would not wait, and the changes which had not come at his beat, came more rapidly than expected. Undeterred by the master's tragic flaws, the men from La Chesnaie, Malestroit and Saint-Méen stood with new companions at the outposts of religious and social reform. The best of their agenda became reality, the rest lives as the memory of the ill-timed, misdirected struggles. [51]

Gregory XVI, Bishop de Lesquen of Rennes, Archbishop de Quélen of Paris, and a number of official Vatican intermediaries, intervened at each phase of this story. If the record shows that Félicité was not dealing with the most flexible and enlightened papacy, the same record equally reveals that every aspect of the case was examined with great care, not only by adversaries, to wit the transcript of case documents published by Louis and M. J. Le Guillou. [52] Roman authorities did not open proceedings against Félicité; he brought the matter to Rome, even before the French bishops took effective action; Roman authorities would have preferred a local solution to a national controversy.

Jean Leflon comments on the role of Gregory XVI: *"Intransigence, lack of form, and somewhat rude methods, had earned Gregory XVI many enemies. Historians have often been too severe toward him. The magnitude and effectiveness of his ecclesiastical work, the reorganization of the hierarchy [etc] must be recognized. ... His doctrinal work is no less considerable. On the then critical and burning question of liberalism, he set the basic principles which have remained those of the Church."* [53] The principles that he laid out guided the Church until experience and persevering good will eventually sorted out the best elements of a troubled period.

Félicité claimed that his judges were not of stature to understand the new politics of a new society. The prophet with eagle vision saw in the distance without reckoning with the reality at his feet. Félicité demanded solutions by his concepts, his way, and in his time. He came to realize that society and the Church do not evolve on demand by the insights of prophetic minds, and he would spend his last days deploring the state of the world. *"A sense of delay and patience were lacking in Lamennais. It is, however, deplorable that minds were dead-set to the point that they could achieve nothing other than crisis,"* writes M.-J. Le Guillou. [54]

Unfortunately, the politics of the time did not help. In Rome, the unification of Italy had not yet liberated the Church from the outdated burdens of civil rule, the perils of statesmanship, the demeaning involvement of the Papal States in European diplomacy. Relationships with European states thrust hard elements into the heart of this drama. The case of Félicité de La Mennais was processed through the Secreteriat of State, not the Holy Office responsible for the supervision of doctrine.

"How do you wish to be remembered?"

Ange Blaize, nephew of Félicité de La Mennais, recalls that his uncle chose his own symbol. "He was telling us one day: *'If I had to choose an emblem for my life, it would not be the reed swayed by the wind, but the oak broken by the storm. I break but do not bend,"* [55] In adopting that stand, he was choosing to travel a lonely road.

Éloi Jourdain remembered him with the highest respect, while acknowledging that his beloved master granted friendship at a price. *"In his affections, he gives his heart to those whom he loves, on condition that they give him their intelligence, and that they open it to him as a vase to be filled by his thoughts. That man knows only disciples, and if you cease to be his, you are no longer but a stranger to him, whatever the intimacy that may have existed between you. He will more readily forgive you the gravest faults of the heart, rather than the objections and the revolts of your mind. How many bonds this man has broken since his escape from the Church! How many friends he has sacrificed!"* [56] John was one of the "sacrificed."

Félicité demanded too much from his followers. The gentle and perceptive Gerbet could no longer bear his contradictions. After "Affairs of Rome," he wrote: *"M. de Lamennais has been the wandering Jew of politics . . . There is not, in the realm of social issues, a solid stone or a vain dust heap upon which he has not successively stood, while proclaiming loudly: 'This is the foundation of the world."* [57]

Jean Leflon outlined the evolution which he expected his disciples to accept. Félicité first presented the Catholic faith and human reason as resting on the same base. Then he exalted the Holy See: *"Without Pope, no Church, without Church, no Christianity, without Christianity, no religion and no society, thus the life of European nations has its source, its only source, in pontifical power."* He shifted after disapproval. *"After having said the King and the Pope, the people and the Pope, he stays only with the people while declaring: 'I am accused of having changed. I have merely allowed thoughts to evolve."*

At the time of his defection, Félicité was guiding Sainte-Beuve closer to religious conversion than is generally supposed. The literary critic wrote thus about the experience. *"He had ceaselessly admonished me directly or indirectly to come to a decision, to believe. But, I ask, what could I do when I suddenly saw him pass from white to black or red, and vault over my head in his testiness, stride over me as in the game of leap-frog*[58] *to fall in one leap from Catholicism to an extreme demagoguery? There was reason for genuine embarrassment and reason to hang one's head."* [59]

Sainte-Beuve had taken *The Words of a Believer* to the publisher for him. Félicité was then changing views altogether and the literary critic found it impossible to *"turn"* with him. He put a halt to the relationship for a while and blamed his guide for defaulting: *"How could you so abruptly abdicate, and was that allowed to you? Note well that there is nothing worse than to elicit faith in souls and to leave them unexpectedly, and to scamper away . . . How many hopeful souls have I not seen, which you were carrying along in your pilgrim's bag, and once you threw down the burden, have remained lying by the wayside."* [60]

The loyal Montalembert tried to reconcile him with Gregory XVI a few months before the publication of *Affairs of Rome*. The early issues of *l'Avenir* had come to him as he was observing O'Connel's liberation movement in Ireland. He had travelled from London to offer his services in Paris. He had worked with Félicité, accompanied him to Rome and stood by him at the departure of Lacordaire. He remained faithful through two encyclicals, deferred his official statement of full submission, and remained an active correspondent in the hope of bringing about the return of his master.

Montalembert had recently married and was on the way to Rome with his young bride when he wrote to Félicité, asking authorization to negotiate his peace with the Holy Father. Mrs. de Montalembart wrote in her souvenirs: *"At each stage of his voyage, Montalembert hastened to the post office expecting a reply from La Mennais. In Rome, he waited a long time for it still: it never came."* On a brief letter received from La Mennais a few months earlier, and dated July 14, 1836, he wrote: *"The last!"* [61] To no one's surprise, John de La Mennais could pierce his brother's resistance no better than Feli's most genuine friends.

"He fell from his horse, wrote Lamartine, "not on the way to Damascus, but on the way to Rome; he became the Saint Paul of another religion." [62] There were those, like Lamartine, who admired him for repudiating the first half of his life to live by new convictions. The pity, bemoaned the same Lamartine, was that he was *"as bitter and ruthless against his former friends as he had formerly been with his new ones."*

Félicité settled in Paris while his and John's books were being sold, and sometimes given rather than sold. He complained about meager returns: *"It does not add to 14 000 francs, net, and the fees are enormous. It would have been better to pitch the books by the window, it would have been shorter and would have spared me infinite cares and worries,"* (To Marion, February 5, 1837). [63] He tried to live by writing and investments, but never regained his previous stature. In business, he remained as luckless as he had ever been. He relied on the continuing sale of previous works, and admitted in 1849 that his translation of the Imitation of Christ and other devotional books had been his principal source of income. [64]

Felicite engaged sporadically in journalism, became Director of the journal *Le Monde* [65] for a few months, founded Le Peuple constituent, and held it until government exactions made it untenable. He repeatedly changed domicile while eking out a frugal existence. Privations and a life devoid of affection eventually became very painful. He was elected Deputy to the Constituent Assembly, April 23, 1848. [66] When the Chamber carried the Falloux Law of March 25, 1850, by 399 votes to 237, he voted against it, even though he had fought for two decades to win the school freedoms affirmed by it. He criticized the government at his own risk and served a year at Sainte-Pélagie prison, Jan. 4, 1841, to Jan. 3, 1842, for criticizing it in *Le Pays et le Gouvernement,* (The Country and the Government).

He contracted new friendships in a world quite unsuited to his nature. Some of them, like the circle of Georges Sand, which he abandoned after 10 years, tried to draw him into deeper associations with them, but they felt resistance, and commented that there was still too much of the priest in him. He could fit more comfortably with other friends, like Barbet, Béranger and Forgues, who understood his vulnerability, sensed his difficulties and helped him in his new roles. [67]

One of his most loyal converts, the baroness Cottu, asked him: *"by what disastrous influence are you following today doctrines against which you have been the most formidable adversary?"* (May 21, 1835). [68] The dear Miss de Lucinière wrote in outrage after the publication of Discussions Critiques during the year of his incarceration: *"And when you were Christian you were telling us in one of your sublime reflections on the 'Imitation of Christ,' Book 3, chapter XVI: 'Calm is in God, it is only there. There is rest, peace, joy and consolation only in him. Now tell me why in your writings you seek to snatch away our faith, the only treasure in which we can find a remedy to our adversities and a support in our weaknesses?"* (May 18, 1841). [69]

The strife cutting across the writings of F. de La Mennais lives on in the authors who write about him. His experience evolved in tightly circumscribed relationships and can be studied only in the interplay of persons at the time, and place of their encounter. Writers who turn to that history without opening to the broader dimensions of the struggle risk confusing readers with self-serving claims, contradictions and fallacies.

---

[1] Dargis, op. cit., pp. 531-607. **Lav**, v. 1, pp.490-540. Boutard, op.,
[2] October. 28, November 4, **Cor gén J**, v. 3, pp 59-61.

[3] J. Laurentie, *Laurentie, Souvenirs inédits, publiés par son petit-fils,* Paris: Bloud et Barral, 1893, p. 227.

[4] Adrien Dansette, *Histoire religieuse de la France contemporaine* (Édition revue et corrigée), Paris: Flammarion, 1948. V. 1, p. 308.

[5] Charles Augustin Sainte-Beuve (1804-1869), **Cor gén F,** v. 6, pp. 231-232.

[6] **Lav,** vol. 1, p.502.

[7] **Cor gén J,** v. 3, pp. 99-100, and at pp. 80-81 in the following. **Cor gén F,** v. 6, pp. 53-54.

[8] André Bellessort, *Sainte-Beuve et le Dix-Neuvième Siècle,* Paris: Perrin, 1927, pages 161-162.

[9] **Cor gén F,** v. 6, p. 69.

[10] See **Cor gén J,** v. 3, pp. 101-106.

[11] Sainte Beuve, *Le Constitutionnel,* September 23, 1861.

[12] Ernest Renan, "M. De Lamennais", *Revue des Deux Mondes,* Août, 1857, pp. 765-795. 781-782.

[13] **Lav,** v. 1, pp. 502-507. **Cor gén J,** v. 3, p. 102.

[14] Boutard, op. cit., v. 2, pp. 60-61.

[15] Louis Le Guillou, *Les Discussions critiques, Journal de la Crise mennaisienne, Genèse et édition du manuscrit 356 de la Bibliothèque Universitaire de Rennes,* Paris: Armand Colin, 1967, pp 8-9.

[16] **Cor gén F,** v. 6, p. 78.

[17] Concerning the Words of a Believer, see Yves Le Hir, *Les Paroles d'un Croyant de Lamennais,* Paris, Armand Colin, 1949. Paul Vuillard, *Les Paroles d'un Croyant de Lamennais,* Amiens, Éditions Edgar Malfère, 1928.

[18] Félicité had shown him only selected excerpts from the manuscript.

[19] **Cor gén J,** v. 3, pp. 105-106. **Lav,** v. 1, p. 504. All this correspondence is published in SA (1960), p. 143, ff.

[20] Bishop De Lesquen shared the contents of the letter with Coëdro and Dinonais at the time of reception. It is apparently at their suggestion that he published it.

[21] **Cor gén J,** v. 3, p. 108. See the letter to Father Ruault, May 28, p. 109. **Lav,** v. 1, p. 505.

[22] **Cor gén J,** v. 3, pp. 108-109.

[23] **Cor gén F,** v. 6, pp. 118-119. **Lav,** v. 1. P. 206.

[24] **Cor gén J,** v. 3, pp. 116-117. See the letter to Miss de Lucinière, July 24, pp. 117-118 and various letters, pp. 116-123.

[25] Boutin, Op. cit., v. 3, pp. 63-115. Dargis., Op. cit., pp. 570-572.

[26] Lecanuet, *Montalembert, Sa Jeunesse (1810-1836), Paris*: Poussielgue, 1903. Pp. 436-440. See the documents in Paul Dudon, Lamennais et le Saint-siège (1820-1854), Paris: Librairie Académique Perrin, 1911. Pp. 336-338.

[27] **Cor gén J,** v. 3, p. 117. **Rop,** p. 327. **Lav,** v. 1, p. 507.

[28] **Cor gén J,** v. 3, p. 130. **Lav,** v. 1, pp. 507-548. **SA (1960),** pp. 112-116, documents, 140-172.

[29] Text in **Cor gén J,** v. 3, pp. 128-130.

[30] **Cor gén J,** v. 3, pp. 572-573. Documents from this section are also available in **SA (1960),** pp. 153-168.

[31] **Cor gén J,** v. 3, pp. 128-129.

[32] **SA (1960),** pp. 167-168. **Cor gén J,** v. 3, p. 146.

[33] **Cor gén J,** v. 3, p. 212.

[34] **Cor gén J,** v. 3, pp. 350-351. **SA (1960),** p. 84.

[35] Henri de Courcy, *Lettres inédites de J.-M.& F. de La Mennais* ...Nantes: Vincent Forest et Émile Grimaud, 1862. Introduction de Eugène de la Gournerie, p. v. **Lav,** v. 1 pp. 535-539. **SA (1960),** pp. 82-86. **Cor gén F,** v. pp. 82-86.

[36] **AFIC,** 018.17.032. Writers without access to the few later letters end the story with the broken relationships without mentioning the apologetic attitude of Bruté de Rémur and the renewal of friendship with John.

[37] Lecanuet, Montalembert, *Sa Jeunesse,* op. cit., p. 446.

[38] (September 7, 1836) **Cor gén J,** v. 3, p. 425.

[39] J.-Marie Peigné, *Lamennais, Sa vie intime à La Chênaie,* Paris: Librairie de Mme Bachelin-Deflorenne, 1864. Repeated in **Lav,** v. 1, pp. 522-523, v. 2, p. 193. (Félicité was in Paris on May 29).

[40] **Cor gén J,** v. 3, pp. 395, 398. **SA (1960),** pp. 77-78. **Cor gen F,** v. 7, p. 601-602.

[41] M. F. De La Mennais, *Affaires de Rome,* Paris: P. D. Cailleux, 1836-1837.

[42] Pages 50 and 53 from the introduction written by José Cabanis for a reedition of the *Affaires de Rome,* pages 9-56. *Affaires de Rome,* Félicité de Lammenais (sic), Lyon: La Manufacture, 1986.

[43] Ibid., and **Cor gén F,** v. 5, p. 771.

[44] Lecanuet, Montalembert, *Sa Jeunesse,* op. cit., pp. 490-491. **Lav.,** v. 2, pp. 201-202.

[45] Charles-Augustin Sainte-Beuve, *Portraits Contemporains,* Paris: Michel Lévy, 1870. Tome 1, p. 270.

[46] "The Fall of de la Mennais" *in Essays Critical and Historical,* London: Longmans Green, 1919, p. 172.

[47] Dudon, op. cit., pp. 382-385.

[48] Adrien Dansette, vol. 1, pp. 291-292 and 309-310.

[49] *Louis Veuillot, Oeuvres complètes, XVI, Deuxième série,* Correspondance, Tome 11. Paris: P. Lethielleux, 1931, p. 175.

[50] **Cor gén F.** vol. 6, pp. 282-283. For Montalembert, vol. 5, 278-309 at the following dates: Jan. 21, 23, 36, Feb. 12, 1833 and beyond.

[51] The former disciples of F. De La Mennais deserve more attention than I can give them here.

[52] See the thorough record in **FL Cond.**

[53] Jean Leflon, *La crise révolutionnaire, 1789-1846.* Paris: Bloud et Gay, 1949, p. 471.

[54] "Postface", in **FL Cond,** p. 750. M. J. Le Guillou further observes that F. de La Mennais hardly understands the fundamental distinction between nature and grace. The condemnation of La Mennais presented by Louis and M. J. Le Guillou deserves careful study.

[55] *Oeuvres inédites de F. Lamennais, publiées* par A. Blaize, Paris: E. Dentu, 1866. Vol. 2, p. 351.

[56] Charles Sainte-Foi (pseudonym of Éloi Jourdain), *Souvenirs de jeunesse, 1828-1835,* . . . Publiés avec une introduction et des notes par Camille Latreille, Paris: Perrin, 1911, p. 57.

[57] See his *Réflexions sur la chute de M. de Lamennais,* par l'abbé Ph. Gerbet. Paris: rue Saint-Guillaume , no. 24, 1838. (172 pages). Also published in *l'Université catholique,* janvier-juillet 1837.

[58] This child's game is also referred to as "saddle-my-nag." Sainte-Beuve refers to it in different texts as *"cheval fondu"* or *"saute-mouton".*

[59] Charles Augustin de Sainte-Beuve, Les grands écrivains français . . . XIXé *siècle, Philosophes et essayistes, II, La Mennais, Victor Cousin, Jouffroy.* Paris: Garnier, 1930, p. 132.

[60] Ibid., pp. 59-60. Chateaubriand in his *Mémoires d'Outre-Tombe* (IV, 12) wrote: *"The guide in his flight abandoned the flock in the night."*

[61] *Lettres de Montalembert à La Mennais. . . .* Publiées par Georges Goyau et P.de Lallemand. Paris: Desclée, de Brouwer, 1932, p. 301.

[62] Alphonse de Lamartine, *Cours familier de littérature,* Paris: Chez l'auteur, 1856. V. 2, p. 271.

[63] **Cor gén F,** v. 7, p. 145.

[64] See **Cor gén F.**, v. 8, pp. 646, 647.

[65] *Le Monde,* from Feb 10 to June 7, 1837; *Le Peuple Constituant,* from Feb. 27 to July 11, 1848.

[66] Alexis de Tocqueville in his Souvenirs (Part II, chapter XI), remembered him as Deputy in 1848, proceeding *"with a pride ready to walk on the heads of kings and hold his own against God."* Lacordaire, elected member of the same Assembly, recalled that his former master turned his eyes away from him.

[67] See the brief essay of Stanislas Clair, *"Lamennais à la rue du Regard."* Paris: rue du Regard, (no date). Livret de 12 pages.

[68] **Cor gén F**, v. 6, p. 905.

[69] Ibid., v, 8, pp. 918-919.

Chapter 22

UNDESERVED LEGACY

The holdings of a dissolved religious congregation

The dissolution of the Congregation of Saint Peter in September 1834, did not exempt John de La Mennais from the consequences of his brother's misadventures. The liquidation of common property required settlements with the diocese, the house of Malestroit could not be closed without his participation, and the original contributions of founding members had to be reimbursed. Divisions over the influence of Félicité and tangled relationships cast suspicion on John and his works. The confusion drove two sisters at Saint-Méen to separate from the Sisters of Providence; in addition, opposition against the schools of the brothers hardened. John's role in the Congregation of Saint Peter kept him at the vortex of unsavory liquidation proceedings.

Adjustments with the diocese and with the members of the former Congregation of Saint Peter took precedence. John was visiting his schools when he advised Bishop de Lesquen a few days after the dissolution that he would prepare detailed accounts and rely on two acceptable negotiators to work out differences, one selected by him, and one by the former members of the Congregation of Saint Peter. When that proposal proved unacceptable, he worked with Father Coëdro for a solution. Father Ruault forwarded letters received for John in Ploërmel as he assembled the elements of a comprehensive report. Claims and counterclaims tested nerves during seven months. [1]

Conflicting interpretations of the original financial agreement explain the tension. Two jurisdictions were involved: the Congregation functioned under the local bishop, while the civil law determined title to collective ownership. The diocese could modify the religious society, but under the civil *Société Universelle des Biens* of November 4, 1825, liquidation required the participation of all signers. No party could unilaterally dispose of common property.

Father Coëdro insisted that the religious congregation that was reorganized in September 1834, automatically inherited ownership of goods as successor to the Congregation of Saint Peter, and insisted that the only required accounting centered on the house of Malestroit acquired in John's name for the Congregation. John's intention was to transfer all common property to the Bishop and to the new society, but only after settling all legally binding obligations with the members of the original civil society. [2] Father Coëdro disagreed to the point of abruptly severing all personal relationships with him.

As financial administrator and last Superior General, John proceeded to draft detailed accounts and to end all matters amicably by reimbursing the members of the *Sociét Universelle des Biens*. He requested financial statements and written observations from those concerned, and coordinated statements in the hope of doing justice to all parties. He convened all council members of the dissolved society to review the findings at Malestroit on February 5, 1835. Father Coëdro begged to be excused for reason of illness, but he sent a delegate. Three members arrived a day late, Coëdro's representative among them. John asked those present to study all observations in good faith to do justice to all parties. Recent experience had not provided guarantees of fairness, so he acknowledged that he could be quick-tempered, and he apologized in advance for any sharp statement which might escape him. [3]

The council members present on February 5 and 6 resolved to deal with all contributions and all property. They decided to yield all the holdings of the society to their former colleagues in the new Congregation, with the proviso that former partners in the original civil society first be indemnified. John pressed Father Coëdro to close the unfortunate affair:

"The time has come to close our sad transactions in one way or another. Please God that it be done quietly and with perfect understanding! But how will they end if you refuse the terms I can reasonably accept, and if you do not even answer the letters which I send? Your silence might prove either your inability to respond, or your intention of intimidating me with the prospect of a lawsuit?" (March 9, 1835). [4]

Father Coëdro reviewed the reports and referred the matter to Bishop de Lesquen. He had neither answered all of John's questions, nor acquainted the prelate with the legalities of the situation. The evasions left John with the embarrassment of explaining the matter from the beginning. The Bishop initially blamed his Vicar General for transferring liabilities too heavily on former associates, but the records supplied by the plaintiffs reversed the balance.

John finally announced his coming to his Bishop: *"I would have done this trip with trust and joy a few weeks ago. I now do it with sad apprehensions. According to what I learn from all quarters, the devil sank his burning claws into this affair and will release his hold with difficulty,"* (April 13, 1835). [5] In the settlement concluded on April 24, the diocese kept full title to the seminary of Saint-Méen; through his seminary, the Bishop guaranteed the pension rights of two former seminary teachers.

John guaranteed payment of the initial outlay in full to all original contributors, including the share of his brother. Two properties were involved: Malestroit and a recently acquired house in Rennes. He offered them to other members in lieu of payment. They refused. John suffered discredit during these negotiations even as he relieved his Bishop and the diocese by accepting the unwanted buildings with all related liabilities as part of his share. He was also sacrificing 18,000 francs of his own resources in the interest of peace. [6] The clerical students of Malestroit moved to the seminary of Saint-Méen, or followed the directives of their bishops. [7]

Misunderstandings aside, personal claims from all parties were moderate and justified. Fathers Coëdro and Ruault, for example, requested no more than their original outlay. John and Félicité having been the largest contributors, over half of the total, were consequently entitled to the largest indemnity. Félicité released everything given to him for the Congregation, but asked for the return of his personal outlay; John did the same, and closed his own account without personal gain.

The Daughters of Providence, Pélagie Le Breton and Father Corvaisier

Who could foresee that the pastoral vision of a dedicated priest, the zeal of an elementary school teacher, and the generosity of a benefactress would further aggravate relationships between John and his Bishop? Nevertheless, such was the case. The priest was Jean-François Corvaisier, (1780-1849) the teacher Miss Pélagie-Hélène Le Breton, (1789-1874), the benefactress Miss Pauline de Bédée.

The Sisters of Charity of Saint Vincent de Paul had been serving in the hospital of Saint-Méen during almost two centuries, when a local priest became preoccupied by the school needs of the region. The sisters were then providing an elementary school for the girls from poor families, however there was no local school for the daughters of middle class parents. Father de La Mennais was twice refused when he attempted to meet this need as the sisters rule required them to accept only the poor. [8]

Funds from parish families and the generosity of Miss LeBreton made the foundation possible. Fully aware of his parishioners' desire for service, Father Corvaisier asked her to found the badly needed school. He rented a section of the Ronsain building and Miss Le Breton opened the school on October 2, 1831. Poverty did not discourage her; she abandoned her independent life, made her home in the building, and furnished it with her personal belongings and from gifts. In 1832, an unexpectedly large donation from Pauline de Bédée to John de La Mennais would transform the school and the life of the teachers.

Pauline de Bédée was preparing to join a religious congregation when the school opened. She decided to eliminate all personal debts and dispose of her fortune before entering a convent. She offered her resources to Bishop de Lesquen, who refused the gift to avoid difficulties with her relatives, but referred her to John who was aware of good works in need of assistance. The gift was a family chateau which Father de La Mennais found useful as an expansion to the seminary, and a home for the sisters who would teach at the local girls' school.

Pauline de Bédée left Father de La Mennais the use of the funds for good works. He invited her to become a Daughter of Providence, but she preferred another congregation. The Augustinian Sisters of Rennes admitted her in their Saint-Yves convent. Father Corvaisier and John de La Mennais considered several projects before agreeing to found a school in Saint-Méen with the Daughters of Providence.

The new school was inaugurated on February 12, 1834, a few weeks before the onset of a new crisis. Miss Bedee had not completed seven months as Superior of the Daughters of Providence at Saint-Méen when Felicite de La Mennais published his *"Words of a Believer"* at the end of April, and condemned by Gregory XVI in June. Bishop de Lesquen dissolved the Congregation of Saint Peter on September 2; Miss Bedee had opened her first school in peace before the departure of Félicité de La Mennais for Rome; she was now caught between contradictory directives as unnamed parties prevailed on parents to withdraw their daughters from the school of the sisters.

Because of Felicite's increasing conflict with Rome, the confusion caused by different parties complicated an already difficult school situation, forcing Father de La Mennais to compromise some of his rights while adding additional burdens to his heavy administrative load, John raised issues of simple justice and invited Father Corvaisier to resolve his claims more judiciously. Caught between two determined negotiators, the Bishop accused Father de La Mennais of defending too sharply the interests of his schools. To end the discussion, John accepted to lose a school, his reputation and financial terms inferior to his investment. A pro forma sale legalized the transfer of the building to the Bishop. [9]

Heartbreak upon heartbreak befell John and his peace-loving Bishop through the destruction of the Congregation of Saint Peter, the closing of the school of the sisters at Saint-Méen, and two financial contests which should never have occurred. The parties involved in these controversies were zealous souls, but the scandal of Felicite confused minds, warped relationships, destroyed friendships.

Bishop de Lesquen was genuinely devoted to the spiritual needs of his diocese. He governed with a generous heart, but lacked the qualities of a gifted administrator. He easily slipped into romantic declarations of openness and cooperation, while taking decisions with little consultation. The vexations drove him to write that it was becoming harder to love his *"dear collaborator,"* the Vicar General. Biographer Laveille comments: *"Msgr. de Lesquen renewed his friendly relations with John, but what anguish was caused by these suspicions, what burdens were assumed by John from those he loved the most!"* [10]

Some friendships survived unscathed, some rivalries soon subsided, but suspicion and persecution lingered on. Doors had slammed shut on a vital Church service for John, but his priestly ministry, and the children in his schools still called for his presence; John would not let hardship, obstructions and persecution keep him from his good works.

───────────────────────────────────

[1] The long and involved documentation is collected in **SA (1960),** pp. 250-322, and Symphorien-Auguste, *À Travers la Correspondance de l'abbé J. M. de la Mennais, Deuxième série.* Vannes: Lafolye et de Lamarzelle, 1938. Pp. 157-182.

[2] **Cor gén J,** v. 2, pp. 346-347, and **SA (1960),** p. 250 includes the full text.

[3] **SA (1960),** pp. 262, 269, passim, and Symphorien-Augusre, deuxième série, op. cit, p. 142.

[4] **Cor gén J,** v. 3, pp. 188-190 and **SA (1960),** pp. 305-306.

[5] **Cor gén J,** v. 3, p. 195, **SA (1960),** p. 316.

[6] **Cor gén J,** v. 3, pp. 199-201, **SA (1960),** pp. 319-322 and Symphorien-Auguste, deuxième série, op. cit., pp. 174-179.

[7] **Lav.,** v. 1, p. 521. It eventually became the home of a community of Augustinian nuns.

[8] Marie Lidou, *Jean-François Corvaisier, Prêtre du diocèse-de Rennes* (1780-1849), Saint-Méen: Les Prêtres de Saint-Méen, les Soeurs de l'Immaculée, 1980.

[9] **Cor gén J,** v. 3, pp. 281-282.

[10] **Lav,** vol. 1, p. 535.

*Statue of John de La Mennais, erected before the Mother
House in Ploermel.*

Mother House of the Brothers of Christian Instruction, Ploermel, Morbihan, France.

Chapel Entrance at Ploermel

City of Paris.

*The Tomb of Venerable de La Mennais in the Community
Chapel in Ploermel.*

Father John de La Mennais, shortly after he passed away.

Chapter 23

THE DEEDS OF A BELIEVER

The Founder's coach

Open highways invited travel between the leading cities of Brittany, and a surprisingly efficient coach service, *(la diligence)* met transit needs. John knew the system well, but he saddled his horse to visit his first schools until his circuit widened. After his return from Paris in 1824, he often rode his private coach with a brother as coachman. The brothers remembered that coach filled with books, papers, the paraphernalia of travel and reading material to fill open time. He lived in that secondary residence for extended periods. Éloi Jourdain recalled his stops at La Chesnaie: *"In some way, his coach had become his apartment; accordingly, he took along a substantial library, pens, ink and paper, and he wrote in transit as if he were sitting at his table."* [1]

Jourdain remembered him as a man of practical sense, understanding fully the constructive use of time. John eventually *became so involved with his visits, that his mail occasionally came addressed: "To Mr. de La Mennais, on the highways of Brittany."* He sometimes paused to write letters along those highways: *"I am writing to you as I sit in my mobile room, but I stopped rolling while my horses graze in the hay and chew their oats."* [2]

> Breton roadways wander fancy free
> Veering round the meadows in their spree,
> Linking life and labor through the day
> Bonding hardy kinfolk leagues away. [3]

Homeland bards lingered by those forlorn lanes which sometimes seemed contrived to retard travelers rather than to lead them on, but John's responsibilities allowed little leisure for poetry and pleasure stops. He rode with the children of his schools in mind. Because he organized so many schools where there were none, he rode rutted dirt lanes angling through the smaller towns of the checkered Breton farmlands. Rain or shine, he ventured through sunken hedgerows, stony runs and muddy roads as heartily as he rolled along the greenery of shaded country byways.

The byways were essential to John's work as he made his rounds, occasionally extending his reach by combining carriers, leaving his mobile home and riding the public coach. He then returned to his own coach before resuming with a fresh team of horses. His letters tell the story: *"I still intend to leave Paris on the evening of Sunday, the 24th ; I will arrive at Vitré on the morning of Tuesday, the 26th , my coach must be waiting there by Monday evening."* [4] His brothers helped him care for his horses: "Find me a not-too-expensive stable for my horses: *"I was not too satisfied with last year's accommodations."* [5] When the horses could not stand the strain, he let them rest and finished his course otherwise: *"My horses will probably not take me from Dinan to Ploërmel, for they are too exhausted. I will therefore board the coach at Dinan for a very early arrival at Ploërmel Saturday morning."* [6]

Place and means mattered less than teachers and schools: *"I will arrive at Quintin during the afternoon of Thursday, May 15: the brothers from Ploeuc, Gausson, St. Donan and Plouguernevel must be notified to meet there on Friday."* [7] He was on his way to Saint-Brieuc when he wrote to Miss de Lucinière, *"I write these few words in haste, for I will soon reenter my home, that is my coach, to travel the highways."* [8]

Determination etched a midwinter report from Lannion about night travel by public coach: *"I reached here after the most perilous voyage of my life, but in which I had no accident; from Brest to Quimper, the horses collapsed six times in very steep hills. And we must thank God for not rolling over. I was traveling by night, first by mail coach, then by regular service. My own coach was waiting for me at Landerneau. I never would have managed with it on such roads."*

■ —————————————————————

His planning left no one out, as shown by a message from Guingamp: *"I will return to Saint-Brieuc on Wednesday, and will leave on Friday for Ploërmel, via Plédran, Ploeuc, Uzel, Alliance and Loudéac ... I might return rather early to Ploërmel on the second. I will then return to Dinan after 10-12 days and will complete my visits along the coast on my way to St.-Brieuc for the distribution of prizes at the Providence."* He occasionally announced travel plans to Father Ruault as *"presumed itineraries."* Circumstance often toyed with his planning. Public officials were unavailable, snow and ice delayed travel, indigestion and fatigue curbed his pace. [9] He sometimes stopped for rest and undisturbed correspondence at his sister's home at Trémigon near Combourg, or at La Chesnaie for work and indispensable peace. There was a single purpose to that activity, and he rejoiced when he could write lines like the following: *"I must leave today for Côtes-du-Nord and Ille-et- Villaine where I will assign nineteen brothers and found eleven new schools,"* (September 6, 1824). [10]

Schools

Though there had been setbacks during John's two-year term in Paris, the number of brothers grew from 24 to 75. The enterprise was human: some of the first schools had failed, experience had taught lessons, but the Congregation was increasing beyond anticipation. Some of the early schools were founded in cities; however, the intended presence was rural, with the single-teacher school the reality of the early years. The 24 brothers of 1822 taught 2,000 children in 19 little schools. [11] Twenty new schools opened during John's absence. [12] The young institute had taken form to the point that he could write in 1825: *"Our traditions are already very strong, and I personally am in the fortunate incapacity of changing any of them."* [13]

Louis XVIII died on September 16, 1824. His Brother, the Count of Artois succeeded him as Charles X. The new monarch, a poor diplomat, too religious for the liberals, kept ministers who continued the policies of his predecessor. Educational needs accelerated the call for teachers, and the number of John's school increased under favorable laws. For John de La Mennais, school openings meant more brothers, more living space at the novitiate, more recruits, and rising costs. A supportive government eased the requirements for opening schools, granting a measure of funding, for a while.

Supplying teachers meant preparing them. [14] The availability of funds paced the restoration of Ploërmel. Over 130 brothers assembled for the retreat of 1825, the first in the new home acquired by Father Deshayes, now being renovated by Father de La Mennais. They came with a new edition of the rule. By April, Father de La Mennais had transformed the 24-page rule of 1823, *(Statuts)* into a 134-page manual, *(Recueil)* in which he had supplemented the preceding edition with prayers, extracts from the writings of the saints, the *Imitation of Christ,* instructions on prayer and the spiritual life, and a list of spiritual readings.

The material restoration at Ploermel being incomplete, the brothers received the community in a chapel still in need of elementary renovations. The two Founders opened the exercises on August 16, 1825. The retreat was to end on the 22nd, but the brothers remained at their new motherhouse until the end of the month. The brothers of the local community served the assembly, the elders leading the way on hospitality by personally serving retreat guests.

The practicalities of life could not be ignored at a time when everything needed attention. The brothers tailored the religious habit from the early years on. When Father de La Mennais bought a bakery, they baked home bread. The project list seemed unending, the brothers even planning a cemetery. One of the workers chided the 25-year-old Brother George at work on the hedge by the cemetery. *"I wonder who will be first in there?"* *"Not I,"* replied the novice, *"there are sickly candidates ahead of me!"* Pneumonia made him the first occupant a few days later, (April 19, 1826).

The context was religious life, but the activities of Ploërmel were all about schools and teachers. Novitiate time was also study time, as John wanted his men ready to help the young. He provided teachers, saw to their instruction, encouraged them to teach one another. Even at this early date, he wanted them to introduce mechanical drawing as a preliminary skill for drafting in the industrial arts. He even set up the beginnings of a vocational training program.

Ploërmel provided teachers for new schools, created the beginnings of a boarding school, even opened its doors as a normal school for lay teachers. The Superior delegated the supervision of construction to Brother Ignatius, and sometimes sent him to oversee the construction of new schools. In 1828, he relied on him to manage the reconstruction of Malestroit for the Congregation of Saint Peter.

A privileged system of public schools was gaining strength across the nation. The government jealously guarded its secondary schools, (the *collèges*,) but the towns could freely support Christian elementary schools, and parents often preferred traditional religious schools to secularized institutions. The government recognized the education of teachers in secular normal schools or in religious novitiates as public services, and for some time subsidized part of the cost with a wavering measure of impartiality. Since 1816, the General Councils of departments were explicitly encouraged to assist the education of teachers in the novitiates of religious congregations. John had an aversion to government intervention, but he soon won the cooperation of public officials, many of whom were friends who valued his work. After the foundation of Ploërmel, growth was very rapid, sustained by need and popular demand.

Félicité complained that he saw his brother too rarely and too briefly, and wrote that the vocation of John was *"to travel about the roadways sowing good works along his course, good works prospering visibly,"* (October 15, 1827). [15] Between 1825 and 1826, John founded sixteen schools as the number of brothers increased from 75 to 110. [16] Statistics for 1827 report 128 brothers and 56 little schools. [17] He wanted his schools worthy of the name, preferring to close those that could not serve their purpose well. Of the little school at Bignan, he wrote: *"This school has been founded, but it nevertheless has been suspended for two years because I would not allow a brother to limit his care to reading and catechism."* [18] He kept some teachers in Ploërmel and a few extra men in the larger schools to replace sick or nonfunctional teachers.

Public assistance was sporadic and Corbière, Minister of the Interior, stopped it abruptly June 18, 1827, with a circular ordering the General Councils of the departments to cut off assistance to all religious corporations. The General Council of the Côtes-du-Nord protested and pleaded for replacement funding: The Council views the circular *"with pain. It particularly feels a deep regret for not being allowed to support the rapid progress made by the Brothers of Christian Instruction. After hardly four years of existence, that institution has three novitiates, 22 operating schools instructing 3,000 children. ... The Council was providing his main source of revenue. Mr. de La Mennais will be unable to support these schools if His Excellency the Minister for Ecclesiastical affairs, does not otherwise restore equal funding,* (July, 1825)." [19] Mr. Prud'homme, [20] one of John's closest friends and supporters then received the following plea: *"You are aware that the General Councils have not given me anything for my novitiates during the last session. At Rennes, they refused to pay even what had been allocated to me. To save my congregation, I must find means to exist independently from politics and the men of the day,"* (July 24, 1825).

A change of government voided the circular after three months. Except for the Council of the Côtes-du-Nord which resumed financial assistance by 1828, the Councils often continued to reject John's repeated appeals for funding. The emergency forced him to measure expenses, to call on friends and benefactors for survival assistance, until the return of better days.

Ploërmel defaults on its contract

In the judgment of Ploërmel historians, the presence of the brothers was a singular advantage to the town. Public administrators should have appreciated the work of John de La Mennais, but Brother Hyppolyte recalls that elements in the population of 1824 had not fully overcome the religious intolerance of two previous centuries. The obstacles raised to the brothers were not as severe as the resistance to the Ursulines, but they came as Father de La Mennais was enriching the town with a prosperous teacher-training center. [21]

When the brothers came to Ploërmel in 1824, Fathers Deshayes and de La Mennais had negotiated the acquisition of the elementary school from the city, a school founded by Father Deshayes in 1818 in a section of the old Ursuline monastery owned by the city. On September 5, 1824, the City Council released ownership of their school under clearly specified terms: If the brothers ceased to provide two teachers, the Founders would pay 12,000 francs, or lose the title ceded to them.

The liberal[22] statesmen installed in Paris after the Revolution of 1830, appointed men of avowed secular loyalties at the control of Ploërmel affairs. John de La Mennais soon realized the change when the city council questioned his rights to the school, though he had fulfilled all contract terms. On November 14, 1830, the City Council decided to fund a monitorial school and to end the annual allocation of 600 francs granted to the brothers. It further asked the mayor to verify the sale and the agreement of September 5, 1824.

Father de La Mennais could hardly believe that the Council could repossess his new organizational center by unilaterally annulling contracts. *"If it is true,"* he argued, *"I would ask ... to be heard by the Council before decisions are made."* The Council heard him on November 30, and December 5. The Superior of the brothers announced that he would not abandon the children entrusted to his care by the parents; he would fund their instruction personally if the Council cuts off salaries. The Council was not prepared with substitute teachers. To avoid interrupting teaching, it voted the *status quo* for 1831, but the Mayor informed Father de La Mennais that the City's lawyer had found no act validating the approval of the original contract. Such local agreements were subject to approval by higher authority. On March 13, 1831, the Council took notice of that "finding," an apparent procedural error, and declared illegal the agreement of September 5, 1824. It advised Father de La Mennais that it would reclaim the locale ceded to him and Father Deshayes in 1824. [23]

The rhetoric in support of the new monitorial school bared the true motives for the decision, the establishment of a Lancasterian method at Vannes. The avowed purpose was to establish a quality monitorial school to *"remove the prejudices deliberately spread among people"* against this *method, and to oppose "the usurped reputation of the Brothers of Christian Doctrine, (sic) who have rendered no services to the nation, since they perpetuate ignorance and prejudice oppose to the happiness of mankind."* The monitorial school opened during September, 1831; though the sub-prefect applauded its success, by 1833, 70 students attended the Lancasterian school and 230 students were with the brothers' institution.

Father de La Mennais was still occupying the disputed quarters on September 1, 1831. The city administrators underestimated their adversary when they asked him to leave. He opposed substance to technicality and refused to leave. He correctly reminded city officials that they had not acquired the school with their own funds, but with funds from the General Council of the Department with the purpose of opening a brothers' school. He denied them this unilateral authority and embarrassed the Mayor with a dilemma: *"How can you say: I send the brothers away and I keep the funds received to install them?"* He then offered to pay the agreed 12,000 F required to keep the building. He sued the Mayor at the tribunal of Ploërmel, affirming that he would not leave without the reimbursement of 13,922 francs owed to him for improvements. The mayor reacted with a counterclaim of 15,000 F in compensation for demolitions and alterations to city property.

According to City Council plans, a monitorial school and part of the military garrison would soon become close neighbors to the brothers. On June 26, 1832, the Council appointed a commission to negotiate with Father de La Mennais, requesting a prompt decision from the tribunal. The possible presence of noisy, unsympathetic neighbors was an embarrassing prospect for the Superior of a religious congregation.

On August 7, Father de La Mennais made an offer to the Council. In exchange for the disputed quarters, he would buy the Saint Nicholas field adjacent to the public market, and build a secondary school for the city on it. Since his building plans were ready, the Commission and the Council could not refuse a new secondary school for quarters in the old convent. Construction began immediately after an official approved the transaction. The Founder delivered the school to the city a year later, on May 28, 1835. The brothers could now pursue their work in peace and the

Rector of the *Académie* of Rennes was satisfied with the opportunity to *"counterbalance in the region the manifest bias of the teaching directed by Mr. de La Mennais."*

Controversy often buzzed about John as he pursued his work with the schools. Brother Casimir recalls his first days in the Institute: *"When I came to Ploërmel in 1830, we had no assigned chaplain. When the good Father de La Mennais returned from his frequent visits to spend a few days, he ate at our table, sat on the same benches, and kept silence as we did. Nothing was served to him that was not served at the common table, with the exception of a little butter. ... I sat facing him, and though quite young, I admired his sobriety and simplicity."* [24] What else was this fifty-year-old priest doing in 1830?

He could share the simple life of his brothers, but he was Superior General of the Daughters of Providence and the Brothers of Christian Instruction while sharing the direction of the Congregation of Saint Peter with Félicité. The priests of the Congregation of Saint Peter saw him regularly, his brothers still more regularly, and he could not pass Saint-Brieuc without visiting the Daughters of Providence and their students. A simple perusal of his letters shows him dealing with Prefects, Mayors, the Rector of the Academy of Rennes, national executives in Paris and parish priests, several of whom built and supported schools from their own resources. In Ploërmel, he could rest with his brothers, even as the City was preparing to repossess the quarters of the old school. While pettiness was spoiling the peace of local communities, the wind of revolution stormed through 1830 and changed the life of the nation.

[1] Charles Sainte-Foi, *Souvenirs de Jeunesse,* 1828-1835. Paris:Perrin, 1911, pages 72-73.

[2] To Father Ruault from Blain, April 15, 1836. **Cor gén J,** v. 3, p. 350.

[3] Author's variation from Breton song lines: *Les chemins bretons sont des fantaisistes,*
    Qui vont de travers au lieu d'aller droit, ;
    ils seront toujours aimés des artistes.

[4] To Father Ruault from Paris, Sept 16, 1837. **Cor gén J,** v. 3, pp. 514-515.

[5] Letter from Saint-Brieuc to Brother Ambroise, May 12, 1828. **Cor gén J,** v. 2, p. 413.

[6] Letter to Father Ruault, July 29, 1845. **Cor gén J,**

[7] From Ploërmel to Brother Laurentie, April 26, 1828. **Cor. gén. J,** v. 2, p. 428.

[8] **Cor gén J,** v. 3, pp. 139-140 (October 12, 1834).

[9] **Cor gén J,** December 11, 1837, v 3, pp. 557-558, June 21, 1838, v. 4, pp. 62-63. See letter of January 14, 1840, v. 4, pp. 278-279.

[10] Letter to Count de Chazelles, **Cor gén J,** v. 2, p. 308.

[11] Thirteen of these were single-teacher schools, 4 had two teachers, 3 had three or more.

[12] P. Friot, **ÉM,** No. 14 (July, 1995), pp. 69-104.

[13] Letter to Father Mazelier, in the context of a response about the priesthood in the Congregation, August 31, 1825, **Cor gén J,** v. 2, pp. 342 and 343.

[14] See generally Rulon, **REH,** Chapter XI, unpublished, and **Chron,** no. 199 (July, 1954).

[15] Letter to the Countess of Senfft, **Cor gén F,** v. III, p. 383.

[16] Philippe Friot, **ÉM,** no. 18 (April, 1997), p. 26.

[17] Including 39 single-classroom schools, 10 two-teacher schools, and 7 with three or more.

[18] The school of Bignan in 1833. **Cor gén J,** v. 3, p. 63.

[19] From **ADCd'A,** as quoted in Rulon, **REH,** Chapter XIV, p. 1

[20] Louis-Jean Prud'homme (1745-1832), printer and former Mayor of Saint-Brieuc, **Cor gén J,** v.II, p. 338.

[21] Brother Hyppolyte Morin, "Mes Souvenirs sur l'Institut des Frères de l'Instruction chrétienne (1852). **AFIC,** 80-01.

[22] Such was the term.

[23] About this contest, see Rulon, **Chron.** No. 199 (July, 1954) 526-530.
[24] As quoted in Rulon, op. cit.

The City of St. Brieuc

Chapter 24

FROM CELLAR TO ATTIC

Elementary schools and the Revolution of 1830

The Revolutions of 1830 stunned Europe, dethroned Charles X to install the **July Monarchy** and changed the Constitution of France. The government shifted to the left under the influence of the new monarch: King Louis-Philippe associated with the Jacobin Club and the liberal bourgeoisie. The events of 1830 tempted Félicité into aggressive journalism which led to feuds in France, conflicts with the Holy See, and the eventual dissolution of the Congregation of Saint Peter.

The government tightened its hold on all schools. The Ordinance of April 8, 1824, had assigned the control of primary schools to the bishops. On April 21, 1828, an Ordinance revoked that authority and the Ordinances of June 16, 1828 interfered with the education of the clergy by consolidating all secondary schools into a single closely supervised category. [1]

The violence of 1830 brought little relief, but the relative calm which followed the Revolution provided time to assess the needs of elementary schools. François Guizot, remembered for his vigorous presence in French politics from 1814 to 1848, surprised the nation with visionary insights as he steered wrangling deputies towards a more broadly available elementary school system and generous concepts of educational freedom. A reform of elementary schools became law in 1833.

The Guizot Law, June 28, 1833

François Guizot[2] was the driving force behind the law of 1833, and the school freedoms which it affirmed. He was born in Nîmes in 1787 of a Protestant lawyer supportive of the Revolution, but nevertheless guillotined as a federalist during the Terror. His mother fled to Geneva to raise her son, but returned to Nimes to allow him to study law in Paris: *'If I gain new knowledge, it serves only to affirm my faith in the Gospel of Jesus Christ, I have never been ashamed of it and never will be."* [3] His Christian faith survived 34 years of assertive politics. After retirement in 1848, he devoted his time to historical writing and active responsibility on the administrative body of the French Calvinist Church.

The Charter of the July Monarchy promised freedom of education; the "Guizot law" of June 28, 1833 codified that freedom for elementary schools. The Law incorporated the major elements of the Ordinance of February 29, 1816, but pressed national objectives far beyond. [4] Creating an effective school system was a challenge. After the law, an unusually thorough report dramatized the reality. Guizot commissioned 490 inspectors to visit all elementary schools late in 1833. The results published by Paul Lorain in 1837, revealed that the importance of good elementary schools was far from universally understood. [5] The legislators of 1833 achieved their goal: in less than 20 years, primary schools for boys increased by over 440%; schools for girls by over 920%, the latter particularly after the law of 1836. By 1850, the nation was ready for the next major school decisions.

John received the prospects for a new law with reservations: *"It is thoroughly absurd, oppressive to the towns and hostile to religious congregations; however, it will be a great advantage to me for it suppresses special authorizations for private schools; as for public schools, our towns will more readily make the sacrifices required of them for my brothers than for lay teachers,"*(February 8, 1833). A few weeks passed and he cheered, *"Hurrah for Mister Guizot!"* [6] He read the law with exuberance. The Guizot Law reminded the nation that *"primary and elementary instruction necessarily include moral and religious instruction;*

that heads of families must always be consulted and honored on the participation of their children in religious instruction."

The Guizot law guaranteed the right of any person eighteen years of age or older to *"engage as a primary instructor and direct any primary school,"* with no requirement other than presenting in advance two documents to the mayor of the locality in which he chooses to teach: (1) a teaching permit for the level of instruction in his school; (2) a character reference, (a "morality certificate") validating the reliability of the candidate as a teacher, the latter to be obtained from the mayors of the towns of the candidate's last three years of residence. A citizen could now open a private school and freely adopt his teaching method and no authority could legally object.

The opening statement specified that primary instruction could be either private or public, the Ministry of Public Instruction determining the basic curriculum. Guizot wanted Church and state to collaborate despite the diminished role assigned to the Church. The Ordinance of February 13, 1830, required towns to provide schools, but the order was a dead letter caught between the executive fantasies of Paris and the inertia of local administrations. The law of 1833 compelled each town to provide a school individually or jointly with others. Towns with a population above 500 must now support a school.

The Law made a decisive attempt at decentralization: the *Université* lost all control over private schools though it retained limited oversight over public institutions which now passed under local control. Cities and towns hiring members of religious congregations contracted directly with teachers instead of through the Superior of the Congregation as was done previously. This provision annoyed religious superiors because it gave headstrong members a basis to resist directives from their Congregation, an occasional annoyance to Father de La Mennais. The authors of the law considered elementary instruction a responsibility towards the children of the nation. [7] They maintained certain controls, but did not compel school attendance and left funding to local initiative. Under the Guizot law, elementary schools became local and religious, though public officials treated public and private schools differently. John had teachers in both categories.

Of laws and men

The promise of educational freedom revived hope, but partisanship could readily travesty the promise. Before 1830, John de La Mennais was often dealing with unsympathetic public officials. [8] A student of the brothers recalled his own experience at Guingamp where he learned to read in a rented room in a public secondary-school building. The City closed their school. *"Brothers and students found refuge in a garret, while the parents built an entirely new school which soon became too small."* [9] The expulsion was due to an instigator who contemptuously resented John's countermove: *"What kind of man is this? I have never met the likes of him! The devil is in him. We drive him from the cellar, and he rushes to the attic!"* [10] Political appointees quickly maneuvered similar schemes in Ploërmel, Tréguier, Lamballe and elsewhere, failing in some cases, succeeding in others.

The Founder opened schools, but he would not let opposition close them without cause, or without a fight. A school founded in Vitré in 1827 had accepted 200 children and refused 100 for lack of space. In 1830, the city administration cancelled the subsidy and expelled his teachers. The brothers moved into hastily renovated quarters though reviled by a barrage of defamation. When the impertinent action of one brother towards a student ignited an explosion of sectarianism, the brothers were required to leave. Thirteen months of persistent negotiations prepared their return with the revocation of the expulsion order. [11]

Opposition hardened after 1830 despite the freedoms guaranteed by the Guizot Law. After 1833, John appealed against unfair men on the basis of a fair Constitution and fair laws. The Ministry of Public Instruction ruled with justice and understanding at the top, but the attitude below at times remained unchanged. François Guizot valued religious congregations as the most dependable auxiliaries of the government in popular education. John de La Mennais could rely on this Huguenot friend to oppose bias and vindicate the civil rights of the members. Guizot invited the Prefect of Ille-

■

et-Vilaine to respect the law in dealing with them: *"Nothing prevents ... the brothers from serving as public school teachers; the law recognizes them when they comply with all the conditions legally required from other teachers"* (June 6, 1834). [12]

The teaching certificate: "Le brevet"

Educational regulations from Paris were more attuned to the situation in the cities than to the needs of rural France. The law added higher elementary grades to the program and eliminated the lower teaching certificate. Opponents quickly wielded the new requirements as a weapon against Christian schools. Since 1808, the Brothers of the Christian Schools and members of other legally authorized congregations with teacher preparation programs could legally substitute a letter of assignment, (referred to as a letter of obedience) for the official teaching permit. The law rated as adequate the apprenticeship provided by religious congregations; school administrators awarded the official permit on presentation of a letter of assignment from the superior of their religious congregation.

The ordinance of March 12, 1831, revoked that privilege for all teaching congregations of men. Directives issued on June 21 specified that the certificate was required only from teachers responsible for a school, and that directors in office were entitled to a certificate without examination. The Guizot law of June 28, 1833 reaffirmed the executive decision of 1831, and eliminated the lower certificate for teachers of basic reading, writing and arithmetic. It also required a certificate from all teachers in higher grades. New teachers assigned to single-teacher schools would now be authorized only under the new rules. John de La Mennais, who was then providing teachers for public and private schools, expected reasonable transition terms.

The issue was not unreasonable standards, but the administration of unwieldy transition terms. It was difficult for the general public to assess the education needs and resources of rural folk deprived of schools during ten to twenty years of revolutionary chaos. John had schools in towns, but many brothers worked in scattered hamlets

His teachers were willing to rescue children from illiteracy, a task made difficult since compulsory attendance was unknown at the time. The Revolution had destroyed the existing school system and a new financial base had to be created to support them, a requirement which the poorer districts were still unprepared to provide. The challenge was to find ways of serving where no one wanted to serve. Families appreciated teachers freely providing an education to their children.

John had no objection to the new higher primary regulations, even accepted new standards as "good," but he resented the abrupt elimination of the lower certificate. He shared his experience with the Minister of Public Instruction: *"Our schools have multiplied and prosper despite a hostile system because they are better adapted to the needs and the ways of the region, and because they earn the full trust of families. ... Our best rural schools are those which I have entrusted to very pious and very zealous brothers properly suited for this task: I have often ached over an assignment when a required certificate determined my choice,"* (November 7, 1837). [13]

He objected to absolute uniformity when needs differed, and he did not confuse aptitude with certificates: *"Let us not be mistaken about it; the most capable man according to the law, is often the most inept to teach in a humble village school; there he will often teach them very imperfectly. The children do not stay in school long enough to make it possible for anyone to teach them anything more than the catechism, reading, mediocre writing, and the skill to solve the simplest arithmetic problems,"* (April 16, 1849). [14] Public administrators were often unprepared for sudden adjustments to the new rules.

Now that the only legal authorization required from teachers *"in whatever capacity,"* was a permit for the higher grades, John organized himself to comply with the law. He scanned his lists, asked his more capable candidates to prepare for examinations, and sent directives to the directors in Ploërmel to make the necessary adjustments. He did not want "a day lost" in the education of apt candidates, and *"zeal redoubled"* in upgrading the learning of more capable men. [15] He had no complaints against examination boards except in cases of unfairness. Conscientious officials served on the same boards with sectarian colleagues who could easily embarrass him and his men by summoning teachers for unexpected examinations, or unfairly disqualifying capable applicants.

When prejudice threatened his work, he sent his men to examination centers known for their fairness. He could write to Guizot in November 1837: *"Since the law of June 28, 1833, we have earned about 30 brevets from the examination commissions."* [16] However, the gains never seemed to catch up with the needs, especially in poorer rural schools where more advanced schoolmasters were not readily available.

Battle scars, hard-won gains

The harassment of some officials and the good will of others forced John to navigate between countercurrents; at times, an undertow of ideological partisanship laid vexing obstructions along his course. Funds were withdrawn, rival schools planted near successful institutions, information withheld and credentials delayed for months. Regulations changed, authorizations for transfers withheld or denied, answers to legal requests for provisional authorizations deferred or never received. At times, transactions stalled even when John had closely observed all proper procedures.

The freedom written into the law did not convert all public officials to fairness. From 1827 to 1832 and to a lesser degree thereafter, liberal public administrators breathed a second wind into the secular monitorial school movement; however, John did not resume the polemic of 1819. [17] John objected to the Lancasterian methodology because as it was sometimes applied, it was bad pedagogy, and because public officials often wielded it as a privileged weapon for the secularization of schools. His teachers occasionally enlisted capable students for recitation, drilling and tutoring

The creation of new normal schools opened a new front, not by the influx of new teachers, for the demand far exceeded the new arrivals, but because public administrators resorted to old tactics with a new twist. The law respected local options by allowing towns to operate a Christian school directed by a religious congregation, or to establish a secular school of its own. However, the application of the school policy was contradictory and at times *"far from the dream of François Guizot and Ambroise Rendu, to create genuine cooperation between the Church and the state in matters of elementary education."*

The public archives reveal that at times, the purpose of the local public normal schools was to *"counter the Brothers of Christian Instruction of John Mary de La Mennais,"* who emerged repeatedly in the Breton school controversies of those years. [18] Among the graduates who later wrote memoirs, there were those who did not hesitate to describe the normal school students of their time as *"men of their times, voltairian, unbelievers, skeptics, even sometimes disrespectful towards religion."* [19]

John did not easily yield when opponents pressured prefects and town administrators to supplant his brothers with new graduates. When local officials closed a public school founded for the town, John re-founded the institution as a private school when he found support from the families. He explained that he would not open a school where the monitorial schoolmaster respected the faith of the young and led a moral life, but the demand for teachers was such that he would not allow opponents to dislodge his teachers. He kept repeating basic arguments: monopoly kills; liberty fosters life and prosperity.

He said in response to an attack by deputy Glais-Bizoin in the Chamber of Deputies, Feb. 15, 1834: *"Is it evil if my schools are so well attended that rooms must be added to receive more students? Am I wrong not to leave a child without instruction in towns where I found schools? Am I to blame if monitorial schools are languishing, remain almost empty almost everywhere, even where I am not competing with them? ... I am astonished to hear accusations of monopoly because I managed to found thirty schools in a land where twelve hundred are needed. One thousand seventy schools are available to Mr. Glais-Bizoin; is his share not good enough?"* [20]. He insisted that opening necessary schools would serve the public interest better than destroying prosperous ones to secularize education.

Hostilities often flared locally, attempt at redress when fairness was not found in the Ministry of Public Instruction. Often, parents and priests mobilized to give him new schools when public authority evicted his teachers from public institutions. [21] He wrote to Deputy de Sivry: *"It is undeniable that the families highly trust the brothers, a fact that cannot be blameworthy. More than a hundred municipal councils voted for them in four months, and requests for them to increase daily,"* (January 17,1834). [22]

John forged on despite the discredit cast by certain ecclesiastics upon his brothers during the years which followed the defection of Félicité: *"Persecution against the work of my brother continues in the diocese.... A number of ecclesiastics in the diocese of Rennes advise, or even forbid parents to send their children to a school of the brothers about to open in a city,"* (August 28, 1833). [23] Some of the same voices were advising parents away from the school of the Daughters of Providence at Saint-Meen.

Others were more discerning and enrollment in the brothers' schools often increased dramatically. Father Ruault wrote: *"I saw requests [for brothers] come not only from all quarters of Brittany, but from all parts of France."* [24] The Congregation increased from 197 members in 1833, to 694 in 1851, the year following the next major school reform. According to available statistics, the schools of the brothers increased in France from 146 to 228 between 1836 and 1851. By then, John de La Mennais was also supplying teachers for the French colonies.

Teachers where there were none

Providing teachers presupposed long-term resources and planning. Some irregular government funding helped; however, it had to be supplemented with private donations and the voluntary economies of teachers serving without adequate salaries. There were those who understood poorly John's strategy of service to the poor. As he visited French schools for the British government, Matthew Arnold admired the work and community life of the Brothers of the Christian Schools.

In Brittany, he encountered the Brothers of Christian Instruction who *"go out singly,"* and he commented that: *"the moment a Brother goes singly and thus is employed in any poor commune, he loses the virtue which religious association confers upon its members, and which is the source of half of its strength."* [25] Arnold was unaware that John de La Mennais did not abandon brothers in single-teacher schools. Though he preferred larger schools to isolated institutions, he was dealing with the reality of small communities straining to support one teacher.

Stable, better-funded schools were a dream of the future, particularly for rural lands. Gabriel Deshayes and John de La Mennais understood the challenges of the moment and joined in a strategy to provide teachers where there were none, bringing literacy and religion to thousands of children who otherwise would have remained unschooled. Their men served wherever they were needed, from cities to forgotten parishes, but one-teacher schools persisted for decades. The needs were such that he avoided cities served by the Brothers of Christian Schools.

Isolation was neither the purpose nor the preferred mode of service. He lodged solitary brothers in the rectories where the company and supervision of the parish priest compensated for the community which could not surround their lives. He visited all of them regularly on location several times a year, and kept in regular letter contact every three months. A printed rule unified the orientation of their lives; in addition, he assembled the entire brotherhood at Ploërmel once a year for the annual retreat.

Shortly after his arrival at Ploërmel, he wrote to Father Mazelier about the distribution of his schools: *"There are very few schools which are not visited every three months; this should be sufficient as they are close to one another. ... I have already referred to my novitiates. They are houses with not less than six brothers, and they serve as support centers for the schools clustered around them. ... I have three houses of that type in the Diocese of Saint-Brieuc. One, Quintin is at the center of the Diocese; the other two, Dinan and Tréguier are at the opposite ends. The brothers working in the region visit occasionally, particularly when I am there; that helps me to abridge my visits,"* (February 1, 1825).

To M. A. Padé, he observed: *"I am careful to link my schools together, and to group them in some way, otherwise they would have no solid base,"* (December 26, 1836). [26] To Father Mazelier he added: *"There is no doubt that schools with two teachers are preferable to single-teacher schools. This year therefore, I took advantage of favorable circumstances which enabled me to assign two brothers where there was only one; but I would not set that policy as an absolute rule, as this would be too restrictive,"* (December 21, 1835). [27] The schools revived hope in a population unaccustomed to regular instruction. The single teacher schools dwindled as better-organized schools generalized, but survived as examples of flexibility to the end of the century.

Parish priests usually treasured the presence of these brothers. [28] They often wrote to the Founder at the time of the retreat begging him not to transfer their teacher. On rare occasions, John protected them from rude relationships; when the brother was the problem, he willingly eased tension with a substitute. He later wrote to Father Mazelier: *"When I dealt with parish priests of difficult or vicious behavior, I sent them brothers of unshakable virtue, and some of these brothers have converted several by their good example,"* (August 31, 1835). [29] Some brothers could bear the inconsiderate attitude of a parish priest and reassured their Superior that there was no need for a transfer. Parish priest, brother and Founder often became close friends; some priests became John's most reliable recruiters when they realized that education awakened a sense of self-assurance, and that the example of brothers inspired a quiet renewal of Christian family life.

John carried out this school mission with a firm vision of the needs of the Church and a practical sense of local and country needs. He founded boarding schools because children from some towns were otherwise deprived of all schooling.He lost little time with theories of education and remained unconcerned with the grand curriculum of contemporary educators. He focused on needs, broadened the local curriculum and raised the level of learning with realistic innovations refined over time. John de La Mennais was changing his ways in a changing elementary-school system while planning for secondary schools.

Secondary schools

The Guizot law opened a new field of action by formalizing higher-level elementary grades, the middle school of later years. Students often considered those classes a preparation to the secondary school, and parents requested Latin lessons. The brothers' rule excluded Latin and the classical languages from their field of action. However, some of them moved on to a higher level curriculum and John entrusted Latin instruction to priests or lay instructors.

John could have oriented more brothers towards secondary schools as he later did, but there was such a strong demand for elementary school teachers that he could never meet all requests. A number of students continued to more advanced work, increasing the need for secondary school teachers. He once thought of continuing the work of his brothers with a separate group for secondary schools. *"I would very much like to do for secondary education what I have done for elementary education, form and educate young men capable of being certified as boarding school masters,"* (December 21, 1836)." [30] New legislation on secondary schools prompted him to share his concerns with Father Mazelier: *"Will the clergy lock itself into its minor seminaries? ...We must hasten to do for secondary education what we have done for elementary education. I am working on it, but alas, what difficulties, what obstacles!"* (June 30, 1837). [31]

Former members of the Congregation of Saint Peter became indispensable participants in his Latin instruction initiatives. In 1835, he proposed an association for good works between former members who had chosen not to continue with the Priests of Saint-Méen. [32] Though the nine associates did not mature into a lasting religious congregation, some of them became teachers of Latin for students preparing for secondary school.

Two conditions were essential to the new enterprise: a large building and a government permit for a teacher to serve as "master of boarding school." At that time, the only adequate building available was the former Malestroit novitiate. John's new company of priests, now reduced to five, worked in Malestroit and Dinan with young men preparing for professional life or for the seminary. In 1838, he reorganized them into a religious congregation with vows; the second Malestroit ended as the first when finances dried up and young men left. [33]

Then, Dinan and ecclesiastical interdiction by two bishops

An entirely unexpected vexation awaited John's new society at Dinan. [34] Dinan had three educational opportunities for boys: a minor seminary, *(Les Cordeliers),* the dwindling public secondary school, and the school of the brothers which had grown to include higher level classes. The mayor proposed to send the twenty city students to the school of the brothers where priests were offering Latin instruction, physics and mathematics. In return, the school would include Latin students not destined to the priesthood, and would admit students from the minor seminary. John invited out of retirement his friend Querret, doctor of science and retired professor of physics and mathematics to the new institution, and obtained his required certificate.

Bishop De La Romagere who still governed the diocese of Saint-Brieuc would have to approve a new *Collège* in his diocese. John explained his plan and De La Romagère approved it with a written declaration: *"I read this text and I approve its content."* However, eight days later, the Bishop declared that his approval was not definitive. In respectful deference to the inconsistencies of his Bishop, he wrote to Querret that the project had to be abandoned.

At that point, the editor of a local newspaper, *Le Dinanais,* published offensive observations against the teachers at the minor seminary. John had no foreknowledge of the article, but rumors raised suspicion that he had inspired it. He denounced the article and denied participation in the affair. Unfortunately, the elderly prelate spoke forcefully from the pulpit against the local clergy and the Municipal Council in the principal church of Dinan. From the same pulpit, he proclaimed an episcopal order forbidding all priests outside of the diocese to exercise their ministry without his formal authorization. De La Romagère named no one, but John understood his position and suspected that his associates, Fathers Chevalier and Mermet would bear the same stigma.

His work in Dinan was threatened, but he did not give up. Realizing that the loss of his students by the municipal secondary school might provoke reprisal from public authority, he met the prelate to explain the consequences of his decree, only to learn that the indirect order was meant for him personally, and for the priests associated with his work. The Bishop planned to expel his brothers from the diocese and replace them with a new congregation of brothers founded and ruled by him.

Relationships with de La Romagère were such that John notified the mayor of the possibility of having to close his own elementary school: *"The decisions which Msgr. declared ready to take would compel me to close my school without hesitation should he persist in such troubling dispositions. At issue therefore are 465 children, two hundred of them educated without charge that I may have to return to their parents.... I would like these poor children to suffer the least inconvenience possible from such a sad and unexpected situation; it is my obligation to notify you of this possibility,"* (October 23, 1838). The Mayor implored him to delay his decision until all appeals fail: *"the city would revolt and the ecclesiastical school would inevitably be suppressed."*[35]

Responsible men deplored his withdrawal from the project, but he explained to Judge Charles Bailly of Dinan: *"What you tell me of the evil to follow from my rupture with the college is quite true, and I deplore it more than anyone. It is obvious that I am acting against my interests in the circumstance, but, a motive of honor determines my decision. It would be a scandal for a priest to become part of a Collège founded on the ruins of a religious community; I prefer to lose everything than compromise my reputation in such matter,"* (September 18, 1840).[36]

The city of Dinan did not share John's submission and restored its own municipal secondary school, though numerous externs from the minor seminary lost their privilege of sharing the courses of the public institution. A vindictive public supervision began to weigh more heavily on the seminary, and its director was compelled to become part of the *Université* to keep his students.

A tangle of negotiations followed, but the episcopal threats returned 465 children to their families, 200 of them attending school without fees. John attempted to negotiate with public officials not to close the school, and sympathetic public administrators supported his efforts. The Bishop finally negotiated with public authority; the seminary kept its authorization, but lost the right to accept non-clerical students. Opponents in the city government vengefully closed the Ursuline school and replaced it with a public institution.

The interdict of Saint-Brieuc still weighed against John. Until 1839, John visited his seventy schools in the department of Côtes-du-Nord without authorization to celebrate mass and hear confessions. Conscious of their spiritual responsibilities, John and Father Chevalier decided to meet at La Chesnaie across diocesan lines the students who wished to meet them for direction and confession. Soon the Bishop of Rennes decided to extend the order of de La Romagère to his diocese, which included La Chesnaie. John was now under the interdict of two bishops for offenses which he had not committed. He wrote to Brother Ambroise from Ploërmel at the time: *"I have many sufferings indeed, but the Lord gives me the grace to bear them without complaint, and without anxiety. From the hour of his birth to his death on the cross, Jesus Our Savior and Model was never without suffering; to share his glory we must share his sufferings,"* (January 5, 1839). [37]

A layman friend and founder of an agricultural boarding school for boys, Count Achille du Cleusieux obtained the forgiving word from the prelate. He compulsively went to the chapel and prayed for half an hour before the prelate started his mass. After his thanksgiving prayers, the Bishop asked why the Count was visiting. *"I came to reconcile you with Mr. de La Mennais,"* replied the visitor. *"Impossible, I cannot forget!"* retorted the Bishop. The Count pointed to the crucifix in the room and replied: *"But He has forgotten, has He not?"* Du Cleusieux then heard the reply of a stunned prelate: *"When do you expect our reconciliation?"* The layman replied without hesitation: *"Today! I know that Mr. de La Mennais is in Saint-Brieuc; allow me to lead him here."* Mr. de La Mennais was accompanying brothers on the way to board a mission ship at Brest, and was then in transit in Saint-Brieuc when the Count surprised him with Mr.

Sébert and explained the purpose of the intrusion. Knowing the character of the prelate, he thought of reconciliation and replied, *"Impossible!"* However, he followed his friend to the episcopal residence where the Count asked for the Bishop. De la Romagère could not conceal his displeasure when du Cleusieux called for the priest. John was seated on a stone marker outside. When he raised his eyes, the old Bishop was standing with open arms on the porch, ready to seal the reconciliation with an embrace. De La Romagère officially lifted the interdict the next day, and published the decision in a circular praising the Superior of the brothers.

The secondary school of Ploërmel

The secondary schools that preoccupied John de La Mennais at the time were meant for young men preparing for the professions, but seminarians were never far from his thought as he struggled to serve young men pursuing career studies. Future priests had been his first students, and he never lost his zeal for their education. The experience of racing from cellar to attic at the closing of his elementary schools paralleled ousters from ecclesiastical schools. Napoleon had closed the ecclesiastical school of Saint-Malo, and the collapse of the Congregation of Saint Peter ended Malestroit as a seminary novitiate, but he attempted several times to found ecclesiastical secondary schools and recruit priests for the ministry. [38]

After the experiences of Malestroit and Dinan, the school of Ploërmel was John's only success with ecclesiastical secondary schools. [39] In 1850, a new law broke the hold of the *Université* on secondary schools and entitled qualified citizens to open secondary institutions as the Guizot law of 1833 had done for elementary private schools. The small group within the boarding school moved to Malestroit and remained there from 1837 to 1843. It continued a quiet quasi-clandestine existence in Ploërmel in the form of preparatory courses, until the law of 1850 authorized its existence. In 1853, John requested Father Ruault to direct a secondary school at the motherhouse of Ploërmel; its official existence began with 39 students though it closed its doors definitively in July of the following year.

John's new secondary school prospered as the *Collège Saint-Stanislas* in Ploërmel from 1850 to 1870. Mr. de La Mennais enriched the curriculum to meet the needs of an increasing student body. Priests taught Latin lessons, but the brothers guaranteed the other preparatory secondary school subjects. The school eventually became a heavy imposition on community life. The Founder intended to separate it from the motherhouse, but he lacked the resources to complete the project before his death.

---

[1] For a summary which reflects the mood, see Félix Ponteil, Histoire *de l'enseignement en Fance, Les grandes étapes, 1789-1964, Paris: Sirey,* 1966, pp. 197-203.

[2] François Guizot, 1787 (Nîmes) - 1874 (Val Richer, Calvados). He served as Minister of the Interior in 1830 and Minister of Public Instruction from 1832 to 1837.

[3] Letter, November 20, 1806.

[4] It applied exclusively to schools for boys, but was later extended to schools for girls, by the Pelet Law of June 23, 1836.

[5] Paul Lorain, *Tableau de l'instruction primaire en France.* Paris: Hachette, librairie de l'Université Royale de France, 1837. Lorain reported with honest realism.

[6] Letter to Father Mazelier, February 8, 1833. **Cor gén J,** v. 3, p. 16. Letter to Father Ruault, April 30, 1833. Ibid. v. 3, p. 28.

[7] See generally P. Chevallier et B. Grosperrin, *L'Enseignement français de la Révolution à nos jours,* Paris, La Haye: Mouton, 1971. 2 v. V.1, pp. 69-74; v.2, pp.121-140. The politics leading to the law are outlined in Maurice Gontard, *L'Enseignement primaire en France, de la Révolution à la loi Guizot (1789-1833).* Paris: Société d'Édition des Belles Lettres, 1959, pp. 493-536.

[8] The Ploërmel experience is reviewed in chapter 24.

[9] **Rop,** pp. 383-384. The author was friend and first biographer of John de La Mennais.

[10] **Lav,** v. 2, p. 40.

[11] **Lav,** v. 2, pp. 40-41. **Cor gén J,** v. 2, pp. 577-580.

[12] As quoted in Rulon and Friot, *Un siècle de pédagogie,* p. 59.

[13] Letter to Mr. Salvandy, **Cor gén J,** v. 3, pp. 542-544.

[14] Reply to questions from Mr. Cochin and Mr. Michel for the Minister of Instruction, **Cor gén J,** v. 6, p. 150.

[15] See his letter to Father Ruault, April 13, 1834, **Cor gén J,** v. 3, p. 94.

[16] **Lav,** v. 2, p. 87. **Cor gén J,** v. 3, pp. 542-544.

[17] The earlier controversy is reviewed in chapter 13.

[18] Gilbert Nicolas, *Instituteurs entre politique et religion,* Rennes: Éditions Apogée, 1993. In sequence, pp. 162 and p. 9. See "Le rival des narmaliens: Jean-Marie de La Mennais," pp. 165-168, passim Note his objections to unfair practices in his report to Ambroise Rendu (July 27, 1839) **Cor gén J,** v. 4, p. 202.

[19] Ibid., as presented on p. 191. See also pp. 172-175. See p. 197 about the 10-year promise.

[20] **Rop,** p. 399. **Cor gén J,** v. 3, pp. 83-85.

[21] See generally, Rulon, **RPH,** pp. 95-147 (unpublished); **Lav,** v. 2, pp.38-58, 79-95, 389-412; **Cor gen J,** various letters for the period; H. C. Rulon et Ph. Friot, *Un siècle de pédagogie dans les écoles primaires (1820-1940),* Paris: Vrin, 1962, pp. 57-65.

[22] **Cor gén J,** v. 3, p. 75.

[23] A dated addition in a letter to Montalembert, August 18, **Cor gén F,** v. 5, p. 456. The Sisters of Saint Meen also complained that the priests were turning parents away from their school. See Michel Lagrée, *Mentalités. Religion et histoire en Haute-bretagne, Le diocese de Rennes,* 1815-1848, Paris: Klincksiek, 1977, pp. 368-369.

[24] Quoted in **Lav,** v. 1, p. 526.

[25] Matthew Arnold (1822-1888), *The Popular Education of France, with notices of that of Holland and Switzerland.* London: Longman, Green, 1861, p. 116. Arnold started his visit in Paris, in March, 1859.

[26] **Cor gén J,** v. 2, p.323, and v. 3, p. 440. See his observations to Father Dupuch, May 23, 1836, v. 3, pp. 361-363. Pierre Zind (Marist brother) offers a representative diagram showing the links between single-teacher schools and Ploërmel through the secondary novitiates and the larger schools nearest to them, in *Les Nouvelles congrégations de Frères enseignants en France de 1800 à 1830.* Le Montet (Saint-Génis-Laval): Chez l'auteur, 1969, pp. 275-277.

[27] **Cor gén J,** v. 3, p. 305.

[28] Matthew Arnold knew little of John de La Mennais' experience. He wrote that the Bishop of Quimper thought that the brothers were *"irksome inmates to the Curés, and not willingly accepted by them."* The extent of Arnold's conversation with the Bishop is difficult to evaluate, but the

parish priests kept requesting brothers and John could never meet the needs of the Bishop's diocese.

[29] **Cor gén J,** v. 2, p. 342.

[30] Letter, December 21, 1836, **Cor gén J,** v. 3, pp. 436-437. **Lav,** v. 2, p. 97, gives December 27 and attributes it "probably to Rohrbacher."

[31] **Cor gén J,** v. 3, p. 491. The brothers of another generation expanded their work to secondary education (with Latin language teaching) when the needs of the students required it.

[32] See his plan of association dated September 17, 1835 and revised in 1838. **Lav,** v. 1, pp. 550-551 and v. 2, p. 101.

[33] Father Mermet, a member of the new society of priests, later organized a teaching clerical society as a Third Order of Saint Dominic in 1852. Lacordaire, the former associate of Félicité de La Mennais at *L'Avenir* who was then leading the French Dominicans approved the project. The tradition of Malestroit thus lived on at Flavigny in eastern France years after the demise of the Congregation of Saint Peter. **Lav,** v. 2, p. 423.

[34] **Lav,** v. 2, pp. 103-124. **Cor gén J,** vols. 3 and 4. The controversy spills over into numerous letters and documents, particularly from the summer of 1837 to the summer of 1840.

[35] Letters to the Mayor and to Father Ruault, **Cor gén J,** v. 4, pp. 100-102.

[36] **Cor gén J,** v. 4, 1840.

[37] **Cor gén J,** v. 4, pp. 17-148. The Superior kept a remarkably active pace in his letters to his brothers during this trial.

[38] **Lav,** v. 2, pp. 630-633. The plan designates the junior seminaries as petits collèges.

[39] H. C. Rulon, **Chron,** No.199 (July, 1954), pp. 587-596. **Lav,** v. 2, pp. 521-525.

Paris

Chapter 25

650 LITTLE GIRLS AT THE PROVIDENCE OF SAINT-BRIEUC

Prosperity in poverty!

Mr. Salvandy, Minister of Public Instruction read the Founder's report: *"In my school, known as the Providence of St.-Brieuc, I have 650 little girls, 570 of them pay absolutely nothing; 80 students pay fees suffice to support the house, but without any profit whatever at year's end,"* (October 13, 1837). [1] The quest for larger quarters had been a constant preoccupation until the purchase of the present *Providence.* The sisters added 200 children in 1819 with the availability of a new home.

The law did not require compulsory school attendance and inspectors repeatedly complained of the apathy of rural populations towards schooling for girls. While they might be indifferent to the education of boys, they often became hostile at the proposal of schools for girls. [2] That resistance did not exist in the cities, certainly not in Saint-Brieuc. John observed in the same report: *"Generally, the education of girls was less neglected than that of boys: now everything is done for the boys and very little for the girls."*

When Miss Cartel began her work in Saint-Brieuc, he supported her work and their cooperation evolved into a highly respected private institution, maintained by the zeal of the sisters and the generosity of benefactors. Parents turned to religious women willing to educate their daughters as there were few reliable schools for them. The Providence never lacked students, and the sisters welcomed with open arms the waifs of Saint-Brieuc neighborhoods, as had the early companions of Miss Cartel, (See Chapter 10.)

Under their Constitutions, the sisters elected superiors for three-year terms. When John left the diocese in 1822, the Bishop appointed a diocesan priest as advisor and chaplain to the Congregation. John, the legal owner of the Providence, continued in his role of Founder and Superior, but unlike the brothers under his direct authority, the sisters elected the Sister Superior to govern at the Providence, under the oversight of a chaplain and the advice of Father de La Mennais.

Ill health excluded the Foundress, Marie-Anne Cartel, from prolonged administrative service; she passed away on October 21, 1821. The sisters elected six superiors ("Mothers") to govern the Congregation during the lifetime of Father de La Mennais. The first, Marie Conan (Mother Marguerite-Marie), served for nine years from 1818 to 1827.[3] Her successor, Esther Beauchemin served for three years and was assigned the care of material interests as treasurer. Poverty was their only treasure, and Divine Providence their only recourse. Before leaving for Paris, Father de La Mennais had asked the chief benefactor of the house to look after his daughters. Mr. Sébert remains unforgettable in that role, but some community incidents bewildered Mother Conan and her sisters.

One Saturday, Mother Conan found herself without funds for the supplies of the day. Never having borrowed, she refused to do so even then. She left with a few coins in her purse, bought one sole for dinner, took the fish to the convent kitchen where it was readied and she cooked the "meal." After the blessing, she served normal portions to the sisters then stood wondering over the unexplainable leftovers, soon sent to an indigent family.[4]

On another day, her purse held a mere 24 francs when a sister needed a dress. She responded immediately, bought the cloth and had it cut. The price was 24 francs She emptied her purse, carried the purchase home then found her 24 francs in her pocket. Convinced that there had been a mistake, she returned to the store, apologized and re-deposited the money only to be told that there had been no error; her coins were still on the counter. She walked home convinced that Divine Providence was working in her favor.

On another occasion, she had nothing to purchase the Saturday provisions as the last coins had been given in charity at the convent door. She expressed her distress to the superior who told her: *"Buy what we need; we will pay when we can."* She replenished the normal provisions and returned home; that very day, unexpected funds came to the convent. The gift covered her purchase and seven hundred francs of outstanding debts. Help kept coming in less spectacular fashion, but Providence and its emissaries were providing means to carry on with unalterable hope.

In 1830, the sisters elected Pélagie Texier, Mother Sainte-Pélagie as their Mother Superior and kept her in office during nine years. The new superior was a progressive woman ready to respond to Father de La Mennais' urging to think of new schools. Demand and numerous vocations encouraged John to open numerous schools with the brothers, but the circumstances of the Daughters of Providence were quite different. His brothers were then the only congregation of men available in the smaller towns, while several congregations of sisters shared responsibility for the few girls' schools. Parish priests directed prospective religious teachers' for the boys to the Brothers of Christian Schools or to the Brothers of Christian Instruction, while the sisters in local service normally recruited teachers for girls.

The Ursulines, the Sisters of Charity of St. Vincent de Paul, the Daughters of Wisdom, the Pauline Sisters, the Sisters of Our Lady of Refuge and the Daughters of the Holy Ghost, among others, were all serving in the diocese of Saint-Brieuc. [5] A variety of other congregations were present in the other Breton dioceses, including the Daughters of the Holy Ghost founded in the diocese in 1706. As the number of Sisters increased, they became available to provide health care and education to the girls throughout Brittany

New schools, changing society

Even after Father de La Mennais's return from Paris, tribulations and prosperity marked the life of the Daughters of Providence. From 1824 to 1841, the sisters founded three schools outside of Saint-Brieuc. The legal status of schools for girls changed, the Constitutions of the congregation were revised, the Congregation obtained legal authorization for them, and the Founder prepared to transfer the ownership of the Providence to the sisters.

The first school outside of St. Briuc was in Saint-Meen, the school founded by Miss Pélagie Le Breton. It became a major heartbreak for them when the scandal of Félicité de La Mennais destroyed the Congregation of Saint Peter, and confused Miss Le Breton. The sisters were maintaining a successful school when Sister Le Breton left, but the confusion was such that the clergy virtually forced the sisters to leave.

The sisters founded the school of Moncontour on October 2, 1833, well before the closure of Saint-Meen. The Founder was quite familiar with these cities as he had been visiting his brothers in Moncontour since 1823. In Saint-Meen, the brothers had been teaching there since 1826, a few years before the reorganization of the seminary by the Congregation of Saint Peter.

The pressure to open schools for girls increased after the government applied the major provisions of the Guizot law to them with the ordinance of June 23, 1836. [6] Until then, Father de La Mennais felt no need to request legal authorization for the Daughters of Providence. He wrote to Guizot, Minister of Public Instruction: *"The Providence of Saint-Brieuc is considered the foremost and best organized school for girls of the Department; on that score, there is but one voice, and through its long years of existence, that school has never had a critic or an enemy. All families without distinction send their children to it with the same eagerness and the same trust,"* (March 31, 1837). [7]

The same positive comments were also written by Father de La Mennais to Salvandy: *"At Moncontour, I have another school administered by religious of the same Congregation; they now have 150 students, but will have 180-200 as they had last year when the school is full ... The house of Moncontour would be given to them if they were [legally] enabled to own it,"* (October 13, 1837). [8] The two schools of the Daughters of Providence were filled before the government began to compel towns to open schools for girls.

John asked the sisters to keep orderly records and began to revise the Constitutions in preparation for legal authorization. The Constitution had been revised for a first printing in 1832; he prepared a second printing in 1837. Because public officials found it easier to work with known organizations, he declared that their model of government was the Constitutions of the Ursulines of Amiens. King Louis-Philippe signed the ordinance of authorization on October 2, 1838. There were 15 Daughters of Providence in 1822, 21 in 1830, and 67 at the death of Father de La Mennais in 1860.

Legal status had advantages. The Ordinance of June, 1836 preserved to the Superior the privilege of assigning sisters to lower primary grades without subjecting them to the examination required for the *brevet*.

Religious congregations often offered the best professional preparation for women. John deplored the needless intimidation of young women by public examiners whose rigor often scared capable candidates from service. When public funds became available, he requested assistance for the Providence where the sisters had already given so much. Despite its services to the public, the private school had never been adequately funded. [9]

"The devil would leave us alone if ... "

After the loss of Saint-Meen, Moncontour was a consolation, a success in the face of nagging contradictions. John asked full use of a home for the sisters, as long as they served in the parish, and he invited Father Le Borgne, the parish priest, to establish ownership as he saw fit. [10]

Unfortunately, the sisters could not avoid interference from Bishop de La Romagère. Elections were coming at the end of Sister Chaplain's term and the Bishop was sending a sister, Sister Le Borgne, the parish priest's own sister to reside with the community as she prepared the renewal of her profession. Sister Le Borgne could not get along with the community of Saint-Brieuc and soon left.

De La Romagère was also thwarting the attempts of John de La Mennais to found a new *collège* in Dinan. Father de La Mennais was preparing to transfer ownership of the Providence to the sisters and asked Mother Chaplain to put all accounts in order and to complete a full inventory of the Providence and Moncontour as required by law. The Bishop was maneuvering to acquire the title of the Providence school for the diocese, even dictating terms of transfer to the Mother General. Father de La Mennais shared with Mother Chanplain some of the vexations interfering with his work including the recent death of the Director of the Guadeloupe mission from yellow fever. He wrote: *"All of this must comfort us, my daughter: if we were not beating back the Devil, he would leave us alone. If our work did not please God, he would not stamp it with the sign of the cross. Courage, my very dear daughter, courage! Forward, says the Lord!"* (January 4, 1839). [11]

The good work of the sisters continued despite the setbacks. In 1840, they founded a school in Combourg, a city that John frequently visited.

Father Ruault warned Father de La Mennais of the frustrations awaiting the Sisters in Combourg: *"Mother Colmache, the first Superior is perplexed because the house of the sisters has been rented and the new one is not ready and will not be ready when they move,"* (July 15, 1844). Nevertheless, the parish priest and the population welcomed them and soon the school began to fill with children. Father de La Mennais supported the initiatives of Sister Colmache by asking his brother-in-law, Ange Blaize, to press local authorities to expedite the construction work and assure that the classrooms were comfortable.

Bishop de La Romagère passed away on February 19, 1841. His successor, Bishop Le Mée, a longtime friend of Father de La Mennais, brought peace. Ecclesiastical obstacles which delayed the transfer of the Providence to the sisters disappeared. Relationships between the sisters, Father de La Mennais and the diocese became what they should always have been.

The words of a friend

In his work with the Daughters of Providence, Father de La Mennais did not forget the other religious congregations of sisters in the diocese of Saint-Brieuc. In some cases, he intervened to restore legal authorization or repossess buildings confiscated during the Revolution, at times to be their advocate in civil matters. The many experience John shared with the sisters deepened his own understanding of religious life; the friendships born in service stayed with him for life.

Father de La Mennais had intervened to legalize the reorganization of the Daughters of Providence, and he had been instrumental in the return of their former convent. Though their school prospered at the *Victoire,* the government still had the power to reoccupy it. The Superior appealed to Father de La Mennais when they received a request for the building from the *Université* preparing the way for a second expropriation. Father De La Mennais appealed to the Minister of the Interior in support of the sisters' request, though nothing John did prevented public administrators from dislodging the sisters a second time. [12]

John was more successful in his efforts to assist Jeanne (Jenny) de Kertanguy and the Sisters of the Retreat in Vannes. Jeanne came to him for advice as she worked to promote spiritual retreats, an activity which led her to the work of Catherine de Francheville, foundress of the Retreat of Vannes.

Closed retreats offered special opportunities to deepen one's commitment to Christian living. The usual format of parish retreats provided teachings, reflection time, time for prayer and special access to the sacraments. They were an invitation to withdraw from one's normal environment to spend reflective time in seclusion following a program of instruction, meditation and devotion. Earlier missionaries had established the movement in Brittany before the Revolution; Jeanne de Kertanguy decided to revive the movement for women.

Catherine de Francheville founded a religious congregation supporting the "Retreat Movement" in 1674. [13] The Revolution destroyed that institution, as it destroyed so many good works a century after her death. Jeanne de Kertanguy was inspired to give her life to that spiritual renewal movement; [14] she eventually succeeded when she was supported by a group of women equally committed to that cause.

She applied for membership in the community and after her novitiate, was assigned to the retreat of Saint-Pol-de-Léon where her personal gifts were soon discovered. She later served as Mistress of Novices and elected Superior General in 1832. As Superior General, she resolved to restore the tradition of the earlier retreat Congregation by restoring the work of Miss de Francheville. It might have been impossible for her to follow that dream without the assistance of Father François-Marie Langrez, a friend of Father de La Mennais. [15] Some fifty letters from her hand between 1834 and 1838 reveal a deepening spiritual relationship. [16] When letters ended, visits continued until the death of Father de La Mennais.

Mother de Kertanguy turned to Father de La Mennais for advice during her term as Superior General. He convinced her that education was the primary need of the times, and that retreat centers would offer more lasting benefits if they were combined with boarding schools for girls. Sister de Kertanguy easily understood the concept; the problem was to gain the acceptance of her Congregation and the agreement of the Bishop of Quimper. After three failed attempts, the daughter of Count Paul-Emile de La Fruglave created the possibility by providing funding. [17]

The foundation of the Lannion retreat center was a transforming experience for a number of retreat communities and for Mother de Kertanguy. Divisions between the older and younger members of her Congregation was her first challenge; the younger sisters, her former novices, were ready to accept the three vows of religious life, while the older sisters clung to their traditions. However, the community was ready to accept the foundation of Lannion. The boarding school opened in September 1836, obtaining full legal authorization the following year.

The different points of view on the vows persisted and Mother de Kertanguy was not spared years of anguish. She was strengthened through the hardest obstacles by the advice of Father de La Mennais who reminded her that *"she needed not only a courage of fire, but a will of steel,"* to be useful to her Congregation. [18] With a community of willing sisters, Mother de Kertanguy was eventually free to reinstate the religious vows and the rules of Catherine de Francheville of Vannes. On September 29, 1845, Mother de Kertanguy sent sisters to open a convent for Retreats in Vannes. In her letters to Father de La Mennais, she opened her soul about her long ordeal and he sustained her by his judicious counsels Maria de la Fruglaye was a major benefactress in the foundation of Mother de Kertanguys Lannion retreat centre. As along-term family friend of Fr. De la Mennais, she also intervened courageously in his favour in a diocese which had closed the doors to his schools at the time of Felicite's controvertial Publications.

---

[1] **Cor gén J,** v. 3, p. 545.
[2] H.-C Rulon and Ph. Friot quote one of many such reports in *Un siècle de pédagogie dans les écoles primaires (1820-1940),* Paris: Librairie Philosophique J. Vrin, 1962. P. 36. The example given is dated as late as 1855.
[3] She was the last foundress to die, March 24, 1858.
[4] These accounts are based on the Annals of the Community. **Lav** v. 1, pp. 310-311.
[5] See René Durand, *Le Département des Côtes-du-Nord sous le Consulat et l'Empire.* Paris: Librairie Félix Alcan, 1926. 2 v., v. 1, pp. 463-474. F. Le Douarec, Le *Concordat dans un diocese de l'ouest.* Paris: Éditions Alsatia, 1958, pp..151-153. The yearbooks of the Breton dioceses for the period provide additional data.

[6] Gréard, *La législation de l'enseignement primaire,* Paris: Delalain, s.d. Vol. 2, p. 251+.

[7] **Cor gén J,** v. 3, p. 469.

[8] Ibid., p. 545.

[9] **Cor gén J,** v. 3, pp.545-546.

[10] Letter (August 5, 1837), **Cor gén J,** v. 3, p. 503.

[11] **Cor gén J,** v. 4, pp. 145-146 and reply from Mother Chaplain (January 7, 1839) **AFIC,** 077-04-003.

[12] **Cor gén J,** v. 4, p. 286. **Lav,** v. 2, pp. 156-158.

[13] Jacqueline Héduit, *Catherine de Franchevilli, Initiatrice et fondatrice des retraites de femmes, Sa vie (1620-1689), Son oeuvre: La Retraite de Vannes.* (Imprimerie Mame à Tours, 1957).

[14] A. du Bois de la Villerabel, *Mère de Kertanguy, 1796-1870.* Paris: Beauchesne, 1925. **Lav,** v. 2, p. 159-177.

[15] On François-Marie Langrez (1787-1862), see L. Kerbiriou, *Au service des orphelines, et Face au tabernacle. La Congrégation de l'Adoration Perpétuelle.* Brest: Imprimerie Le Grand, 1926. He founded the Congregation in 1821. Marguerite Le Maître was the directress of the first orphanage.

[16] Copies in **AFIC,** 048-02-001+, and several related files.

[17] Three proposals failed to incorporate a school, each for a different reason. Mother de Kertanguy was planning the foundation of new retreat centers at the time. Mr. de La Mennais suggested the opening of a retreat house with a boarding school for girls in Saint-Servan and offered the help of the Daughters of Providence to start the school. The concept was new, but the General Council of the little Congregation accepted the principle. The project had to be abandoned when the revolt of Félicité de La Mennais confused relationships between the Bishop of Rennes and the two La Mennais brothers. The commitment of Mother de Kertanguy to restore the Retreat of Vannes matured and her determination to combine retreats with boarding schools intensified until a generous friend offered to help

[18] From a brief manuscript biography of Jeanne de Kertanguy, Superior General of the Daughters of the Blessed Virgin of the Retreat of Vannes, p. 15. **AFIC,** 048.01.001. Also cited in Du Bois de La Villerabel, *Mère de Kertanguy,* op. cit. p. 342. Biographer Laveille applies a similar expression to John de La Mennais in **Lav,** v. 1, p. 271.

Chapter 26

OVERSEAS !

Unexpected call

When Father François Mazelier requested a few teachers to assist his new congregation of brothers in southeastern France, Father de La Mennais responded that he was not inclined to disperse his troops: *"Mr. Deshayes, my venerable and saintly friend, has been bolder and more fortunate; he recently told me the story of his trip to Digne."* Indeed, in their request for legal authorization in 1821, John de La Mennais and Gabriel Deshayes declared that they had no intention of serving beyond the five departments of ancient Brittany. Fifteen years later, Father de La Mennais was still reluctant to send brothers far from the home front: *"Will I be converted later? That is not likely, for I have the head of a true Breton, and those heads are hard,"* (June 30, 1837).[1]

He must have written with subdued chuckles, for the government was then inviting him to send brothers to the French Colonies, and the Minister of Education, François Guizot was asking him what he could do for the education of slaves in the Caribbean: *"I would like to receive information about what you could do if you were helped, really helped in the education of slaves in our colonies. No one is more convinced than I that liberation is possible only after we have helped these miserable people to live for a long time in a religious atmosphere. In the English colonies, it is in Antigua where emancipation has been most successful, even though it was sudden, because the Moravian brothers had been established there during a century and had exerted a strong influence upon the black population,"* (November 8, 1836). [2]

The Breton heart of John de La Mennais was not *"hard"* enough to dismiss the call of captive souls on Caribbean plantations. He wrote to Father Ruault on December 11, 1837: *"Our brothers boarded yesterday; today they must be far at sea: God protect and bless them!"* [3] He later learned that indolent winds had kept his brothers in port during a few days, but soon five brothers were passengers on *La Girafe* bound for the Island of Guadeloupe. They had volunteered for the slave islands without fully realizing what awaited them. Their Superior had prepared the mission with his customary foresight.

The formal request came in August 1836 through Mr. Lorois, Prefect of Morbihan, at the suggestion of Admiral Victor Guy Duperré, Minister of the Navy and the Colonies. [4] His successor, Admiral Rosamel also believed that only a religious congregation could win the trust of the black population. The government had to contend with the curse of slavery until emancipation in 1848. Though Louis XIV had issued orders to treat slaves humanly, colonial executives allowed serious abuse to continue. Chains, whips, fetters, extended lockup (sometimes in total darkness), and the iron collar, terrorized the insubordinate into docility. As late as 1845, Brother Arsène could report to the Founder from Pointe-à-Pitre the torture of three *"thieves"* bound naked, face down, and whipped 29 lashes. Shreds of flesh and spattered blood disgraced the scene, but the victims held their screams until the last stroke. [5]

John understood the gravity of the request. He scrutinized the terms of the government contract, inquired about the experience of the Brothers of the Christian schools and other missionaries, sat through repeated interviews and consultations with ministerial officials in Paris, and pursued a sustained correspondence with Mr. De Saint-Hilaire, Director of the Colonies in the Ministry of the Navy. The call of a helpless people was irresistible to a superior who had refused brothers to numerous French bishops. The August retreat of 1837 ended without mention of the new mission because he had not received the official acceptance of his terms before 150 brothers had returned to their schools. When the official invitation came, he immediately informed those who were still in Ploërmel, and quickly held a list of fifty-two volunteers. He needed five and had confidentially decided on four.

Guizot's reference to emancipation on the neighboring British islands a decade before France abolished slavery in its colonies was quite appropriate. Empty promises of abolition by the French Revolutionists and by Napoleon floated in the winds of 1838, at the time the British emancipated their slaves on British Domenica. The island lay between Guadeloupe and Martinique; freedom could no longer be postponed for the slaves in the French colonies

The slaves of the French planters heard the freedom songs of their brothers and sisters across the waves with menacing impatience. No effective preparation for emancipation had been made and the white population was at risk. Slaves freely swinging machetes could easily turn from the work fields to the cities. The Negro population was tired of false promises, and the colonial administration realized the power of 80,000 machete-wielding blacks against 20,000 whites on Marinique, and 95,000 blacks against 35,000 whites on Guadeloupe. A revolt in 1822, a crop fire on Martinique in 1831 cautioned against delay, and recurring disturbances compelled reform. [6]

Conscious of its ineffectiveness, the government acknowledged the civilizing influence of the Church and called its missionaries to service. It reorganized the colonial administration, revised budgets and funded the work of the clergy through the decades preceding the arrival of the brothers. The parish branch of the Fathers of the Holy Spirit had received government subsidies to prepare diocesan clergy and their own members for the mission parishes of the colonies. Churchmen came as agents salaried by the government, but politics and involvement of Government in church appointments cut into their freedom. The brothers came after a reshuffling of colonial services. The Brothers of the Christian Schools came first in 1817, establishing a permanent mission on the island of *Réunion,* (the former Bourbon Island) in the Indian Ocean. However, they opted not to return to Guadeloupe where they had opened schools before the Revolution.

The Daughters of Saint Paul came to administer the military hospital, and the Sisters of Saint Joseph of Cluny came to teach the girls two decades before the arrival of the brothers. The few available monitorial schools were utterly insufficient for the boys. The brothers were called to serve with members of other congregations as civil servants.

Because of the Brothers' work in the mission, the government assisted the novitiate of Ploërmel, funding studies on the basis of the number of teachers preparing for the colonies. Teachers were "paid" from the colonial budget, and the French navy guaranteed their transit. Over the years, the plan enabled John de La Mennais to supply teachers to French lands as diverse as Guadeloupe, (1838) Martinique, (1839) Senegal, (1841) Saint-Pierre-et-Miquelon, (1842) French Guiana, (1843) and Tahiti, (1860) one establishment a year from 1838 to 1843, a far leap for a society originally meant for service in the five departments of ancient Brittany. Tahiti was the last assignment opened before the Founder's death. [7]

Guadeloupe (1838)

The island of Guadeloupe consists of two islands fanning out from a narrow isthmus, *(la Rivirère Salée)* like the wings of a butterfly, but there was little to flutter about in that land of plantations. African slaves grew sugar cane for wealthy planters. The island and its neighbors were reputed to be the purgatory for the planters, heaven for their wives, hell for their slaves. The island group known as the Lesser Antilles was discovered for Spain by Columbus in 1493. France took possession of Guadeloupe in 1635, and dispossessed the natives of the land in favor of colonists who thrived only on slave labor. The English occupied it at the end of the century, but returned it to France in 1816.

The first five missionary brothers sailed from the land of evergreens and temperate winters, into a world of palms, scorching heat and hellish sugar cane fields. The government had requested ten brothers, five each for Guadeloupe and Martinique. The Founder prudently cut the number to five for a first settlement on Guadeloupe, with the expectation that these early missionaries would adjust to the situation, and then prepare a new settlement on the island of Martinique. Though major problems would soon surface, John had chosen them carefully for experience, stable character and religious spirit. Three had directed schools; Brother Antonin, the Director, held the official teaching permit recently required of school directors in France.

The Founder travelled with them to the chateau of Keranroux, where Count de La Fruglaie and his daughter, Marie, always welcomed him. They were at Brest on December 3, waiting in a hotel until the tenth for the boarding call, then lived on board until favorable winds moved the "Girafe" out of port on January 7. The five brothers landed at Basse-Terre, port of entry and capital of Guadeloupe a month later. Two months after taking leave from Father de La Mennais, they entered a tropical city of 11,600 souls. Some 7,500 slaves lived at the side of a few whites and freed slaves.

The colonial government opened a first school at Basse-Terre where life would test the brothers' ability to adjust to a difficult climate and a region known to them only through reading and instruction. A residence and a building that could be transformed into a school awaited them when the Girafe docked on February 7, 1838. The brothers entered their new home with mixed feelings. Brother Léonide wrote of classrooms in vermin-infested lean-tos; Brother Antonin, the Director, described a residence and classrooms in rented structures with two small yards and a garden. The whole complex was an incongruous cluster of acceptable living and teaching space in lean-tos, and buildings in obvious need of repair. The location was on the street of the new city, where elevation and the proximity of a river valley blessed it as the coolest spot in the city. When the essential furniture arrived, 120 boys filled three narrow classrooms. The planning was not ideal, but no better facility seemed available; the following year, the classrooms were enlarged and repaired.

There was concern in Ploërmel until the brothers sent their first report. The windless month lost in the harbor of Brest, and a second month of idleness on the waves of the Atlantic, prevented Brother Antonin from sending an early report, confusing busy men accustomed to the discipline of school and community life.

Brother Antonin was not gifted with natural authority; he reported the independence of his community and his brothers complained about his erratic behavior. He could not regain his influence and community dissention continued, though the brothers managed to open a highly successful school. The island administrators and the clergy praised the work of the new teachers, but in June, Brother Antonin lost control and asked Brother Judicaël to return to France. In mid-July, yellow fever began a merciless sweep across the island; by mid-November, yellow fever had taken 50 lives from the Girafe's passenger list, and 500 from a garrison of 600 soldiers.

Three brothers fell bedridden, but they providentially recovered. A fourth, Brother Antonin, was not spared. Despite the epidemic, he had zealously and carelessly continued his work providing the material needs of the school and the community. The fever claimed his life on October 4, after eleven days of cruel sufferings. The school continued despite the loss of two teachers, but the dissention continued. There was discord, a refusal to teach by some, and the eventual return to France and departure from the Congregation of the three last men of the first team. The first member dismissed by Brother Antonin returned to France, directed a few schools and died in the Congregation. Insubordination and the epidemic had taken a merciless toll. Was the mission venture a loss cause? [8] Not for Father John de La Mennais, and not for the brothers in Brittany!

Martinique (1839) To the north of Guadeloupe, beyond Dominicana where the British had recently liberated their slaves, Martinique was still waiting for the teachers promised by Father de La Mennais. Between 1838 and 1840, new missionaries led by Brother Frédéric replaced the first team on Guadeloupe, and other volunteers opened a first school in Martinique. An invitation from the Sisters of Saint Joseph of Cluny in French Guiana turned the attention of the Founder south, and by April 1839, three brothers were landing at Pointe-à-Pitre, a city of fifteen thousand people living in a jumble of huts built on unstable volcanic land. The missionaries who landed at Pointe-a-Pitre suffered vexations at the hand of administrators who had earlier insistently pleaded for their services.

The competition raised by the new teachers to the island's monitorial schools displeased the local Director of the Interior who responded by raising obstacles to the brothers. Though life was very demanding on the local population, the government insisted on a small tuition for school admission though earlier it had promised free-tuition. The cordial attitude of the Governor failed to temper local pettiness; eventually patience triumphed, and within three months the highly respected institution had enrolled 150 students.

Soon, five other brothers were welcomed at Fort-Royal, Martinique, (now Fort-de-France) the chief port of the French Caribbean, the capital city and residence of government administrators. Since the brothers' residence was not completed, the Governor lodged them in his home in Saint-Pierre until they could enter their own residence in Fort-Royal. While waiting for their school to be completed, the brothers provided religious instruction to the women of the area.

French Guiana (1843)

As the missionaries were establishing a base on the West Indies, six brothers in transit were held up off Cayenne. The delay permitted them to pay their respects to the Apostolic delegate who tried to keep them for his mission. He could not change their destination, but Ploërmel soon received a formal invitation to send him teachers.

After the Revolution, France began to use French Guiana as a penal colony. It received some 500 political prisoners in 1798, and slavery was reintroduced after 1803. The consequences of deportation, slavery, administrative neglect weighed more heavily on this forsaken, unhealthy land than upon other Caribbean colonies. Missionaries were a blessing to the population as they cared for its distressed population more than other government agents. The Revolution destroyed the early work of the missionaries, but later the French government called upon them to reorganize parishes, restore social services and direct schools.

In 1837, a public elementary school in Cayenne served 123 students, 111 of them black. The school was located in a discontinued

Jesuit institution, the only school for boys in the colony when Father de La Mennais received his request for teachers. The Sisters of Saint Joseph of Cluny, and the Brothers of the Christian Schools had answered the government's call for teachers as early as 1823; the brothers left seven years later, but the sisters were still present when three brothers from Ploërmel arrived on February 1, 1843.

The goal of the missionaries was to hasten the development of this inland jungle, starting in the capital. After enduring the brothers opened their first school in Cayenne, on March 7. While Father de La Mennais was dealing with a variety of requests at home and abroad during this period, three Caribbean slave colonies in the French Antilles had become privileged mission territory for the Brothers of Christian Instruction. The Founder's designs for these forsaken people matured as emergency needs called for a proliferation of schools, teachers and a central authority.

Brother Ambroise; Chief Administrator

By August 1840, despite the initial setback in the missions, the brothers had proven themselves and won the confidence of parents, students, and most government officials. Admiral Duperre, Minister of the Marines was pleased to write to Father de La Mennais: *"Of all the means taken to prepare for the social transformation of the slave population in the missions, none is more effective than an increase in the number of institutions directed by the Brothers of Ploermel; the legislative branch agrees with me, and has provided funding to implement this plan"* [9]

To prove his point, the minister requested from Father de La Mennais, 18 brothers for the Antillies, and 3 for Senegal. The request confirmed the effectiveness of the missionaries' transforming presence, yet it placed a burden on the founder as he had no intention of dismantling his schools in Brittany. His solution was to request additional funding from the Ministry of the Marines, to pay for the education of young men unable to fund their education, yet eager to join the community of brothers.

In order to consolidate the Brothers' presence in the missions, Father de La Mennais sent Br. Ambroise as one of the nine brothers leaving for the missions in December, 1840 on the frigate Andromede. Brother Ambroise had already proven his mettle during his 18 years of leadership in the school of Treguier.

Ambroise[10] was a favorite of Father de La Mennais, a straight arrow, a person of impeccable integrity and good common sense. He was also a person with unquestioned commitment to religious life while totally dedicated to any work assigned to him. Despite these strengths, he experienced serious opposition in his new role as he was brutally frank, often lacking tact and gentleness. He was a person of modest intellectual capacity, though effective as a leader through his own personal example. His specific task was to represent the founder in the missions, to serve as his eyes and ears though his weekly reports, and to coordinate decisions.

The new director of the missions landed in Martinique in March of 1841, immediately assuming full responsibility. He soon realized that though the teachers' academic work was highly appreciated, there was much that needed improvement in the religious behavior of the brothers. Years without any real supervision had led to an unacceptable use of alcohol and tobacco, many brothers seriously relaxing their religious obligations.

In his customary way, Ambroise attacked the matter directly, forcefully, antagonizing many of the hard-working missionaries. Fortunately, Ambroise's honesty and examplary behavior over time won the support and admiration of most of the brothers, though for sometime, Father Evain, a chaplain sent to provide religious support, disorganized the mission by attempting to usurp the authority of Ambroise. At first, the founder did not realize what was happening, since Father Evain had left France with the full confidence of Father de LaMennais. When John eventually realized the situation, he recalled Evain bringing tranquility to the area.

After 1840, the laws in the colonies permitted slaves to attend school without cost; however, the plantation owners were very reluctant to allow their slaves to be instructed for fear of insurrection; in addition, they did not want to lose the fruits of their free labor. Since the slaves could not go to school, Br. Arthur Greffier and Marcellin-Marie in Martinique, and Br. Hyacinthe Fichou in Basse-Terre, Guadeloupe started to instruct the slaves by visiting the sugar plantations after school hours or on Saturdays. After 1845, the government required this service from slave-owners, and the brothers were then paid for this service. In addition, other brothers now joined these pioneers as catechists.

Fortunately, these three early apostles treated the slaves as they treated the white plantation owners, recognizing them as children of God. Within a few years, they were able to win concessions for the slaves: reduction in their hours of work, a more substantial diet, and amelioration of penal policies. In addition, the missionaries served as spokespersons for the slaves until the 24th of May, 1848, when slavery was finally abolished in all of the French colonies.

The service of missionary brothers was so appreciated by the slaves, that when an angry well-armed band of slaves threatened the destruction of Port Royal on the island of Saint Pierre, the government called upon Br. Arthur to face the rebels. Though Arthur was convinced he was being sent to his death, he accepted the challenge. The much abused slaves listened to him and returned to their fields. In a similar situation three years later, when rebellious workers torched the city, the slaves themselves hauled water pumps to control the flames when the fire reached the residence of the brothers. [11]

Having appreciated the services of the missionaries in the Antilles, the government then requested brothers for all of the other French colonies. Father de La Mennais responded by sending brothers to the tropical lands of Saint-Louis in Senegal in 1841; to the frigid coast of Saint Pierre-et-Miquelon in 1842; to the forest plateau of Guyanne in 1843, and to the island paradise of Tahiti in 1859-1860.

At the death of the founder, 65 brothers were serving in 23 schools in Guadeloupe, 52 brothers in 21 schools in the Martinique, and 14 brothers in 4 schools in French Guiana. Though the demands for religious teachers remained high in Brittany, the Founder so pitied the slaves who had been brutalized by harsh labor, that he often listened more sympathetically to the

Minister of Marines asking for teachers for slave colonies, than to bishops requesting brothers in their diocese. [12].

[1] Symphorien-Auguste, *À travers la Correspondance de l'abbé J. M. de la Mennais.* La Prairie, Québec, Canada: Imprimerie de Sacré-Coeur, Septième série, 1960. Pp. 180-181.

[2] François Guizot, *Mémoires pour servir à l'Histoire de mon temps.* Leipzig: F. A. Brokhaus; Livorno: A. Guillaume, Vol. III, 1860. P. 374. **Cor gén J,** v. 3, pp. 416-417.

[3] **Cor gén J,** v. 3, pp. 557-558.

[4] 1775-1846.

[5] **Lav,** v. 2, pp. 255-256.

[6] See Philippe Delisle, *Renouveau missionnaire et société esclavagiste. La Matinique:* 1815-1848 Paris: Publisud, 1997, pp. 30-76.

[7] On the missionary experience of the brothers, see generally, Paul Cueff, **ÉM**, No. 1 (July, 1987). Lav, v. 2, pp.218-347. Symphorien-Auguste, *À travers la Correspondance de L'Abbé J. M. de la Mennais,*troisième série. Vannes: Lafolye et de Lamarzelle, 1939. Quatrième série, La Prairie (Québec, Canada), 1953.

[8] At Ploujean near Morlaix .

[9].Merleau, J.M. de La Mennais, p. 185.

[10].Ibid., pp. 185-187.

[11].Ibid., p. 195.

[12] Drouin, J. M. de La Mennais, p. 56.

Chapter 27

NO ONE LOVED HIM MORE

Deepest Anguish

In addition to the natural bonds of family, during ten years John worked intimately with Felicite at La Chenaie, even providing him much of the educational materials which he used brilliantly in his highly effective philosophical works. In addition, John had been Feli's guide and counselor during more than 15 years, and he had provided him valuable resources when his ill-used funds were depleted. After his break with the Church, he adamantly refused to have any contact with John, as even his presence was a reminder of the past.

John remained hopeful that time would heal Feli's deep wounds and that his smoldering faith would again burst into flame, allowing the bonds of family to be renewed. This dream would never be realized, remaining an anguishing pain that festered during the last twenty years of John's life.

Unless one understands the radical transformation that took place in the life of Felicite de La Mennais after his censure by Rome, and the deep wound of a proud, sensitive person rejected in his most sincere effort, one could not understand the chronically lonely younger brother refusing the hand and the heart of an older brother. Yet, during 20 years, Feli adamantly refused the extended hand, and even the entreaties of family and friends. Feli could not reconcile with his brother before he reconciled with his

Church; he would die without the support of Church officials, as he would die without the presence of his tearful brother.

Severed bonds, abiding hope

"When I left La Chesnaie, eight months ago, I left it firmly resolved never to see it again. No place on earth would ever be more painful to live in, even for a moment, than that one. I miss but one thing, the grave that I had chosen there for myself. I know not where my bones will lie. That matters little, as long as under the earth which will cover them, they be protected from the eyes of the one who has constantly been so fatal to me," (January 26, 1837). [1] So wrote Félicité to Marion, the manager of La Chesnaie about his abrupt departure. [2]

The letter acknowledged none of John's generosities, not the years of shared enterprise, not the support in illness, not the repeated financial assistance. Neither did the letter acknowledge the sacrifice of the Congregation of Saint-Méen for the foundation of the Congregation of Saint Peter, nor the personal risks taken to salvage the defensible elements of his writings. John became *"the one who has constantly been fatal"* to him, (January 26, 1837) *"the person whom you know,"* and *"who should not be mentioned,"* (May 28, 1837).

"Rather than suffer the torment of a relationship without real union, I prefer to abandon the only abode I have on earth, live in a garret where my strength is rapidly declining, deprive myself of the only true pleasures which I know," replied Félicité to Marion who was asking him to reconcile with his brother. Feli explained his attitude thus: *"I have no feeling which appears contrary to the Christian duty of charity; but at the same time, I believe that neither the esteem, nor the affection on which close and lasting relationships are founded can ever be reborn. Be not mistaken, the circumstances which brought about the final rupture were only the last drop of water which caused the vase to overflow; it had long been full. I long knew the character of the one with whom you urge me to reestablish my former relationships, and it is not without anguish that I felt the fatal influence which he exerted on my entire life. I have suffered much for him, and I have always kept silence, and I was always telling myself*

that it was a burden which perhaps God was laying on me that I must bear. I do not deny the good qualities which he otherwise possesses, but they are not sufficient reason for me to reestablish bonds without charm because they would be without illusion. Let him go his way, I will walk along mine; that is the way to journey in peace," (February 15, 1840).[3]

The joint ownership of La Chesnaie would generate misunderstanding. John resented Félicité's early suggestion of convening new friends on the estate. After 1836, the writer undertook major transformations on the land without attention to income. Insolvency soon involved the innocent Marion who mediated differences between the two brothers. John explained that his obligations to his schools prevented him from sharing more than his own half of the expenses, and he advised his brother to measure expenses by income from the land.

When Félicité requested a settling of accounts at the separation of 1836, John replied to Marion: "1) *I have long abandoned to him my share of common profits. 2) I was entitled to half the value of wood cutting. I abandon it in his favor. 3) The unpaid dues of tenant farmers total 8,000 francs. Of that sum, no more than 2,000 F will presumably be reimbursed in land, the 4,000 others in cash: 2 000 of that sum are mine, I abandon those also. 4) Many of the books transported to Paris were undeniably mine; their minimum value amounts to 7,000 F; I have reduced that value by half to render all quibbling impossible. They at least have some value which must be deducted from what I owe Féli for the debt of 7,500. He is not entitled to claim full payment for those 7,500 F. without considering what I otherwise yield on all the items of our contract."* (February 18, 1837).[4] He instructed Élie de Kertanguy, his intermediary for his books that: *"If my brother wants to cancel anything from those 3,500 F, or the full amount,"* he was willing to cede it" (Jan. 18, 1837).[5] John asked the mediator to bring these matters to his brother's attention again, and instructed him to do everything in his power to close the sad affair in peace.

In January 1842, after serving his prison sentence, Félicité had second thoughts about staying away from La Chesnaie. John informed Miss de Lucinière about the prospects of his brother's return: *"Féli proposed* (through an intermediary) *to pay me to rent La Chesnaie, if I accepted to release it to him. I consented on the firm condition that it be gratuitous from me, and I expressed my most loving and cordial feelings. I do not know if he will even reply,"* (July 17, 1842).

John had instructed his brother-in-law Ange Blaize to make the offer through his son: *"I beg you to ask Ange to tell Féli, on my behalf, that I yield to him the total and absolute use of la Chênaie without any reservation. He may dispose of it alone as he wishes as though I were no longer of this world! The only matter to which I will not consent, is to receive a single centime for it . . . Poor Féli, how content I would be to know him with us, even were I condemned never to tell him, heart to heart, how much I have always loved him and how much I love him now!"* (July 8, 1842).

Félicité unbendingly rejected anything likely to reopen relationships: *"How could I accept the least condescension? It is impossible, as you can see. . . . Were I to accept, I would find myself in one of the two following positions, either to be forced to closer relationships which I find repugnant for a thousand reasons, or to be indebted to the one with whom I do not want any relationship,"* (July 21,1842). [6] Joint ownership continued, as did the frustrating claims due to Félicité's poor accounting and spotty financial memory. The writer complained loudly when proceeds from La Chesnaie came late from the manager who could not transfer revenues before tenants settled accounts.

Vigilant intermediaries

Bonds of family and friendship long remained the only links between John and his estranged brother. Marie and Ange Blaize, her spouse, lived at Trémigon, not far from Combourg. They kept a loving relationship with Félicité who cherished their home and that of Marion as a relief from his arid Parisian existence. He visited them until age, health and stubbornness riveted him to Paris. There, Miss de Lucinière, the unwavering friend since the London years, kept her door open to him, even offered him lodging, which he refused. She respected his independence without hesitating to deplore the extravagant inconsistencies of his existence. She wrote to him, invited him for meals as frequently as she could, occasionally arranged meetings with friends. Her devotion never slackened and her letters to Ploërmel kept John informed.

John initially learned that the disaffected priest was seen praying discretely in church. Miss de Lucinière found him confused, but detected traces of faith in him as she wrote that he attended mass regularly, observed abstinence, and vindicated a Catholic priest discredited at a Protestant funeral, (October 3, 1836). [7] Such remnants of his religious past slowly vanished. Félicité accepted to see Father Rohrbacher late in 1837; the former director of studies at Malestroit described his former master as *"the same man,"* but lost in his thinking, perhaps still open to change. The most basic Christian teachings seemed no longer to matter. [8]

Later, in 1847, Felicite agreed to speak with Father Ventura, who had provided for him in Rome. The meeting took place in the presence of the Abbé Martin de Noirlieu and a few ecclesiastics at the residence of Father Deguerry, parish priest at Notre Dame in Paris. Félicité spoke like a book about his new religion of humanity. Ventura held his own in a two-hour rebuttal. Overwhelmed by the logic, Félicité left precipitously, begging Ventura not to be so severe with him. [9] The teachings on the divinity of Christ, Christianity, the Church, dogma, the Eucharist that he had upheld during the first two decades of his priesthood had vanished from his beliefs. [10]

John learned about such interventions during more than a decade. Though attempting to maintain some reason for hope, Felicite's eroding faith deepened his anguish, though John's hope of restoring a lost relationship survived the most disheartening news. He was refused admission when he knocked at his door unannounced in March, 1840. Félicité left unanswered the letter he wrote to express his sorrow, (March 25, 1840). A friend who occasionally met him in Paris during those years witnessed *"the pain he suffered in the proximity of a brother he could no longer embrace."* [11] The sufferings of that brother worried him as it always had: *"I learned indirectly that my poor brother was at Trémigon: I was told that he was very weak, and that he had been carried to his room in a seat when he left the coach: the news broke my heart—Let us pray more than ever for him,"* (June 20, 1846). [12]

Apoplexy disabled John in 1847. He informed his brother of the stroke and reaffirmed his affection as soon as he could: *"I really thought about you at that moment, which I thought might have been the last. I need to tell you that my friendship, which has never changed, nor weakened, is stronger than ever, and that my heart is filled with the desire that one day, we may be reunited in heaven as we have so long been united by the same faith on earth,"* (December 18, 1847). This time, the brother John had so often assisted in illness replied: *"I learn from Ange, who leaves to visit you tomorrow, about your sad accident, and which I hope will not cause the consequences you fear."* He added, that were it not for failing health, he would accompany his nephew on the visit; he closed with the following words: *"I am pleased to embrace you, and to reassure you of my old, sincere and very tender affection,"* (December 26, 1847). John thanked him for the reply that broke a decade of horrid silence, (January 5, 1848).

The peevish resolve to avoid returning to La Chesnaie never destroyed Félicité's interest in the sanctuary of his best achievements. He occasionally conceded that he might live there if he could obtain sole ownership. When age prevented Marion from continuing his services, he asked Ange Blaize (senior) to request new caretaking arrangements from John. A postscript added by him to a letter of Ange Blaize, (January 19, 1848) and a letter about the administration of La Chesnaie, (February 1) came to Ploërmel as the last lines from the hand of Félicité seen by John. Silence followed a friendly letter the following year, (February 18, 1849);[13] prayer for a beloved brother never died in John's heart.

Death closed channels of communication. Archbishop de Quélen expired on December 31, 1838. Anne de Lucinière *(Ninette),* whose friendship never died, passed away on January 26, 1844, Marion in 1848, Marie on March 31, 1851 and her husband Ange Blaize in April 1852. Félicité remembered him as *"the oldest, the most constant, the most devoted of his friends."*

Information about Félicité came through their children: Ange, Hippolyte and their sister, Augustine de Kertanguy, whose spouse Élie, a trusted young assistant of Félicité, had passed away at 34 in 1847. The nieces of Miss de Lucinière, Hélène and Antoinette, (Madame de

Grandville) inherited the loyalty of their aunt. Friends, such as the Baroness Cottu, Fathers Rohrbacher, Martin de Noirlieu and a few other priests obligingly manifested their concern. The letters continued until the end, bringing distressing news corroborated by the press. Whatever definable Christian doctrine remained with him did not transpire in his public declarations. With friends worrying about the drift of his faith, Félicité withdrew behind defensive, unbreachable barricades.

Firm directives, divided loyalties

Declining health stirred the last flurry of communications. Félicité resented the visitors brought to his door and set down formal funeral instructions for Auguste Barbet a month later: *"I want to be buried with the poor, as are the poor. Nothing must be placed on my tomb, not even a simple stone. My body must be taken directly to the cemetery, without being presented in any church. No death notices must be sent."* Only six persons were to be notified: *"M. Béranger, M. de Vitrolles, M. Émile Forgues, M. Jh. D'Ortigues, Mme. (widow) Élie de Kertanguy."* John was the obvious exclusion. As illness reduced his means, Félicité appointed Auguste Barbet to manage his home: *"I declare as a formal decision that my friend Mr. Barbet alone will be in charge of administering my household and all of my interests, including visits."* He clarified the last directive to Barbet, verbally: *"Observe my instructions well, interpret them broadly. Do not let any priest enter my room."*

These directives and the visitors of his last days reflected the contradictions of his life and the conflicts generated by his writings. Faith and friendship called to his side those who had shared his life; others who came realized that Félicité resolutely excluded from his presence anyone likely to recall the past; there were few exceptions.

Félicité had converted the Baroness Cottu and kept a sustained correspondence with her during 26 years. When news spread that her spiritual guide was weakening, she came on January 24, and passed into his room before she could be stopped. She spoke unrecorded words to him and knelt in prayer by his bed, but he turned his head away. [14] He directed that she not be allowed to return. On January 25, Fathers Martin de Noirlieu and

Ventura were refused admission, as Rohrbacher was on another occasion. Félicité was told about the visits afterwards and reaffirmed his instructions. On the 29th, the abbé Dancel came on the part of Archbishop Sibour of Paris, asking Félicité to sign a written retraction. Barbet consulted Félicité who refused to consider such a request.

The chosen company of the last days

John was then confined to his room in Ploërmel by his doctor's orders. At the first alarm, he wrote to his nephew Ange Blaize: *"I beg you to leave immediately for Paris. Go as representative of the family and do not fail to coordinate your interventions with Hélène and her sister, with Mr. De Vitrolles and Father Martin de Noirlieu. Alas! Alas! I can do no more, I only have tears and prayers,)* (January 30, 1854). [15]

Félicité was weak when niece Augustine de Kertanguy arrived from Brittany on February 3, 1854. He greeted the timid but courageous woman and assured her that he would call for her because he wanted to speak to her after regaining his strength. There were occasional brief visits for her and a few others who had so often been turned away. Her return to Brittany had been set, but she postponed her departure because of his illness. On the fifteenth, she asked for the delayed visit; her uncle promised to notify her as soon as possible without specifying a date. The interval was difficult for Félicité; Barbet pointed out that references to religion disturbed him and that he did not wish to see her.

He nevertheless admitted Augustine on Sunday, the 19th. She described the conversation as peaceful. Félicité referred to her affairs in Brittany, acknowledged that *"it was over,"* spoke of resignation to the will of God: *"I will be well when I rest with him."* He obviously wanted all troubling conversation avoided. After a moment of silence she expressed John's desire to come despite his inability to travel. He replied: *"It was better for him not to come."* She explained John's suffering because of his brother's present condition: *"Dear Féli, my uncle John suffers so much, he has been unable to sleep for several nights. A word from you would be so good for him; I beg you, allow me to say it to him on your behalf. He regained composure and told me, as he would have formerly: 'Tell it to him.' I then told him: "I will tell my uncle John many things on your behalf." "'Yes,' he answered very affectionately,"* (Letter to John the next day, February 20, 1854). [16] She managed to introduce religious and devotional considerations in the conversation. At the suggestion of her confessor, she presented him a statement of abjuration which he rejected.

The report of Barbet was quite different. He wrote of raised voices, of imprudent talk upsetting the sick uncle who complained: *"My niece wants to save my soul by killing me."* Barbet and doctor Jallat attributed to her visit the grave relapse of the following day. In a letter to John, the reports circulated about her: *"You no doubt know everything that several newspapers have said about the visit which I made to my uncle Sunday. Several persons have gone as far as to say that I raised my voice, and M. de Lamennais likewise, to the point of drawing the attention of persons in the house. I can certify that this is so far from the truth that the persons who accuse me would be embarrassed to know what I said unless they had stayed very close to me. If it is true that my uncle Féli became delirious, the persons who approached him would have done well to notify M. Rostant who told Mrs. Cottu yesterday that my uncle had always remained conscious,"* (February 26). [17]

The end was imminent when John wrote to her: *"I have not been able to sleep for three weeks; the most painful anxiety torments me. I have an intense desire to go to Paris, and I no longer sleep! Tell my poor Féli on my behalf, what I would tell him if I were there. -- Beg him, conjure him in my name, to think about his soul, about the Church which he loved so much, about his poor old brother John, who loves him more than ever, and who begs him to call to his side a sincere priest moved by faith and charity, who prays for him like another brother!"* (February 23, 1854). [18]

No visitors were allowed to see Félicité again until he took a turn for the worst. On Sunday, February 26, Barbet opened the room to all who wished to see him. According to the official report, at one thirty in the afternoon, Félicité was ready with a codicil to his testament. He had been preparing a complete edition of his works. Fearing that his niece, as universal heir, might yield to conscience and advisors, and bar publication, he dictated instructions in the presence of four of his friends, and signed a statement entrusting his unpublished works to Émile Forgues with the order to publish everything. Later, at a quarter to five in the afternoon, he sent for Forgues. Armand Lévy went to call him and the dying insisted: *"Be firm, they will try to circumvent you."* Forgues vowed: *"I will publish everything."* [19]

These transactions were in progress when Barbet sent for Augustine at three in the afternoon. As she entered the room, her first words were, *"Féli, do you want a priest? You want a priest, don't you?"* Her uncle replied, *"No."* The Niece continued: *"I beg you!"* But he replied in a firm voice: *"No; no; no; give me peace."* She approached the bed shortly afterwards and said: *"Do you need anything?"* He replied: *"I need nothing at all, except to be left in peace."*

When Mrs. de Grandville arrived, she approached the bed and said: *"I am Antoinette, do you recognize me?"* He answered, *"Perfectly, I am pleased to see you ... but I must attend to my friends."* [20] The niece and her friend were allowed to remain in the room after promising to attempt nothing further. They stayed at the end of the divan. They deplored the situation during the evening, saying: *"It is very sad to see someone die, and die like this,"* for *"after all"* added the niece, *"he is the one who made a Christian of me."* Armand Lévy replied: *"The first thing is that the will of the dying be respected."* *"Indeed,"* replied the niece, *"and his will is unfortunately too evident."* At 9:15 in the morning of February 27, Félicité expired

Augustine wrote to John the very next day: *"I could not witness the last breath of our dear Féli. ... I spent the night at his side; I left at about seven in the morning. He seemed still strong and I thought I could leave. ... I asked Mrs. de Grandville to come with me. ... We had time to eat something and to attend mass, and I was in church, praying for my uncle when he appeared before God. I did everything in my power to fulfill your wishes. I did not lose courage. Faith, your prayers, the deep affection I have for you sustained me,"* (February 28, 1854). [21]

Farewell!

John knew little of recent developments when he decided to visit his brother. The parish priest of Lannion, Father Urvoy de Kermoalquin, who had offered to accompany him, summarized the tensions surrounding the moribund: *"I am sending you a letter which may convince you to leave for Paris, where your presence seems necessary,"* (February 24, 1854).[22] Troubled by correspondence about Félicité's isolation, he disregarded his doctor's objections and decided to travel. Father Ruault, his assistant in Ploërmel, dared not object. Félicité lay in his casket when John's coach left for Paris at noon on February 28, flanked by Father Colin, and Brother Donat, the usual coachman of the old coach with whom he visited his schools. He learned in Rennes that Félicité had passed away the preceding day.

At ten minutes to eight in the morning of the next day, Wednesday, March 1st, public undertakers came for the casket of Félicité, set on a "paupers" hearse and brought it to the cemetery of *Père Lachaise* through an increasing assembly of observers. Rumors of planned agitation had alerted public authority. The government avoided the expected disturbances by not announcing the proceedings. The police came in force to control manifestations, few persons allowed to pass the cemetery gate. The casket was taken to the ghastly ditch opened to absorb the remains of the poor. The grave digger who lowered it in the paupers' grave asked: *"should there be a cross?"* Barbet answered: *"No."* The tomb remained unmarked according to the wishes of the deceased. No other words were spoken.[23] Thus ended the curt formalities before the police dispersed the cortège. Barbet and friends would have exhumed him, but niece Augustine de Kertanguy, the designated heir, refused permission. She loved her uncle, but she would not allow a memorial to his sad destiny over his remains.

These events had all taken place by the time John returned to Ploërmel grief stricken. He would later write *"rather dead than living."* Father Ruault wrote to Ange Blaize: *"He thinks of nothing other than his poor brother, and nothing can distract him from that thought, night and day! And what cause for consolation could we suggest to him?"* (March 6, 1854).[24]

After 18 years of separation, John wanted to recall the joys and sorrows of life with his brother. On June 18, 1854, four months after Félicité's funeral, he revisited La Chesnaie accompanied by a few friends. The chapel built by Félicité had been closed for the past twenty years. He had it opened to offer the holy sacrifice at the altar where his brother had celebrated his last mass. He came out after a prayer of thanksgiving, walked across the silent terrace, raised his head toward a well-known window and called in hopelessness: *"Féli! oh! Féli!."* Overcome with grief, he collapsed taking with him Brother Philéas who was assisting him. Weakness abridged the visit; distraught, he re-entered his coach and returned to Ploërmel.[25]

Emile Forgues unwittingly revived the lingering pain. He was writing a biography of Félicité to accompany the publication of his manuscripts and he twice turned to John for personal letters and documents. The first request came through the Baron de Vitrolles. Father Ruault replied that retrieving papers associated with the recent tragedy would reopen unhealed wounds.

Father de La Mennais replied personally when Forgues repeated the request after the death of de Vitrolles shortly afterwards: *"The inexpressible pain which I bear is not the type that suffering slowly alleviates and finally destroys. At the age we had reached, the tomb was expected to open soon for one of us, and the other was to follow closely. ... I could not forget those happy times when my poor brother and I were closely united by the bonds of the same faith, and the same hopes which made our two hearts into one; those times when the absence of a few weeks seemed like years. Those wrenching souvenirs break my heart when I associate them with the end of my unfortunate brother. -- How do you expect me, sir, to be able , in such a condition of mind and heart, to sift through variously dispersed papers, each word of which would be as a dagger wound for me?....The remnant of life which I have, would not bear it. ... Oh! If to save my beloved brother would have required the sacrifice of the little I own, even the sacrifice of my life, God knows with what heart I would have done it!"* (November 29, 1854).[26]

[1] **Cor gén F,** v. 7, p. 143. (The letter is misdated 1836).

[2] Jean-Baptiste-Louis Marion (1772-1848), manager of the La Chesnaie for the two brothers. Félicité left La Chesnaie in May, 1836.

[3] **Cor gén F,** v. 7 at Feb 15.

[4] Abridged statement. Full text in **Cor gén J,** v. 3, pp. 461-462. **Lav,** v. 2, pp. 207, 208, n.2., and **SA (1960),** pp. 86-87.

[5] Letter, Élie de Kertanguy to Marion, **Cor gén J,** v. 3, p. 447.

[6] **Cor gén J,** v. 4, pp. 563-564, 557. **Cor gén F,** v. 8, pp. 174-175. **SA (1960),** pp. 81, 89 and 90.

[7] **Cor gén J,** v. 3, p. 395, note the next letter from the Archbishop of Paris to de Lucinière, pp. 395-396. **Cor gén F,** v. 7, p. 601.

[8] See her letter, **Cor gén F,** v. 8, pp. 960-961, and John's reply, **Cor gén J,** September 10, 1842, v. 4, pp. 586-587.

[9] O'Connel died in Geneva, May 15, 1847. Ventura came to Paris for the funeral oration.

[10] Information about these interventions is dispersed in the writings of the participants and in numerous sources. Among them, see the following, Dudon, op. cit., pp. 365-372; **Lav,** v. 2, pp. 204-217; **Cor gén F,** v. 7, pp. 647-648, 677-678; v. 8., pp. 939, 949, 966; **SA (1960),** pp. 77-91.

[11] **Cor gén J,** v. 4, p. 310. S. Ropartz, friend and first biographer. **Rop,** p. 460.,

[12] Letter to Father Ruault, **Cor gen J,** v. 5, p. 484.

[13] **Cor gén F,** v. 7, p. 676; v. 8, pp. 1042, 528, 539-41, 543, 1045, 1088. **Rop,** pp. 465-470; **Lav,** v. 2, pp. 486, 490.

[14] By some accounts, she entered his room twice that day.

[15] **Rop,** p. 474. Ange Blaize, *Essai biographique sur M. F. de La Mennais,* Paris: Garnier, 1858, p. 163.

[16] **SA (1960),** p. 98.

[17] A. Roussel, op. cit., *"Derniers jours et mort de Lamennais,"* pp. 46-47.

[18] **Cor gén F,** v. 8, p. 869, note 45. **SA (1960),** pp.101-102. **Lav,** v.2, p. 579.

[19] **Cor gén F,** v. 8, pp. 870-872.

[20] The incidents of that day are based on Barbet's account, **Cor gén F,** v. 8, p. 871.

[21] **SA (1960),** p. 102.

[22] **SA (1960),** p. 100.

[23] Friends would have reburied him in a lot purchased for that purpose by Barbet, but Marie refused permission on the advice of her confessor.

[24] **SA (1960), p. 103.**

[25] **Lav,** v. 2, p. 587, and other accounts.

[26] Alfred Roussel, *Lamennais, d'après des documents inédits,* Rennes: Hyacinthe Caillière, 1893. 2 volumes. V. 2, pp. 441-444.

Chapter 28

COME FAITHFUL SERVANT

It was not until 1847 that Father de La Mennais' health started to decline noticeably, suffering chronic pain from gout, making walking difficult. During more than twenty years, he walked with a cane and a hernia obliged him to use a support bandage. However, he refused a companion on his many journeys, and even in his old age, he hardly reduced his activities.

On December 15, 1847, after a very tiring trip to Guingamp, he was struck by a stroke as he started the celebration of mass. He became paralyzed on his right side, losing most of his speech. He was rushed to his room and a doctor was called. As was customary at the time, he was bled though he remained paralyzed and unable to speak. Two brothers came from Ploermel to care for him until the end of the month when he had improved sufficiently to be taken to his residence at the mother house. Though Father tried to celebrate the liturgy daily in Ploermel, it was very difficult for him to express a number of words, difficulty for him to write, and he remained weak, ever fatigued. [1]

At the summer retreat, though Father de La Mennais thought that he was well enough to preside as he always did, he suffered a serious anthrax infection in his right shoulder, forcing him into complete rest. Already weakened by the stroke, the infection again brought him to death's door. Many friends rushed to see him one more time, Bishop LaMotte from Vannes among the first visitors. Before going to Father's room, the bishop addressed these words to the brothers: *"This is without doubt the last time that I will see your Father. After God, you owe him everything else. Through respect for his memory, maintain the practice of charity and humility that he taught you, and be most loyal to his successor, whoever he is."* [2]

Though Father eventually recovered, the stroke, the infection, the gout, weakened his resistance and made him more impatient, at times sharp in his reprimands. A few minutes later he would apologize, ask forgiveness for his insensitivity, often with tears in his eyes. During the following year his health improved noticeably; however, he realized that his full strength would never return and that he needed to share responsibility with others. In addition, he became more careful about his diet, and took the habit or retiring shortly after eight in the evening, reading in bed until he fell asleep. By the end of the year, he had regained his normal composure.

Last Will and Testament, Ministers

As early as 1843, Father de La Mennais had written his Last Will and Testament clearly stating how the Superior General should be selected when he died. Father's Will stated that shortly after his death, a Council of five members would elect the Superior General for a period of three years. At the end of a three year term, all the brothers with perpetual vows would meet to elect the Superior General for a term of five years. However, in 1843, Father de La Mennais did not list the five members who would form the original Council.

Forewarned by the stroke of 1847, as soon as he had recovered sufficiently from the stroke and the anthrax attack, he listed the five brothers who would serve as members of the original Council, though the names were kept in a secret codicil to be revealed only after his death. The five brothers selected were: Brothers Louis, Hippolyte, Joseph-Marie, Bernardine and Yves-Joseph. Brother Yves-Joseph was listed as a substitute in case either Brother Ambroise or Brother Paulin had not returned from the Missions. [3]

During the retreat of 1848, Father de La Mennais read his Testament to the brothers, though again he did not name the individuals whom he had selected as members of the first Council. To provide more credibility to his decision, he asked all the Bishops of Brittany to ratify this decision, which they did immediately. To help the brothers clearly understand the process that would be used at his death, he included this information in the Rule of Life that was printed in 1851.

Though the founder's condition had improved, he was still too weak during the following two or three years to maintain his policy of visiting his schools and his communities, so he named Br. Porphyre as his "*Visitor.*" In addition, he asked one of his priest friends to remain in Ploermel during the whole year to relieve him of some of his priestly responsibilities.

With these additional helpers, Father de La Mennais thought that he could resume his personal correspondence with the brothers; this was a poor decision as his weakened condition and the ever increasing number of brothers in the community soon overwhelmed him with work. Br. Hyppolyte trusted him sufficiently to write: "*I do not understand how you can think that at 70 years of age, you are able to respond alone to so many letters and to assume the responsibility of so many stressful matters. Even with your good will, your courage, your full-time work, you cannot respond in time and you annoy people whom you leave without an important decision.*" [4]

By 1853, the paralysis in his hands was such that he could hardly write, unable to properly hold a pen. Only then did he surround himself with additional aids, calling them 'Ministers.' He remained alert and fully interested in his work, though it was more difficult for him to respond immediately to a delicate situation, and soon his memory started to fail. The Ministers appointed on the 28th of September, 1853, were five brothers he trusted to help him in his work, freely assigning them to any responsibility he could not fulfill himself.

Father selected Br. Julien as his fulltime personal secretary and responsible for the brothers earning a degree; Br.Cyprien was given the responsibility of the Novices and construction projects; Br. Hippolyte became responsible for the official correspondence and official documents;

Br. Bernardine was appointed to teach at the Novitiate and support Br. Cyprien in his work; Br. Ambroise was given responsibility over the brothers in manual labor. The ministers were utilized as trusted aids who could be called upon to assume almost any charge that Father could no longer fulfill; they were even asked to make school visits, a task often relegated to Br. Ambroise or Br. Julien.

Letter of Praise from Rome

In addition to organizing a replacement process for himself, the founder wanted to provide more stability for his men by obtaining approval of the Congregation by Rome. With this in mind, Father de La Mennais sent a formal request for approval on the 4th of October, 1848: *"My age and my infirmities tell me that very soon my earthly pilgrimage will be ended. I have but one remaining wish: that your Holiness bless the Institute of the Brothers of Christian Instruction, by approving in whatever form you deem appropriate, the Constitutions of the Congregation. This precious blessing would still my fears, and allow me to die in peace encouraged by the paternal blessing of the Vicar of Christ."* [5]

In 1848 when the letter of request was sent to Rome, the Congregation had already more than 600 members, more than 300 of them with perpetual vows, and it administered 183 schools. However, the founder waited two years and a half for an answer from Rome, and when the Pontifical brief arrived, it did not approve the Congregation nor did it approve the Constitution, though it provided an apostolic blessing for the Founder and his Congregation. Since the Brothers made only the vow of obedience, Rome could not grant recognition to the Order, as the three vows of religion were required for formal approval of a valid Roman Congregation.

The Papal Brief published on the 1st of February, 1851 stated: "To our Beloved Sons, Greetings and Apostolic Benediction.

Your outstanding charity for poor children, especially children from rural areas, and your ardent zeal for their Christian education, zeal that is blessed by the Lord, has produced in this region of France and even in the faraway missions outstanding fruits; such wonderful results cannot but earn our highest praises. This brief encourages the Founder and his Congregation to pursue the work so well initiated and ends with our blessing: "We beg for you prosperity and consolation, and as a token of our paternal love for you, dear son, we offer you our apostolic blessing from the deepest recesses of our heart." [6]

Though the brief was not the full recognition that he sought, the Papal Blessing brought Father de La Mennais deep peace and the recognition that he needed to show his brothers that their educational work had received approval and encouragement from the highest authority in the Church, counteracting the criticisms of others and associating the name of La Mennais with approval, not condemnation.

New Edition of the Rule, Visitors

In 1835, Father de La Mennais had given his brothers a third edition of the Rule of Life, an enlarged version that clarified some matters, offered advice to local superiors, and provided specific information for communities with multiple membership.

On June 17, 1851, Father wrote to Br. Ambroise: *"We are now reprinting the Rule of Life; it will be far more complete than the previous edition. All the brothers wanted me to have this work done before I die; I trust you will be satisfied with the new edition."* [7] The Rule went from 160 to 244 pages, and included both the Apostolic Brief and the Founder's Last Will and Testament. Along with more detailed information about the rules and regulations for the Congregation, it contained a special segment for the brothers in the missions.

As early as 1851, Father de La Mennais had asked a number of his Ministers to visit his schools and communities; however, by 1857, realizing that he was becoming progressively weaker, he formalized the process of having someone assume that specific responsibility. In a special circular letter dated March, 19, 1857, he wrote: *"From the early days of our Congregation, as long as my health allowed me, I have never ceased regularly visiting our schools and communities. Since I am now obliged to rely on others to assume this task, I want this salutary practice to be maintained by making it part of our Rule of Life."*

Final Days

Following the health crises experienced by Father de La Mennais from 1847 to 1850, his physical condition improved sufficiently to allow him to remain involved in all major decisions, ever helped by his trusted *'ministers.'* Though physically he never fully recovered from his stroke of 1847, until 1859 he remained the guiding force in the Congregation, but as with individuals his age, he became more easily upset by change. He lost the flexibility of a vigorous mind, suffering a failing memory, at times misplacing documents or not responding to important requests in a timely manner.

By 1859, his health and his mental condition had deteriorated to the point that most important decisions were now taken by others, and when he suffered another stroke on September 30, 1860, he was unable to return to any administrative responsibility. Most of the important decisions of the Community were now taken by Br. Cyprien, his trusted secretary who was supported by the ministers.

Father continued to try to recite his breviary until the end, but he said his last mass at Easter of 1860. He read with difficulty, often able to recite but a few psalms, finding more comfort in the recitation of the Rosary. Realizing that he was on his last days, he dictated one final letter to the brothers: *"Every year which ends, brings us closer towards eternity; without doubt, the one starting will be the last for many of us. Are we prepared?... As with the apostles, I say 'it is time to wake from your sleep, the Lord is near.' Pray and console the Church by your virtues and encourage each other to utilize the days at hand to sow abundantly to reap abundantly in heaven."*[8]

A few days after dictating the letter to Br. Cyprien, during the evening of December 21, he suffered his final stroke. The following day he was administered the last sacraments to which he responded firmly with tears in his eyes. When the brothers kneeling by his bedside realized that his condition was deteriorating further, they asked for a final blessing, a solemn slow gesture of love expressed for all his brothers. Then seeing Br. Cyprien at his bedside, he whispered, *"My son, complete my work."*

His last words were spoken to the two brothers who were helping him to readjust himself in his bed: *"Oh, thank you, thank you my dear children, I am causing you such trouble; I am most grateful to all of you. Pray my children, pray."*

After receiving the final Sacraments following the stroke of the 21st of December, he alternated between periods of calm and moments when the fever made him delirious, his frail body shaking with convulsions; at that time, he sought comfort in his Rosary. He quietly breathed his last around ten in the evening on the 26th of December, 1860.

On hearing of Father de La Mennais' death, the Bishop of Nantes expressed sentiments that were repeated by a multitude of friends, well-wishers, admirers: *"I loved M. de La Mennais with particular affection, and I revered him as one of the most faithful servants of God and the Church. He was one of the most active reformers in the Church following the horrible days of the Revolution, and he rendered the Church of France immense benefits by founding an institute which has brought educational blessings to our towns and villages. Your Congregation is being deprived of a pious, gifted Founder, but now receives a powerful intercessor before the Lord."* [9]

During five days, an endless stream of people sought to pay their respects to one who had served France and her colonies with so much love, by touching his hands, his garments, his rosary. Friends and admirers now requested special blessings from one now trusted to serve as an advocate for the people, particularly for the little children he loved so dearly, and who often loved him as a father.

On December 31st, an overflow crowd solemnly celebrated Father de La Mennais' last rites in the large granite chapel of Ploermel. As chapel bells tolled, more than 200 priests and 800 religious marched behind his remains to the modest cemetery plot he had selected for himself, after refusing the chapel crypt burial that had been planned for him. Father de La Mennais' personal work was now ended, but his educational work continued, entrusted to the brothers and sisters who had generously responded to his invitation to serve the Lord in the extended field of education.

The Mission Continues, Daughters of Providence, Brothers of Christian Instruction

At the Founder's death, there were 60 Daughters of Providence located in five centers of Brittany, most working in the field of education; in addition, in Combourg, the Daughters of Providence were providing health and social services to the population. The Congregation of religious sisters had been administering its own affairs during almost all of its history, as the Order had always elected its own Superior General and administrative team.

The Brothers of Christian Instruction founded with the very early leadership of Father Gabriel Deshayes had remained in the field of education and support services for education. At Father de La Mennais' death, the Brothers numbered more than 850; 154 were serving in the missions at that time, 125 were living at Ploermel serving as administrators or support and formation personnel, and 570 brothers worked in various locations in France, almost all of them in Brittany.[10]

In addition, there were about 150 Novices and temporary professed brothers studying in Ploermel, bringing the total number of professed religious at the death of Father de La Mennais to about 1,000. These religious taught in 297 schools in France, all except two located in Brittany, and teaching to 25,700 students.

The 154 brothers in the missions, taught in 51 schools to 5,800 students and 4,900 adults. In addition, in the missions, there were 20 brothers working fulltime as catechists, teaching to almost 3,000 adults.

Father de La Mennais' influence was so strong and his authority so absolute, that a number of brothers and friends of the community feared for the future of the Congregation at his death. However, the Last Will and Testament had clearly stipulated how authority should be transmitted at his death, and the five brothers suggested as members of the first Council of the Congregation had been very well selected. [11]

As determined in the codicil of the Last Will and Testament, the brothers who were named as original members of the Council were: Brothers Louis, Hippolyte, Cyprien, Ladislas and Joseph Mary; they immediately assumed responsibility. Less than a month later on January 24th, 1861, the Council elected Br. Cyprien as Superior General for a term of three years, again as previously determined.

Br. Cyprien had played such a vital, supportive role in the last years of the Founder's life, and his talents were so well recognized, that he was very well received by the Brothers; the fears of instability in the Congregation proved chimerical. Three years later, again as had been stipulated in the Last Will and Testament, the brothers with Perpetual Vows assembled in Ploermel to select for the first time their own Superior General for a period of five years. Br. Cyprien was confirmed in his role, providing long-term stability to the Congregation.

The Founder never explained why he had adopted the particular process he choose to provide leadership in the Congregation following his death; however, it was probably to assure stable leadership and avoid confusion at that critical time. By having the Council select the Superior General, it narrowed the choice to a proven candidate and prevented potential conflict over authority. In addition, by providing a three year first term for the Superior General, it offered a testing period during which the brothers themselves could evaluate the leadership skills of the person selected by the Council, or provide redress if necessary.

Despite a number of threatening crises in both Congregations, the long-term stability of both Congregations offers the greatest testimony that can be given to the Founder. As long as the Daughters of Providence and the Brothers of Christian Instruction *"strive to make Jesus Christ known,"* as was the wish of their Founder, they will be sustained and thrive; should their mission and vision be lost, human wisdom and human energy alone will not assure their success.

[1] Rulon, Petite Histoire, p. 209. As usual, Rulon's assessment is on target.
[2]. Merleau, op. cit., p. 238.
[3] *Rulon, op. cit.*, p. 160
[4] Idem, p. 161.
[5].Ibid
[6] Merleau, op. cit., p. 210.
[7] Rulon, op. cit., p. 162.
[8] Merleau, op.cit, p. 262.
[9] Rulon, op. cit., p. 380.
[10] Drouin, op.cit., p. 68.
[11] Rulon, op.cit, p. 405

Appendix

ELEMENTARY SCHOOLS AFTER THE FRENCH REVOLUTION

(A supplement to Chapter 9)

Broken school tradition

Schools became part of the life of John de La Mennais from 1802 until his death in 1860. He was still preparing for his own ordination when he began to teach in the ecclesiastical secondary school of Saint-Malo; from then on, he managed to provide for the education of future priests whenever possible. He began intensive work with Christian elementary education in Saint-Brieuc, first by restoring the schools of religious teaching congregations, then by founding two religious congregations of teachers, a commitment which led him to promote Christian elementary schools during two-thirds of his active life. Government so resolutely influenced schools during the four decades of his direct involvement with popular education, that an understanding of the role of government in education is helpful in understanding the role and the difficulties faced by John de La Mennais.[1]

The illiteracy of youth was profound especially in rural France, and particularly in matters of religion. The children of Brittany were among the neediest of the poorly provided rural lands. In his Code universitaire, Ambroise Rendu outlined the average school attendance for 1817. The norm for France was that one child in thirty attended school at least part of the year. The record shows variations of 1 in 8 for Haute-Marne and Bas-Rhin, 1/23 for the region of Paris, and 1/190 for the (rural) Massif central area. The region of Brittany, administered by the *Académie* of Rennes, reported 1/567.[2]

In November 1800, the chemist Chaptal included the following reminders in a report to Napoleon: "In the times which preceded the Revolution, the nature of public instruction required a few reforms; but it cannot be denied that the teaching method was admirable. --- The system of public instruction existing today is essentially bad. There are hardly any primary schools anywhere". [3] In 1804, he reminded the Emperor that "before the Revolution, primary schools existed almost everywhere". [4]

The Revolution had not helped. The lawmakers of the Revolution never seemed to tire of conceptualizing national school plans. By expelling priests and religious, and destroying the revenues of the dioceses, religious orders, noble families, societies and financing foundations which supported them before 1789, they had ruined the schools but they failed to replace them. When Matthew Arnold visited the schools of France for the British government, he asked François Guizot what the French Revolution had contributed "to the cause of popular education". Guizot answered: "A deluge of words, nothing more" [5] The revolutionaries handed down an ideology and paper dreams, not a school system.

Centralized control: the Imperial University, 1808

Napoleon established a national system of public education only after his major military victories. There was no lack of forethought as the system was preceded by elaborate consultations and some fifteen advisory reports. The law of May 10, 1806 stipulated that a corporation, the Imperial University, would be organized and entrusted exclusively with instruction and education throughout the Empire. The government was to submit the plan to the legislators during the 1810 session.

The Emperor anticipated his own timing, bypassed the procedure he had outlined and created the *Université impériale* by decree. The new authority was not a cluster of faculties in one location, but a supreme ministry of education. The decree of March 17, 1808 subjected all schools to its control: "No school, no teaching establishment whatever, will be organized outside the Imperial University and without the authorization of its chief (Article 2)". A Grand Master would oversee the ambitious enterprise. The organization was complete, even down to primary schools for introduction to reading, writing and arithmetic, (Art. 5).

A monopoly was complete, the central executive would appoint administrators to oversee and regulate all the schools of the nation. The traditional role of the Church was officially safeguarded. All the schools of the *Université* must base their teaching on (1) the precepts of the Catholic religion and (2) loyalty to the Emperor, to the imperial monarchy, depository of the welfare of peoples, and to the Napoleonic dynasty, guardian of France and of all the liberal ideas proclaimed by the Constitution (Art. 38). The Emperor had published his understanding of "the precepts of the Catholic religion" in his imperial catechism of 1806 which emphasized the civic virtues of paying taxes, serving in the military, respecting the public order and submitting to the Emperor as God's representative,.

Secondary schools

The government opened secondary schools soon after the Revolution. A secondary school was referred to as a collège. A private secondary school administered by priests was an ecclesiastical school, (or a *collège ecclésiastique*). Such private schools could not open without government authorization even though they served as a preparation to the priesthood. Whatever their names, the ecclesiastical schools of the period were in effect minor seminaries often admitting young men not destined to the priesthood.

The Emperor's decree on the *Université* clearly stated that "teaching in the seminaries depends on archbishops and bishops, each in his own diocese; they appoint and revoke the directors and professors; they are simply bound to conform to regulations for seminaries." Neither this text nor the safeguards of the Concordat of 1801 protected minor seminaries from regimentation. Napoleon's government listed them as secondary schools, (*collèges*), and subjected them to its own rules.

The control stratagem interfered with the education of the clergy. Decrees limited the number of minor seminaries per diocese, verified the intentions of students, required loyalty oaths from teachers, lowered the authorized number of students. Such intrusions continued during the Restoration, particularly with the nasty ordinances of June 16, 1828. Controls took on a particularly invasive character when the government obliged the schools to teach the "Four Gallican Articles of 1682" to young men preparing for the priesthood. [6] John resisted such rulings, but no controls frustrated him more than government supervison of elementary schools.

Elementary schools

Napoleon privileged the education of his soldiers. He created a few schools for the daughters of his men, and was known to declare that the education of a man began twenty years earlier with the education of his mother. He favored municipal secondary schools and abandoned elementary instruction to local initiative. During the fifteen years which followed the Revolution, he did little more than study needs and options. René Durand observes that "destruction and magnificence waste the money exacted from taxpayers," leaving but "miserable resources for public instruction." Elementary instruction was the object of pompous circulars from imperial executives, redundant directives from prefects, promises from the *Université* and a scarcity of resources. With respect to primary instruction, "the record of the imperial government can be summed at zero." [7]

Sad consequences followed. For want of a better livelihood, unqualified, at times disreputable men were the only schoolmasters willing to accept the paltry salaries offered for their lessons, poor models of civic pride and Christian life. Vagrants offered their lessons where stable instructors were lacking. The ambulant schoolmaster and seasonal schools of rural France were then far from rarities, justifying the government's need for the supervision of teachers.

Regulation was the legal task of the *Université*. Its executives were asked to guarantee the integrity and aptitude of schoolmasters, the establishment of normal schools for the preparation of teachers, and in a general to suggest the best teaching methods. The measures which followed kept even the lowest levels of education under supervision. For decades the Emperor, then the King and his ministers, would govern the schools by decrees and executive orders. Ministers of the interior would issue circulars, local officials would intervene with directives, supervisory boards and inspectors, school directors, teachers, buildings, books and programs, etc. The king created a ministry for Ecclesiastical Affairs and public Instruction on August 26, 1824. The new authority established its control over elementary and secondary schools on April 31, 1828.

The men who drafted such measures intended no harm. Taken as a whole, the role of government could be beneficial, and often was. As in other countries, the scheme of government regulatory activity could easily enmesh all aspects of schooling in counterproductive procedural drudgery which would often frustrate John de La Mennais. Firm legislation reorganized schooling in 1833 and 1850, easing but not altogether casting off the yoke of centralization. Local difficulties would frequently arise from the interpretations, the bungling or the ill will of lower officials in carrying out well meant but overwrought legislation.

The French government officially authorized two teaching methods in its schools: (a) the simultaneous method of classroom teaching, in opposition to an older practice of instructing students individually and (b) the monitorial system of mutual instruction as practiced by Bell and Lancaster. The Ministry of the Interior immediately adopted the national objectives of the new society, urged and in some cases required the use of the new method. The system spread throughout the nation, in peace or in controversy, depending on the attitude of local sponsors. Some Catholic priests adopted it as did some religious orders.

---

[1] The information assembled in chapter 9 eliminates the need for repeated interruptions of the narrative. Most of the following text would otherwise have to be interspersed through the text.

[2] As summarized in Raymond Tronchot, L'Enseignement mutuel en France de 1815 à 1833. (Privately printed Multigraphed doctoral thesis, Sorbonne University, 1972). Tome 1, first part, pp. 9 ff.

3 Jean Antoine Chaptal (1756-1832) was then Minister of the Interior for the Consulate. His report of 18 brumaire, year IX (November 8, 1800) was published in the Moniteur, No., 49, year IX. See his biographical notice in F. Buisson, Dictionnaire de Pédagogie et d 'Instruction primaire, Paris: Hachette, 1882. (Also in the 1911 edition.)

4 Note to the Emperor. As quoted in Eugène Rendu, M. Ambroise Rendu et l'Université de France, Paris: Fourat et Dentu, 1882. P. 23. (e) F. Le Douarec, Le Concordat dans un Diocèse de l'Ouest,Paris: Alsatia, 1958. P. 149.

6 See Chapter 19 about the Ordinances of June 16, 1828, and the interference with the preparation to the priesthood through the regimentation of minor seminaries.

7 René Durand, Le Département des Côtes-du-Nord sous le Consulat et l 'Empire (1800-1815), Paris: Librairie Félix Alcan, 1926. Vol.1, pp.592-594. See generally, 511-594.

BIBLIOGRAPHY

JEAN-MARIE DE LA MENNAIS

HERPIN, EUGÈNE. *L'Abbé Jean-Marie de La Mennais, ses grandes Idées et ses grandes Oeuvres.* Ploërmel: Imprimerie Saint-Yves, 1878.

LA MENNAIS, JEAN-MARIE ROBERT, DE, 1780-1860. *Correspondance générale.* Textes réunis et annotés par F. Philippe Friot. Presses Universitaires de Rennes, 2001-2002. 7 v

LAVEILLE, AUGUSTE-PIERRE, 1856-1928. *Jean-Marie de la Mennais (1780-1860).* Paris: Poussielgue, 1903. 2 v.

MARECHAL, CHRISTIAN. *La Famille de :a Mennais sous l'Ancien régime & la Révolution.* Paris: Perrin, 1913. 345 pp.

[MIRECOURT, EUGÈNE DE,] pseudonym of Charles Jean-Baptiste Jacquot. *L'abbé Jean-Marie de La Mennais, Fondateur de l'Institut de Ploërmel, par l'Auteur des Cotemporains.* Paris: Brayu et Retaux; Vannes: Lamarzelle, 1876. (Hommes illustres du clergé de France au XIXe siècle).

PERRIN, PIERRE. "Félicité, Jean-Marie de La Mennais et lUniversité. Leurs idées pédagogiques pour la defense de la liberté de l'enseignement, de 1806 à 1860." Brest: Université de Bretagne Occidentale, Mai, 1998. 454 pp. Unpublished doctoral dissertation.

_____. *Les idées pédagogiques de Jean-Marie de la Mennais,* 1780-1860. Presses Universitaires de Rennes, 2000. 221+[6] pages. Adapted from his doctoral dissertation.

ROPARTZ, SIGISMOND. La *Vie et les Oeuvres de M. Jean-Marie Robert de la Mennais.* Paris: Lecoffre,[1874]..xi, 489 p.

FÉLICITÉ DE LA MENNAIS

[BARBIER, HIPPOLYTE]. "M. *de La Mennais*" in *Biographie de Clergé contemporain*. Paris: A. Appert, 1841. V. 1, pp. 146-180.

BLAIZE, ANGE. *Essai biographique sur M. f. de La Mennais*. Paris, Garnier, 1858. xix, 282 p.

_____. *Oeuvres inédites de F. Lamennais*. Paris: E. Dentu, 1866. 2 v.

BOUTARD, CHARLES. *Lamennais, sa vie et ses Doctrines*. Paris: Perrin, 1905-1913. 3 v.

La Condamnation de Lamennais. Dossier présenté par M. J. Le Guillou et Louis Le Guillou. [Paris: Éditions Beauchesne, c1982. ISBN: 2-7010-1036-5] 754 pp.

DARGIS, ANDRÉ. "La Congrégation de Saint-Pierre." Belgique: Université Catholique de Louvin, Faculté de Théologie, 1971. (Unpublished doctoral thesis.) 651 pp + Voume annexe (Documents), 119 Pp. Mimeographed.

DUDON, PAUL. *Lamennais et le Saint-Siège, 1820-1854; d'après des documents inédits et les Archives du Vatican*. Paris: Pe3rrin, 1911.

DUINE, FRANÇOIS MARIE. *La Mennais, sa Vie, ses Idées, ses Ouvrages*. L\Paris: Garnier, 1922. 389 p.

FEUGÈRE, ANATOLE. *Lamennais avant L'"Essai sur l'Indifférence"; d'après des documents inédits* (1782-1817). Paris: Bloud, 1906.

GERBET, PH. *Réflexions sur la chute de M. de la Mennais*. Paris: Ph. Gerbet, rue Saint-Guillaume, no. 24, 1838; Paris: l'Université Catholique, 1837.

FORGUES, É[MILE] D[AURAND]. *Oeuvres posthumes de F. Lamennais, Pubbliées selon le voeu de l'auteur.* Paris: Paulin et Cevalier, 1859. 2 v.

LA MENNAIS, HUGUES FÉLICITÉ ROBERT, DE, 1782-1854. *Correspondance générale.* Lextes annotés par Louis Le Guillou. Paris: Armand Collin, 1971-1981. 9 v.

_____. *Affaires de Rome. Paris: P. D. Cailleux,* 1836-37. See the introductions accompanying the following editions: *Amélie Hoiss, Histoire d'un livre, 'Affaires de Rome' par F. de Lamennais* (1836) ... Dijon: Imprimerie Bernigaud & Privat, 1933. *Affaires de Rome,* Lyon: La Manufacture, 1986. Introduction de José Cabanis,

_____. *Essai sur l'indifférence en matière de religion.* 1817+

_____. *Paroles d'un croyant,* Paris: Renduel, 1834. See the introductions in Yves *Le Hir, Les paroles d'un croyant de Lamennais, Texte publié sur le manuscript autographe, avec des variants, une introduction et un commentaire,* Paris, Colin, 1949. *Paroles d'un croyant,* Introduction et notes de Louis Le Guillou, Paris: Flammarion, 1973.

LE GUILLOU, LOUIS. *'Les Discusssions critiques', Journal de la crise mennaisienne; Genèse et édition du manuscrit 356 de la Bibliothèque Universitaire de Rennes.* Paris: Armand Colin, 1967.
_____. *L'Évolution de la pensée religieuse de Félicité Lamennais.* Paris: A. Colin, 1966.

MARECHAL, CHRISTIAN. *LA Jeunesse de La Mennais, Contribution à l'étude des origins du Romanticisme religieux en France au xixe Siècle.* Paris: Perrin, 1913. 719 p.

ROUSSEL, ALFRED. *Lamennais et ses Correspondants inconnus.* Paris: Téqui, 1912. vii, 455 p.

VIDLER, ALEC R. [ALEXANDER ROPER], 1899-____ *Prophecy and Papacy, a study of Lamennais, the Church and the Revolution.* London: SCM press, 1954. (The Birkbecy Lectures, 1952-1953). 300 pages.

WHITE, RUTH L.*L'Avenir de La Mennais, Son role dans la presse de son temps.* Paris: Editions Klincksieck, 1974.

RELIGIOUS HISTORY AND BIOGRAPHY

BOUDON, JACQUES-OLIVIER. L'épiscopat *français à l'époque concordataire* (1802-1905). Origines, formation, nomination. Paris: Éditions du Cerf, 1996. 589 pp.

FRAYSSINOUS, DENIS-ANTOINE-LUC. *Les vrais principes de l'Église Galicane.* Paris: Adrien Le Clère, Imprimeur de N. S. P. le Pape, 1818.

GARNIER, ADRIEN. *Les Ordonnances du 16 juin 1828, d'après des documents inédits tirés des Archives du Vatican et des Archives nationales.* Paris: J.de Gigord, 1929. xvii, 250 pp.

GAUGH, AUSTIN, 1926-. *Paris and Rome, The Gallican Church and the Ultramontane Campaign,* 1848-1853. Cambridge University Press, 1986. French translation by Michel Lagrée, *Paris et Rome, Les Catholiques français et le Pape au XIXe siècle.* Paris:Éditions de l'Atelier, 1996. 319 pp.

GUIDÉE, ACHILLE (S. J.) *Notice historique sur le P. François Renault de la Compagnie de Jésus mort le 8 décembre, 1860.* Paris: Charles Douniol, 1864.

LE DUAREC, F. *Le Consulat dans un diocese de l'ouest. Monseigneur Caffarelli et le Préfet Boullé.* Paris: Éditions Alsatia, [1958].

SÉVRIN, ERNEST. *Les Missions religieuses en France sous la Restauration.* Paris: Vrin, 1948, 1959. 2 v.

TERRIEN, JACQUES. *Histoire du R. P. de Clotivière de la Compagnie de Jésus.* Paris: Poussielgue, 1892.

EDUCATION

GENERAL

BENAERTS, L. *Le Régime consulaire en Bretagne. Le département d'Ille et Vilaine durant le Consulat (1789-1804)* Paris: 1914. (Thèse de doctorat ès lettres)

BERTIER DE SAUVIGNY, G. DE. *Histoire de France.* Paris: Flammarion, 1977.

BRACHET, VICOMTE DE. *La Terreur dans l'Ouest. Le Conventionnel J-B. Le Carpentier (1759-1829).* Paris: Librairie académique Perrin, 1912.

HAIZE, JULES. *Une commune bretonne pendant la Révolution. Histoire de Saint-Servan (Ille-et-Vilaine) de 1789 à 1800. Saint-Servan: J. Haize;* Paris: Honoré Champion, 1907.

HERPIN, EUGÈNE. *Saint-Malo sous la Révolution, 1789-1800. ...* St.-Malo: Maurice Guérin, [1931].

MANET, FRANÇOIS. *Biographie des Malouins célèbres, nés depuis le 15e siècle jusqu'à nos jours; Précédée d'une notice historique sur la ville de Saint-Malo, depuis son origine.* Saint-Malo: Chez l'auteur, rue des cimetières; et H. Rottier, Imprimeur-Libraire, 1824. Also, Marseille: Lafitte Reprints, 1977.

NETTEMENT, ALFRED. *Histoire de la Littérature française sous la Restauration. 4ë edition.* Paris: Lecoffre, 1888. 2 v.

PRAMPAIN, ÉDOUARD. *Saint-Malo hostorique.* Amiens: Piteux Frères, 1902.

F

Forgues, Émile

L

La Mennais (Family). Officially: Robert de La Mennais
La Mennais, Gratien-Claude, (May 2, 1785-summer, 1818)
La Mennais, Gratienne-Jeanne Lorin de, (1750-1787) John's mother.
La Mennais, Hugues-Félicité, ("Féli" in the family) (June 19, 1782-February 27, 1854)
La Mennais, Jean-Marie, (September 8,1780- December 26,1860)
La Mennais, Louis-François Robert, see Robert
La Mennais, Louis-Marie, (Sept. 12, 1776-Dec. 17, 1805)
La Mennais, Marie-Josèphe, (February 24, 1784-March 31, 1851) see Blaize
La Mennais, Pierre-Jean, (June 24, 1778-1784)
La Mennais, Pierre-Louis Robert de, (1743-1828) John's father.
Le Carpentier, Jean-Baptiste, (1759-1829)
Leo XII, Annibale Sermattei Della Genga, (1760-1829), Pope (1823-1829)
Le Saout, Parish priest of Saint-Malo
Lorin (Family)
Lorin, Bertranne-Marie Roce, (1716-1803) John's maternal grandmother..
Lorin, Félicité-Simone-Jeanne Lorin, see Des Saudrais
Lorin, Gratienne-Jeanne, see La Mennais.
Lorin, Pierre, Sieur de La Brousse, (1719-1799) John's maternal grandfather.
Louis XIV, (1638-1715), King of France (1643-1715)
Louis XVI, Louis-Auguste, (1754-1793), King of France (1774-1791)
Louis XVIII, Louis-Stanislas-Xavier, (1755- 1824), King of France (1814-1824)
Louis-Philippe 1st, (1773-1850), King of France (1830-1848)

M

Malo, Saint, 6th century.
Maupertuis, Pierre-Louis Moreau de, (1698-1759)
Michelot des Saudrais, Josseline

N

Napoléon 1er, Napoléon Bonaparte, (1769-1821), Emperor of France (1804-1815)
Napoléon III, Charles Louis Napoléon Bonaparte, (1808-1873), Emperor of France (1852-1870)

P

Padet-du Dréneuf, Marie-Thérèse, (1718-1744), John's paternal grandmother.
Perruchot, Mayor of Saint-Malo
Pius VI, Gianangelo Braschi, (1717-1799), Pope (1775-1799)
Pius VII, Barnaba Chiaramonti, (1742-1823), Pope (1800-1823)
Pius VIII, Francesco Saverio Castiglioni, 1761-1839), Pope (1829-1830)
Pius IX, Giovanni Maria Mastaï Ferretti, (1792-1878), Pope (1846-1878)
Prairier, Jean (Father-in-law of François Robert III)
Pressigny, Gabriel Cortois de, (1745-1823)

R

Rivières, Marie Yver, (1691-1717)
Robert, François (II), Sieur de La Touurelle, then Des Saudrais (1624-1671)
Robert, François (III), Sieur des Saudrais, (1664-1694/5?)
Robert, François (IV), Sieur des Saudrais, then de La Mennais, (1691-1742)
Robert, Louis-François, Sieur de La Mennais, (1717-1804) John's paternal grandfather.
Robert de La Mennais family, see La Mennais
Robespierre, Maximilien-Marie-Isidore de, (1758-1794)
Roce, Bertranne-Marie, see Lorin
Rochambeau
Rohrbacher, René François, (1789-1856)

S

Sauvage, Amélie
Surcouf, Robert, (1773-1827)

V

Vielle, Louis, (1765-1856)
Villemain, (maid), deceased, 1818.